井上雄彦

Takehiko Inoue

MICHAEL JORDAN PLAYED HIS LAST GAME THE
OTHER DAY. HE PLAYED IN A CHARITY GAME
HOSTED BY SCOTTIE PIPPEN AT CHICAGO STADIUM
WHEN ITS LONG HISTORY CAME TO A CLOSE. THERE
WAS ONLY ONE REASON WHY MJ, WHO HAD MADE
THE TRANSITION TO BASEBALL, DECIDED TO PLAY IN
THIS GAME—THE FINAL GAME OF HIS CAREER WAS
NOT PLAYED IN CHICAGO. AFTER PROVING THAT HE
WAS STILL THE BEST PLAYER IN THE GAME, HE
KISSED THE BULLS LOGO PAINTED ON THE COURT.
HE WAS AMAZING TILL THE END.

*Note: This forward was written after Michael
Jordan's first retirement in 1993 and before his
subsequent return to basketball in 1995.*

Takehiko Inoue's *Slam Dunk* is one of the most
popular manga of all time, having sold over 100
million copies worldwide. He followed that series
up with two titles lauded by critics and fans
alike—*Vagabond*, a fictional account of the life
of Miyamoto Musashi, and *Real*, a manga about
wheelchair basketball.

SLAM DUNK
Vol. 21: Win/Loss

SHONEN JUMP Manga Edition

STORY AND ART BY TAKEHIKO INOUE

English Adaptation/Stan!
Translation/Joe Yamazaki
Touch-up Art & Lettering/James Gaubatz
Cover & Graphic Design/Matt Hinrichs
Editor/Mike Montesa

© 1990 - 2012 Takehiko Inoue and I.T. Planning, Inc.
Originally published in Japan in 1994 by Shueisha
Inc., Tokyo. English translation rights arranged with
I.T. Planning, Inc. All rights reserved.

Printed in the U.S.A.

Published by VIZ Media, LLC
P.O. Box 77010
San Francisco, CA 94107

10 9 8 7 6 5 4 3 2 1
First printing, April 2012

Vol. 21: Win/Loss

STORY AND ART BY
TAKEHIKO INOUE

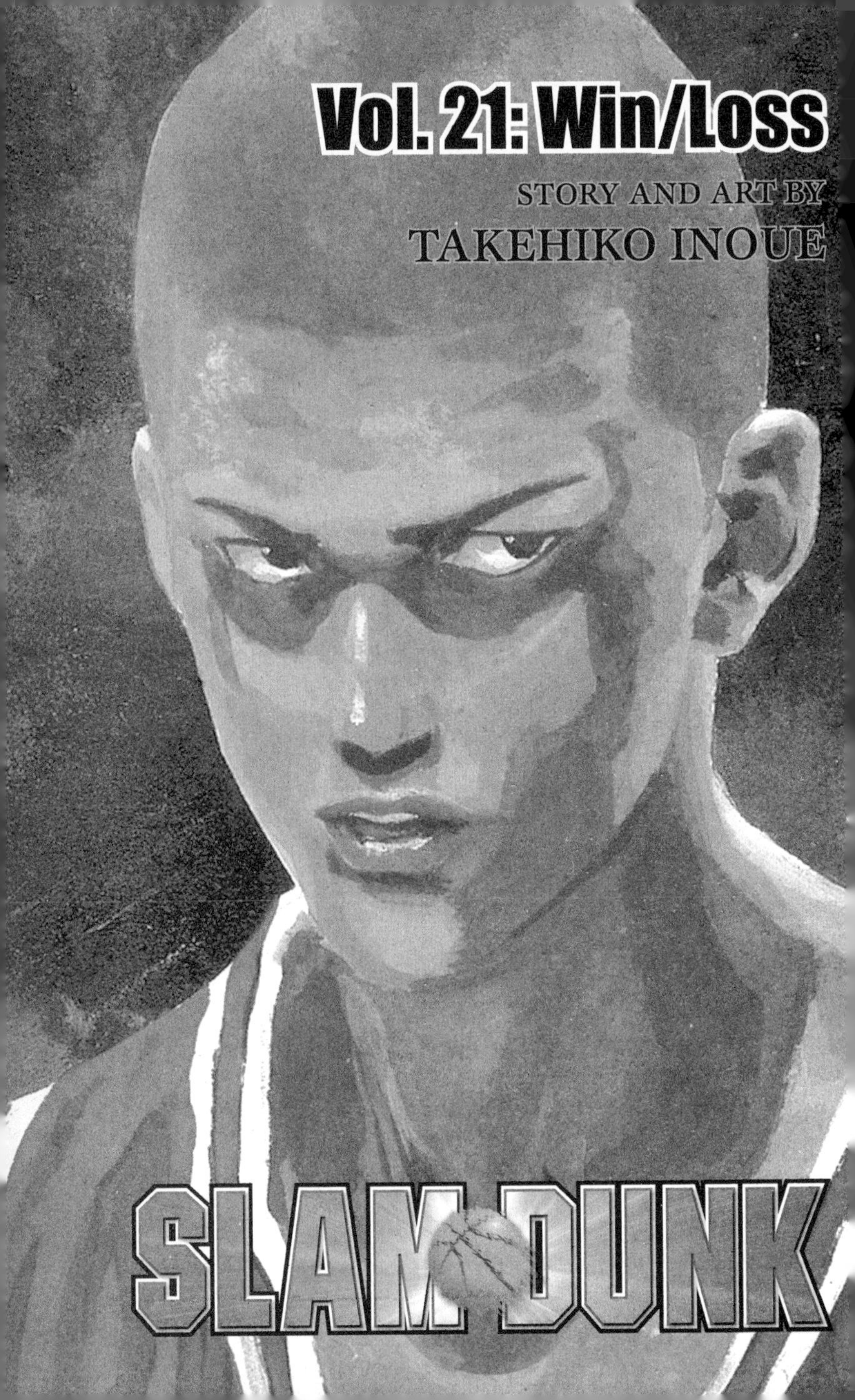

SLAM DUNK

Character Introduction

Hanamichi Sakuragi
A first-year at Shohoku High School, Sakuragi is in love with Haruko Akagi.

Haruko Akagi
Also a first-year at Shohoku, Takenori Akagi's little sister has a crush on Kaede Rukawa.

Takenori Akagi
A third-year and the basketball team's captain, Akagi has an intense passion for his sport.

Kaede Rukawa
The object of Haruko's affection (and that of many of Shohoku's female students!), this first-year has been a star player since junior high.

Uozumi

Sendoh

Ayako
Basketball Team
Manager

Ryota Miyagi
A problem child with
a thing for Ayako.

Hisashi Mitsui
An MVP during
junior high.

Our Story Thus Far

Hanamichi Sakuragi is rejected by close to 50 girls during his three years in junior high. He joins the basketball team to be closer to Haruko Akagi, but his frustration mounts when all he does is practice day after day.

The team sets its sights on the Nationals after playing their first practice game and advancing through the prefectural tournament.

In the game for the final spot in the National Tournament, Shohoku leads Ryonan but, thanks to Sendoh's brilliant play, Ryonan chips away at the lead, narrowing it down to only one point. Then Mitsui collapses, putting Shohoku in a tough spot. With less than three minutes remaining and Ryonan gunning hard for a win, Shohoku's got to give it everything they've got!

Vol. 21
Win/Loss

Table of Contents

#180	Mitsui Remorseful	7
#181	Newbie Sakuragi	27
#182	Newbie Sakuragi 2	46
#183	Four Eyes	67
#184	Win/Loss	87
#185	The Nationals	107
#186	Star of Aichi	126
#187	Freshman Punk	147
#188	Hikoichi Returns to Osaka	167

MITSUI REMORSEFUL

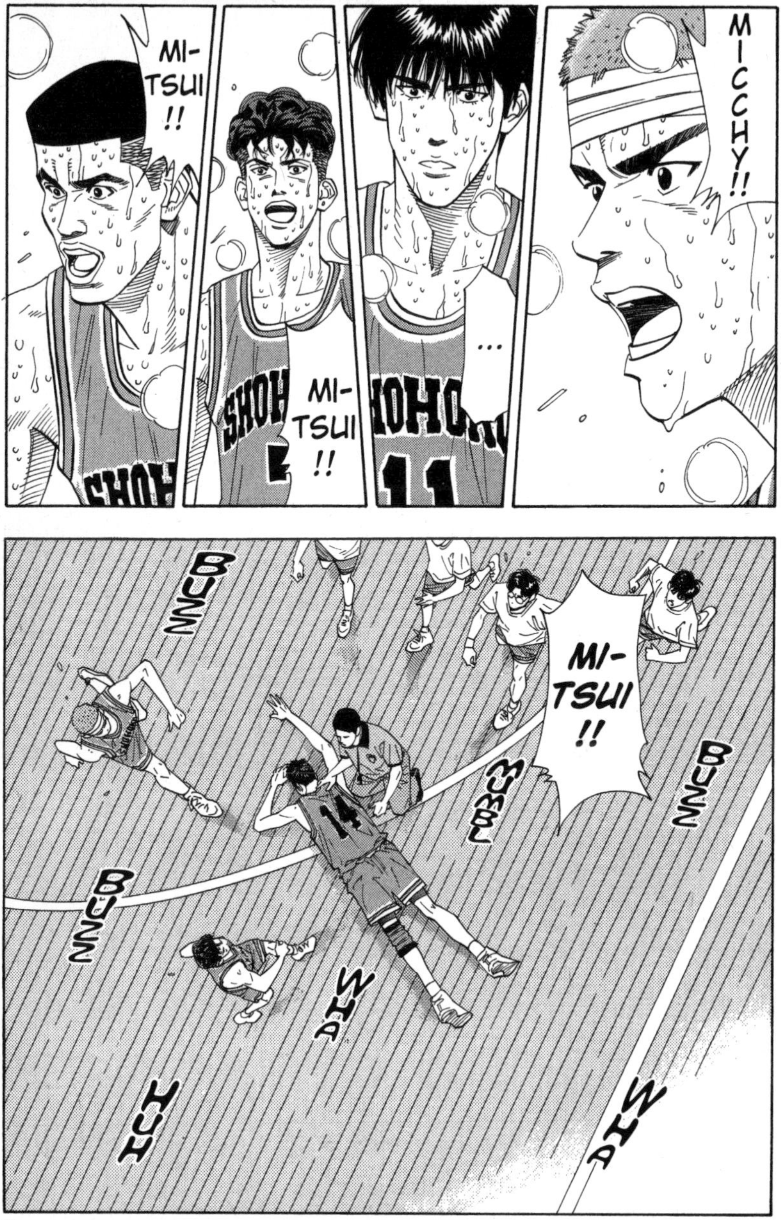
MICCHY!!
...
MI-TSUI !!
MI-TSUI !!
BUZZZ
MI-TSUI !!
MUMBL
BUZZZ
BUZZZ
WHA
WHA
HUH

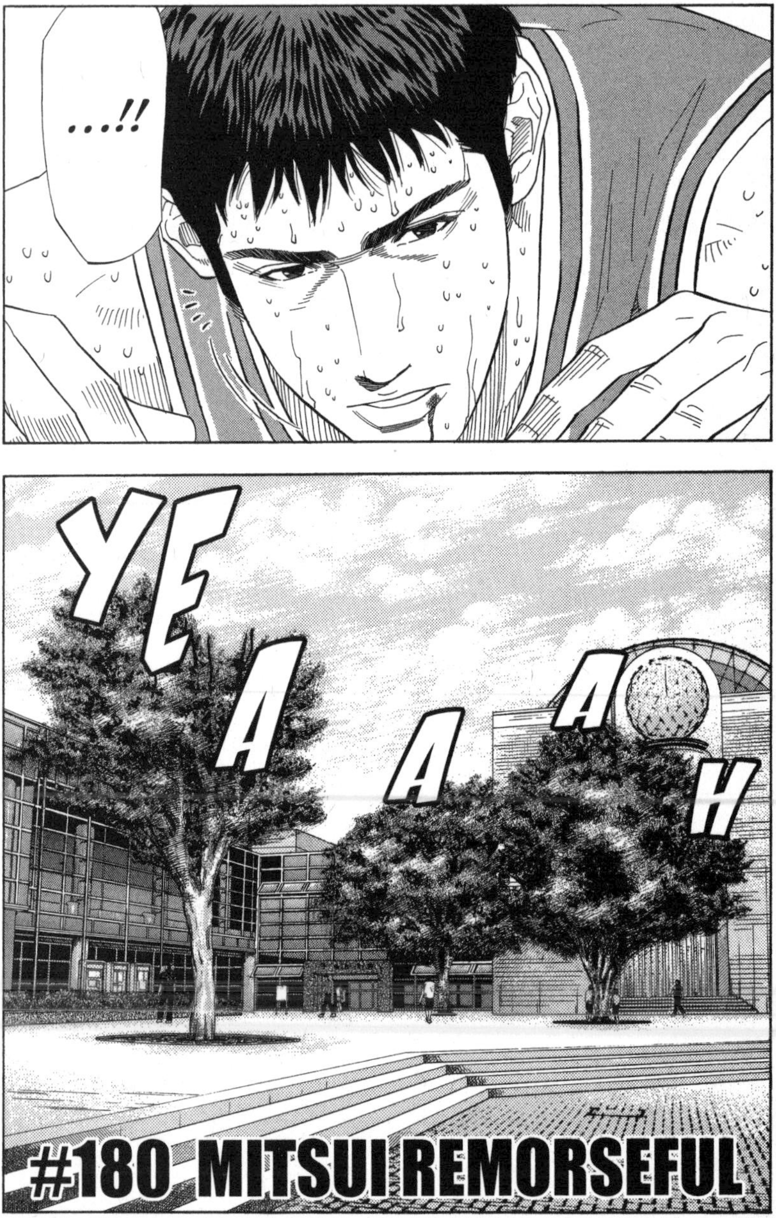
...!!
YEAAAAH

#180 MITSUI REMORSEFUL

READ THIS WAY

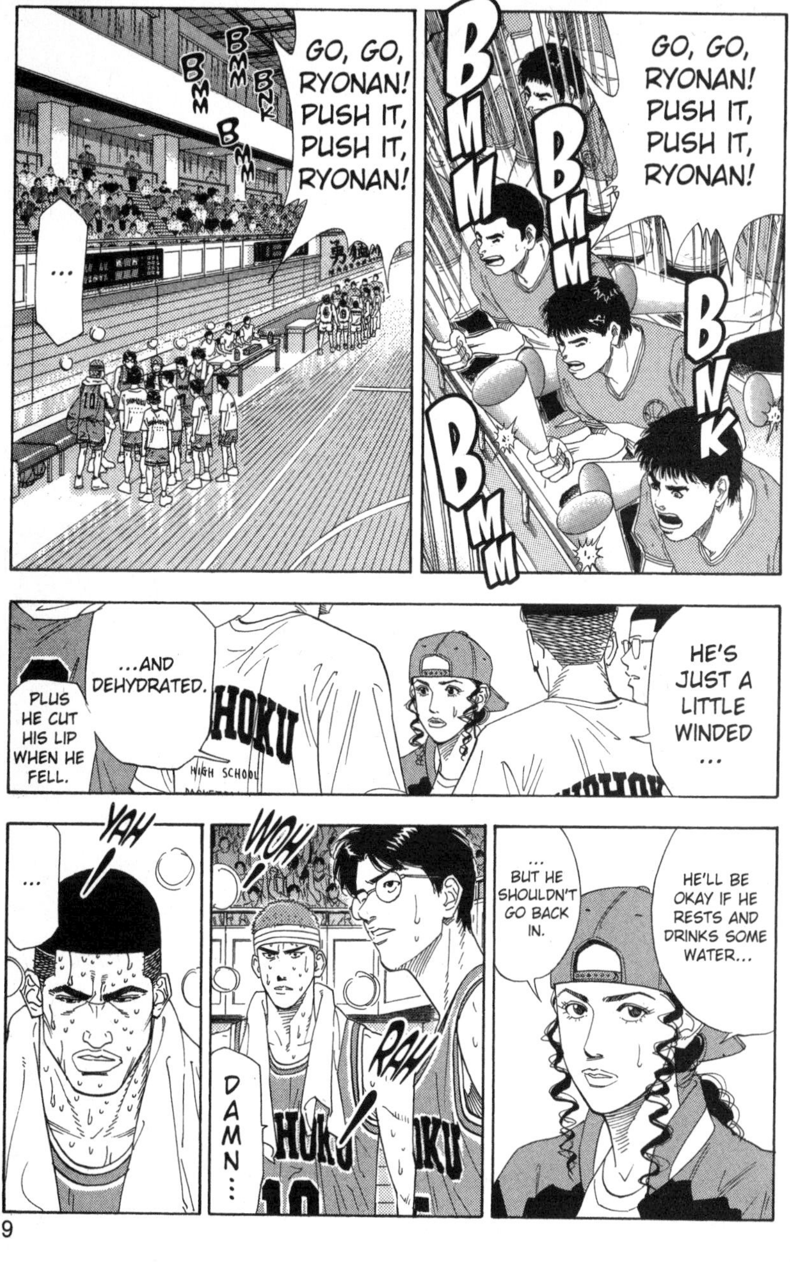

GO, GO, RYONAN! PUSH IT, PUSH IT, RYONAN!
BMM
BMM
BNK
BMM
GO, GO, RYONAN! PUSH IT, PUSH IT, RYONAN!
BMM
BMM
BNK
BMM
...
HE'S JUST A LITTLE WINDED ...
...AND DEHYDRATED.
PLUS HE CUT HIS LIP WHEN HE FELL.
HE'LL BE OKAY IF HE RESTS AND DRINKS SOME WATER...
... BUT HE SHOULDN'T GO BACK IN.
WOH!
RAH!
DAMN...
YAH!
...

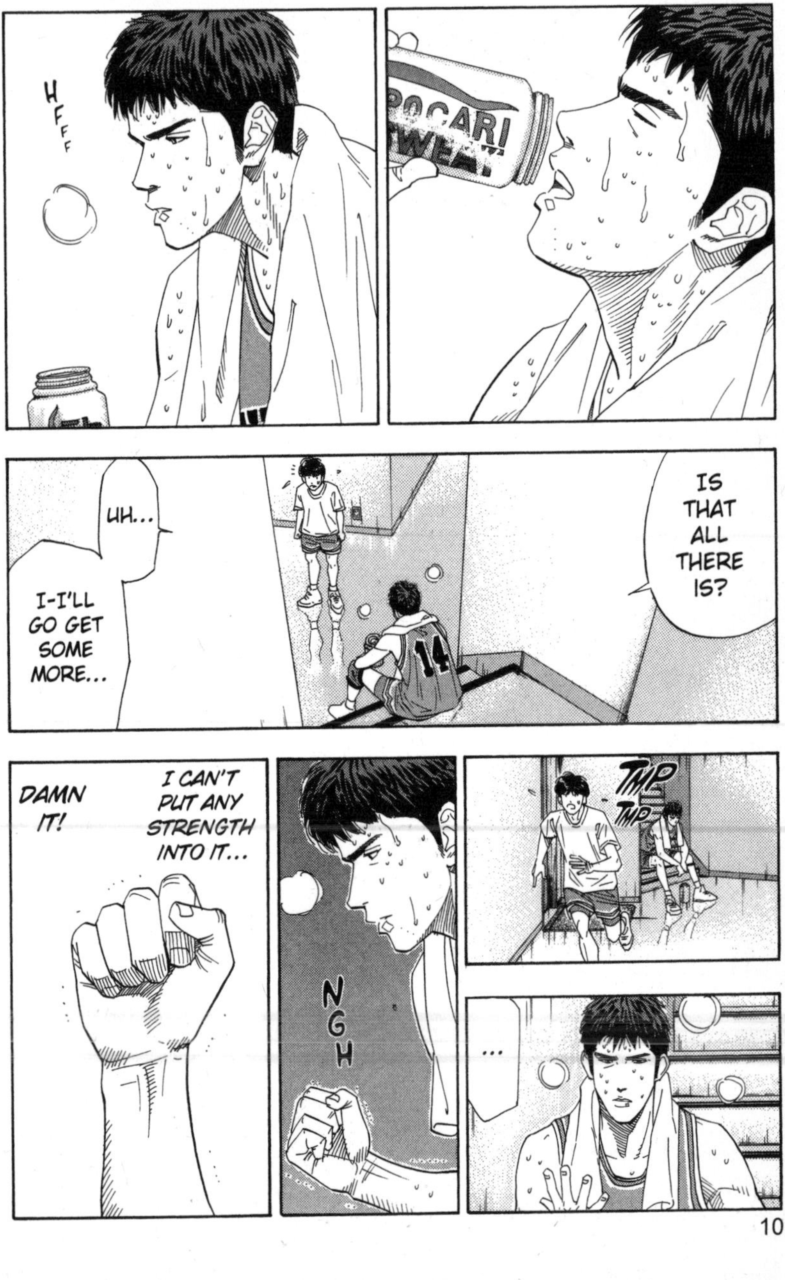
POCARI
HFFF
IS THAT ALL THERE IS?
UH...
I-I'LL GO GET SOME MORE...
TMP TMP
...
NGH
I CAN'T PUT ANY STRENGTH INTO IT...
DAMN IT!

READ THIS WAY

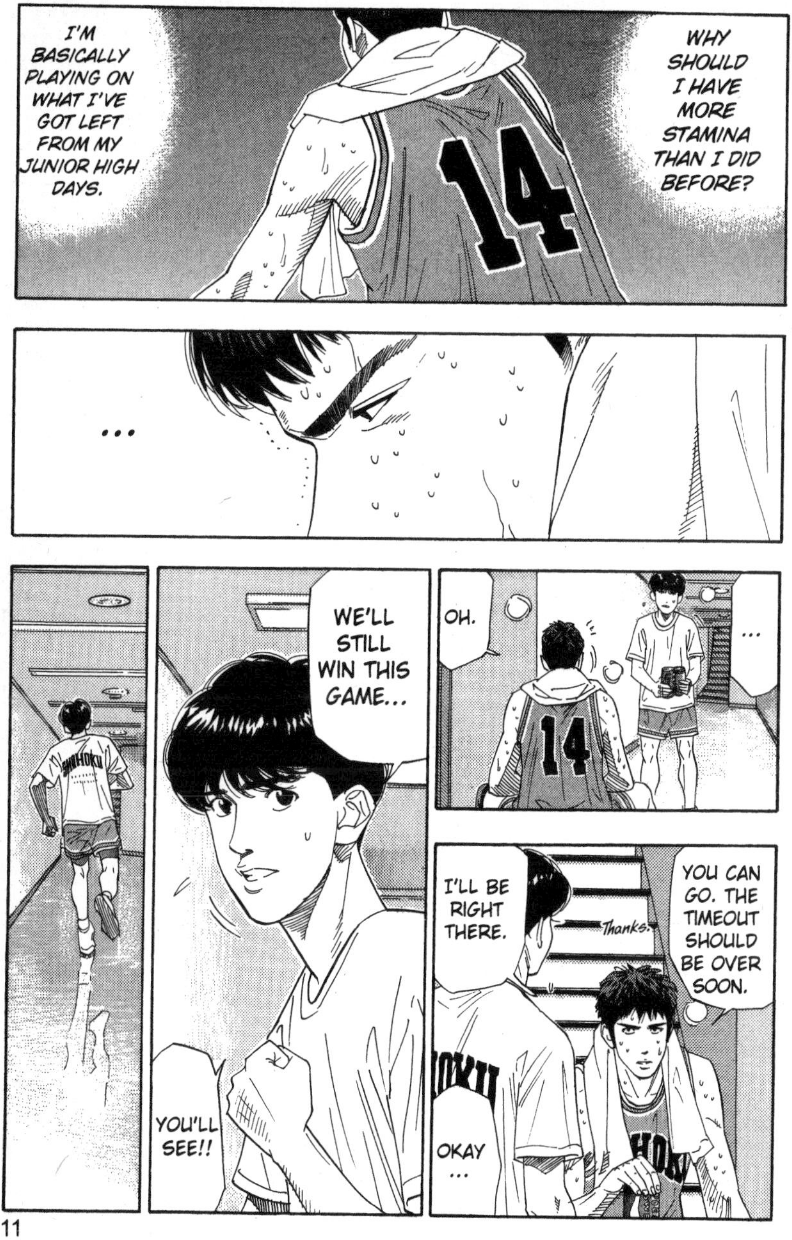
WHY SHOULD I HAVE MORE STAMINA THAN I DID BEFORE?
I'M BASICALLY PLAYING ON WHAT I'VE GOT LEFT FROM MY JUNIOR HIGH DAYS.
...
...
OH.
YOU CAN GO. THE TIMEOUT SHOULD BE OVER SOON.
Thanks.
I'LL BE RIGHT THERE.
OKAY ...
WE'LL STILL WIN THIS GAME...
YOU'LL SEE!!

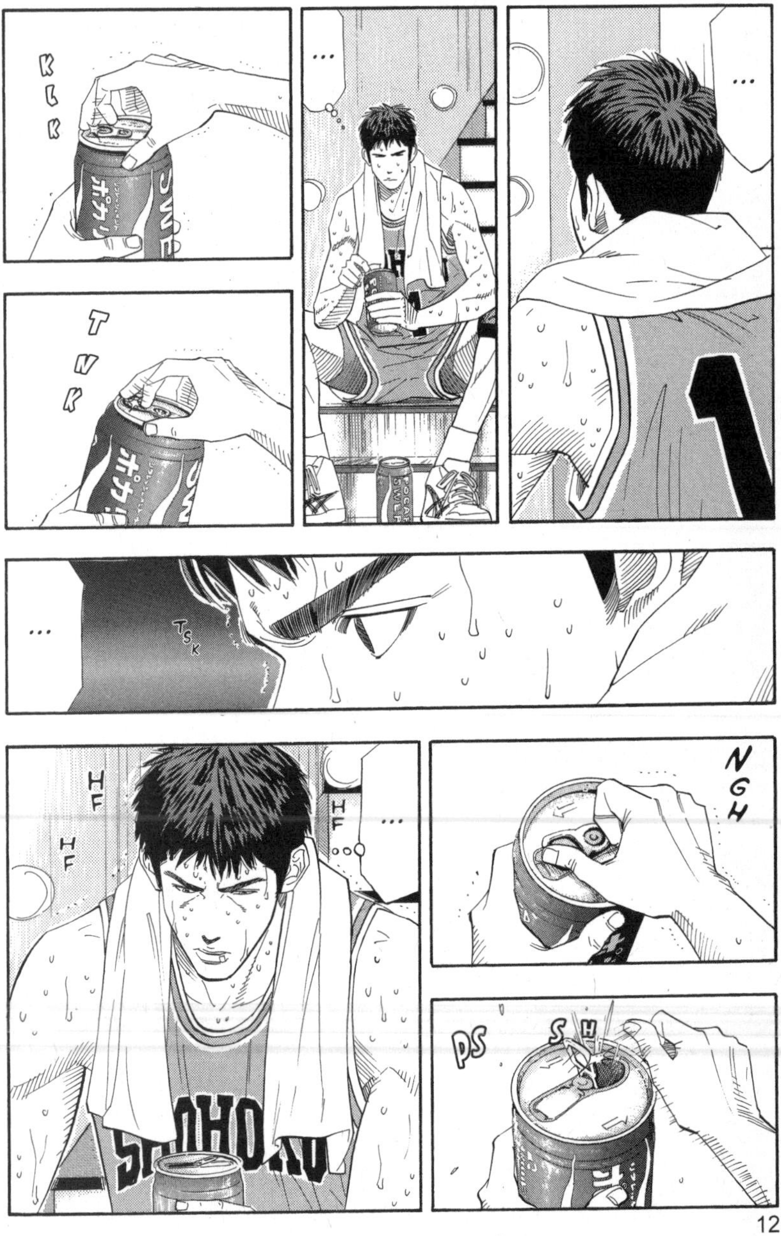
...
...
KLK
TNK
TSK
...
NGH
PS
SH
HF
HF
HF
...

READ THIS WAY

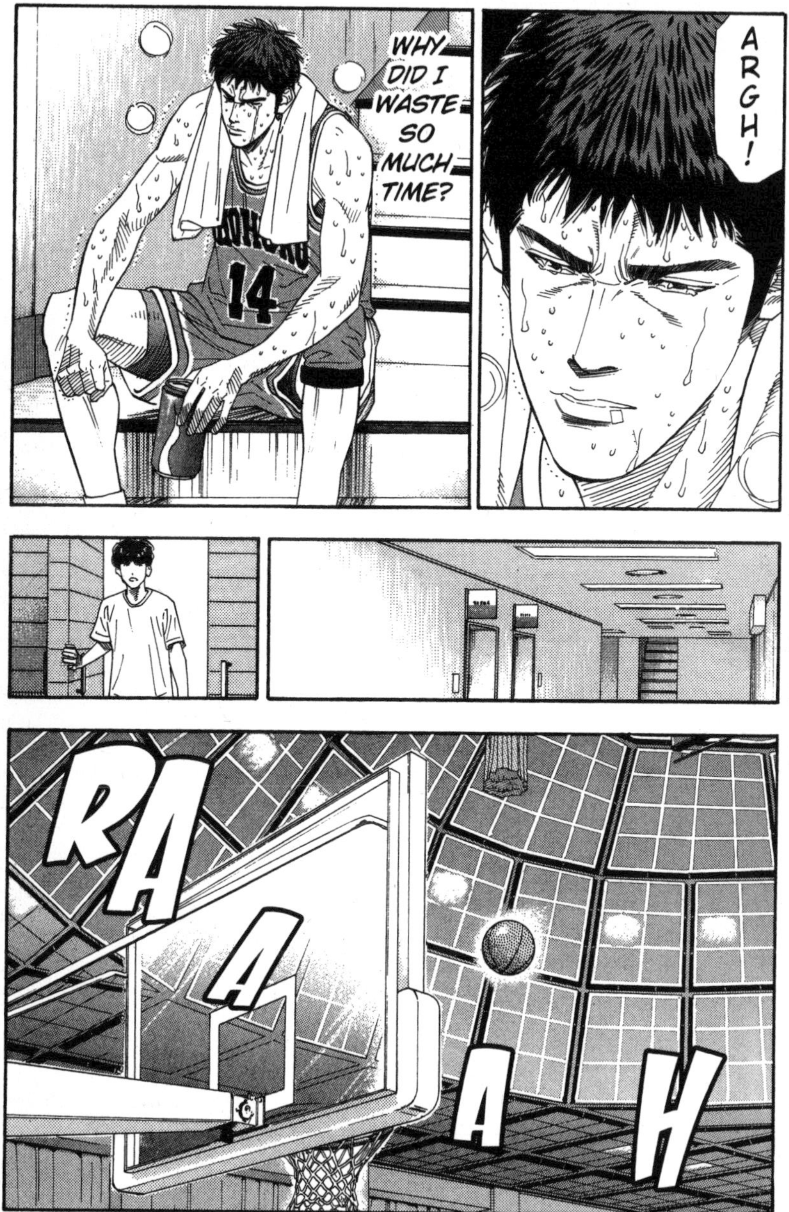
ARGH!
WHY DID I WASTE SO MUCH TIME?
RAAAH

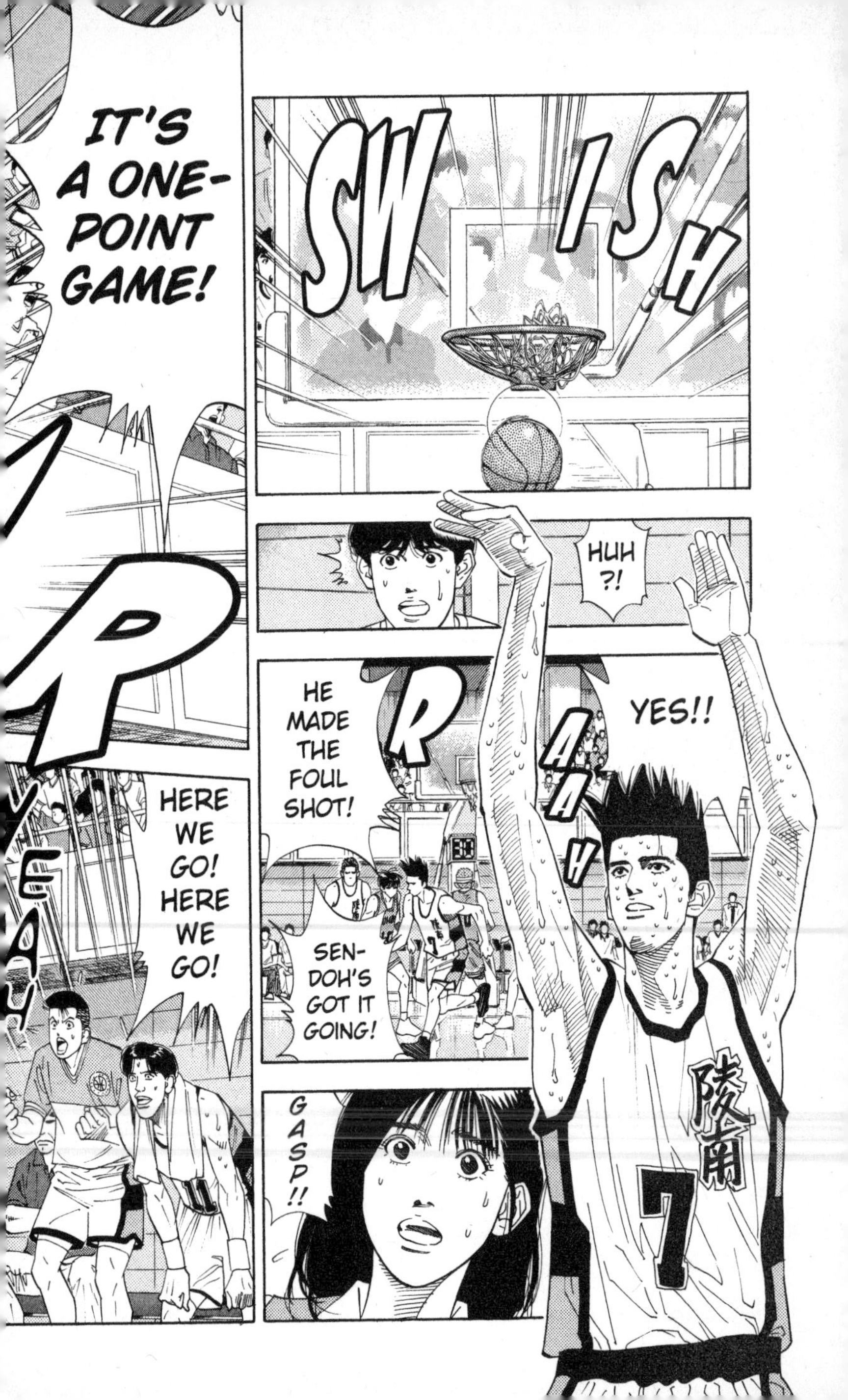
SWISH
HUH?!
YES!!
RAAAH
HE MADE THE FOUL SHOT!
SEN-DOH'S GOT IT GOING!
GASP!!
IT'S A ONE-POINT GAME!
HERE WE GO! HERE WE GO!

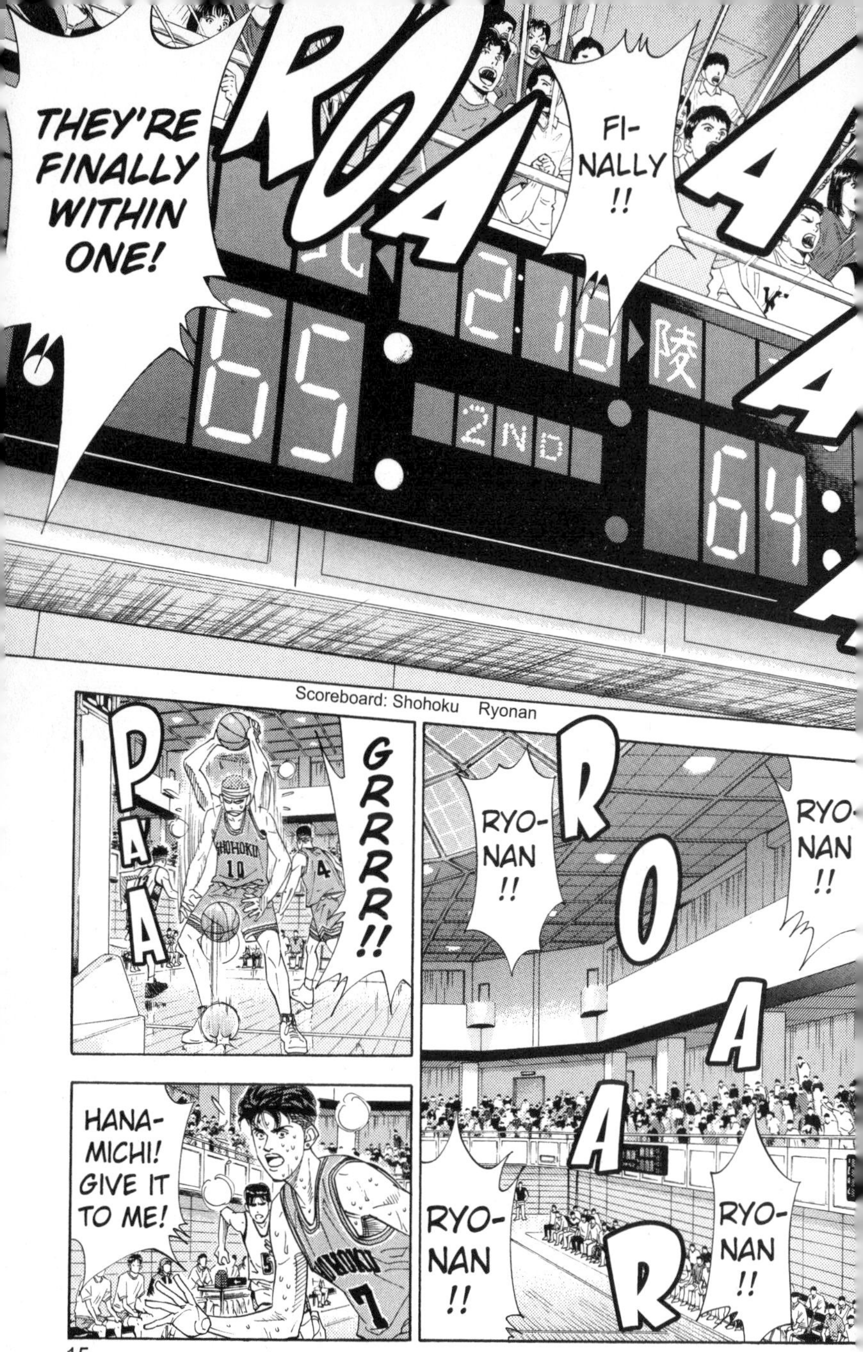

FI-NALLY!!
ROAAAA
2:18
陵
65
2ND
64
THEY'RE FINALLY WITHIN ONE!
Scoreboard: Shohoku Ryonan
RYO-NAN!!
RYO-NAN!!
ROAAR
RYO-NAN!!
RYO-NAN!!
GRRRRR!!
PAA
HANA-MICHI! GIVE IT TO ME!

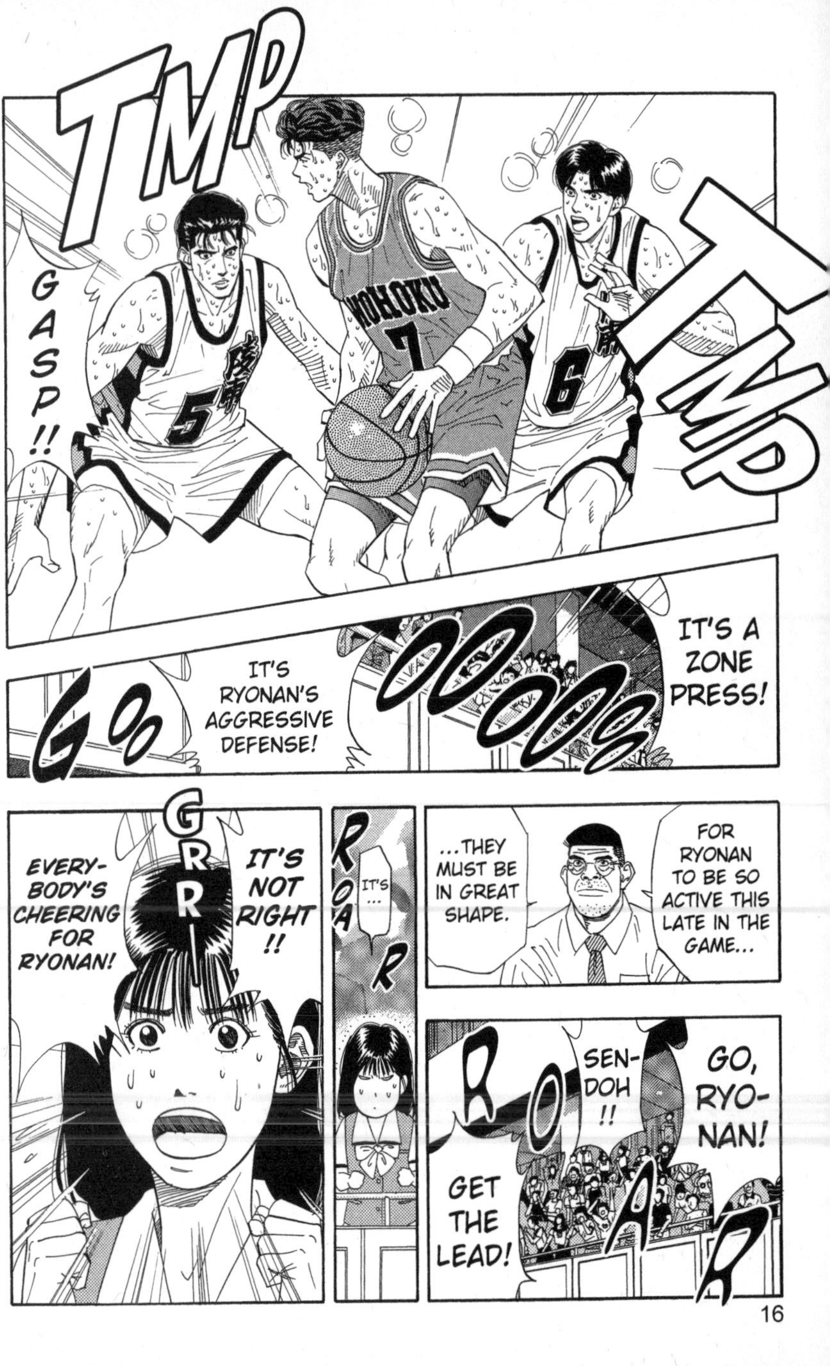
TMP
TMP
GASP!!
IT'S A ZONE PRESS!
OOOOO
IT'S RYONAN'S AGGRESSIVE DEFENSE!
GO
FOR RYONAN TO BE SO ACTIVE THIS LATE IN THE GAME...
...THEY MUST BE IN GREAT SHAPE.
GO, RYO-NAN!
SEN-DOH!!
ROAR
GET THE LEAD!
ROAR
IT'S...
GRR
IT'S NOT RIGHT!!
EVERY-BODY'S CHEERING FOR RYONAN!

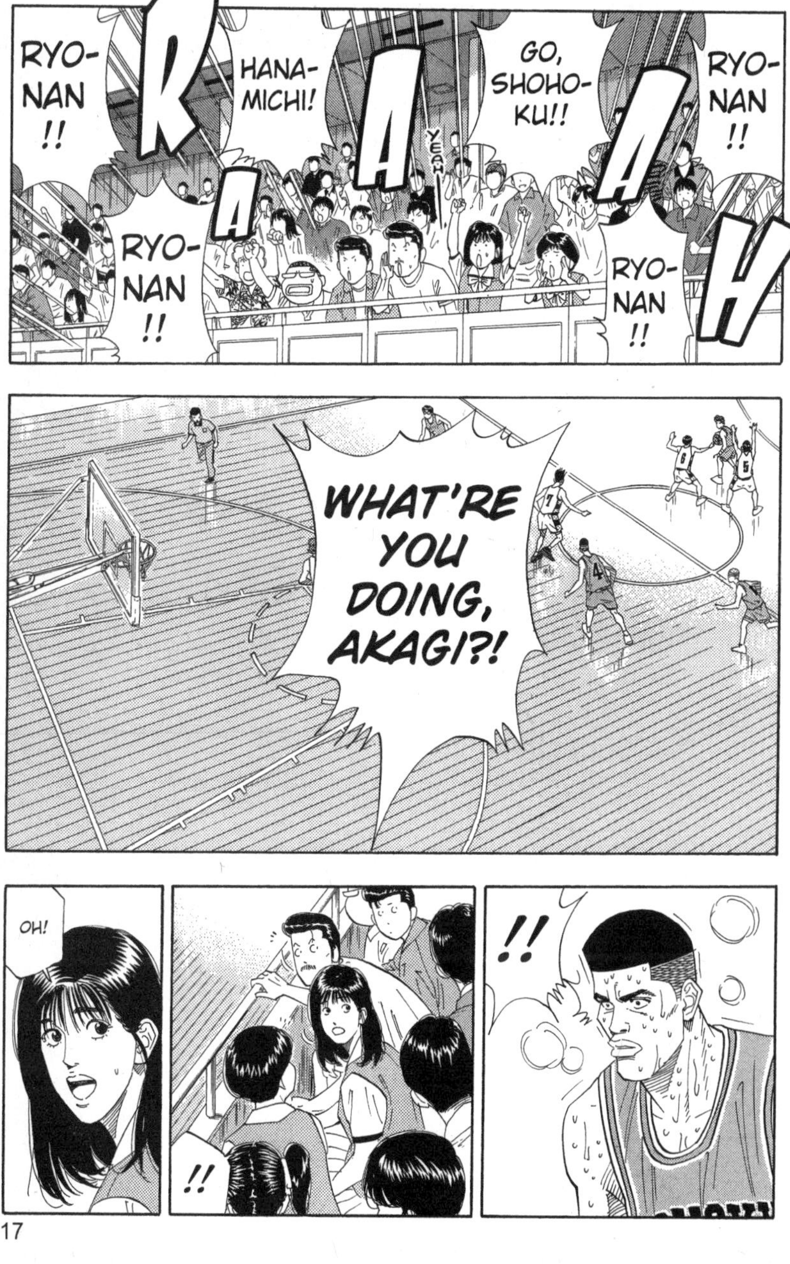
RYO-NAN!!
GO, SHOHOKU!!
HANA-MICHI!
RYO-NAN!!
RAAAH
YEAH
RYO-NAN!!
RYO-NAN!!
WHAT'RE YOU DOING, AKAGI?!
!!
!!
OH!

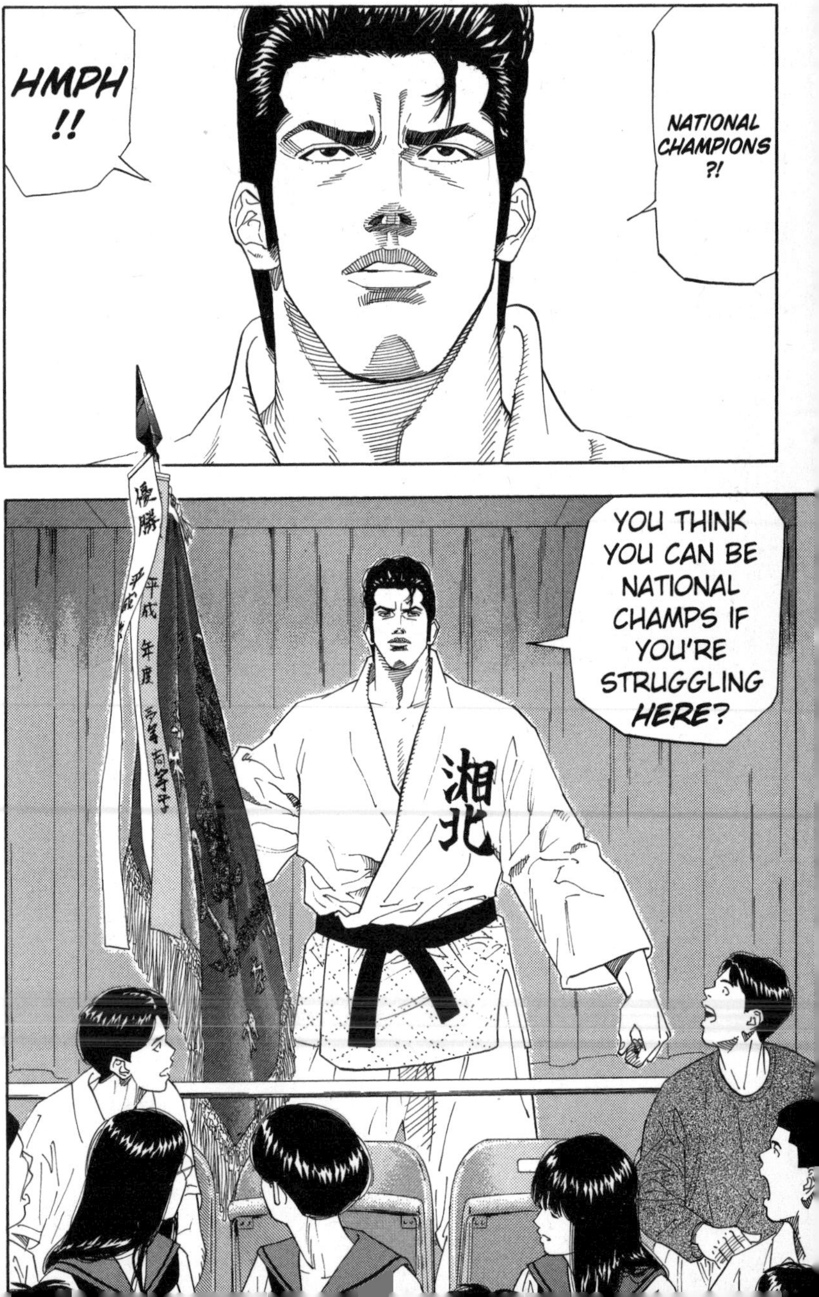
NATIONAL CHAMPIONS ?!
HMPH !!
YOU THINK YOU CAN BE NATIONAL CHAMPS IF YOU'RE STRUGGLING HERE?
優勝
湘北

READ THIS WAY

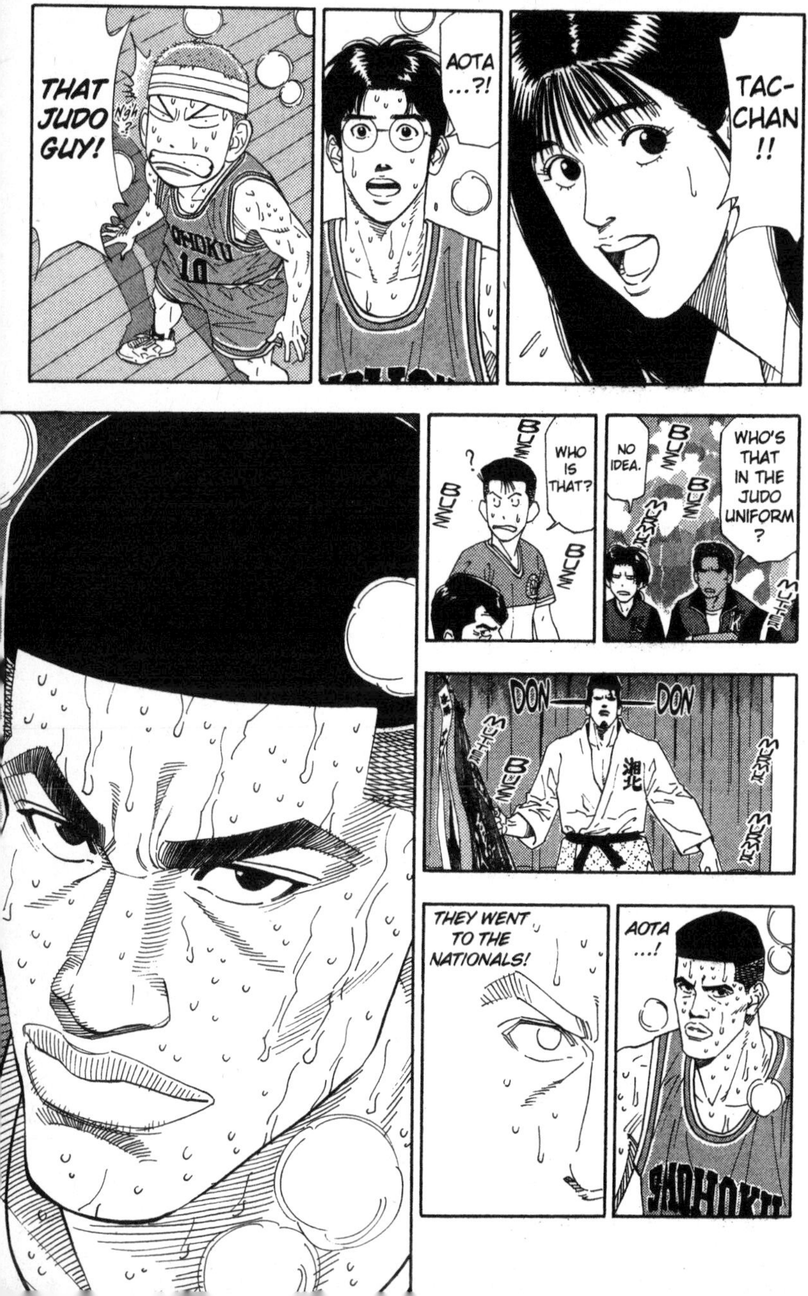
TAC-CHAN!!
AOTA ...?!
THAT JUDO GUY!
Ngh?
WHO'S THAT IN THE JUDO UNIFORM?
BUZZ
BUZZ
NO IDEA.
MURMUR
MUTTER
WHO IS THAT?
BUZZ
?
BUZZ
DON
DON
MURMUR
MURMUR
BUZZ
MUTTER
AOTA ...!
THEY WENT TO THE NATIONALS!

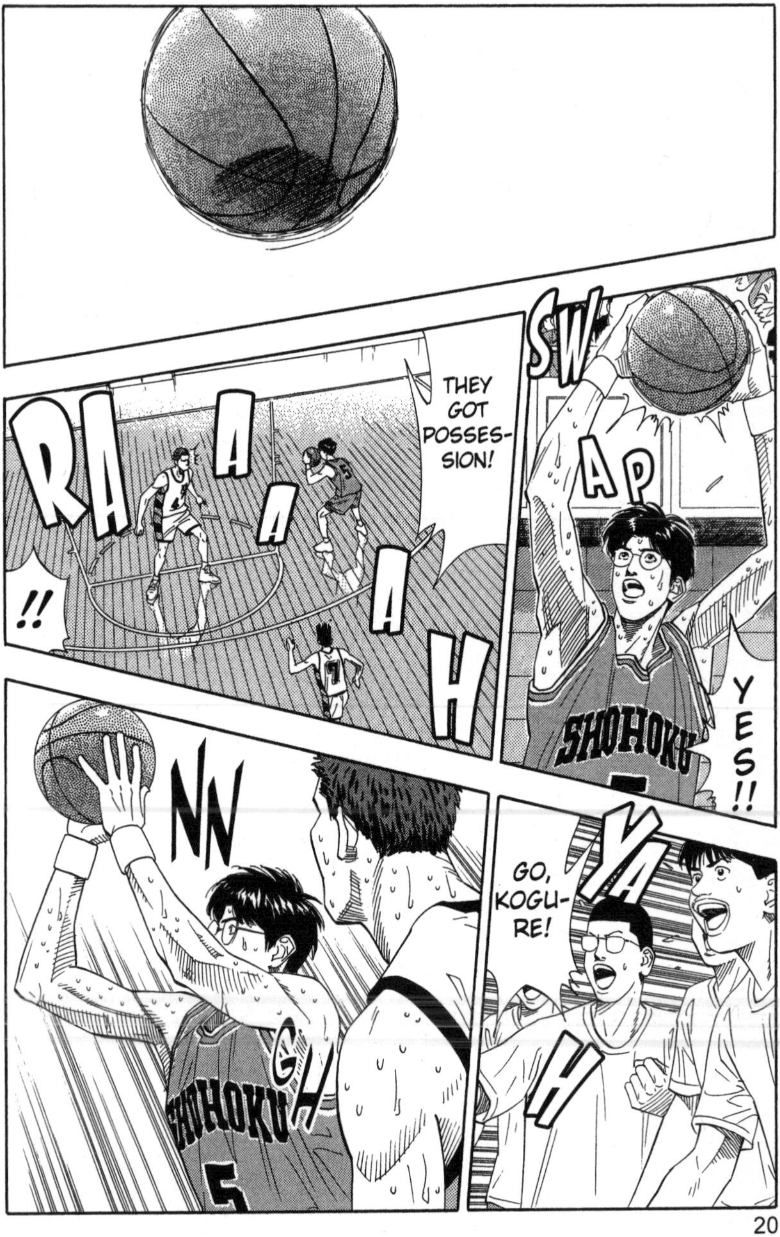
SWAP
YES!!
THEY GOT POSSESSION!
RAAAAH
!!
GO, KOGURE!
YAH
NNGH

READ THIS WAY

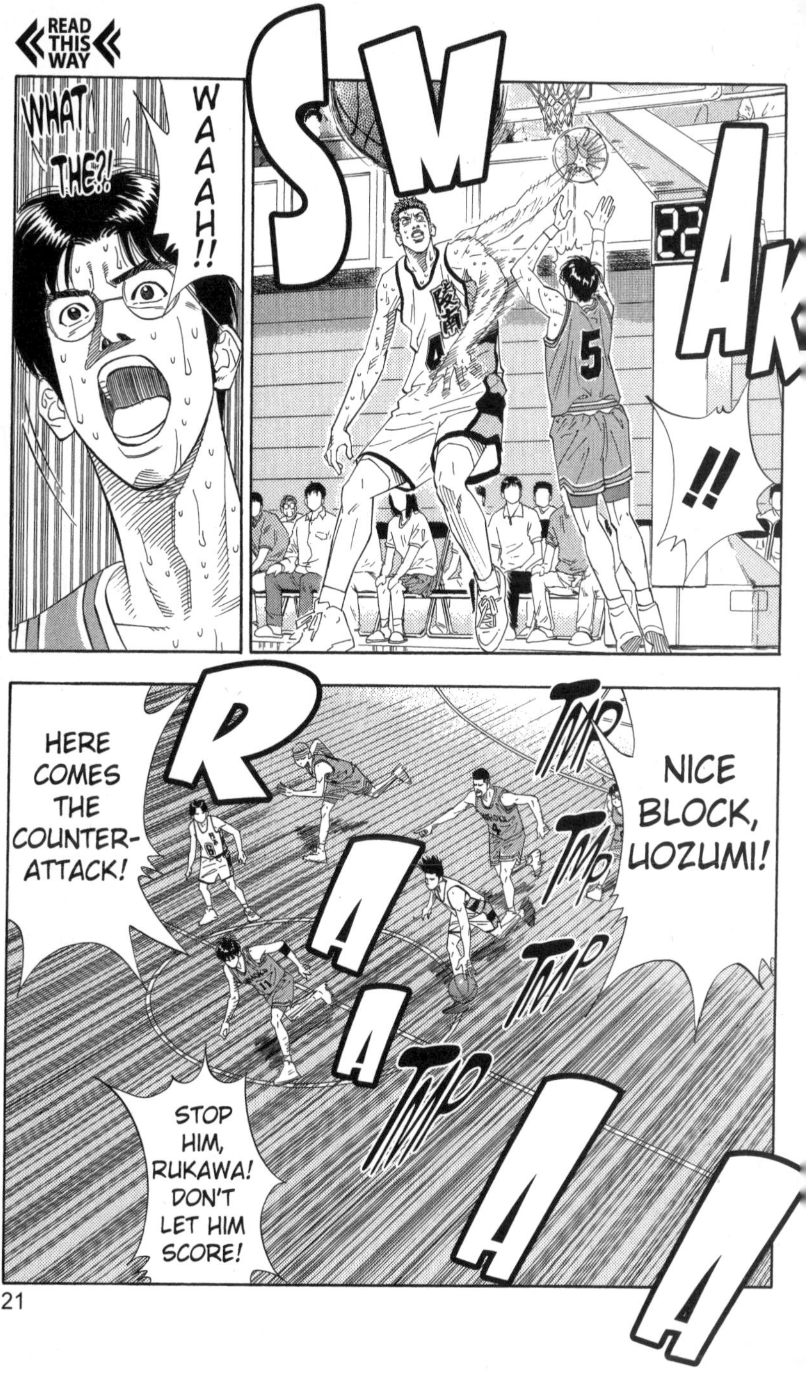

SMAAK
!!
WAAAAH!!
WHAT THE?!
NICE BLOCK, UOZUMI!
TMP TMP TMP TMP
RAAAA
HERE COMES THE COUNTER-ATTACK!
STOP HIM, RUKAWA! DON'T LET HIM SCORE!

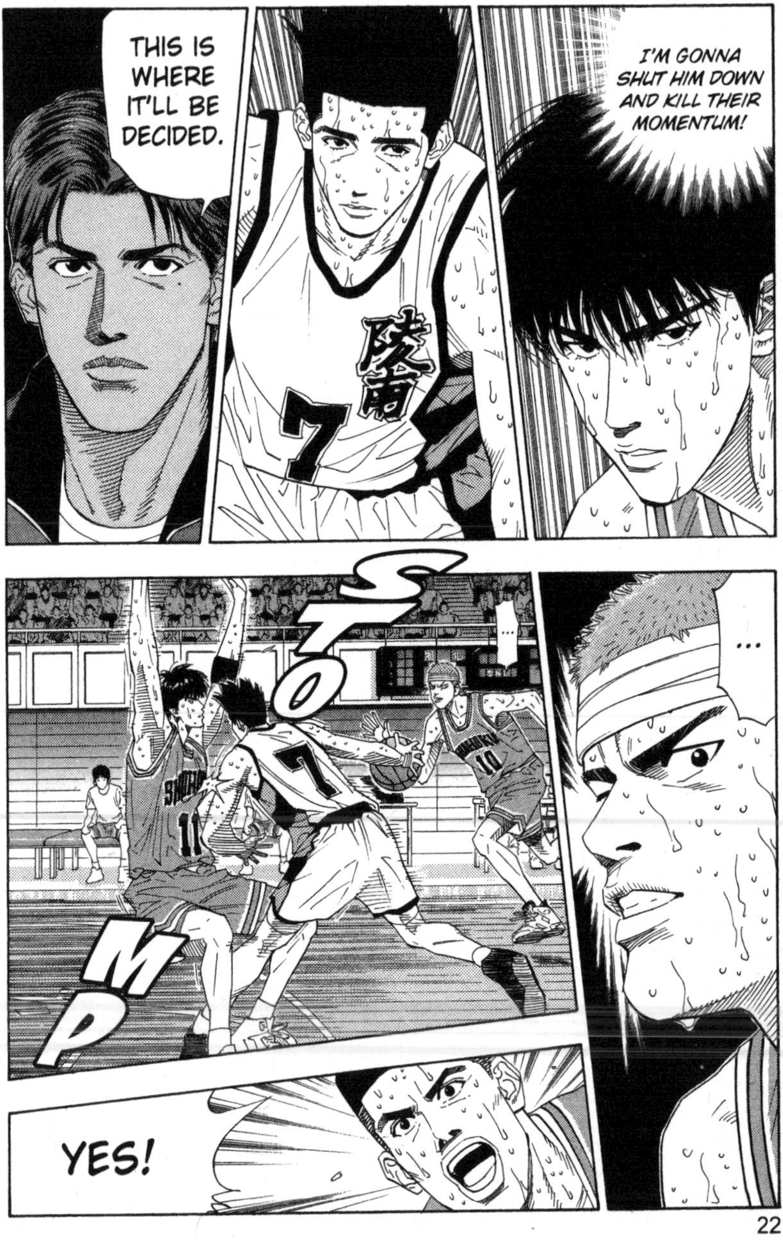
I'M GONNA SHUT HIM DOWN AND KILL THEIR MOMENTUM!
THIS IS WHERE IT'LL BE DECIDED.
...
!...
STOMP
YES!

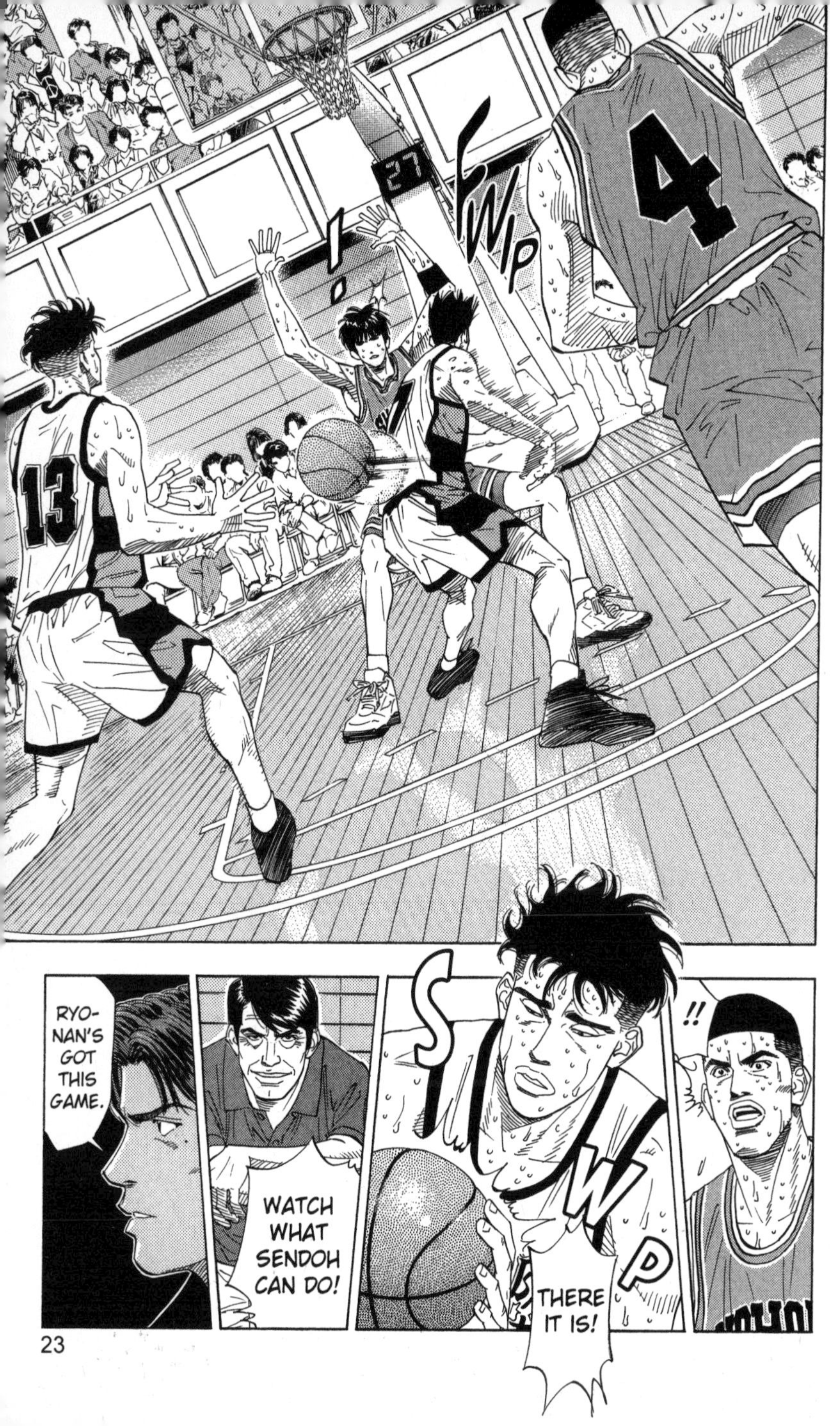
FWIP
!!
SWP
THERE IT IS!
WATCH WHAT SENDOH CAN DO!
RYO-NAN'S GOT THIS GAME.

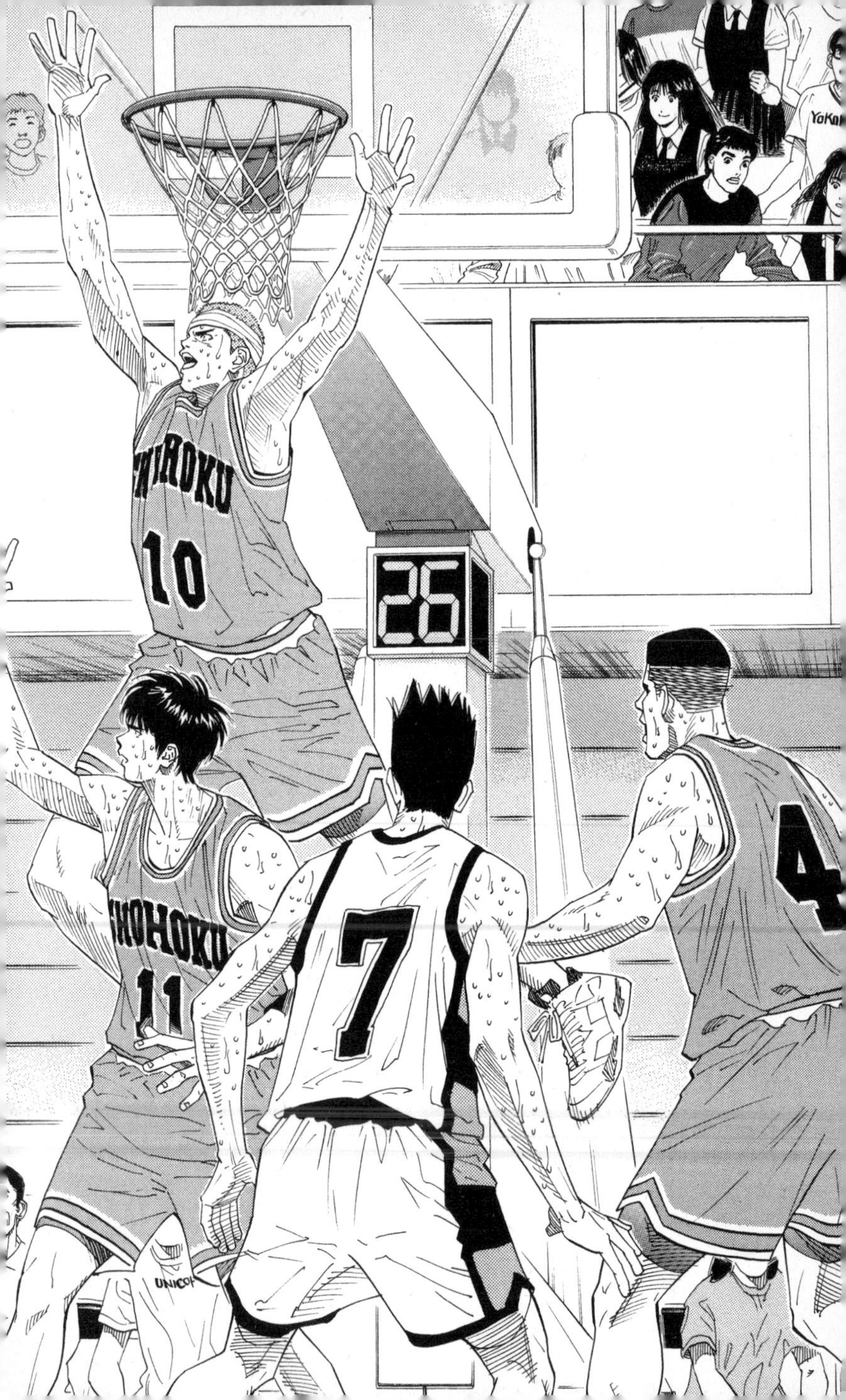
10
26
SHOHOKU
11
7

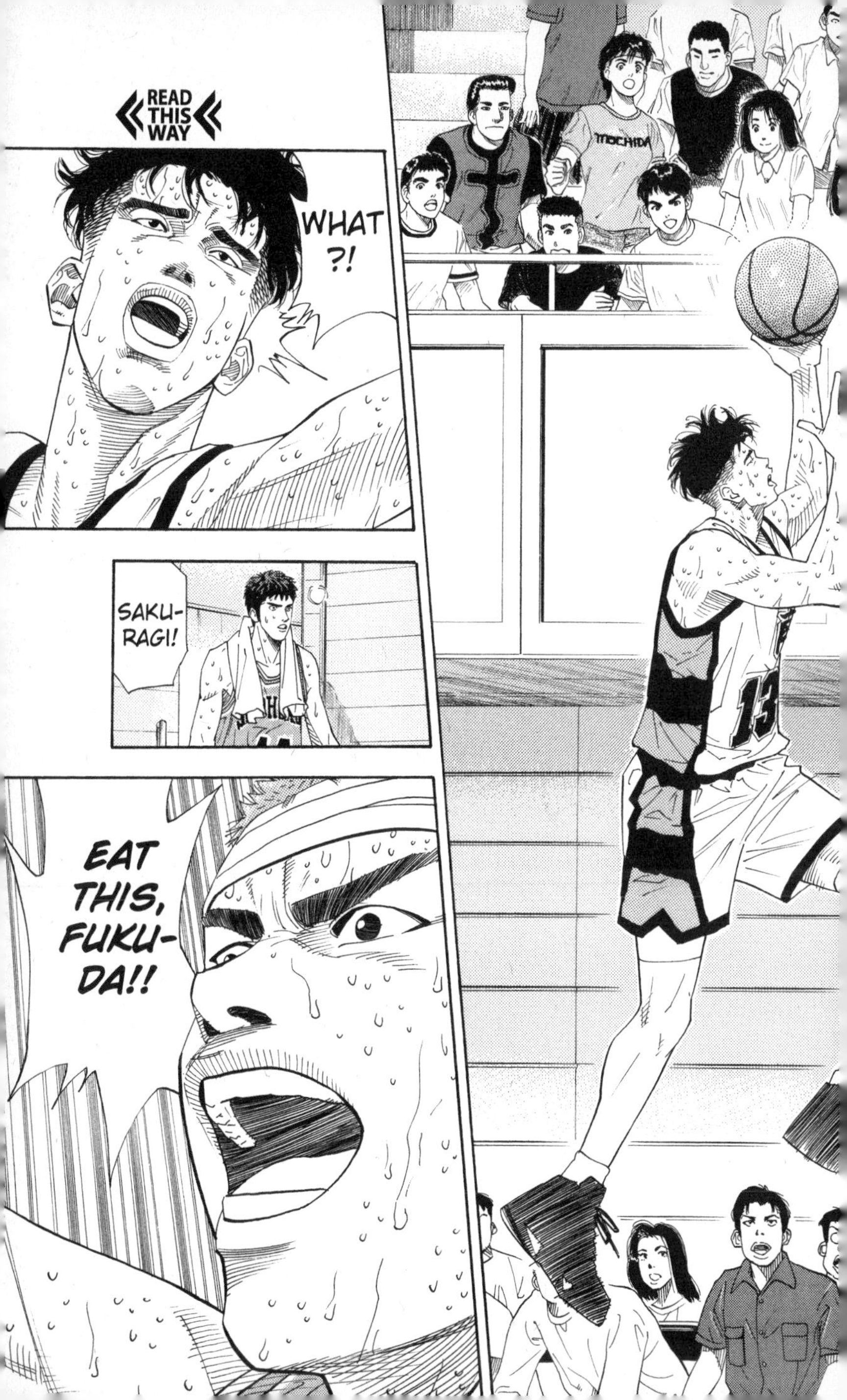
READ THIS WAY
MOCHIDA
WHAT ?!
SAKU-RAGI!
EAT THIS, FUKU-DA!!

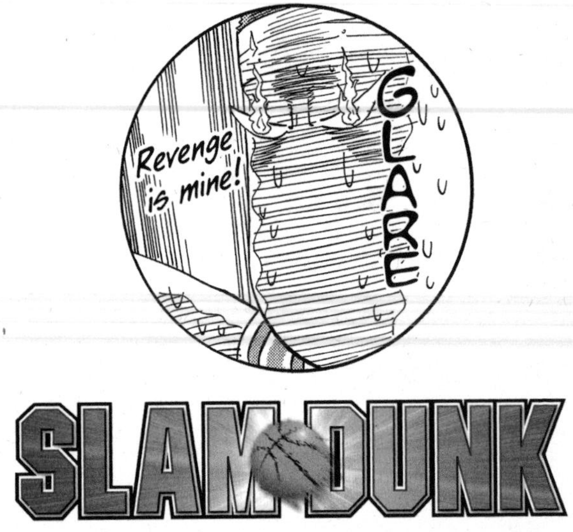
GLARE
Revenge is mine!

SLAM DUNK

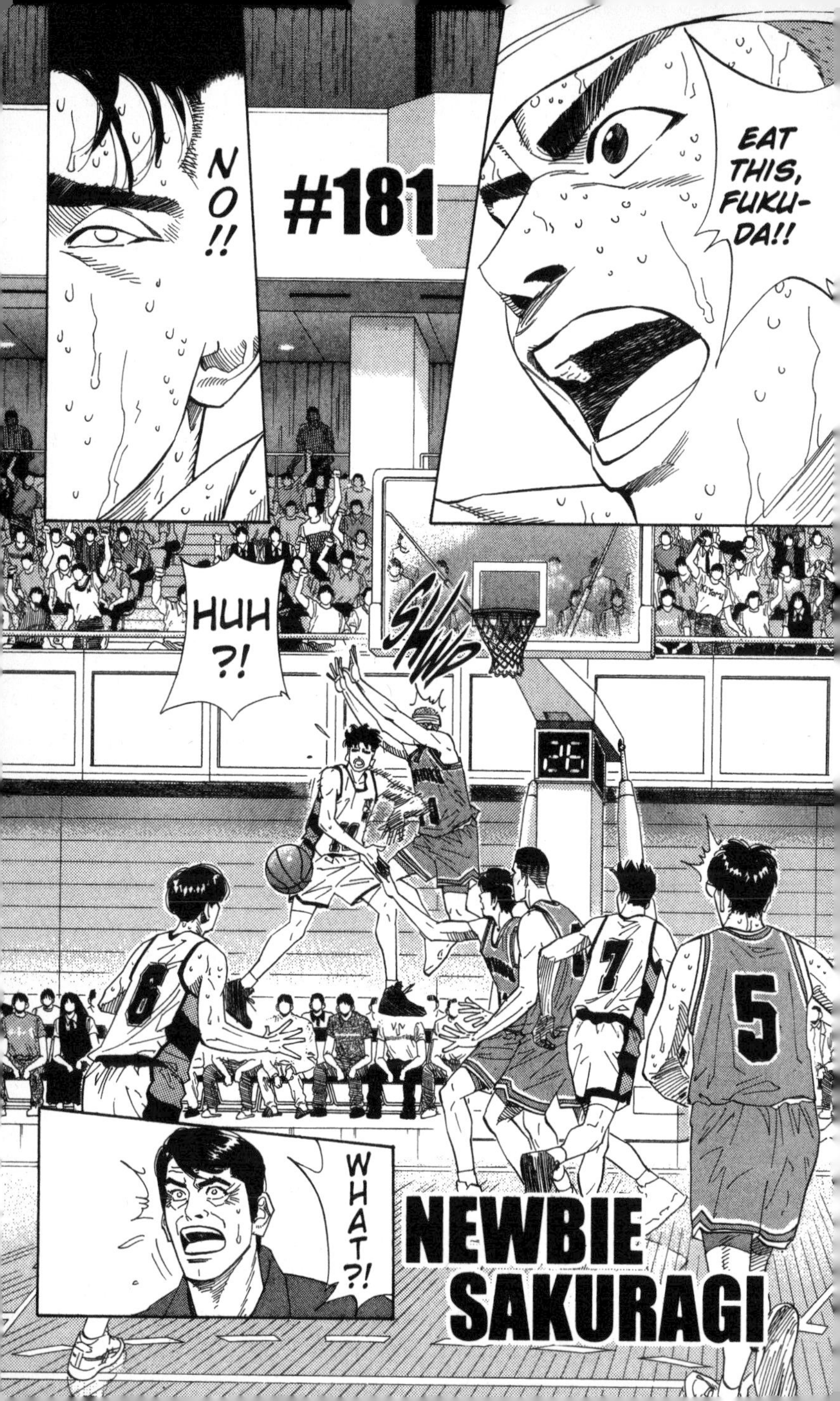
EAT THIS, FUKU-DA!!
#181
NO!!
HUH ?!
SHWD
NEWBIE SAKURAGI
WHAT?!

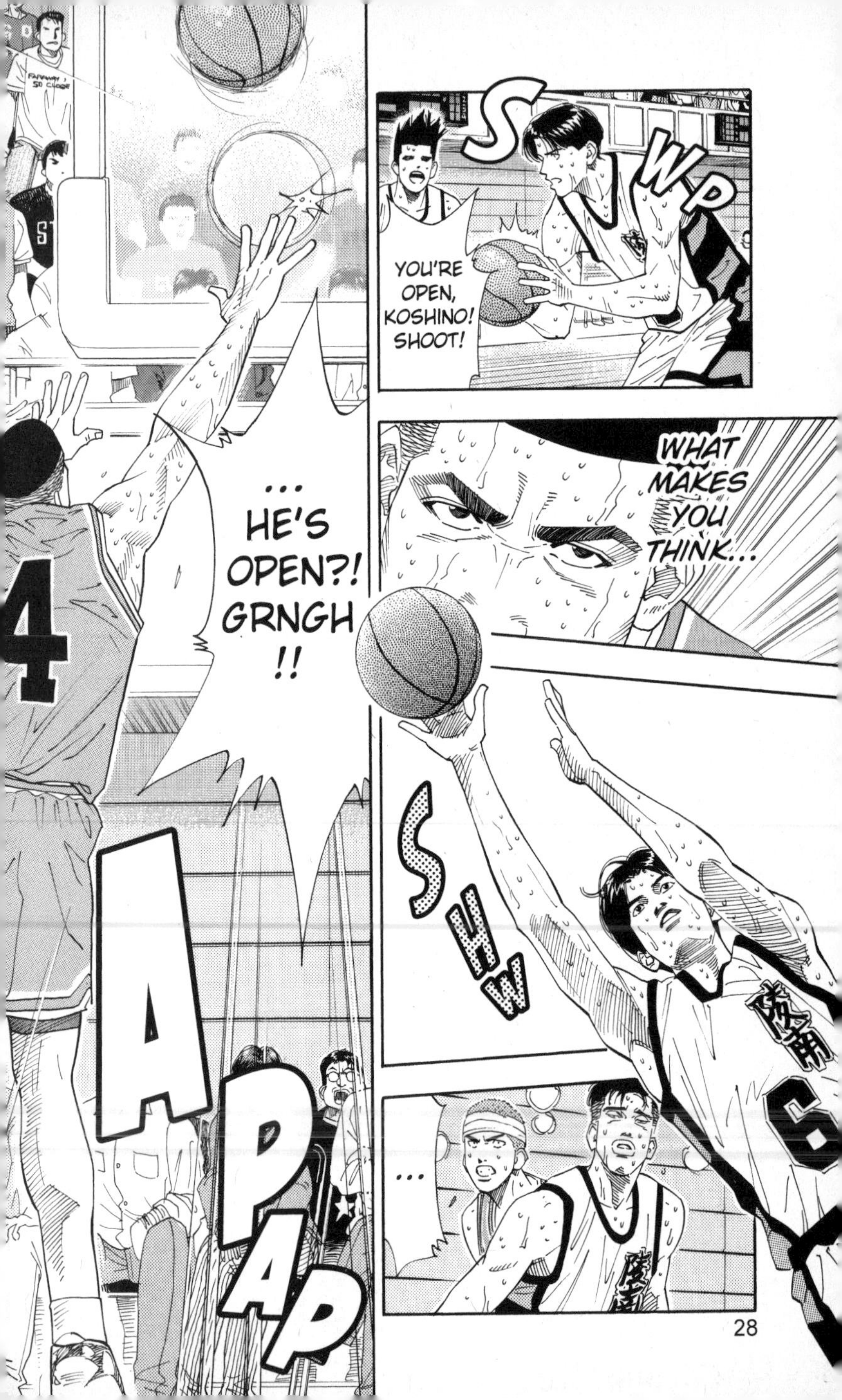
SWP
YOU'RE OPEN, KOSHINO! SHOOT!
WHAT MAKES YOU THINK...
SHW
...
... HE'S OPEN?! GRNGH !!
APAP

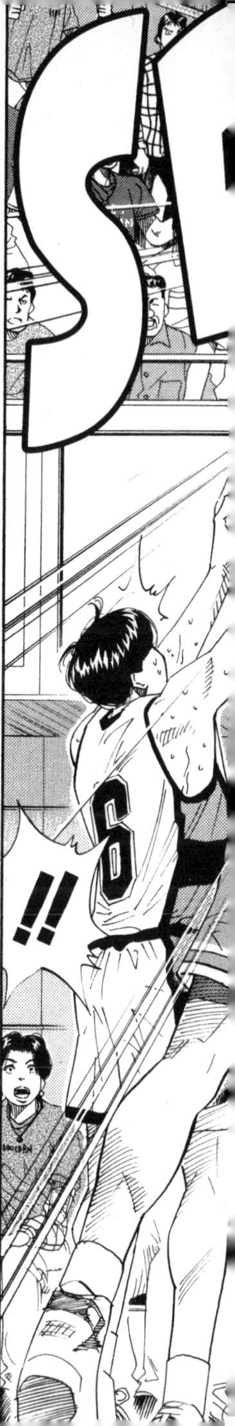
!!

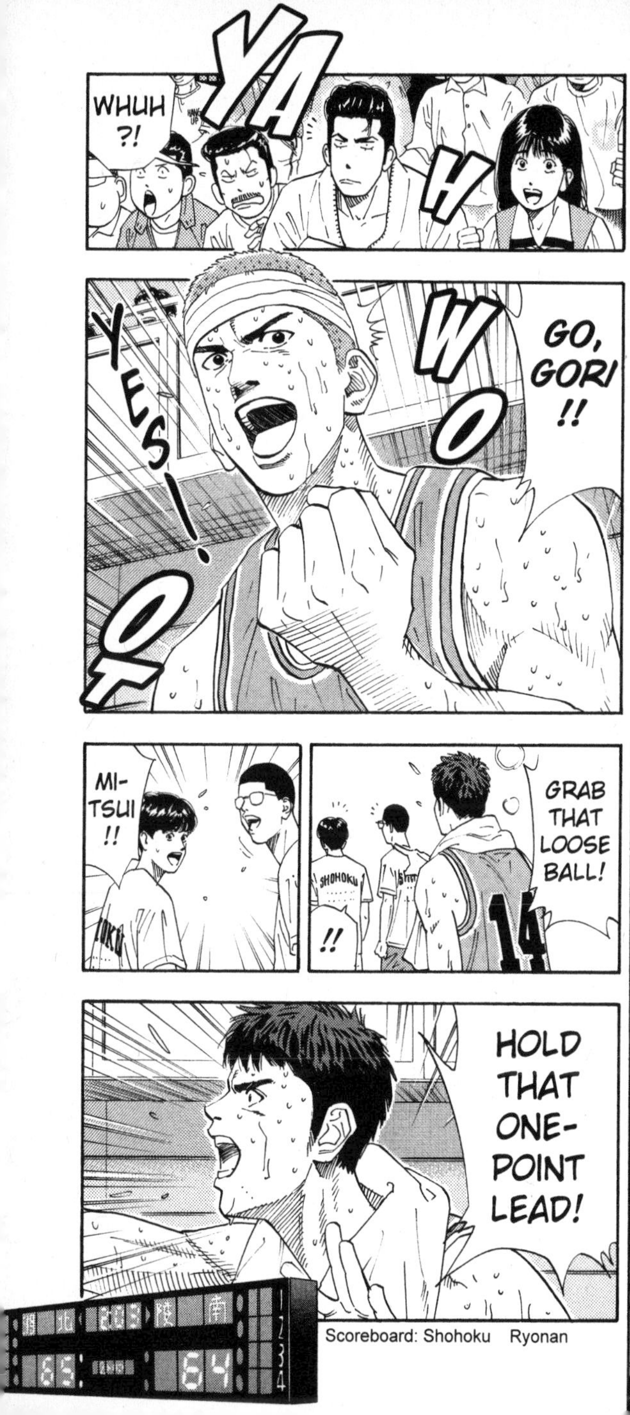
YA
H
WHUH ?!
GO, GORI !!
WO
YES!
OT
GRAB THAT LOOSE BALL!
!!
SHOHOKU
14
MI-TSUI !!
HOLD THAT ONE-POINT LEAD!
1
2
3
4
65
64

Scoreboard: Shohoku Ryonan

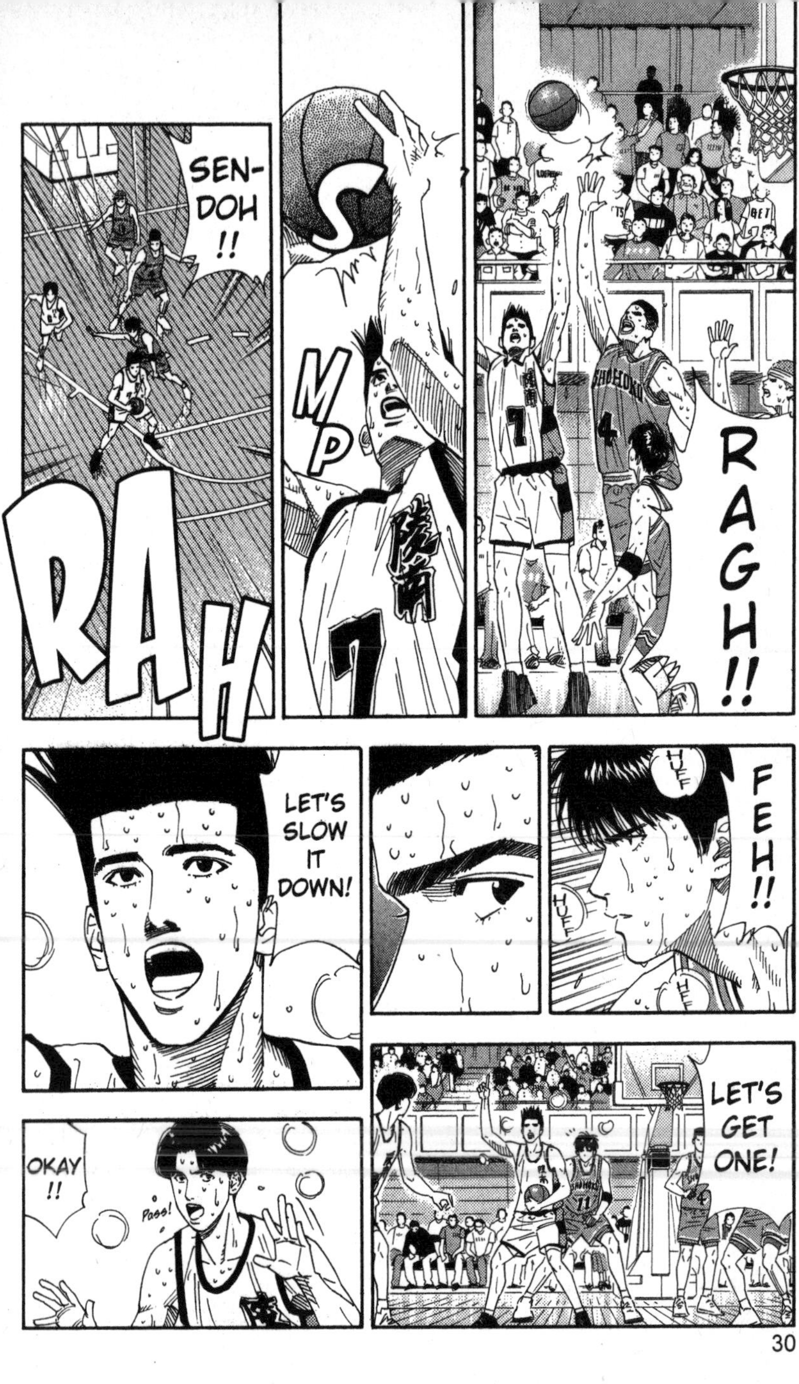
RAGH!!
SMP
SEN-DOH!!
RAH
FEH!!
HUFF
HUFF
LET'S SLOW IT DOWN!
LET'S GET ONE!
OKAY!!
Pass!

READ THIS WAY

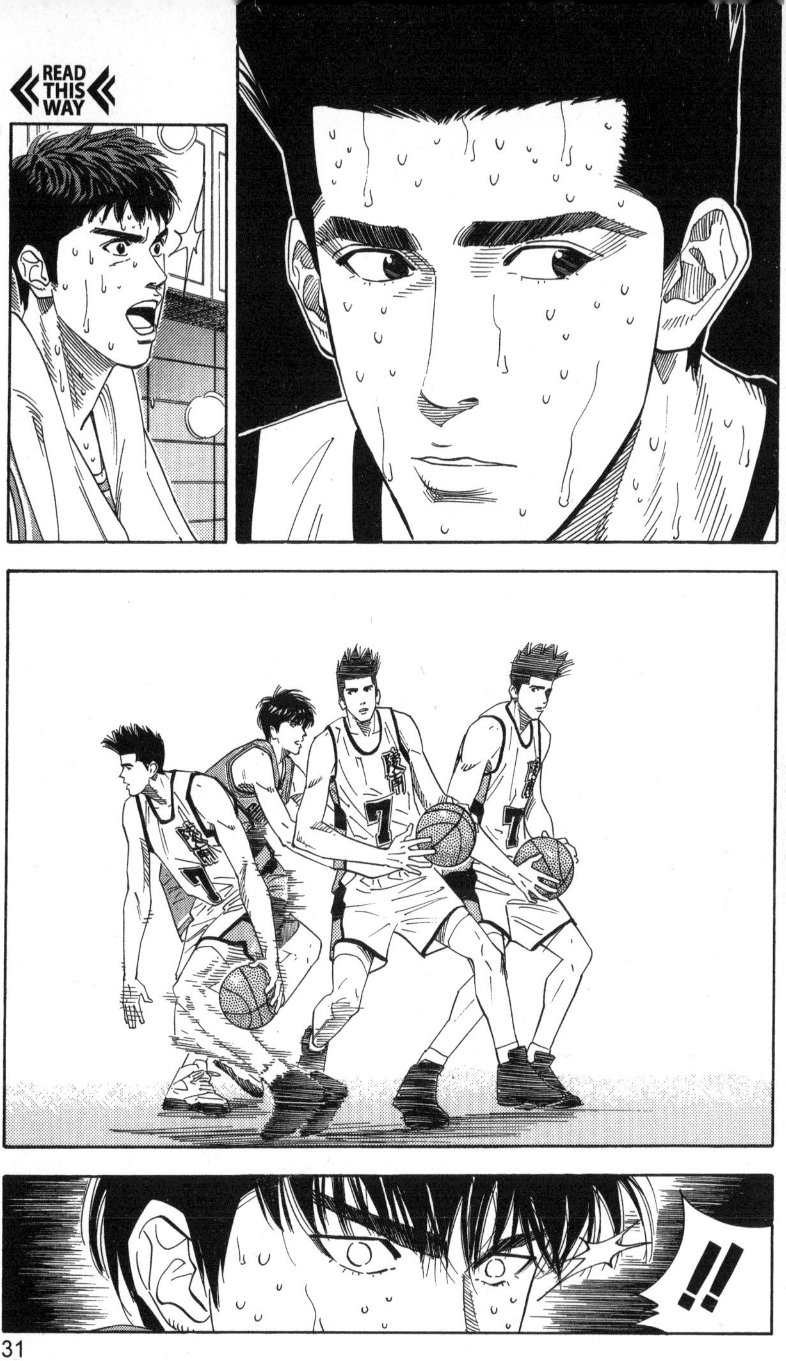
!!

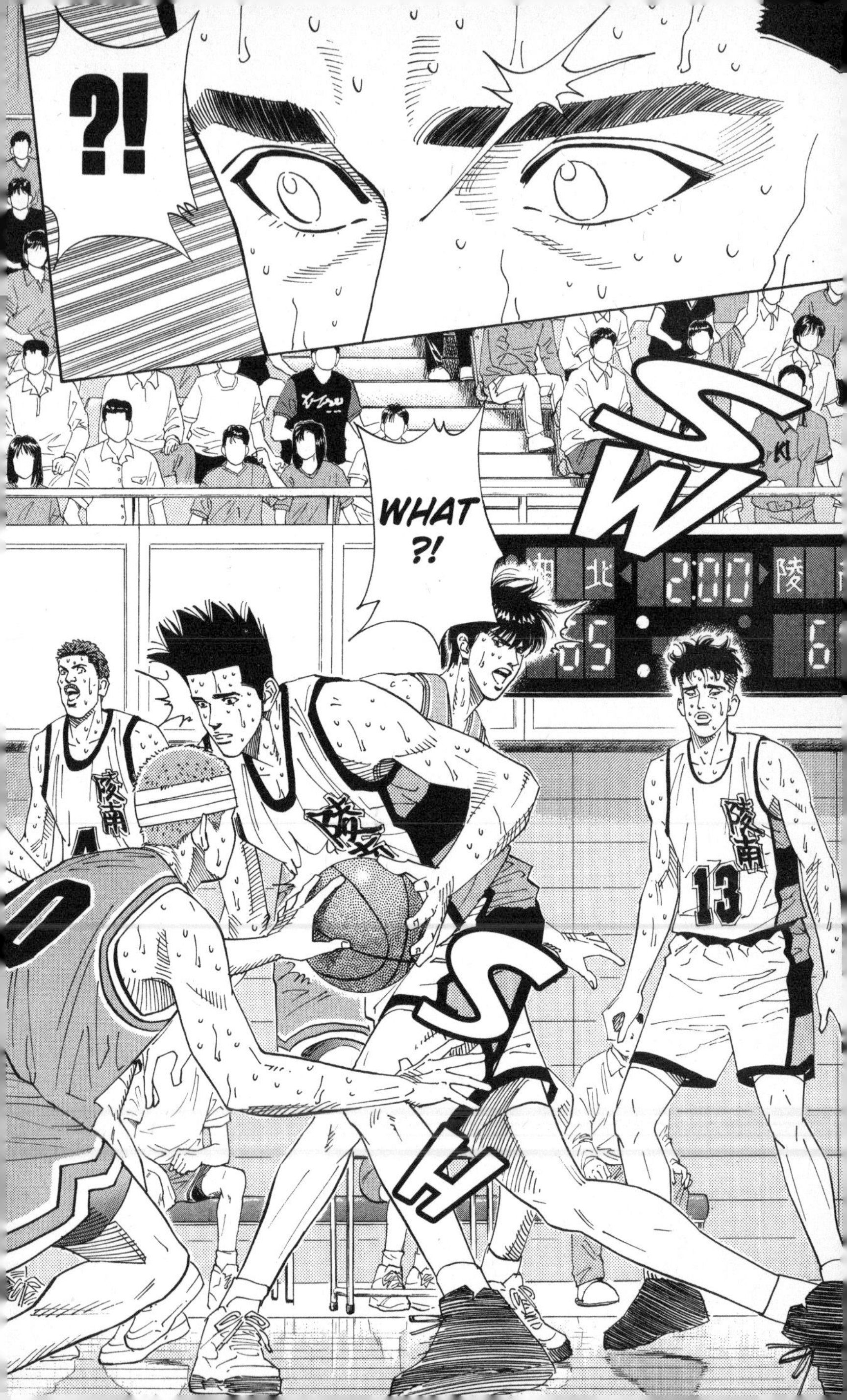
?!
WHAT ?!
SW
SH

READ THIS WAY

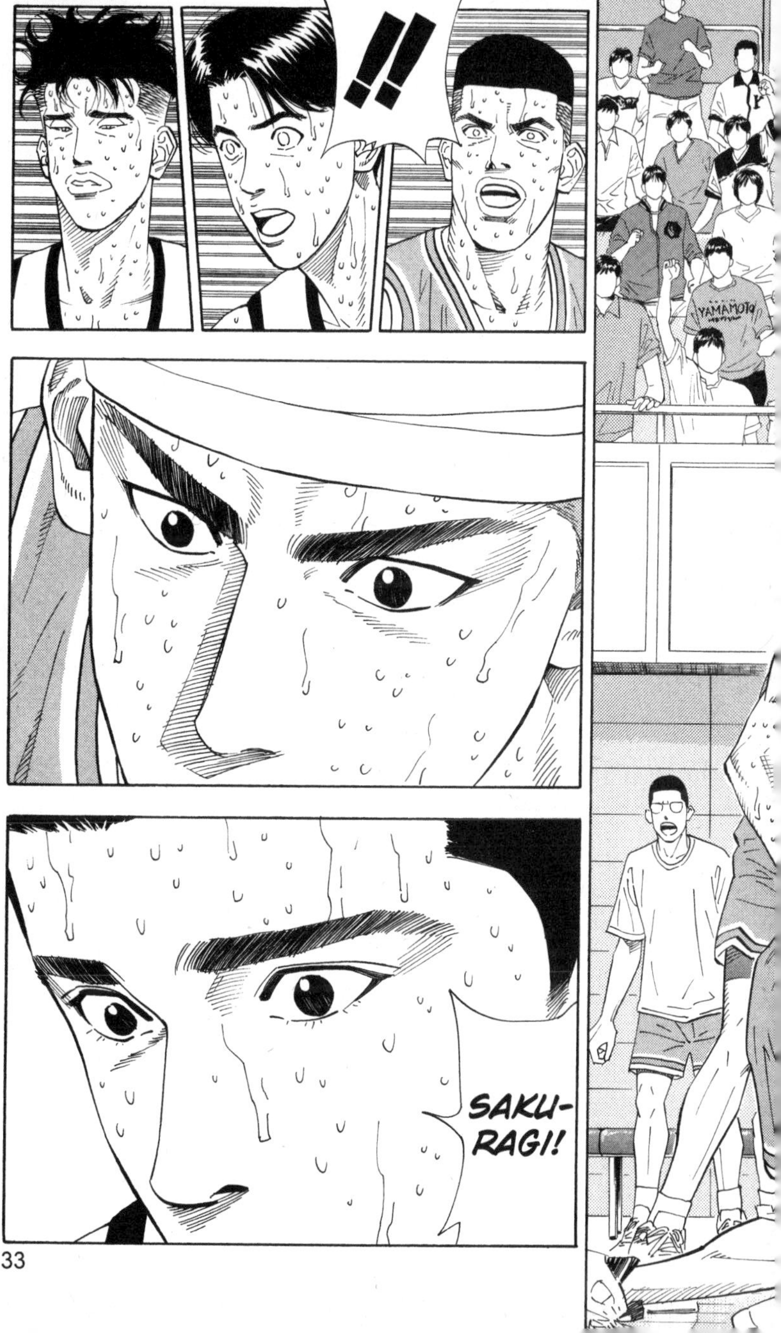
YAMAMOTO
!!
SAKU-
RAGI!

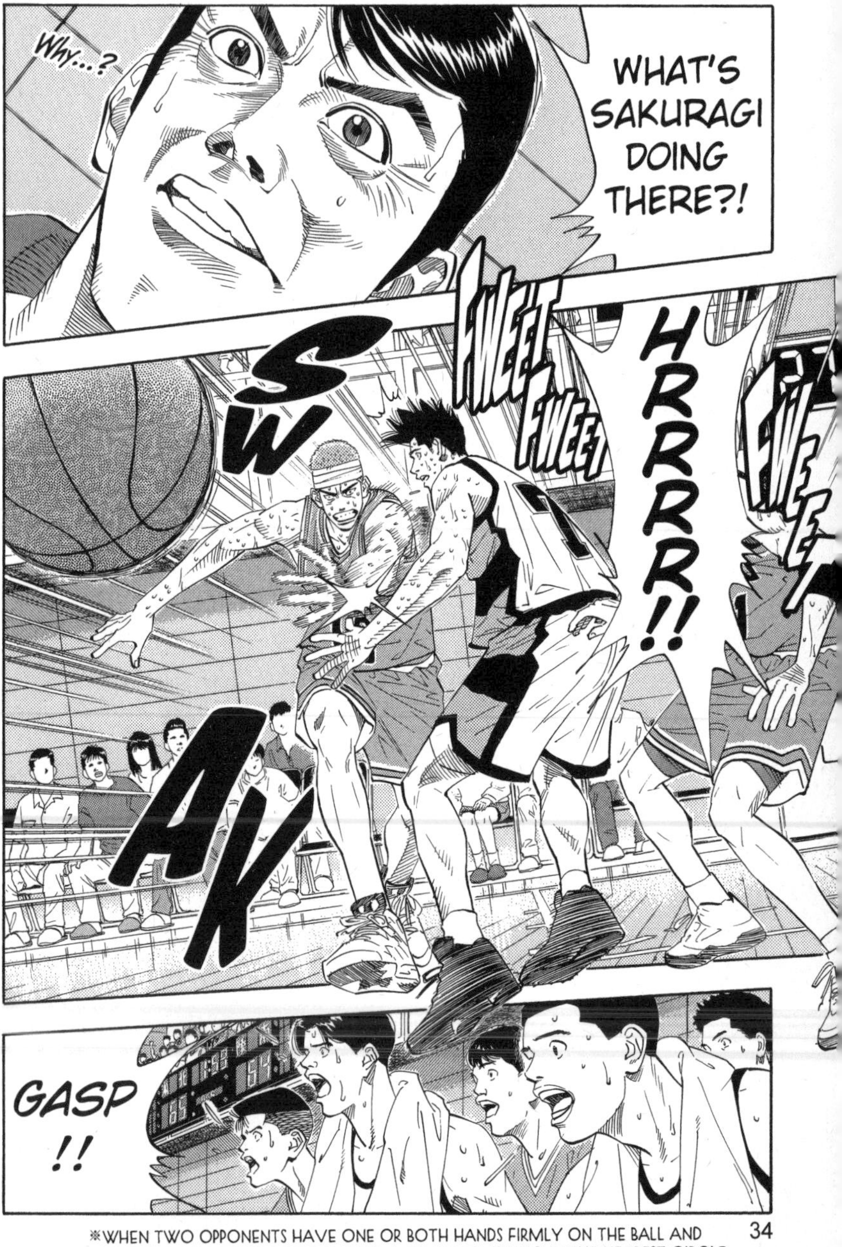
WHAT'S SAKURAGI DOING THERE?!
Why...?
FWEET
HRRRR!!
FWEET FWEET FWEET
SWAK
GASP!!

※WHEN TWO OPPONENTS HAVE ONE OR BOTH HANDS FIRMLY ON THE BALL AND POSSESSION CANNOT BE DETERMINED, A JUMP-BALL IS HELD IN THE NEAREST CIRCLE.

READ THIS WAY

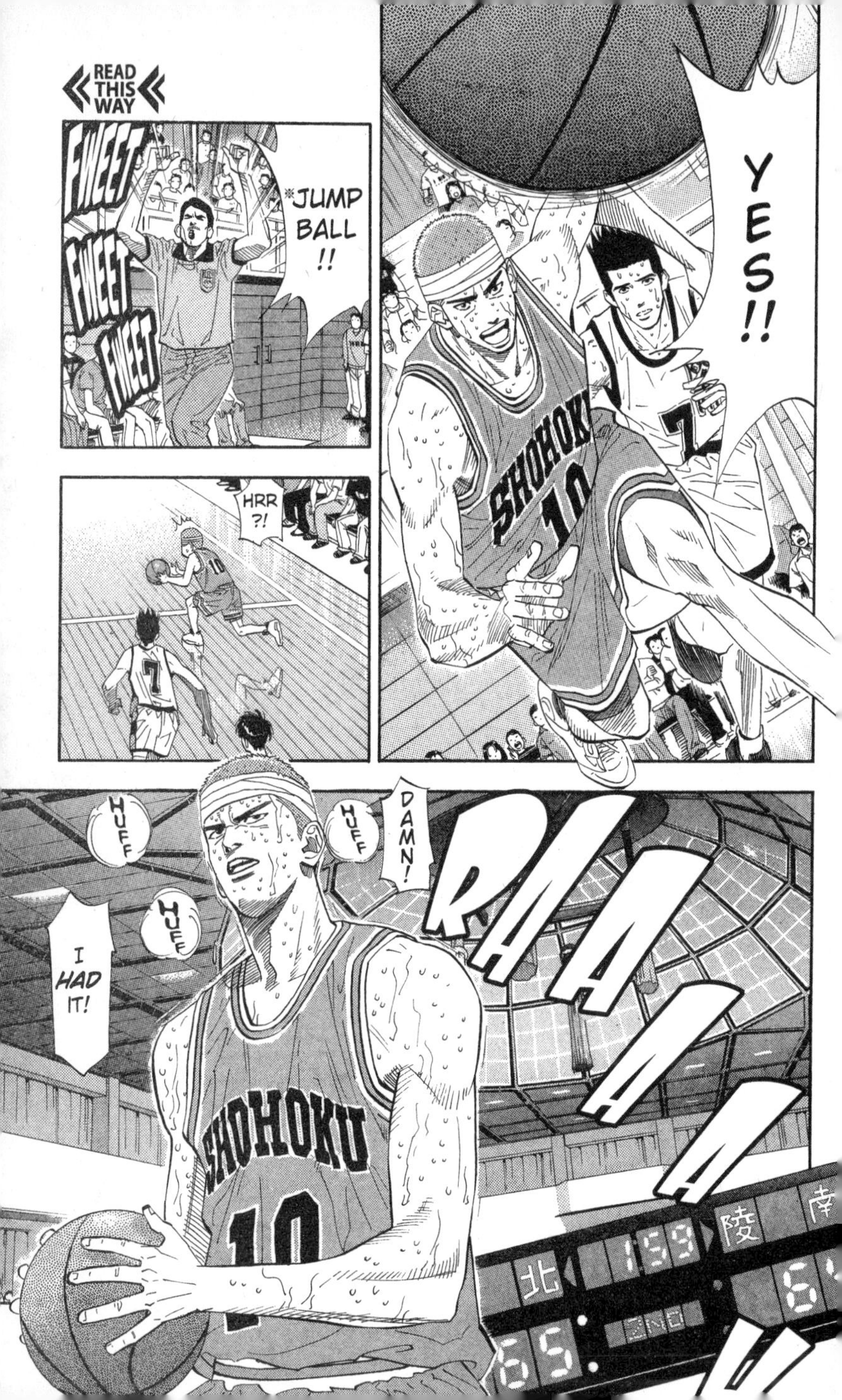
YES!!
FWEET FWEET FWEET
※JUMP BALL!!
HRR ?!
RAAAA!!
DAMN!
HUFF
HUFF
HUFF
I HAD IT!

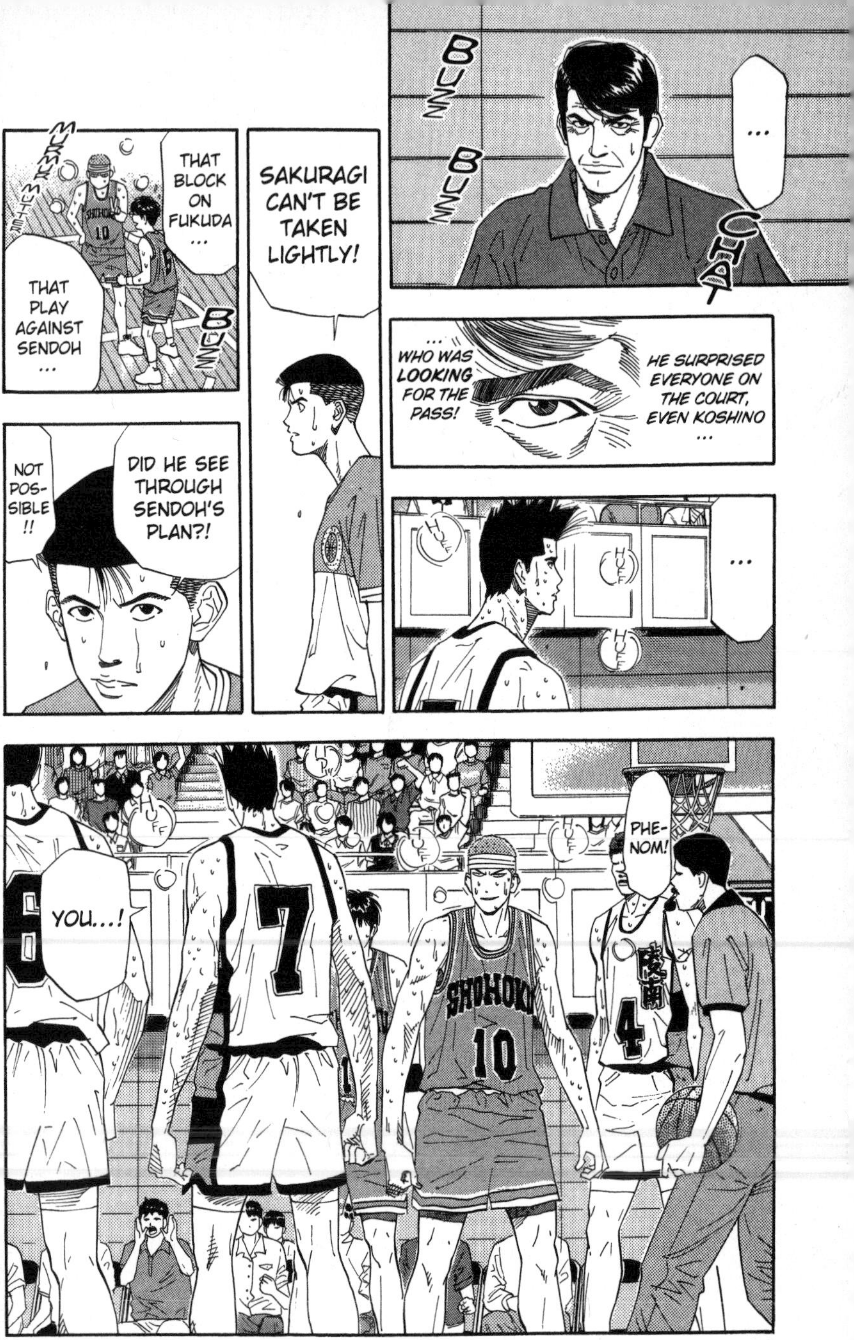
...
BUZZ
BUZZ
CHAT
HE SURPRISED EVERYONE ON THE COURT, EVEN KOSHINO ...
... WHO WAS LOOKING FOR THE PASS!
HUFF
HUFF
...
SAKURAGI CAN'T BE TAKEN LIGHTLY!
MURMUR
MUTTER
THAT BLOCK ON FUKUDA ...
THAT PLAY AGAINST SENDOH ...
BUZZ
DID HE SEE THROUGH SENDOH'S PLAN?!
NOT POSSIBLE!!
PHENOM!
HUFF
HUFF
YOU...!

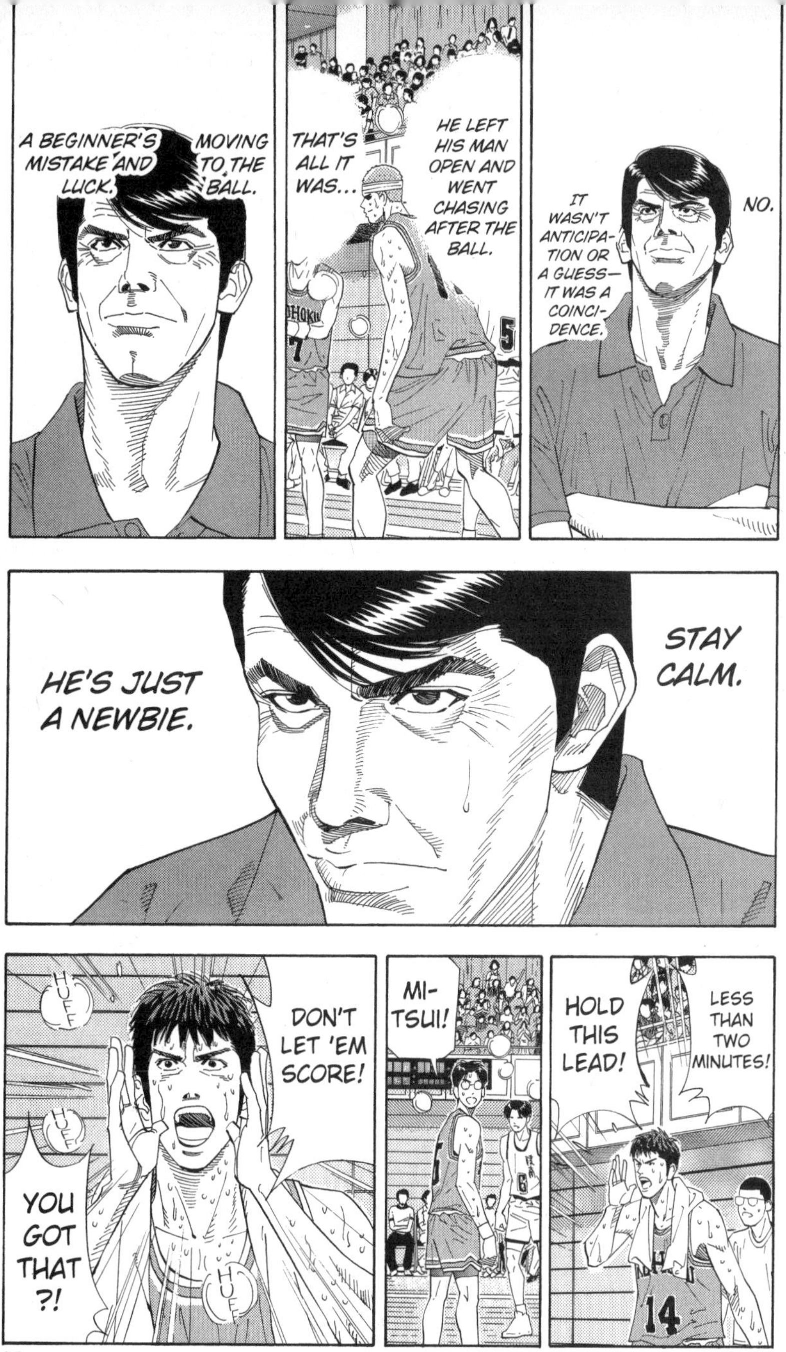
NO.
IT WASN'T ANTICIPATION OR A GUESS— IT WAS A COINCIDENCE.
HE LEFT HIS MAN OPEN AND WENT CHASING AFTER THE BALL.
THAT'S ALL IT WAS...
MOVING TO THE BALL.
A BEGINNER'S MISTAKE AND LUCK.
STAY CALM.
HE'S JUST A NEWBIE.
LESS THAN TWO MINUTES!
HOLD THIS LEAD!
MI-TSUI!
HUFF
DON'T LET 'EM SCORE!
HUFF
YOU GOT THAT?!

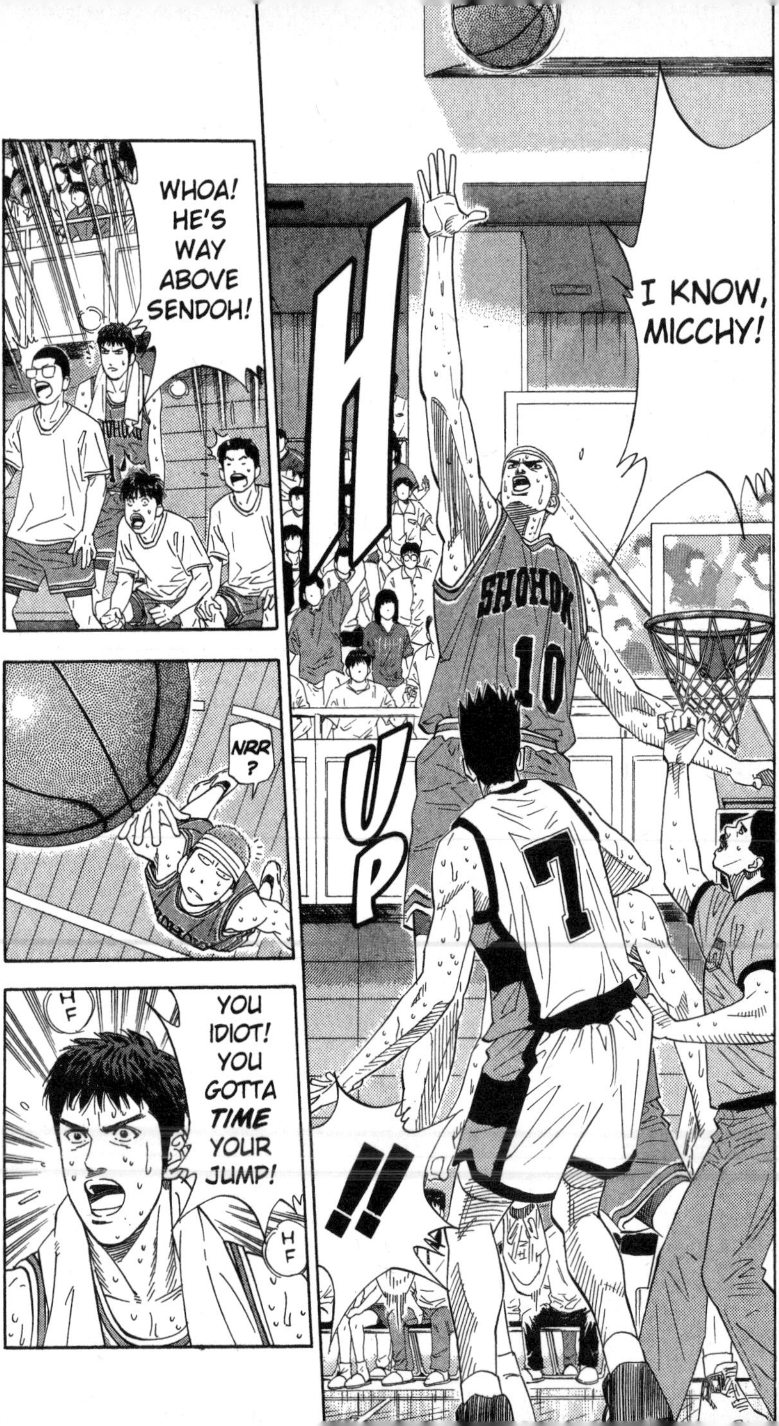
I KNOW, MICCHY!
HUP
!!
WHOA! HE'S WAY ABOVE SENDOH!
NRR ?
HF
YOU IDIOT! YOU GOTTA TIME YOUR JUMP!
HF

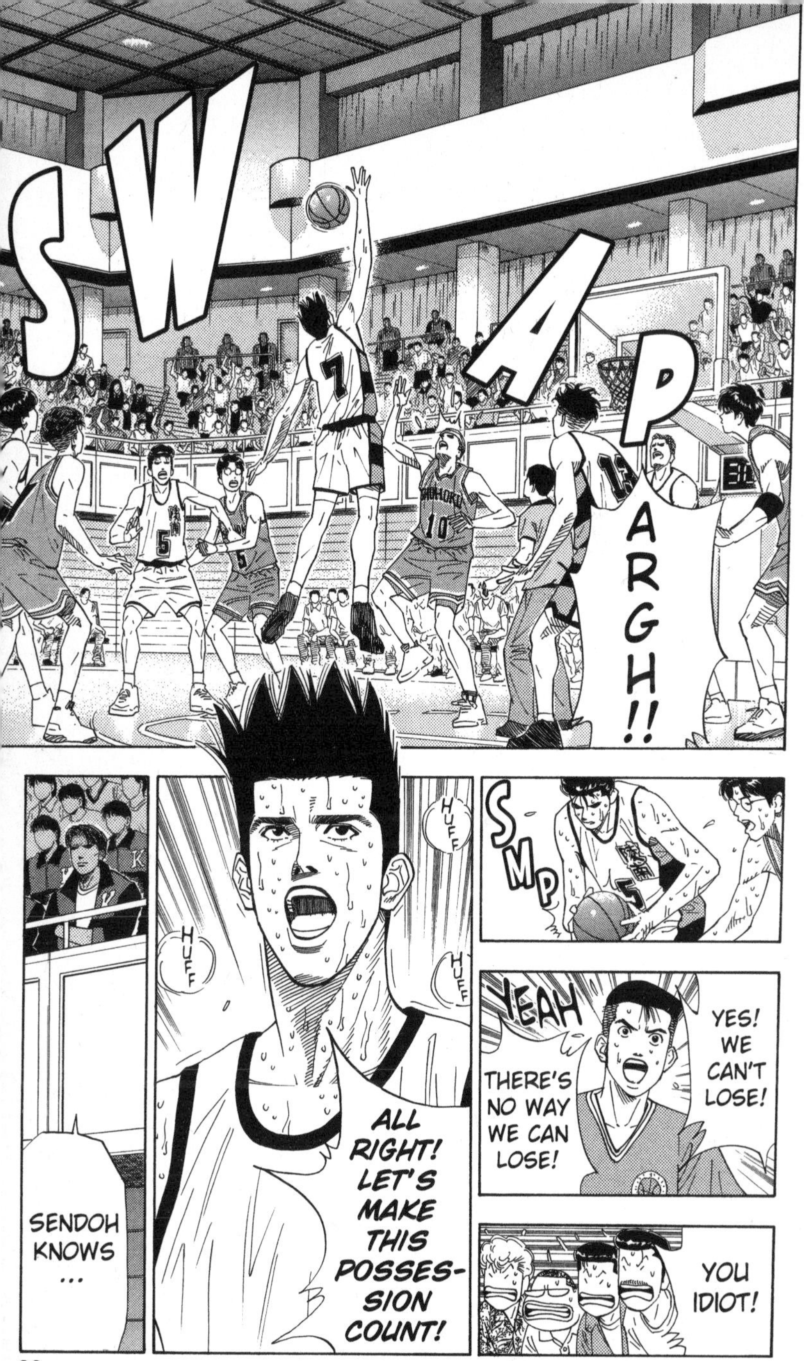
SWAP
ARGH!!
SMP
YEAH
YES! WE CAN'T LOSE!
THERE'S NO WAY WE CAN LOSE!
YOU IDIOT!
HUFF
HUFF
HUFF
ALL RIGHT! LET'S MAKE THIS POSSES-SION COUNT!
SENDOH KNOWS ...

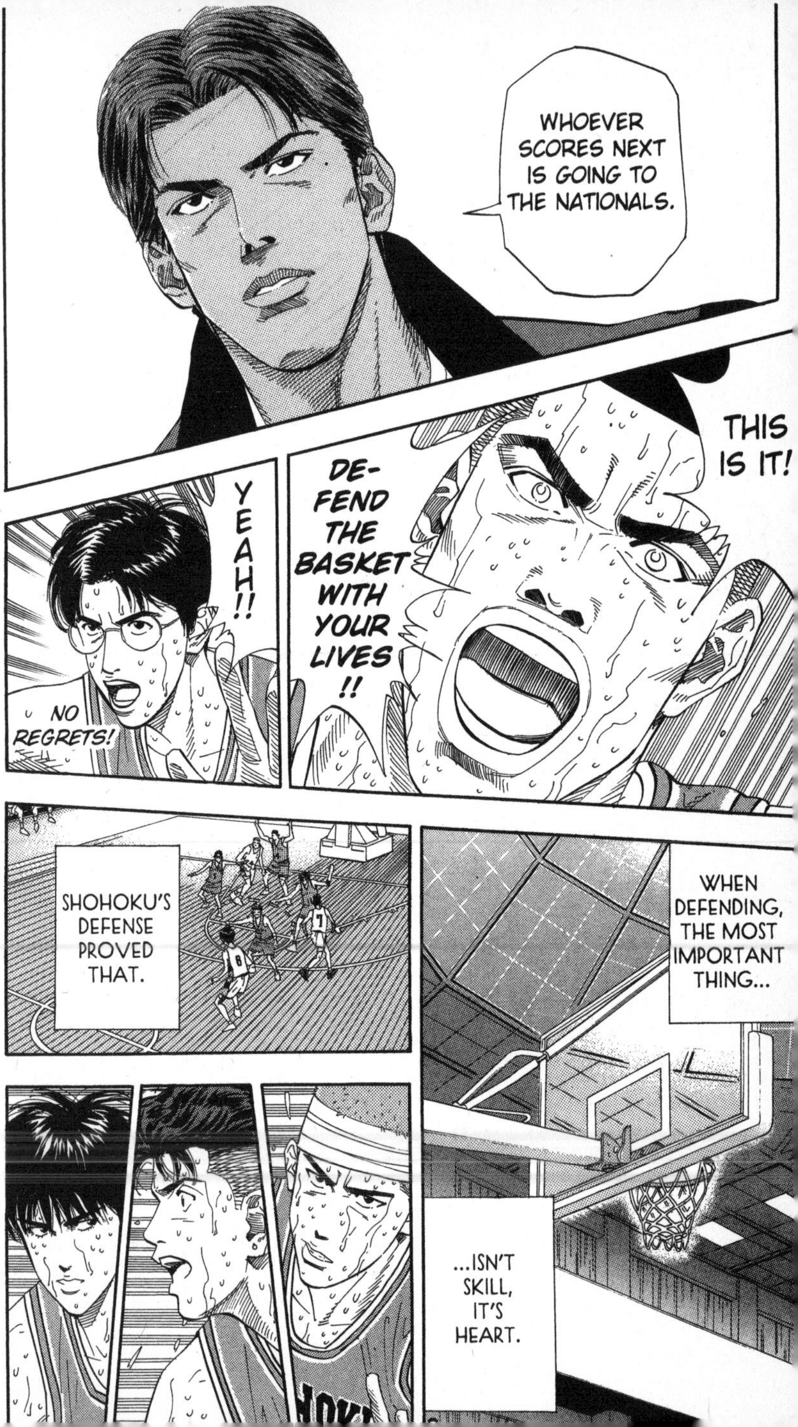
WHOEVER SCORES NEXT IS GOING TO THE NATIONALS.
THIS IS IT!
DE-FEND THE BASKET WITH YOUR LIVES!!
YEAH!!
NO REGRETS!
WHEN DEFENDING, THE MOST IMPORTANT THING...
...ISN'T SKILL, IT'S HEART.
SHOHOKU'S DEFENSE PROVED THAT.

READ THIS WAY

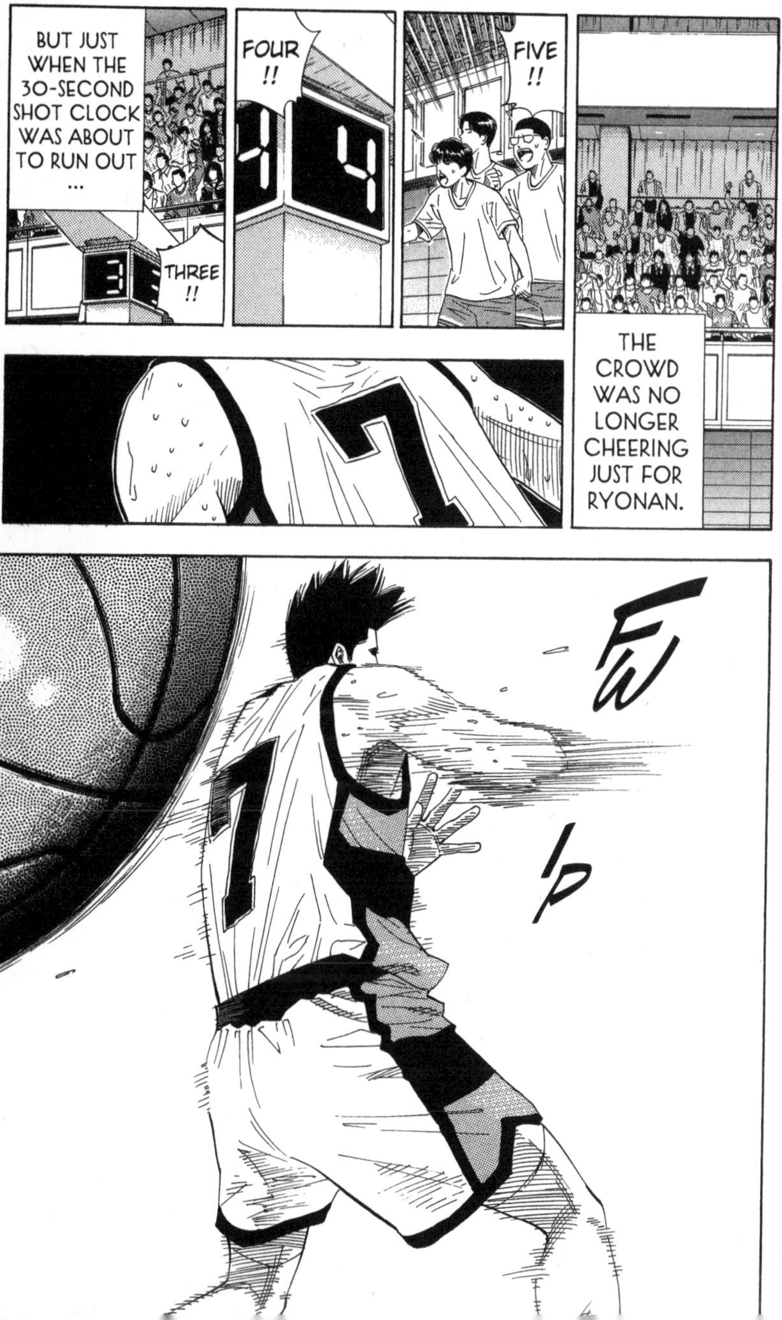
THE CROWD WAS NO LONGER CHEERING JUST FOR RYONAN.
FIVE !!
FOUR !!
BUT JUST WHEN THE 30-SECOND SHOT CLOCK WAS ABOUT TO RUN OUT ...
THREE !!
FW
IP

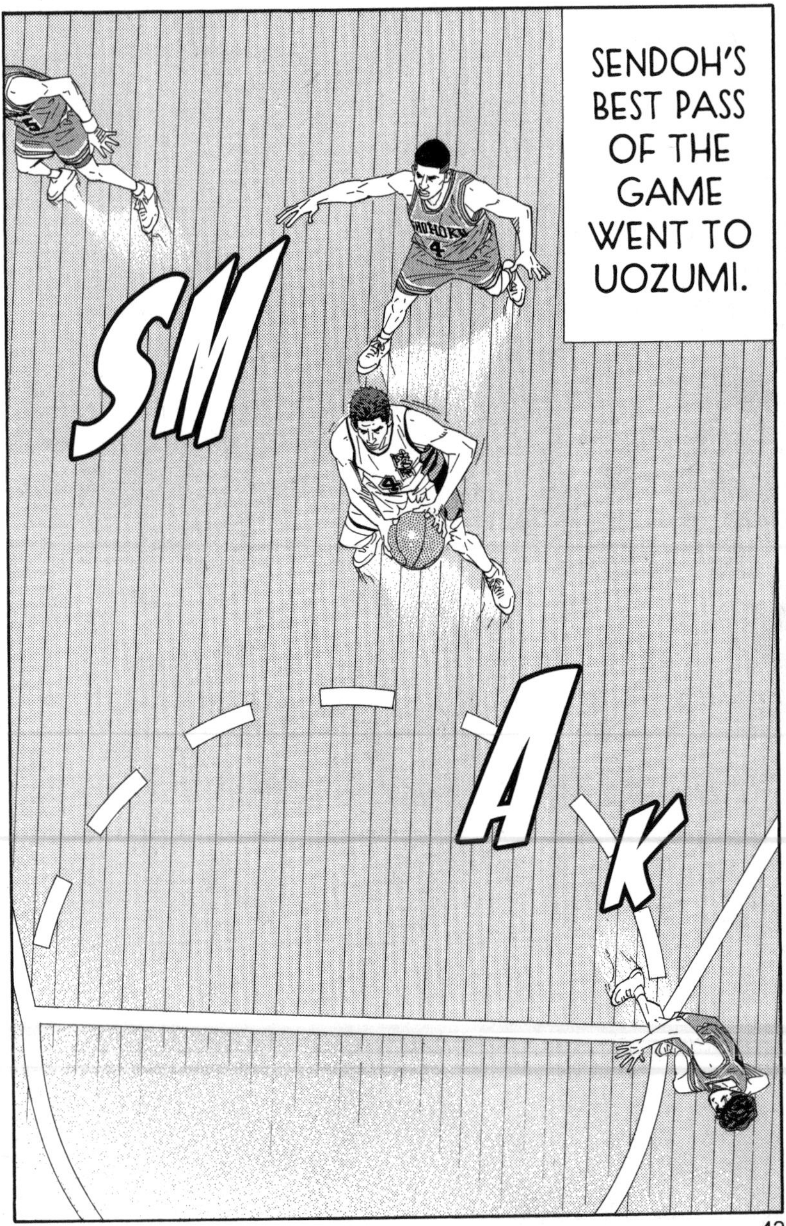
SENDOH'S BEST PASS OF THE GAME WENT TO UOZUMI.
SMAK

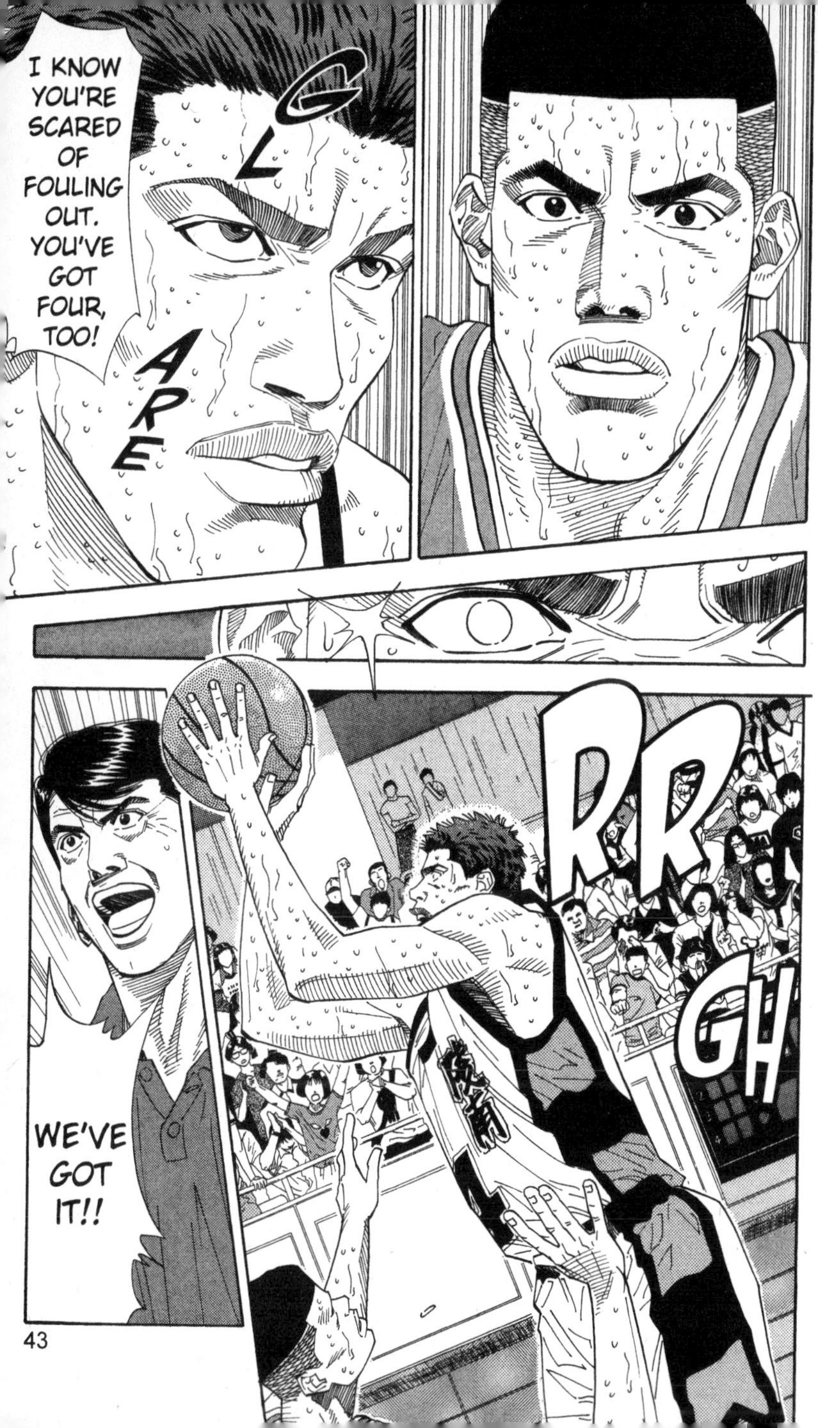
I KNOW YOU'RE SCARED OF FOULING OUT. YOU'VE GOT FOUR, TOO!
GLARE
RRGH
WE'VE GOT IT!!

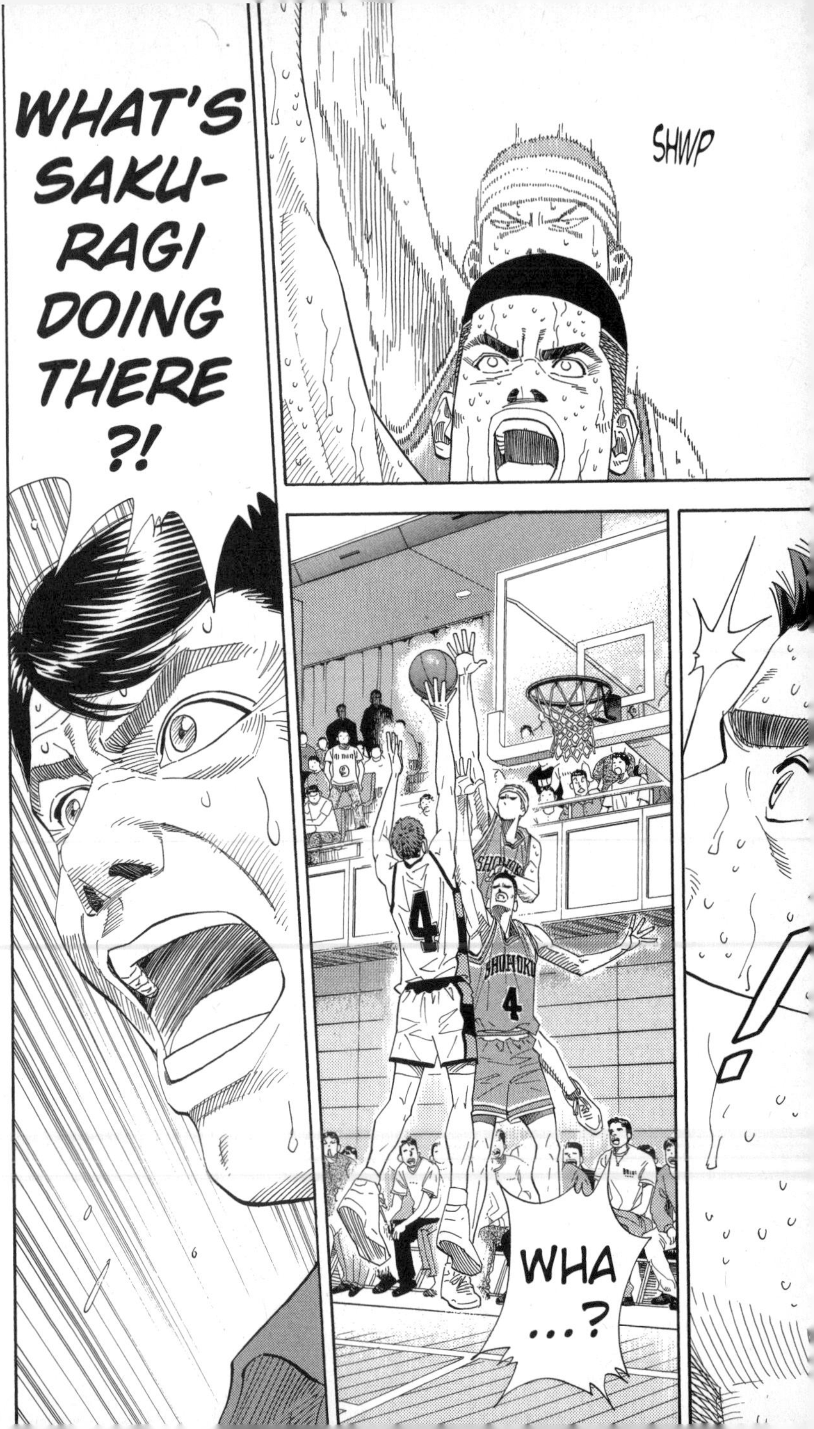
SHWP
WHAT'S SAKU-RAGI DOING THERE ?!
WHA ...?

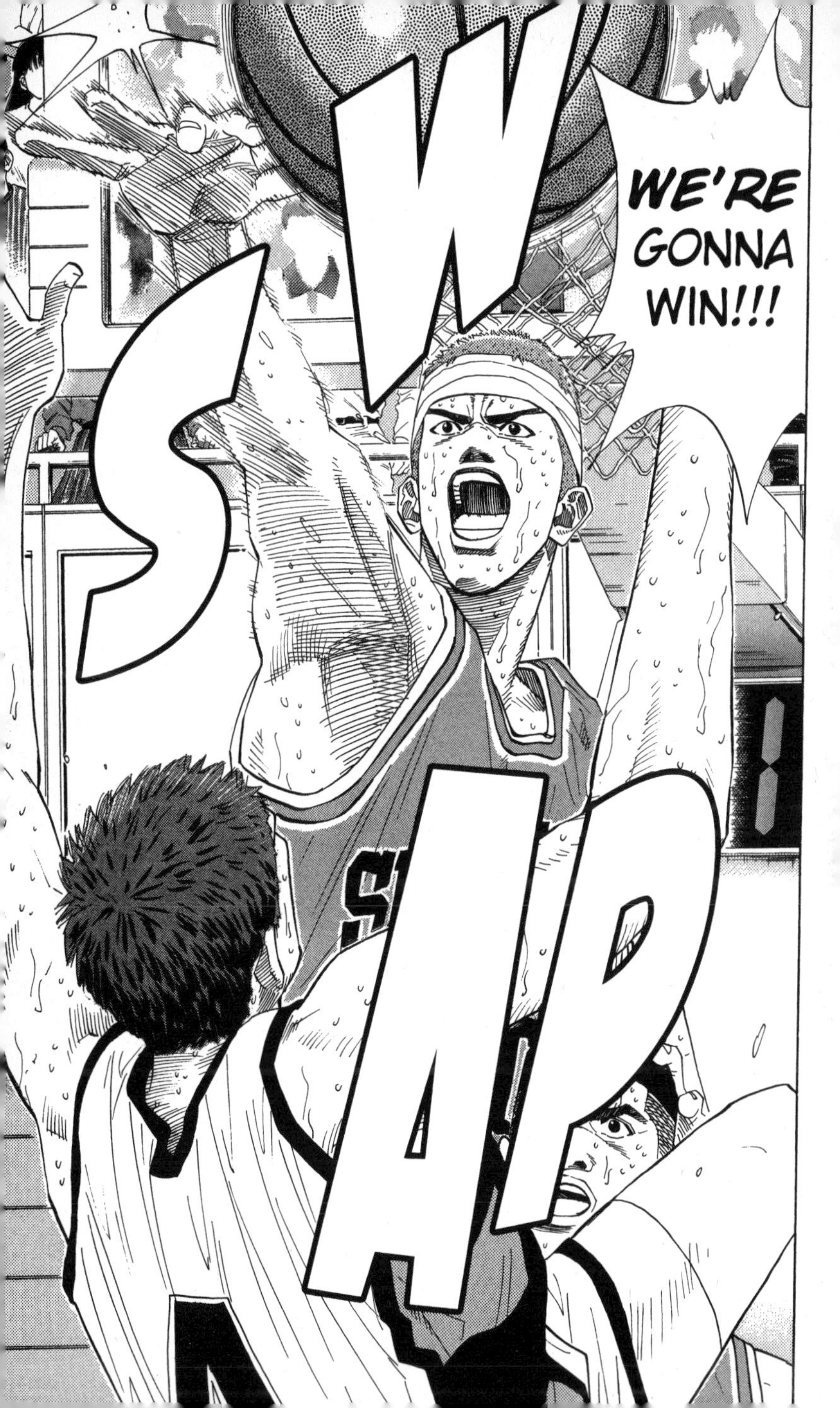
WE'RE GONNA WIN!!!
SWAP

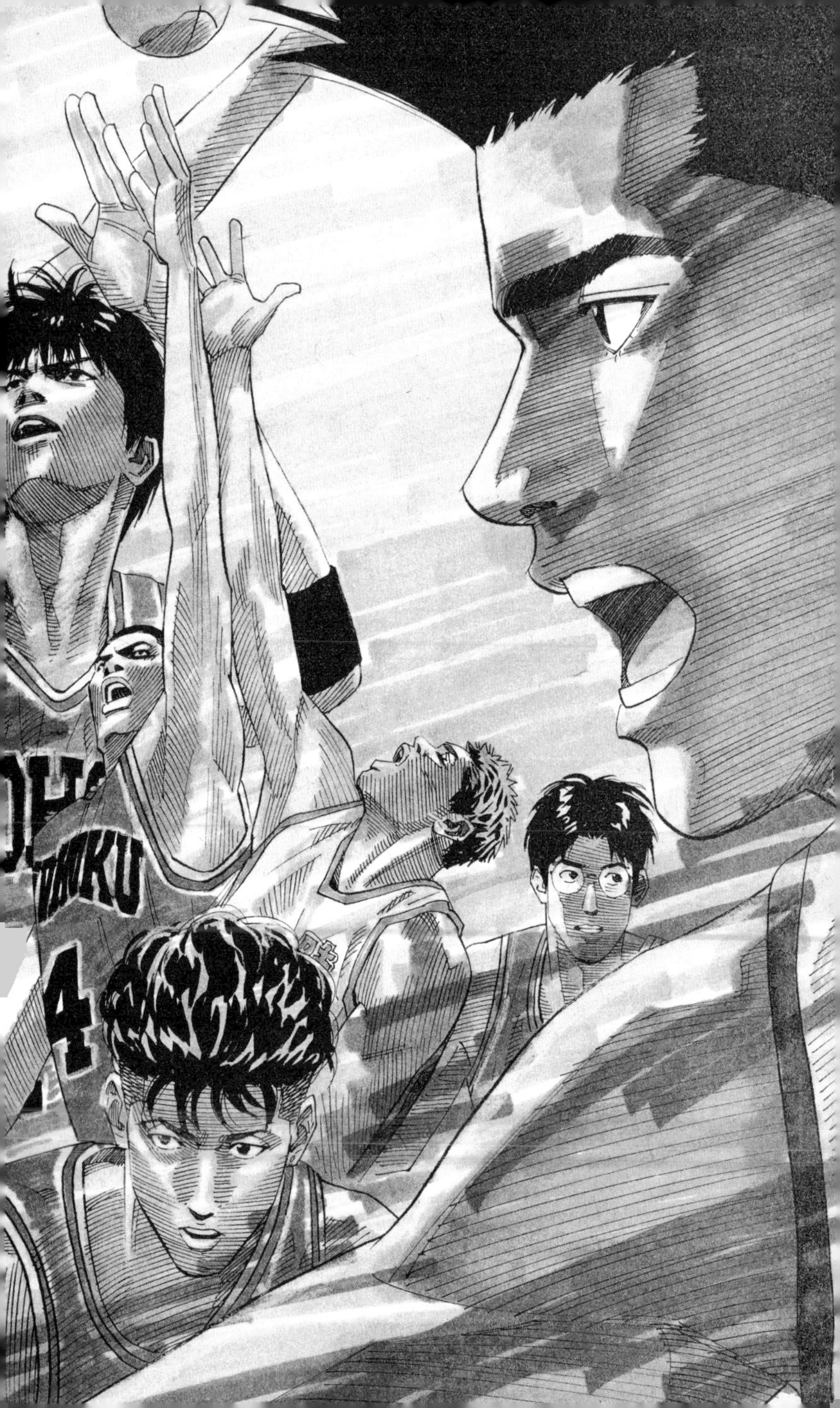

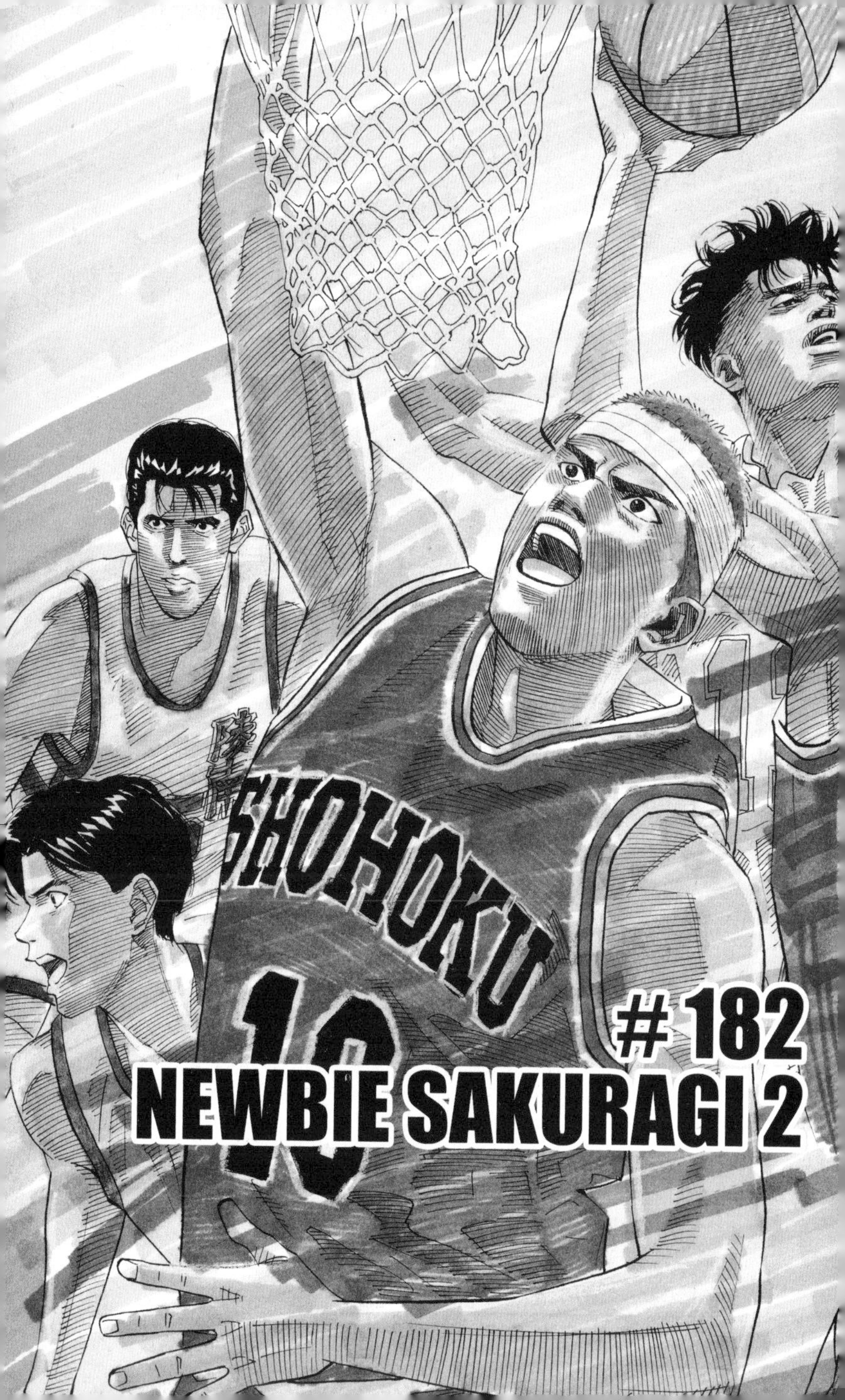
SHOHOKU
10

182
NEWBIE SAKURAGI 2

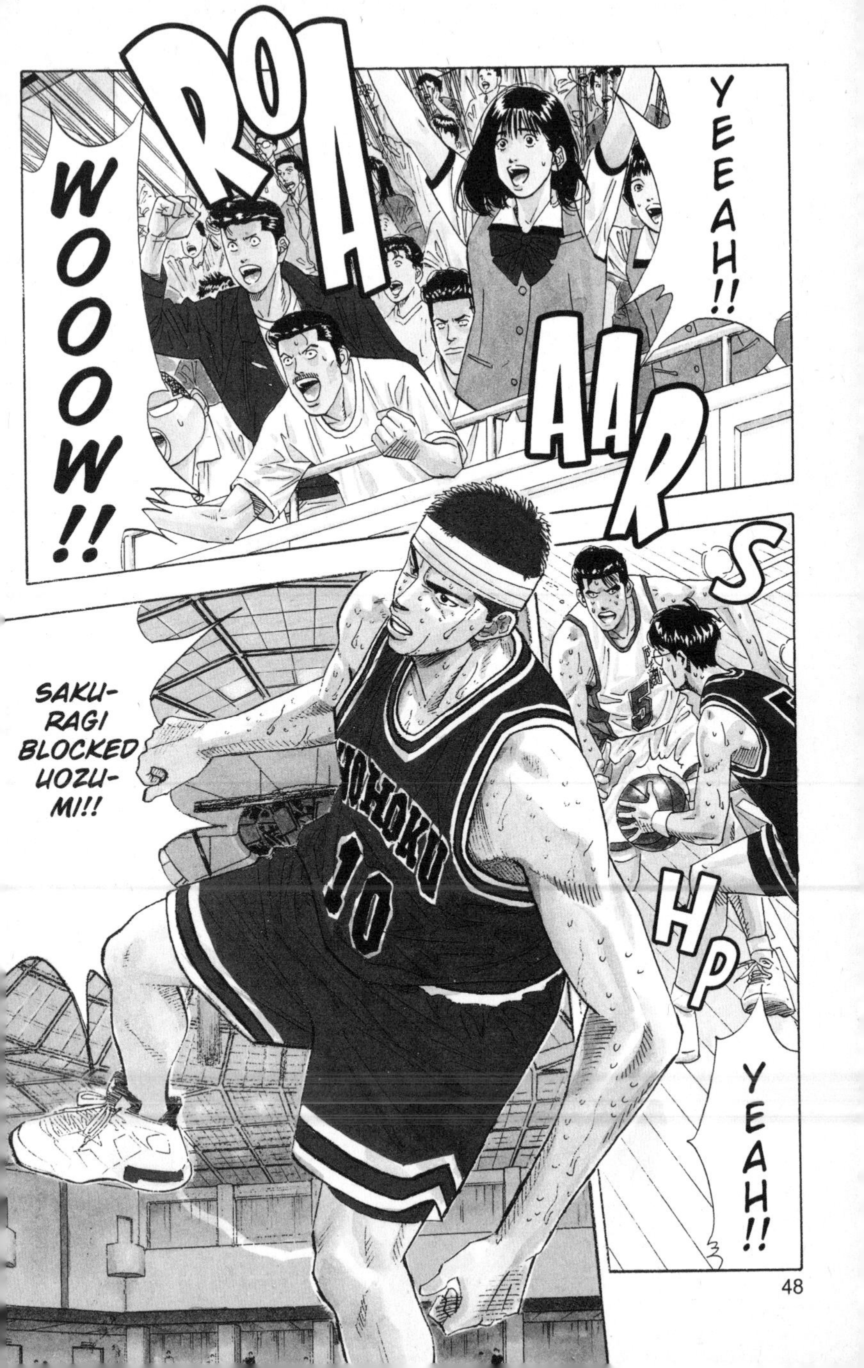
YEEAAH!!
ROA
WOOOOW!!
AAR
S
HP
YEAH!!
NOHOKU 10
SAKURAGI BLOCKED UOZUMI!!

READ THIS WAY

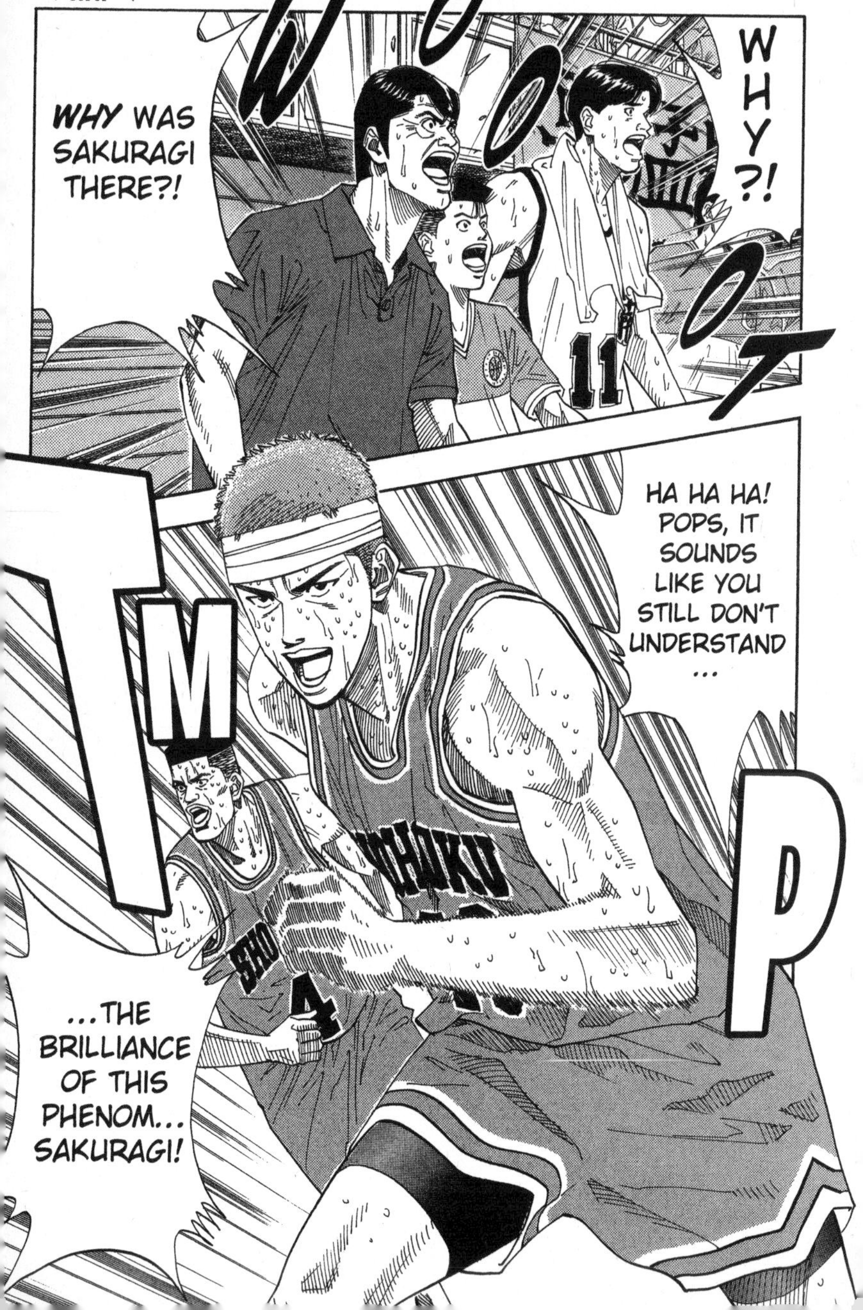
WOOOOT
WHY?!
WHY WAS SAKURAGI THERE?!
TMP
HA HA HA! POPS, IT SOUNDS LIKE YOU STILL DON'T UNDERSTAND...
...THE BRILLIANCE OF THIS PHENOM... SAKURAGI!

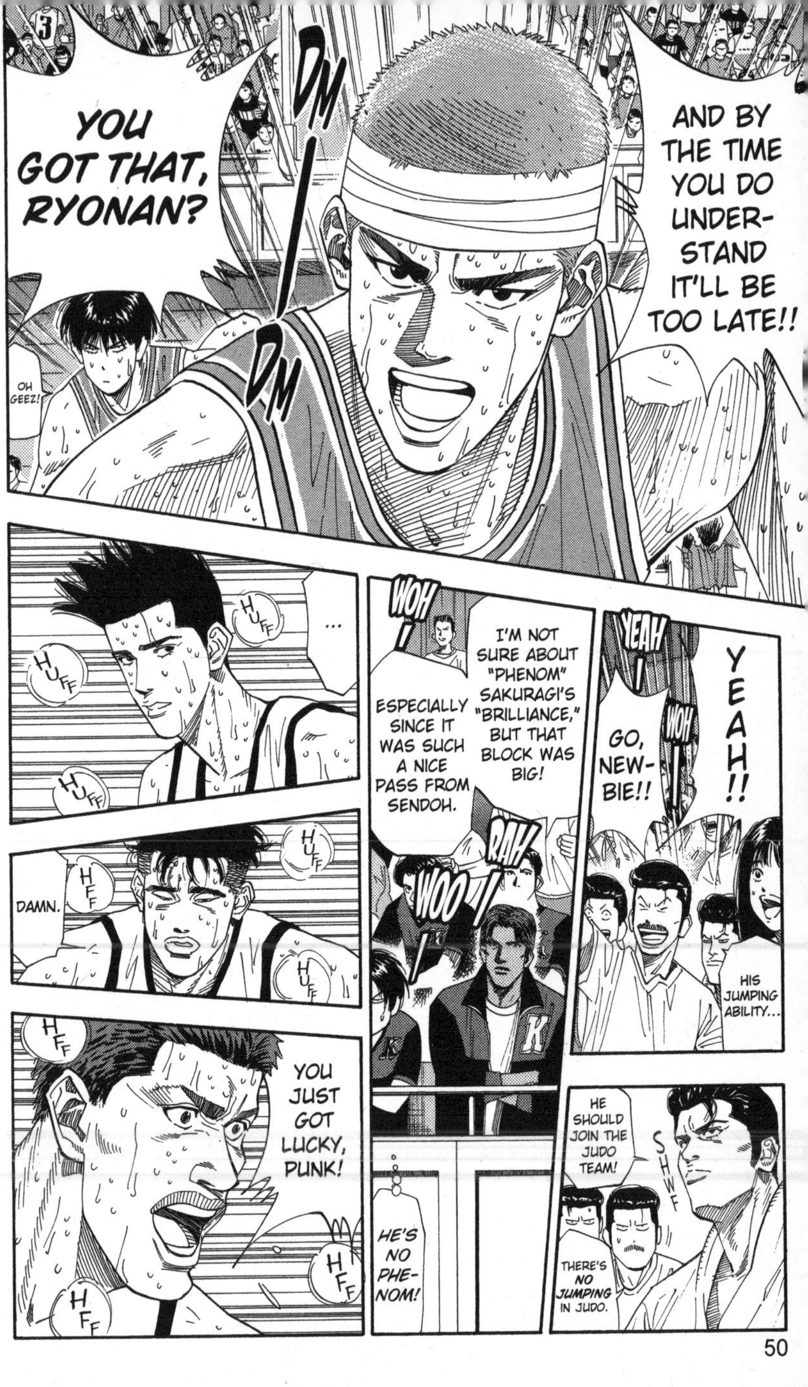

AND BY THE TIME YOU DO UNDERSTAND IT'LL BE TOO LATE!!
DM DM
YOU GOT THAT, RYONAN?
OH GEEZ!
YEAH
YEAH!!
WOH
GO, NEWBIE!!
HIS JUMPING ABILITY...
HE SHOULD JOIN THE JUDO TEAM!
SHWF
THERE'S NO JUMPING IN JUDO.
WOH
I'M NOT SURE ABOUT "PHENOM" SAKURAGI'S "BRILLIANCE," BUT THAT BLOCK WAS BIG!
ESPECIALLY SINCE IT WAS SUCH A NICE PASS FROM SENDOH.
RAH
WOO
HE'S NO PHENOM!
...
HUFF
HUFF
HUFF
HUFF
HFF
DAMN.
HUFF
HFF
YOU JUST GOT LUCKY, PUNK!
HFF
HFF

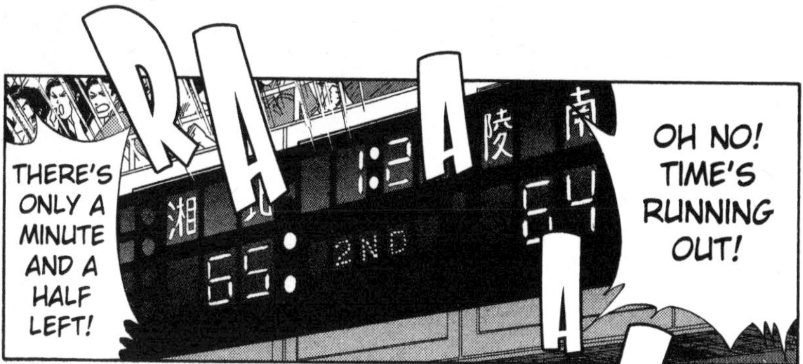
RAAAAAH
OH NO! TIME'S RUNNING OUT!
THERE'S ONLY A MINUTE AND A HALF LEFT!
湘北
陵南
65
64
2ND
Scoreboard: Shohoku Ryonan

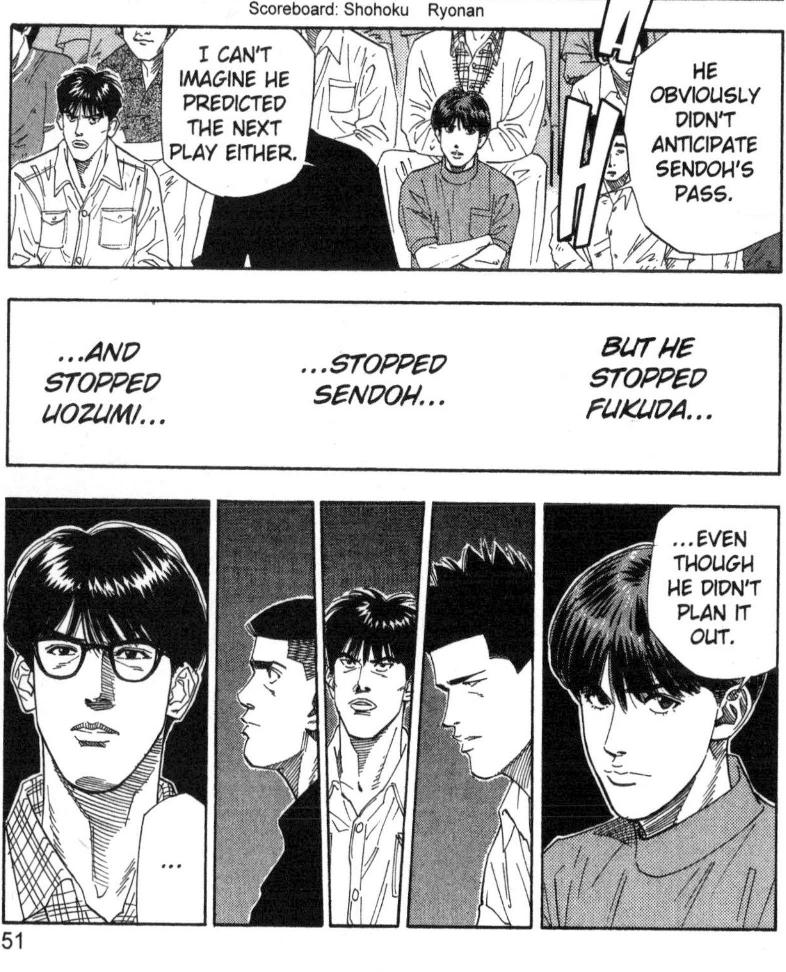
HE OBVIOUSLY DIDN'T ANTICIPATE SENDOH'S PASS.
I CAN'T IMAGINE HE PREDICTED THE NEXT PLAY EITHER.
BUT HE STOPPED FUKUDA...
...STOPPED SENDOH...
...AND STOPPED UOZUMI...
...EVEN THOUGH HE DIDN'T PLAN IT OUT.
...

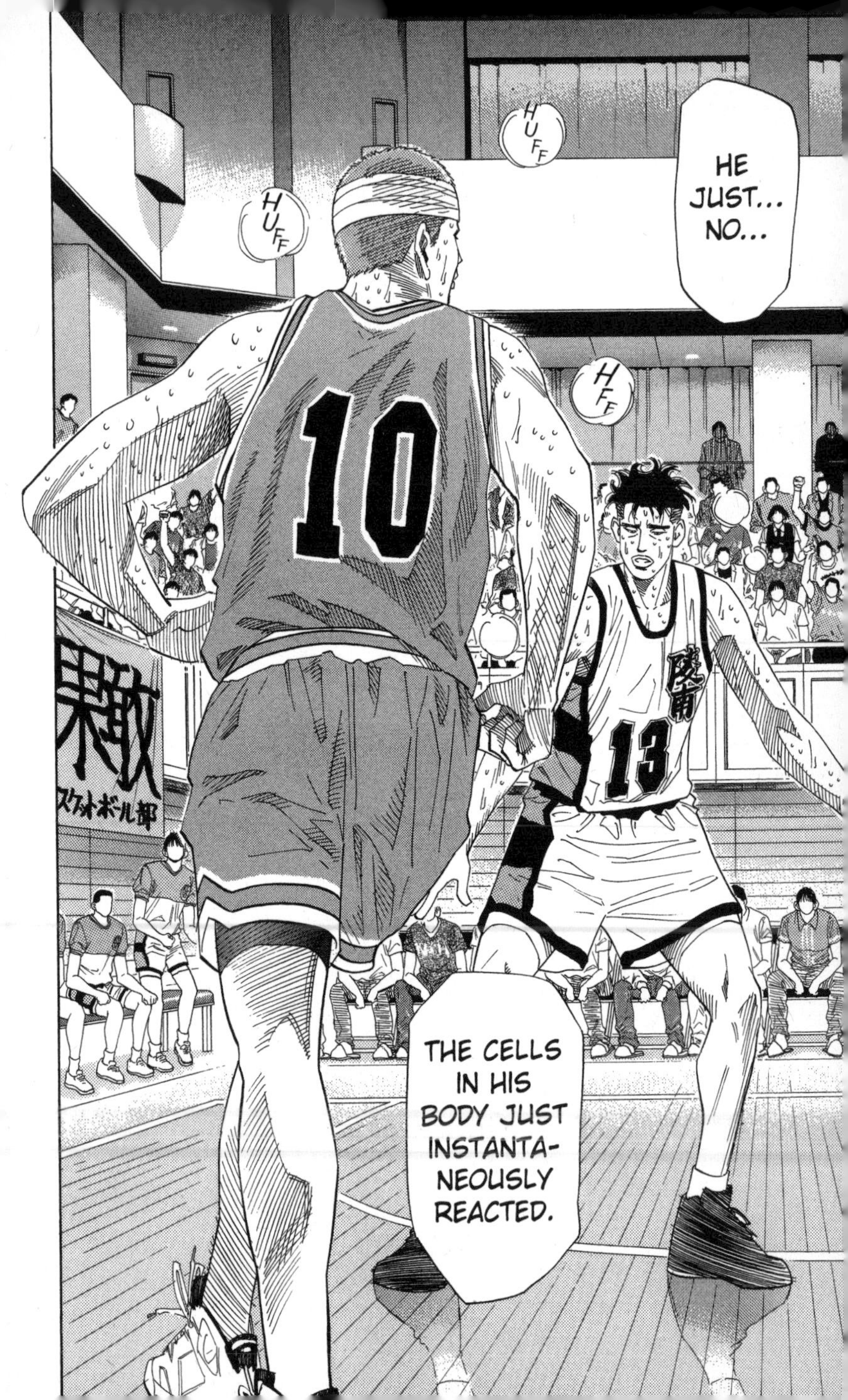
HE JUST... NO...
HUFF
HUFF
HFF
果敢
THE CELLS IN HIS BODY JUST INSTANTA-NEOUSLY REACTED.

READ THIS WAY

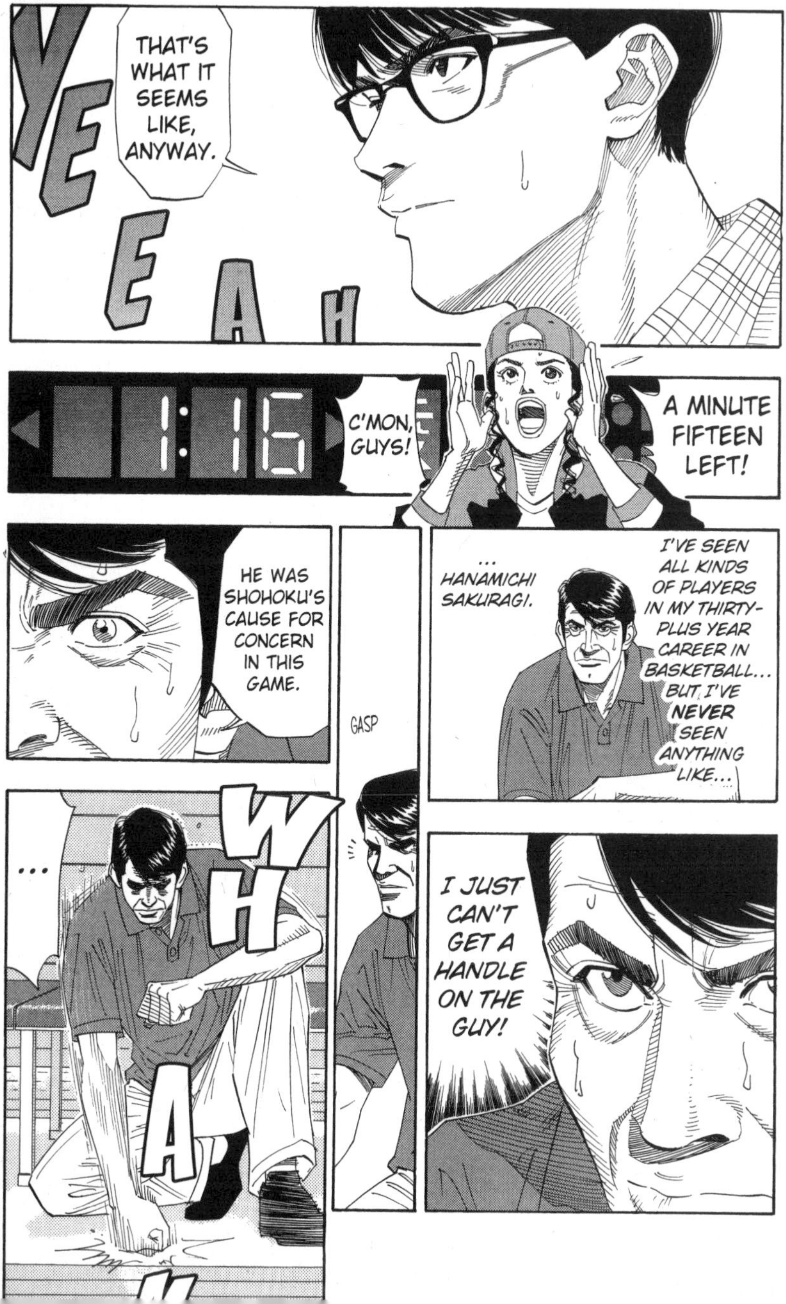
THAT'S WHAT IT SEEMS LIKE, ANYWAY.
YEEAH
A MINUTE FIFTEEN LEFT!
C'MON, GUYS!
1:16
I'VE SEEN ALL KINDS OF PLAYERS IN MY THIRTY-PLUS YEAR CAREER IN BASKETBALL... BUT I'VE **NEVER** SEEN ANYTHING LIKE...
... HANAMICHI SAKURAGI.
GASP
HE WAS SHOHOKU'S CAUSE FOR CONCERN IN THIS GAME.
I JUST CAN'T GET A HANDLE ON THE GUY!
WHA
...

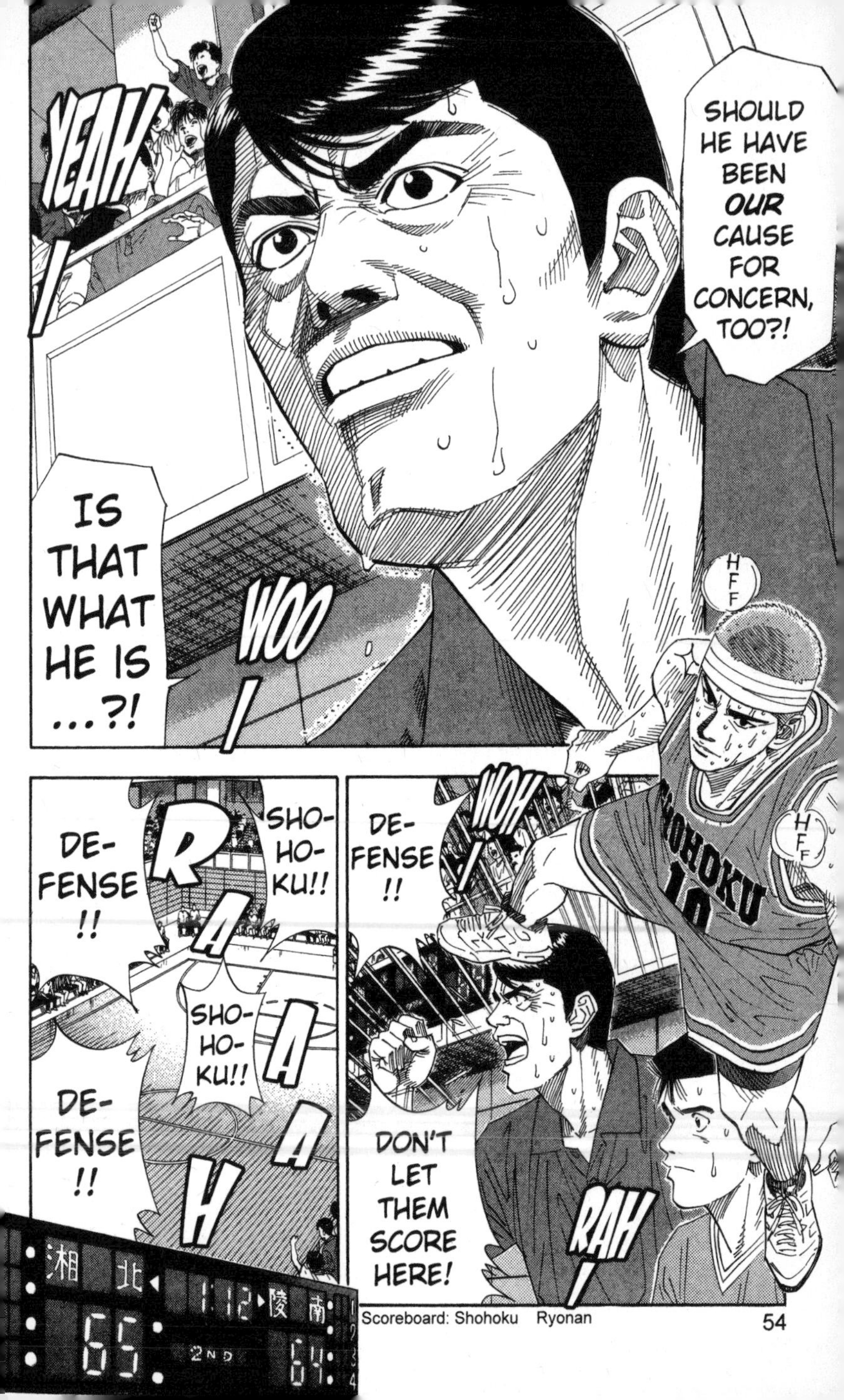
SHOULD HE HAVE BEEN *OUR* CAUSE FOR CONCERN, TOO?!
YEAH!
IS THAT WHAT HE IS ...?!
WOO!
HFF
HFF
WOH!
DE-FENSE!!
DON'T LET THEM SCORE HERE!
RAH!
SHO-HO-KU!!
RAAAH
DE-FENSE!!
SHO-HO-KU!!
DE-FENSE!!
湘北
1:12
陵南
65
2ND
64

Scoreboard: Shohoku Ryonan

READ THIS WAY

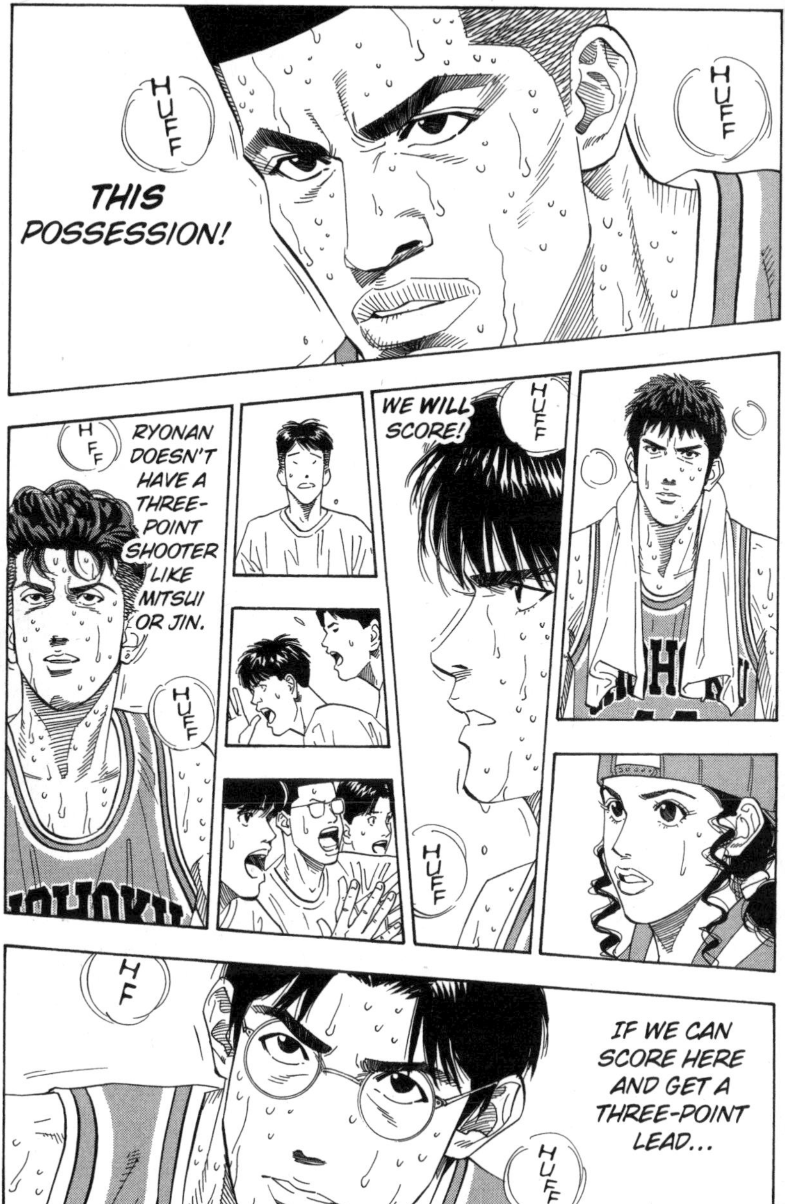
HUFF
HUFF
THIS POSSESSION!
WE WILL SCORE!
HUFF
HUFF
HFF
RYONAN DOESN'T HAVE A THREE-POINT SHOOTER LIKE MITSUI OR JIN.
HUFF
IF WE CAN SCORE HERE AND GET A THREE-POINT LEAD...
HUFF
HF

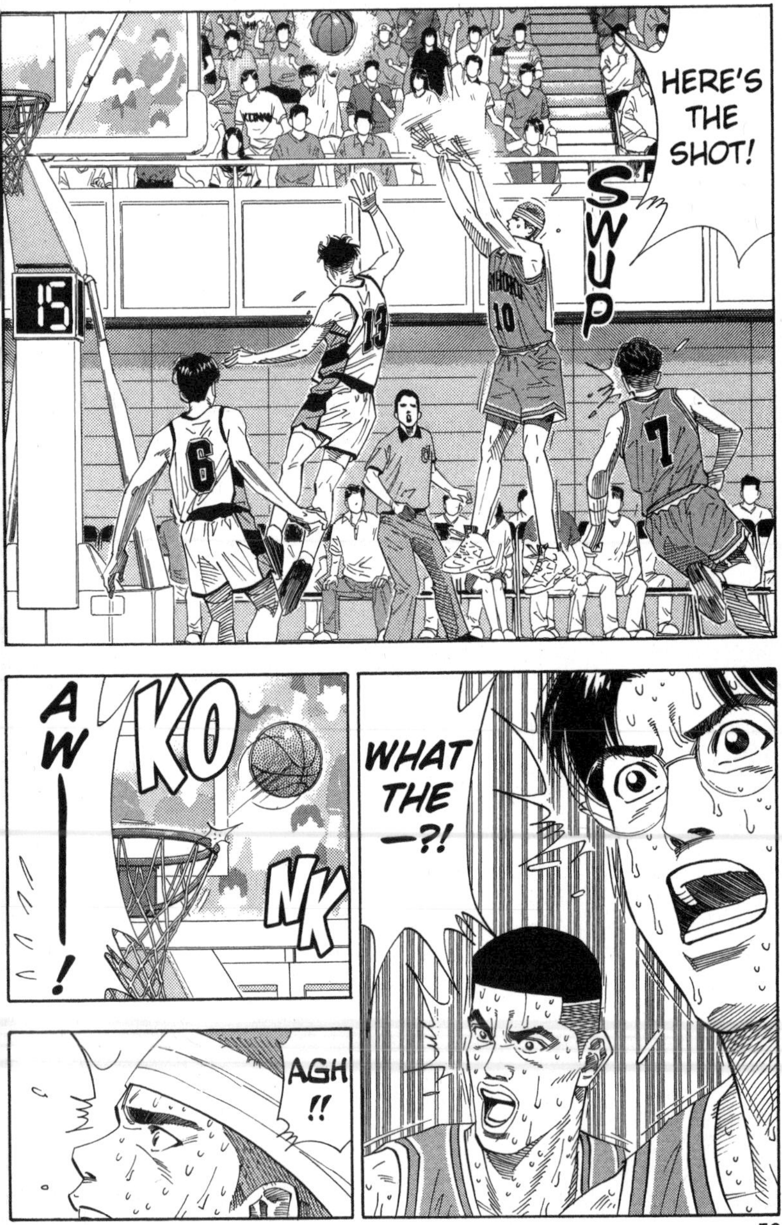
HERE'S THE SHOT!
SWUP
WHAT THE—?!
KO
NK
AW—!
AGH!!

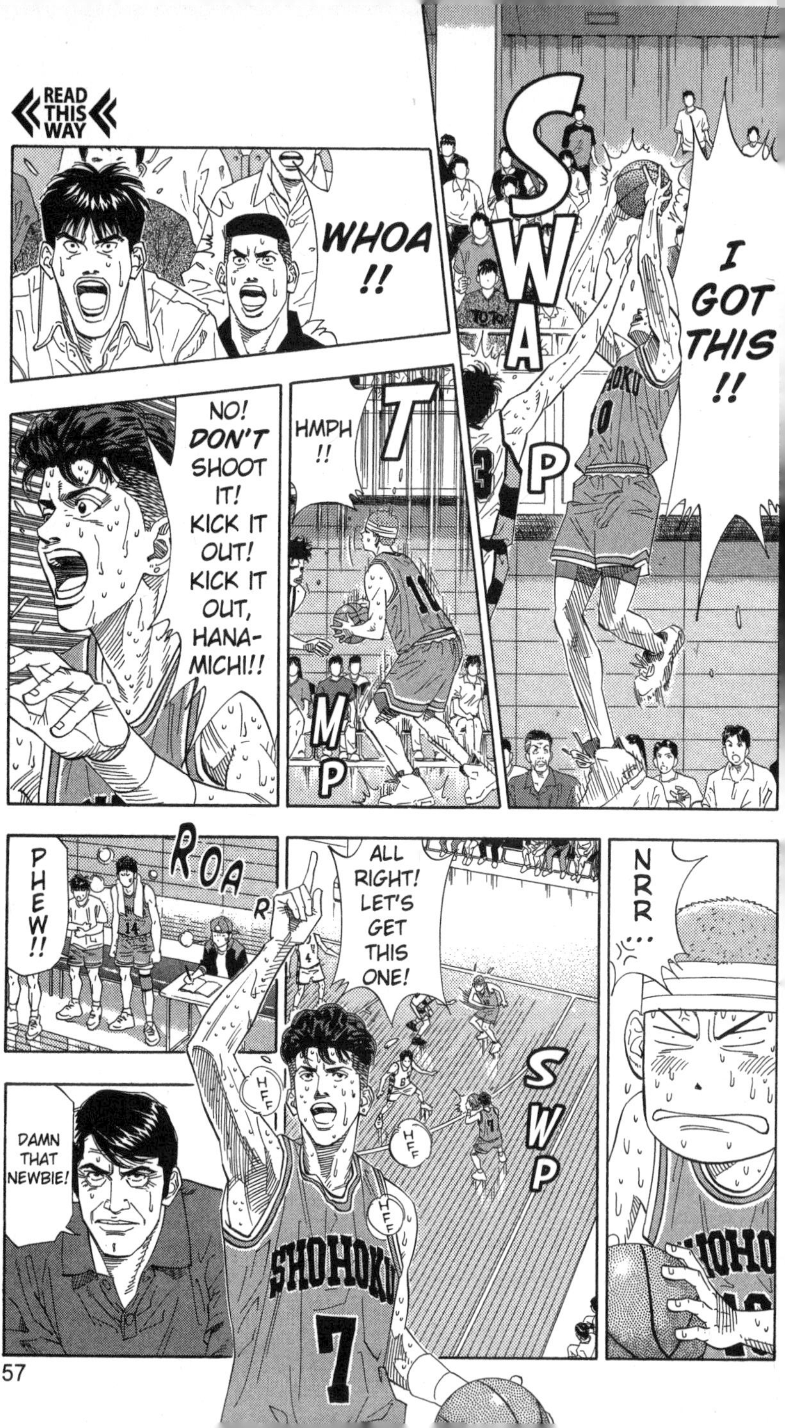
READ THIS WAY
SWAP
I GOT THIS!!
WHOA!!
HMPH!!
TMP
NO! DON'T SHOOT IT! KICK IT OUT! KICK IT OUT, HANAMICHI!!
NRR...
ALL RIGHT! LET'S GET THIS ONE!
HFF
HFF
HFF
SWP
ROAR
PHEW!!
DAMN THAT NEWBIE!

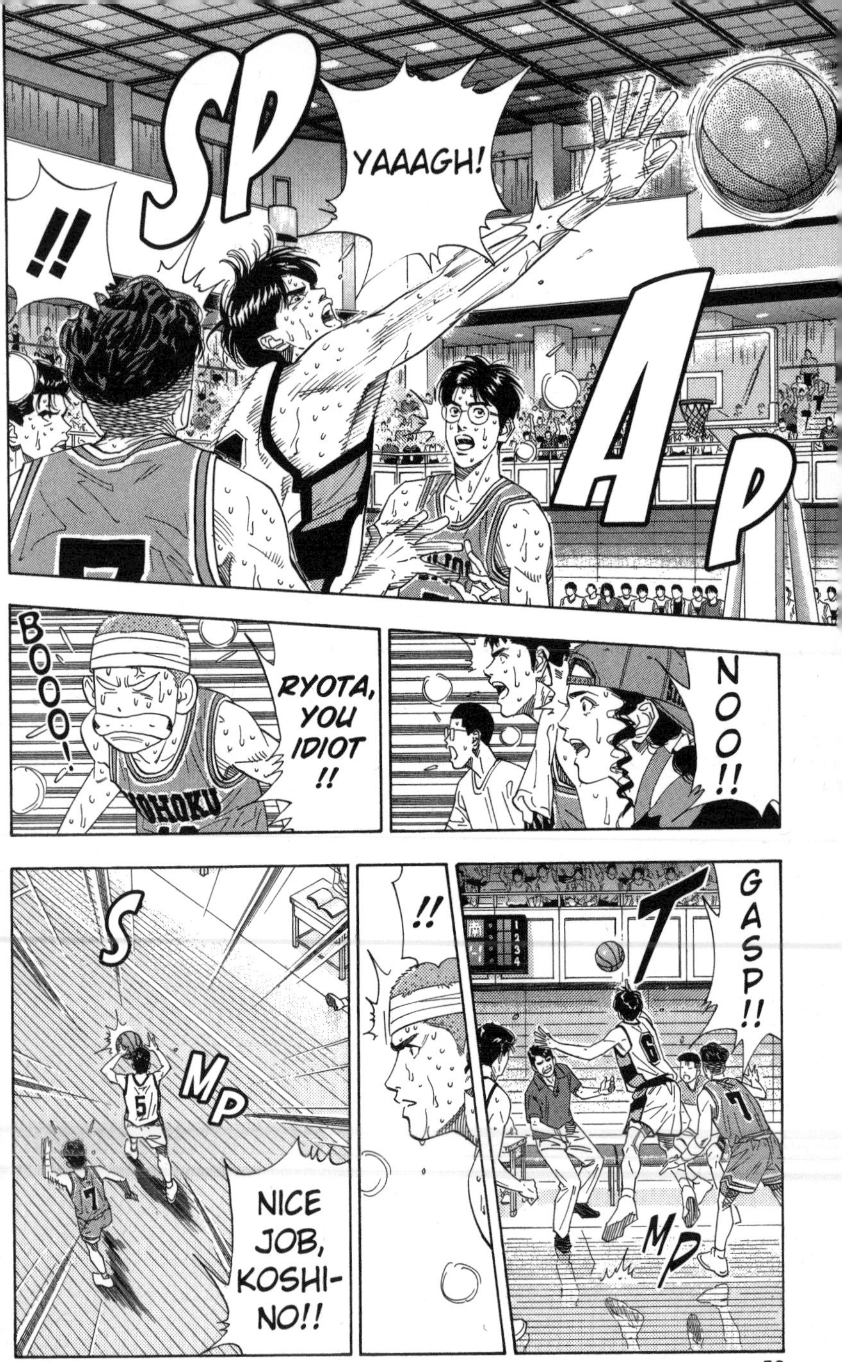

YAAAGH!
SP
AP
!!
NOOO!!
RYOTA, YOU IDIOT!!
BOOOO!
GASP!!
T
MP
!!
S
MP
NICE JOB, KOSHI-NO!!

READ THIS WAY

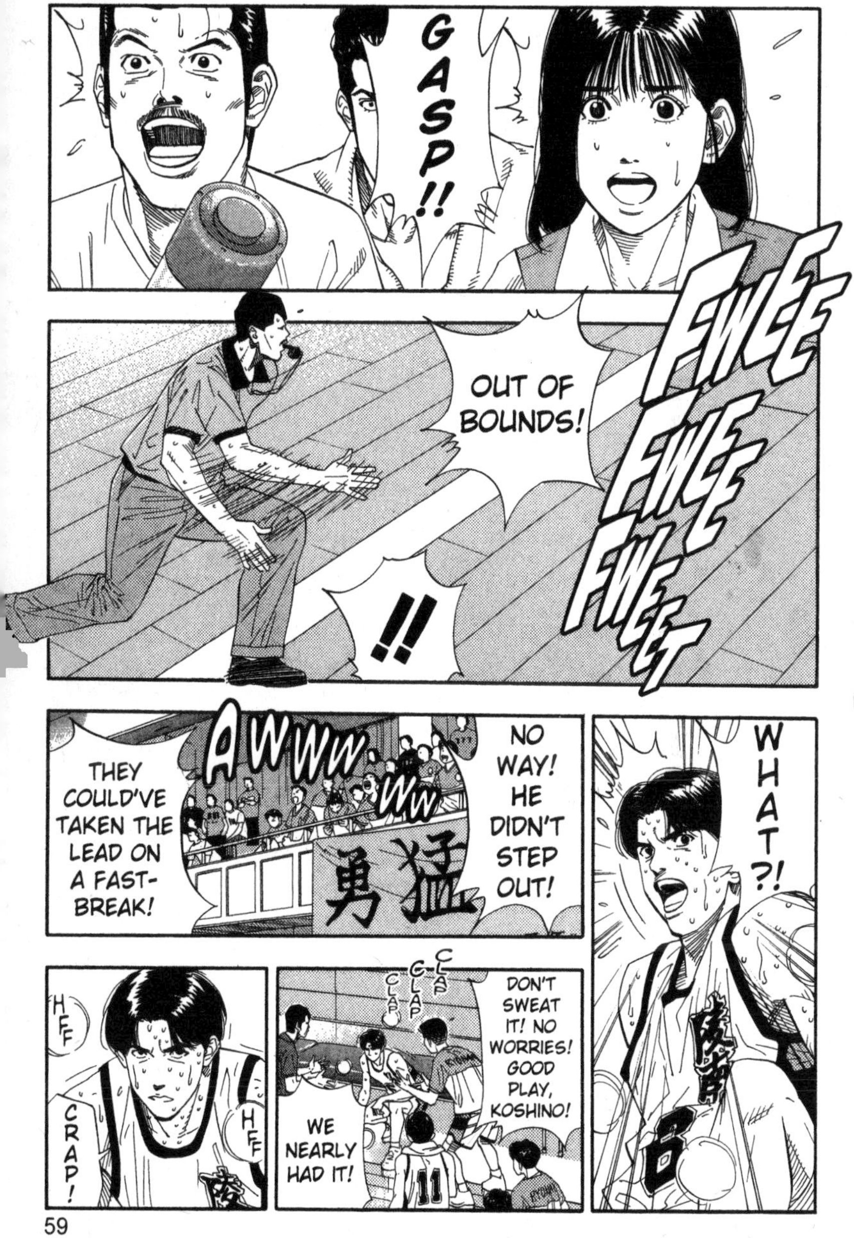
GASP!!
FWEE FWEE FWEET
OUT OF BOUNDS!
!!
WHAT?!
NO WAY! HE DIDN'T STEP OUT!
AWWWWWW
勇猛
THEY COULD'VE TAKEN THE LEAD ON A FAST-BREAK!
DON'T SWEAT IT! NO WORRIES! GOOD PLAY, KOSHINO!
CLAP CLAP CLAP
WE NEARLY HAD IT!
HFF
HFF
CRAP!

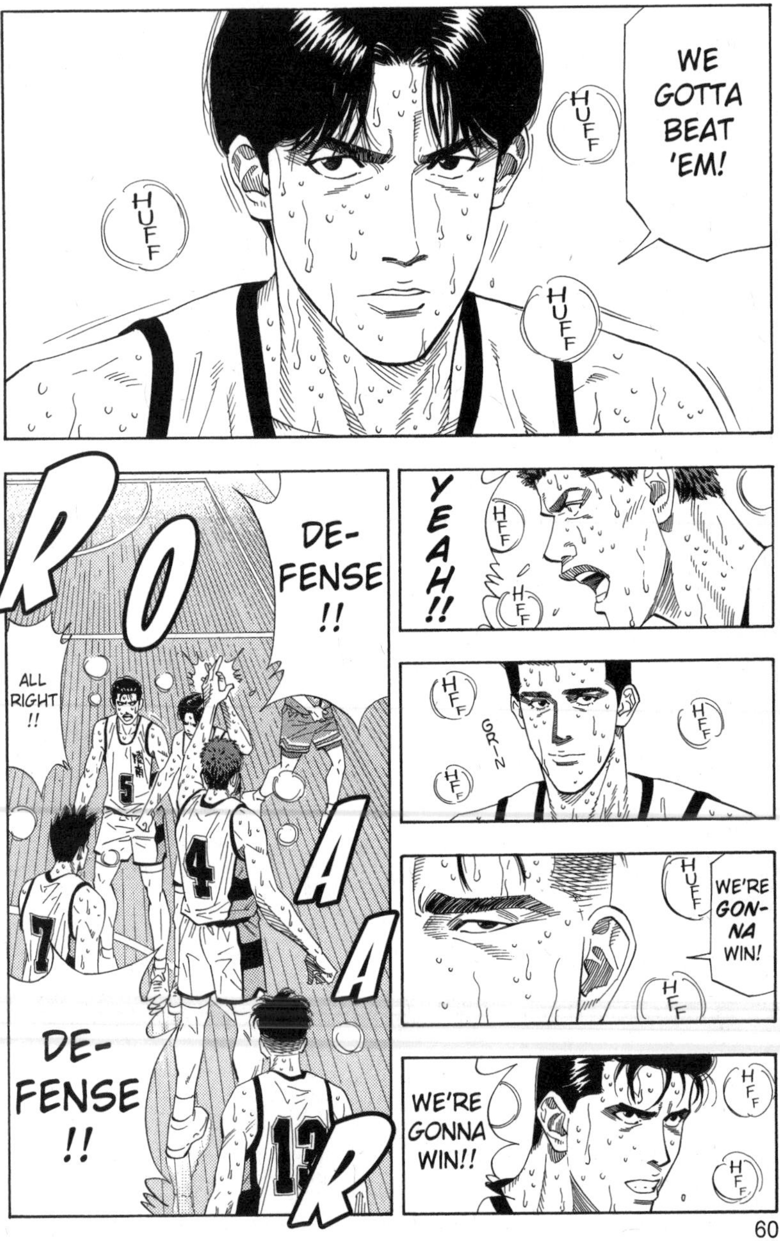
WE GOTTA BEAT 'EM!
HUFF
HUFF
HUFF
YEAH!!
HFF
HFF
HFF
GRIN
HFF
HFF
HUFF
WE'RE GONNA WIN!
HFF
HFF
WE'RE GONNA WIN!!
HFF
DE-FENSE!!
ROAAR
ALL RIGHT!!
DE-FENSE!!

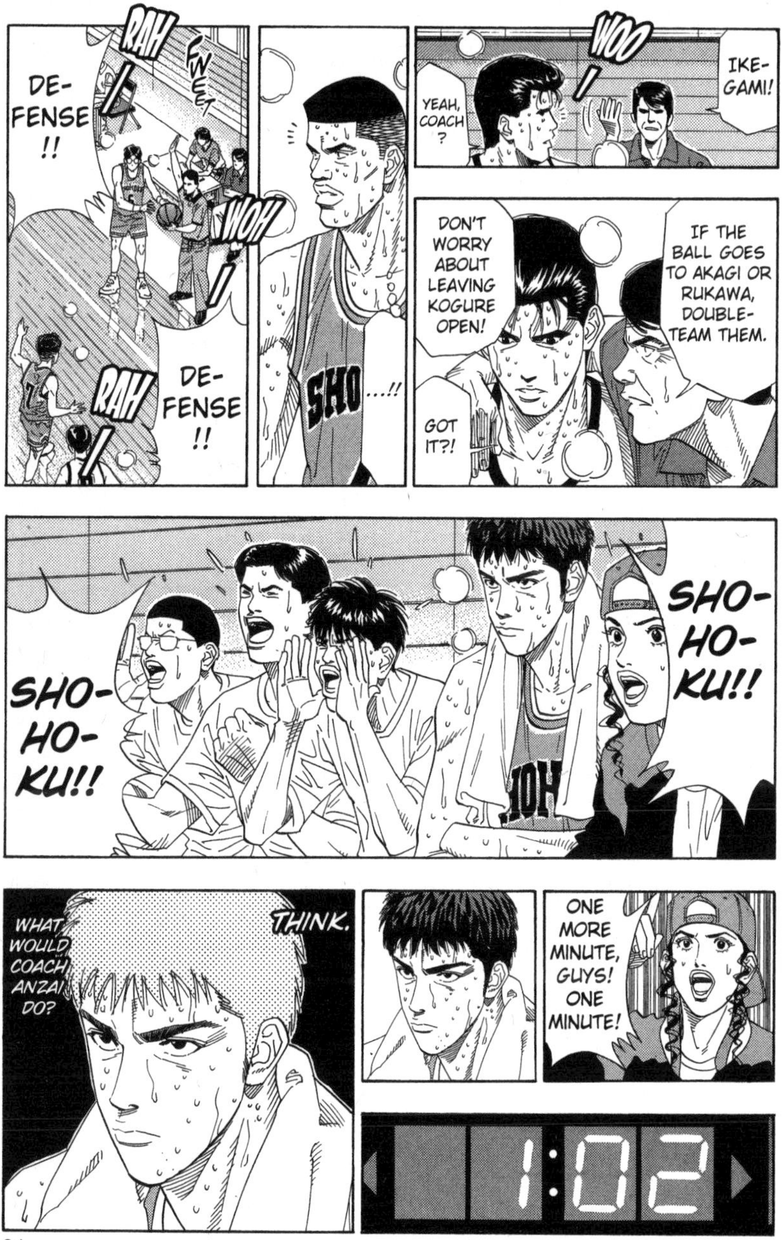
IKE-GAMI!
WOO!
YEAH, COACH?
IF THE BALL GOES TO AKAGI OR RUKAWA, DOUBLE-TEAM THEM.
DON'T WORRY ABOUT LEAVING KOGURE OPEN!
GOT IT?!
...!!
RAH!
FWEET
DE-FENSE!!
WOH!
DE-FENSE!!
RAH!
SHO-HO-KU!!
SHO-HO-KU!!
ONE MORE MINUTE, GUYS! ONE MINUTE!
1:02
THINK.
WHAT WOULD COACH ANZAI DO?

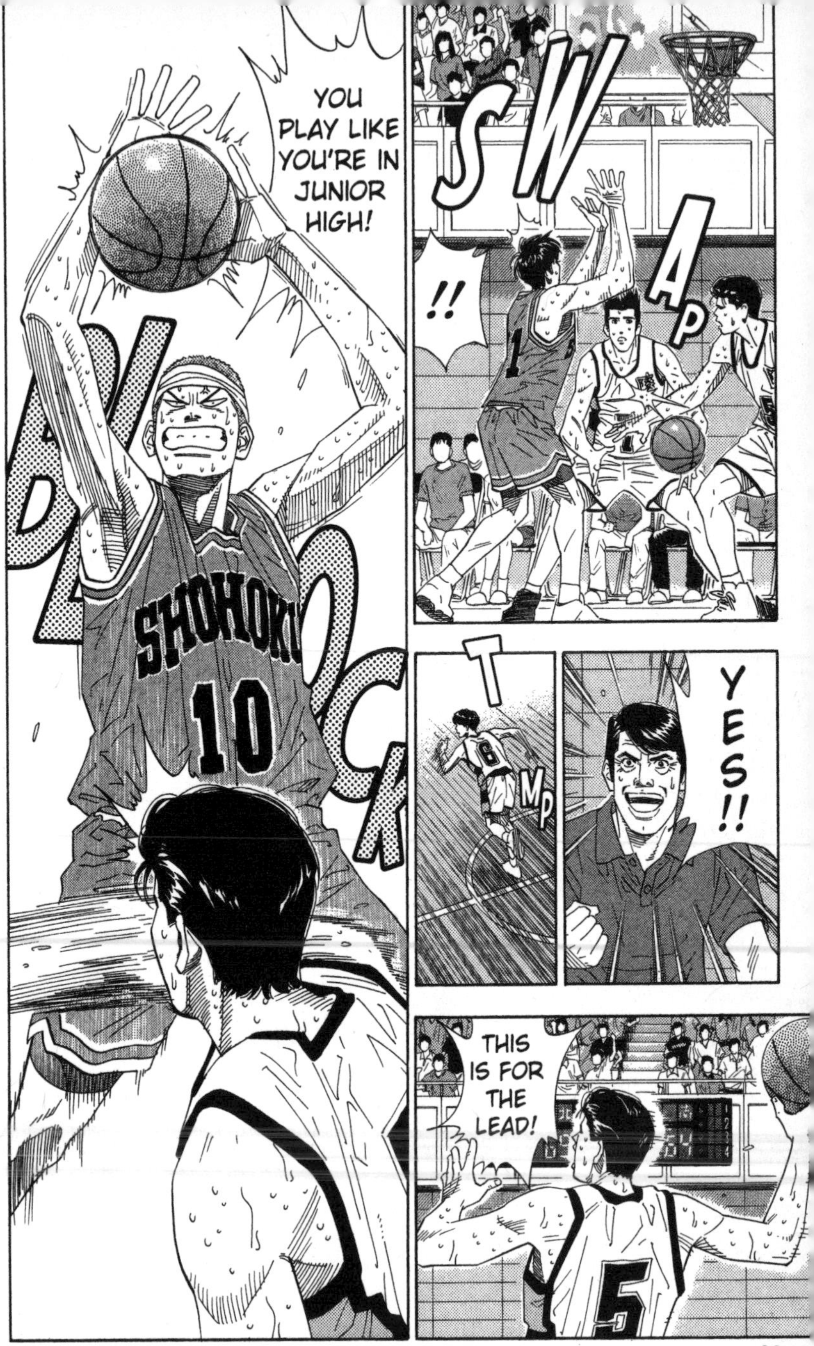
SWAP
!!
YES!!
TMP
THIS IS FOR THE LEAD!
YOU PLAY LIKE YOU'RE IN JUNIOR HIGH!
SHOHOKU

READ THIS WAY

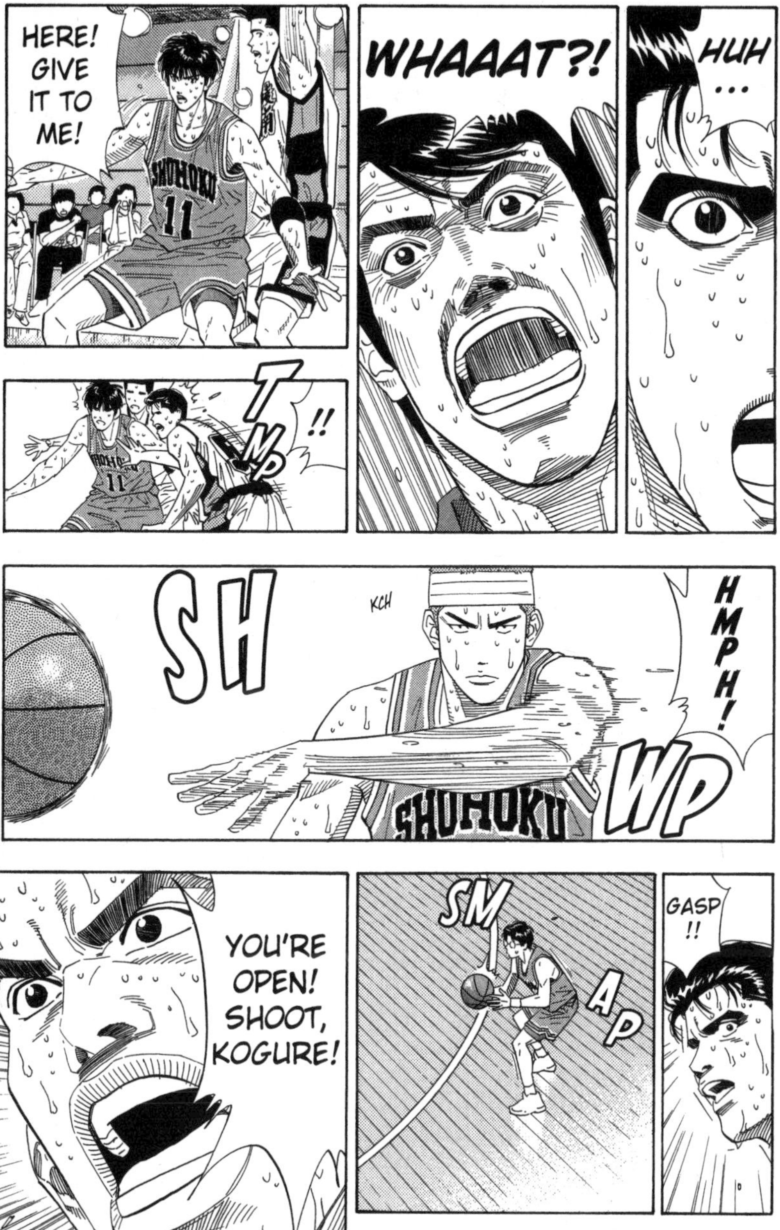
HUH ...
WHAAAT?!
HERE! GIVE IT TO ME!
TMP
!!
HMPH!
KCH
SH
WP
GASP !!
SM
AP
YOU'RE OPEN! SHOOT, KOGURE!

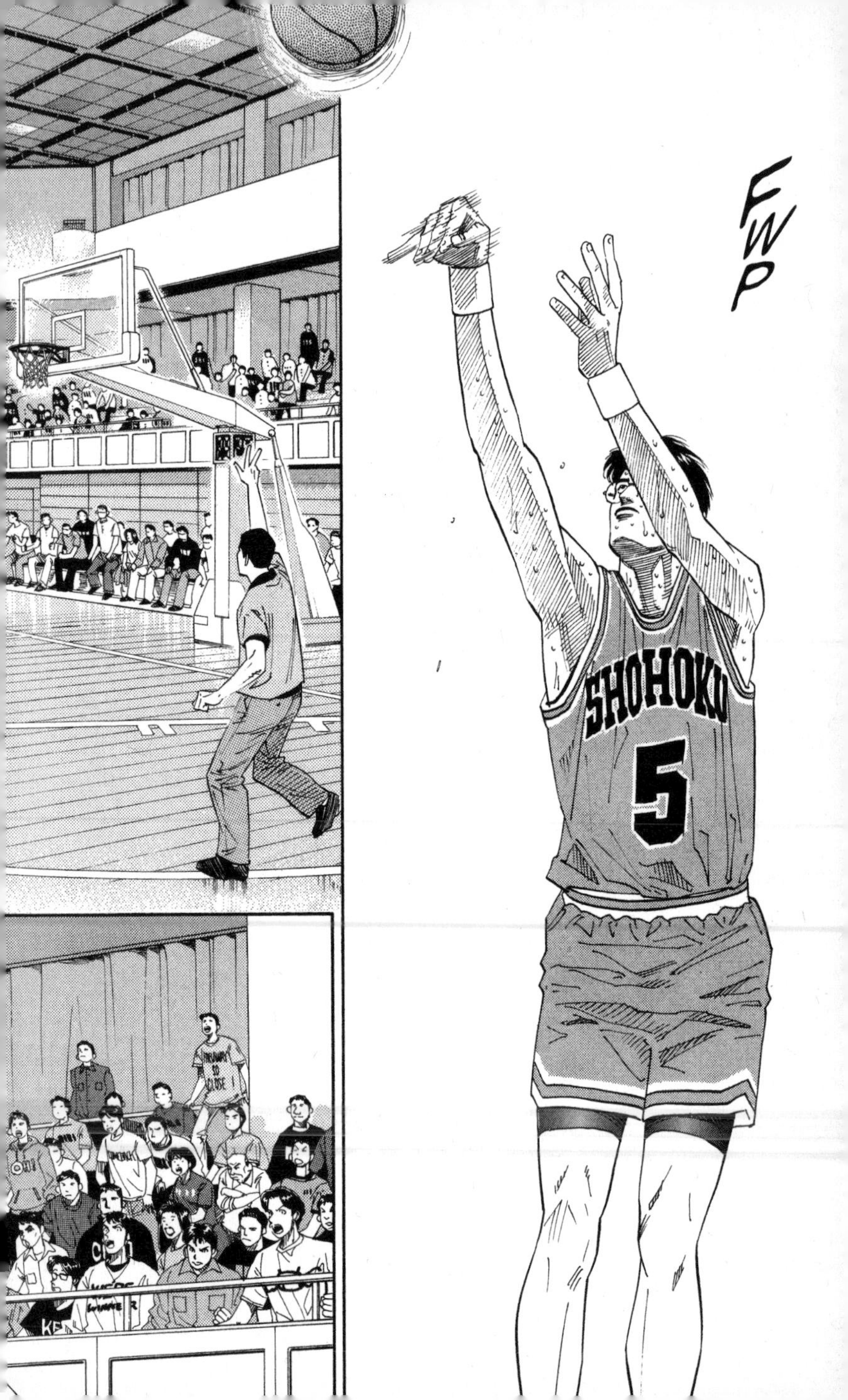
FWP
SHOHOKU
5

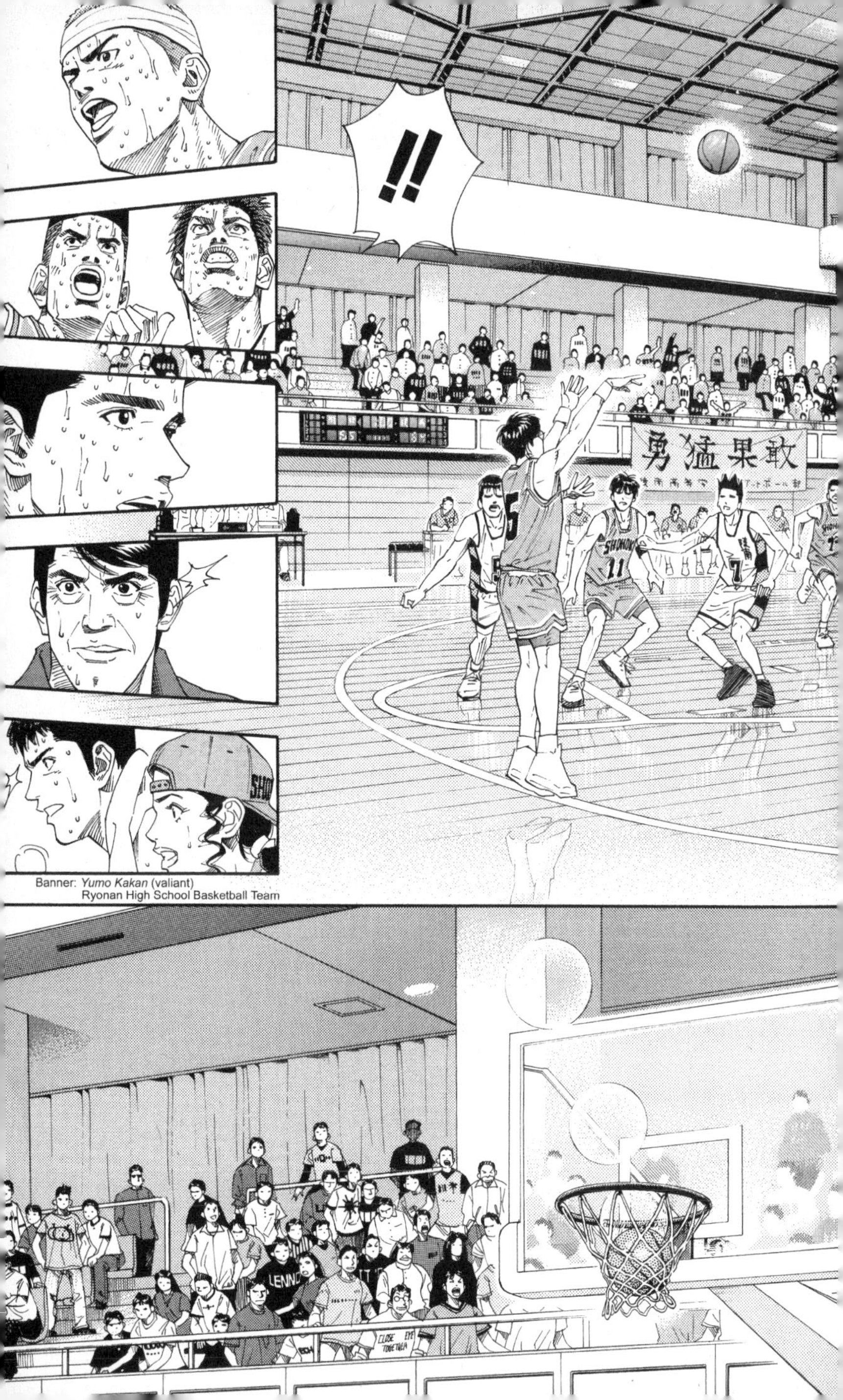
!!
勇猛果敢
SHOHOKU
Banner: *Yumo Kakan* (valiant)
Ryonan High School Basketball Team

SWISH

SLAM DUNK

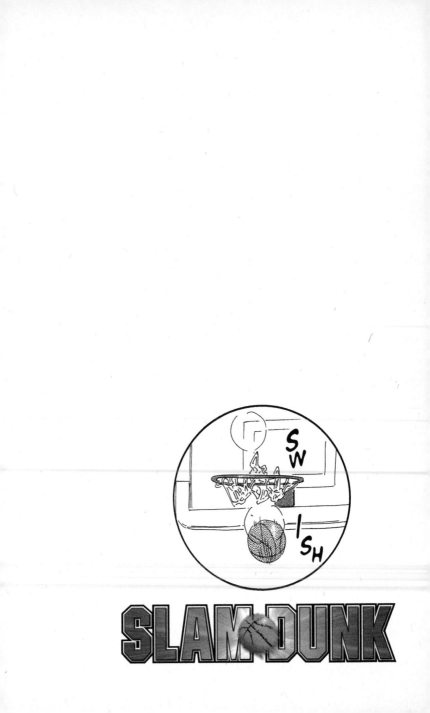

#183

FOUR-EYES

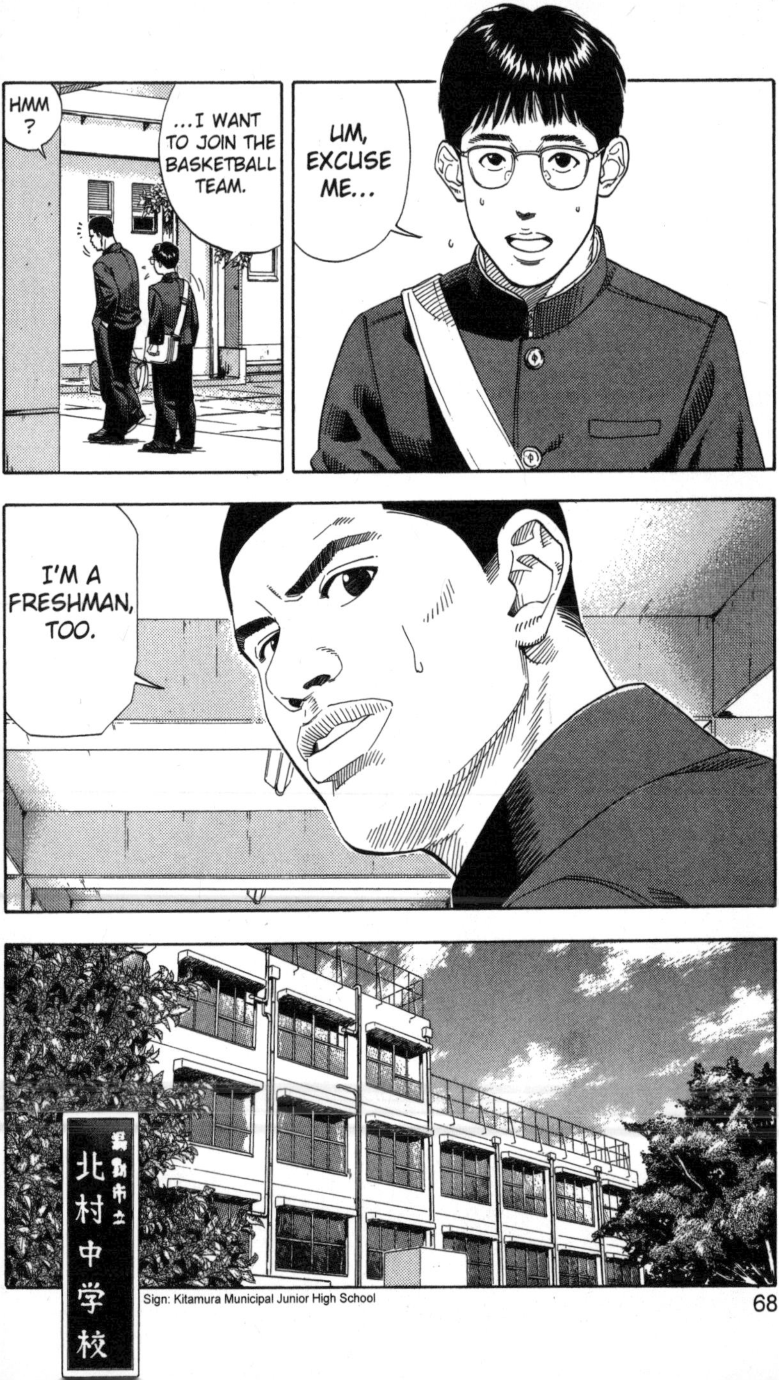
UM, EXCUSE ME...
...I WANT TO JOIN THE BASKETBALL TEAM.
HMM?
I'M A FRESHMAN, TOO.
北村中学校
Sign: Kitamura Municipal Junior High School

READ THIS WAY

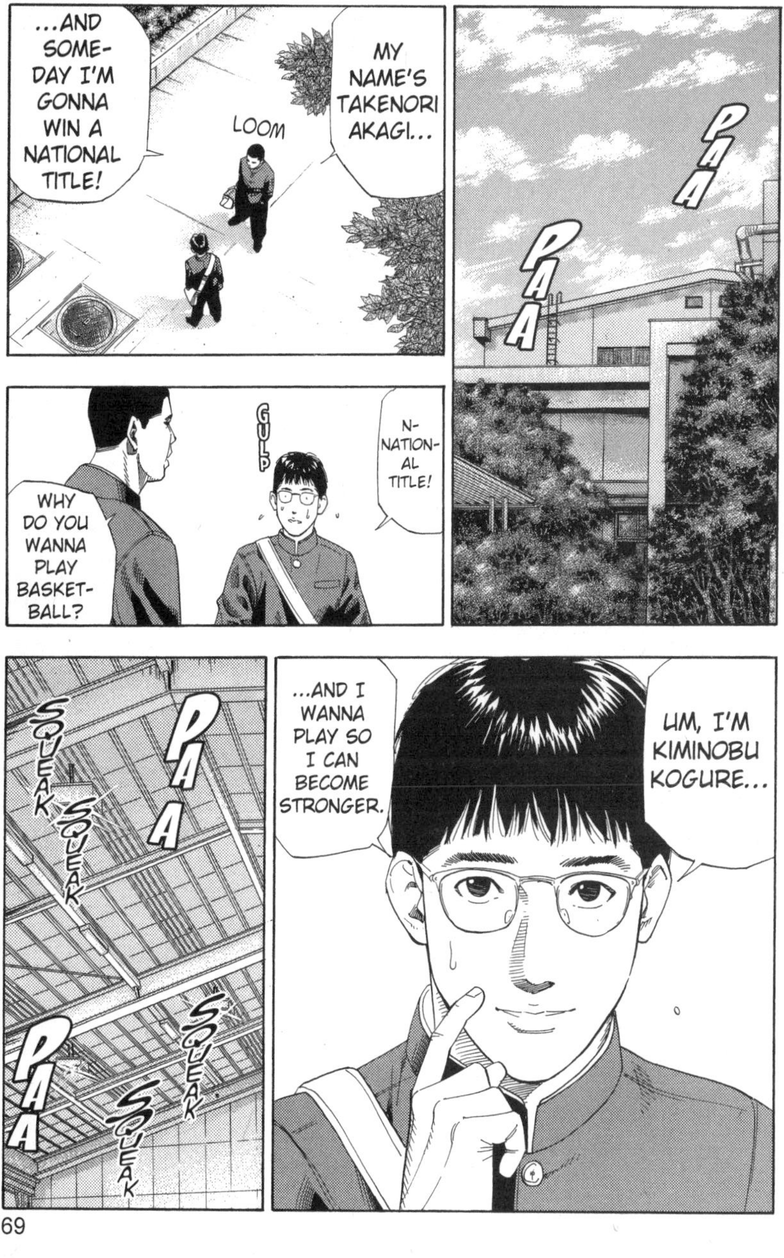
PAA
PAA
MY NAME'S TAKENORI AKAGI...
LOOM
...AND SOMEDAY I'M GONNA WIN A NATIONAL TITLE!
N-NATIONAL TITLE!
GULP
WHY DO YOU WANNA PLAY BASKETBALL?
UM, I'M KIMINOBU KOGURE...
...AND I WANNA PLAY SO I CAN BECOME STRONGER.
PAA
SQUEAK
SQUEAK
SQUEAK
SQUEAK
PAA

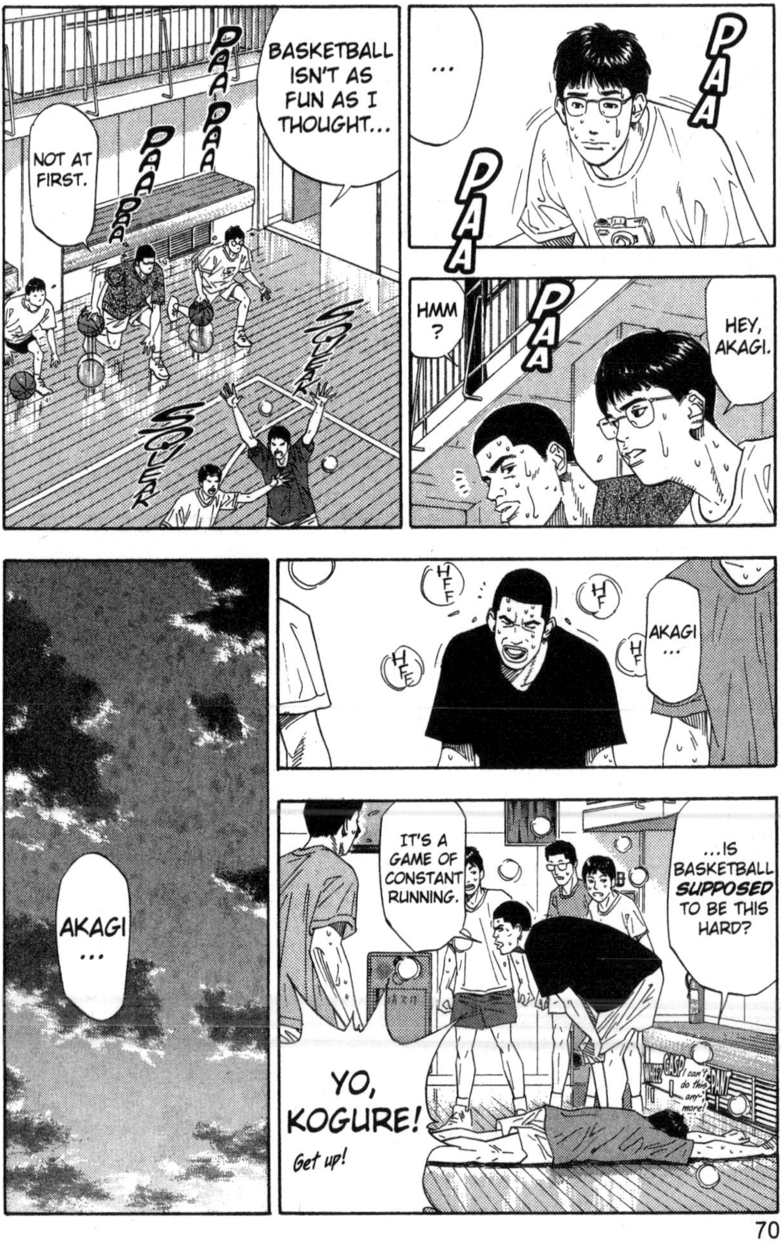
PAA
...
PAA
HEY, AKAGI.
HMM ?
PAA
BASKETBALL ISN'T AS FUN AS I THOUGHT...
NOT AT FIRST.
PAA PAA PAA PAA
SQUEAK
SQUEAK
AKAGI ...
HF
HF
HF
HF
...IS BASKETBALL SUPPOSED TO BE THIS HARD?
IT'S A GAME OF CONSTANT RUNNING.
GASP! I can't do this any-more!
YO, KOGURE!
Get up!
AKAGI ...

READ THIS WAY

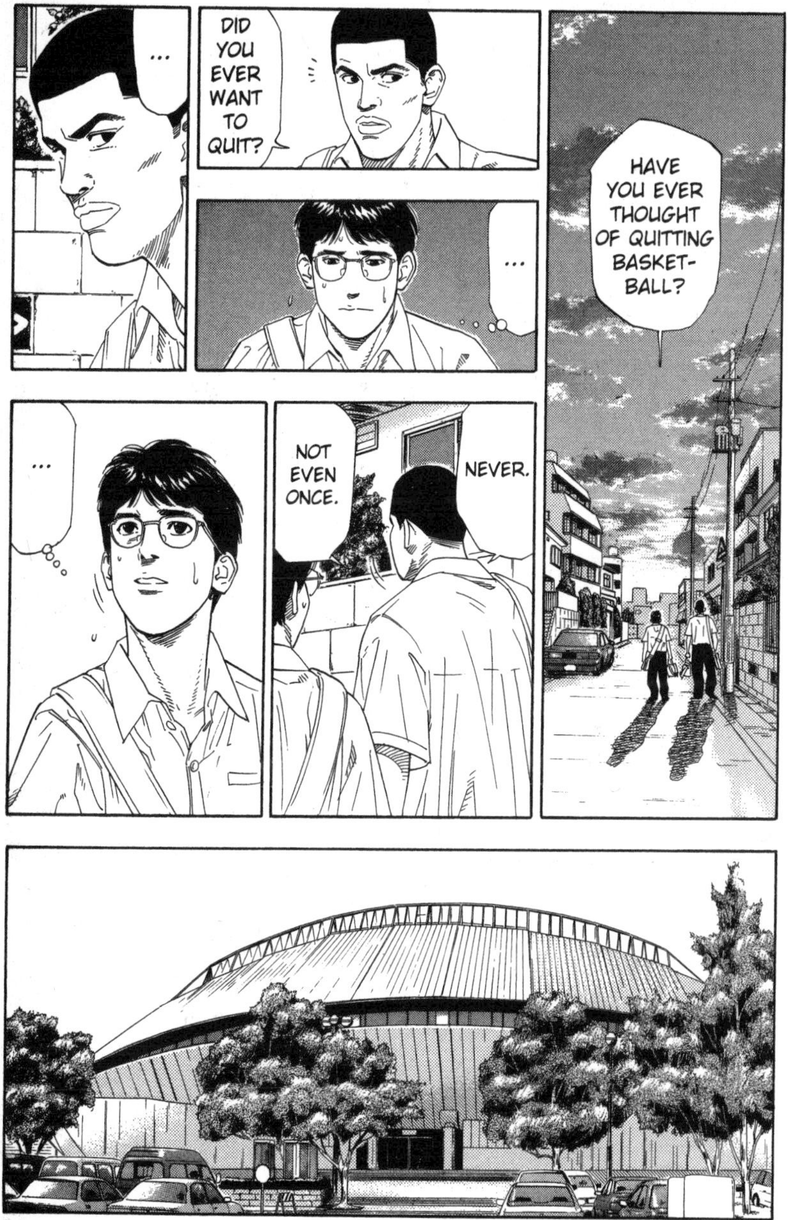

HAVE YOU EVER THOUGHT OF QUITTING BASKET-BALL?
DID YOU EVER WANT TO QUIT?
...
...
NEVER.
NOT EVEN ONCE.
...

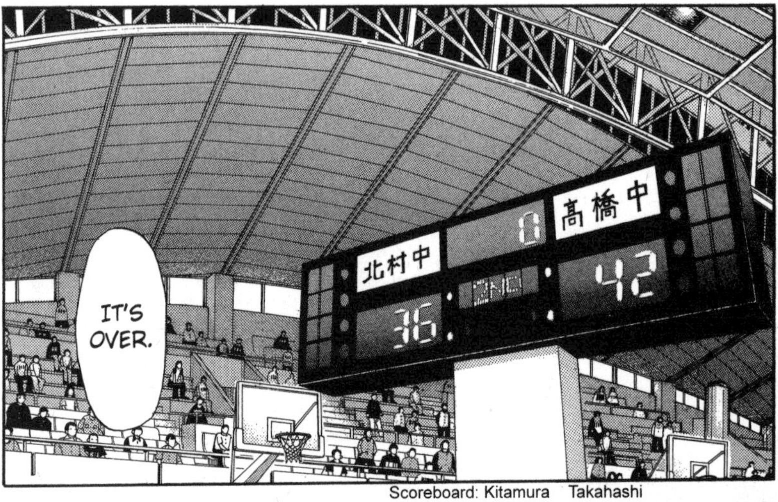
高橋中
0
北村中
2ND
42
36
IT'S OVER.
Scoreboard: Kitamura Takahashi

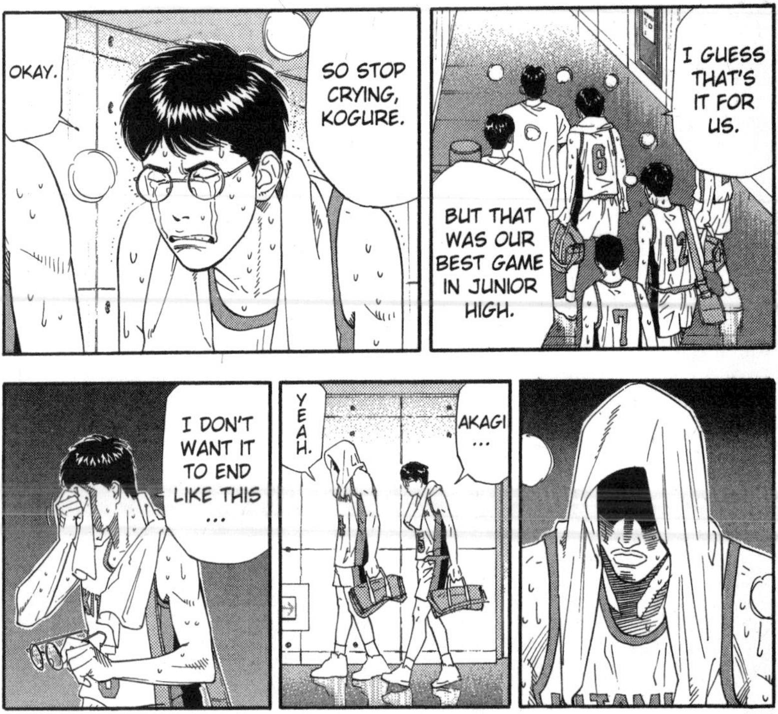
I GUESS THAT'S IT FOR US.
BUT THAT WAS OUR BEST GAME IN JUNIOR HIGH.
SO STOP CRYING, KOGURE.
OKAY.
AKAGI...
YEAH.
I DON'T WANT IT TO END LIKE THIS...

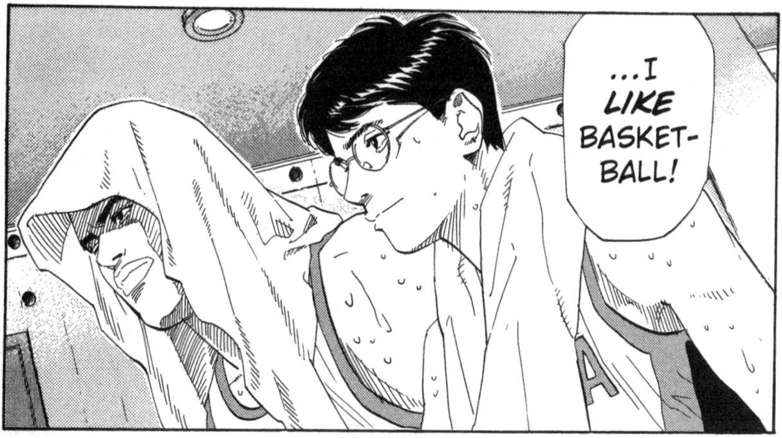
...I *LIKE* BASKET-BALL!

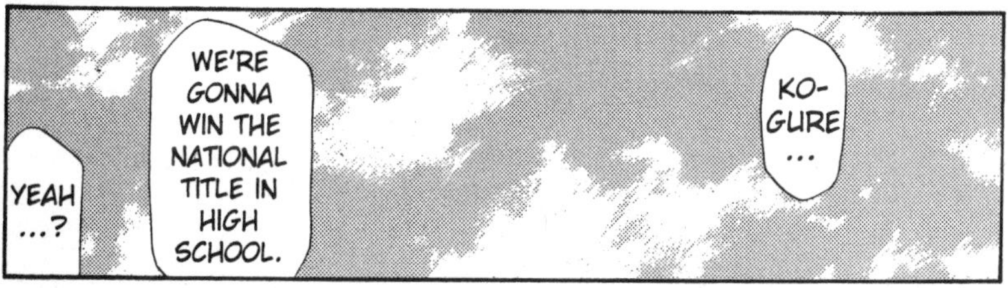
KO-GURE...
WE'RE GONNA WIN THE NATIONAL TITLE IN HIGH SCHOOL.
YEAH...?

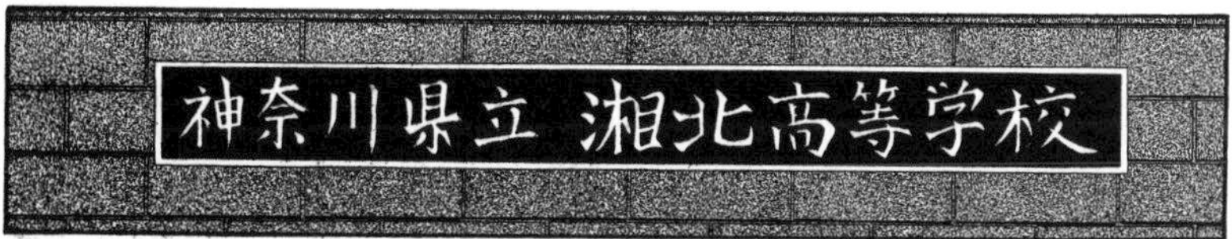
神奈川県立 湘北高等学校

Sign: Kanagawa Prefectural Shohoku High School

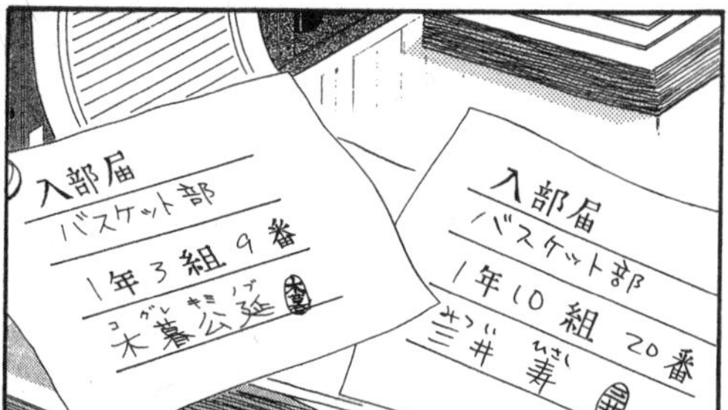
入部届
バスケット部
1年10組 20番
三井寿
入部届
バスケット部
1年3組 9番
木暮公延

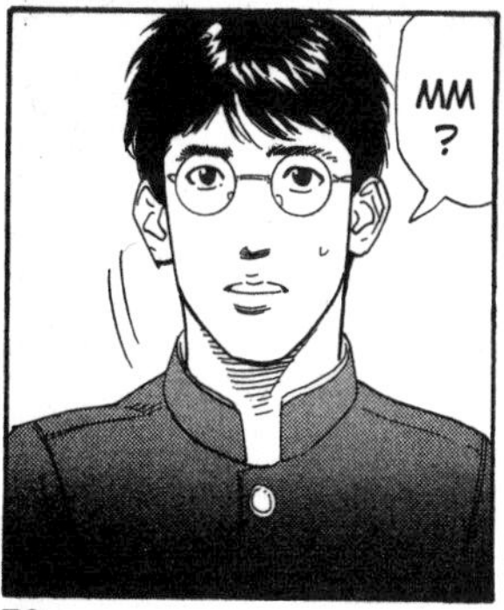
MM?

Paper L: Sign-up Sheet
Basketball Team
Year: 1 Class: 3 Number: 9
Kiminobu Kogure

Paper R: Sign-up Sheet
Basketball Team
Year: 1st Class: 10 Number: 20
Hisashi Mitsui

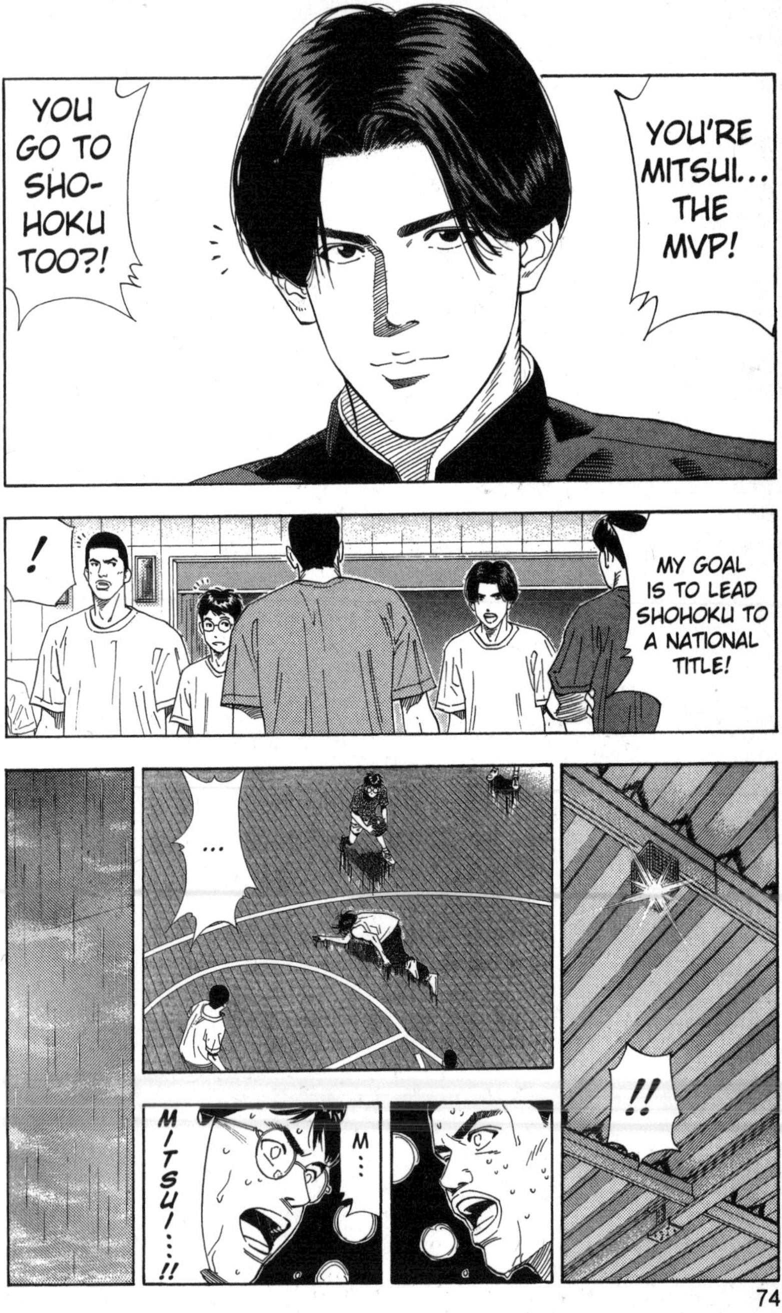
YOU'RE MITSUI... THE MVP!
YOU GO TO SHO-HOKU TOO?!
MY GOAL IS TO LEAD SHOHOKU TO A NATIONAL TITLE!
!
!!
...
M...
MITSUI...!!

READ THIS WAY

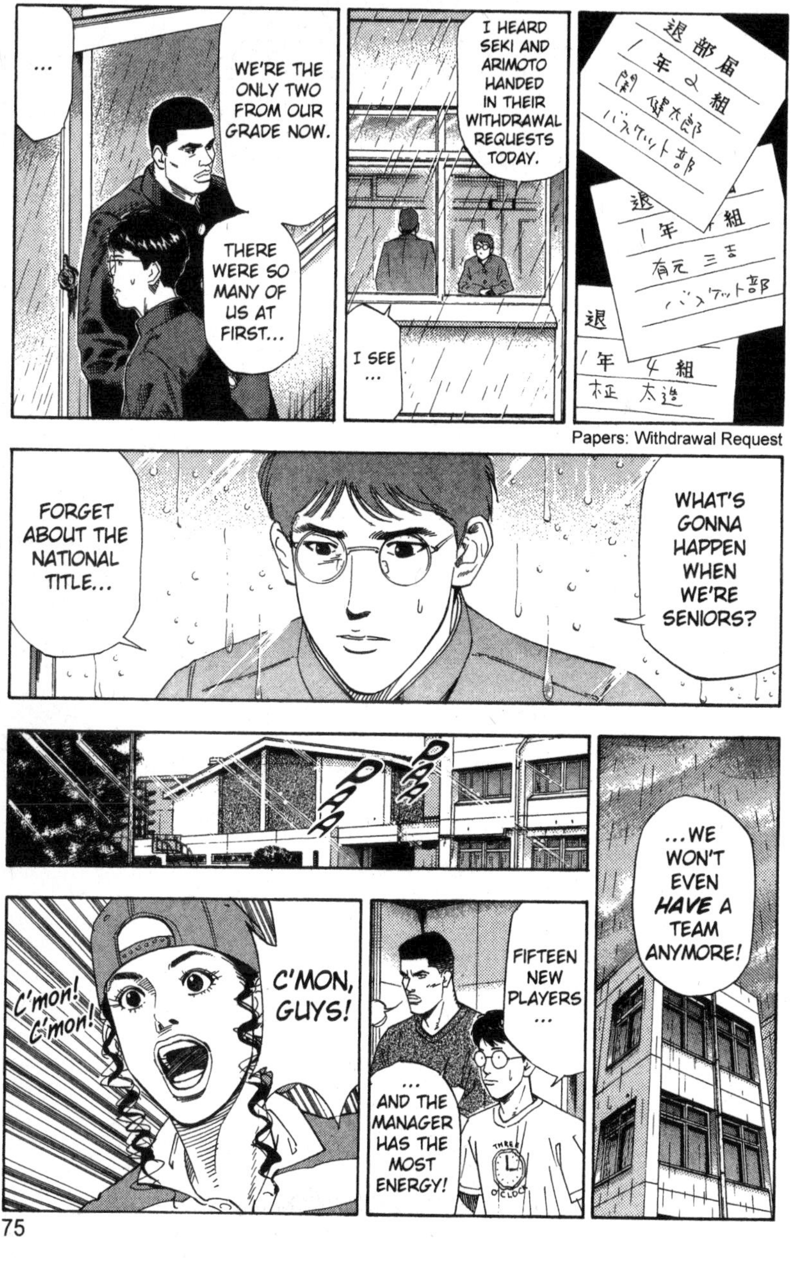
退部届
1年2組
関 健太郎
バスケット部
1年
有元 三吉
バスケット部
1年4組
I HEARD SEKI AND ARIMOTO HANDED IN THEIR WITHDRAWAL REQUESTS TODAY.
I SEE...
WE'RE THE ONLY TWO FROM OUR GRADE NOW.
THERE WERE SO MANY OF US AT FIRST...
...
WHAT'S GONNA HAPPEN WHEN WE'RE SENIORS?
FORGET ABOUT THE NATIONAL TITLE...
...WE WON'T EVEN *HAVE* A TEAM ANYMORE!
FIFTEEN NEW PLAYERS...
...AND THE MANAGER HAS THE MOST ENERGY!
C'MON, GUYS!
C'mon! C'mon!
THREE O'CLOCK
Papers: Withdrawal Request

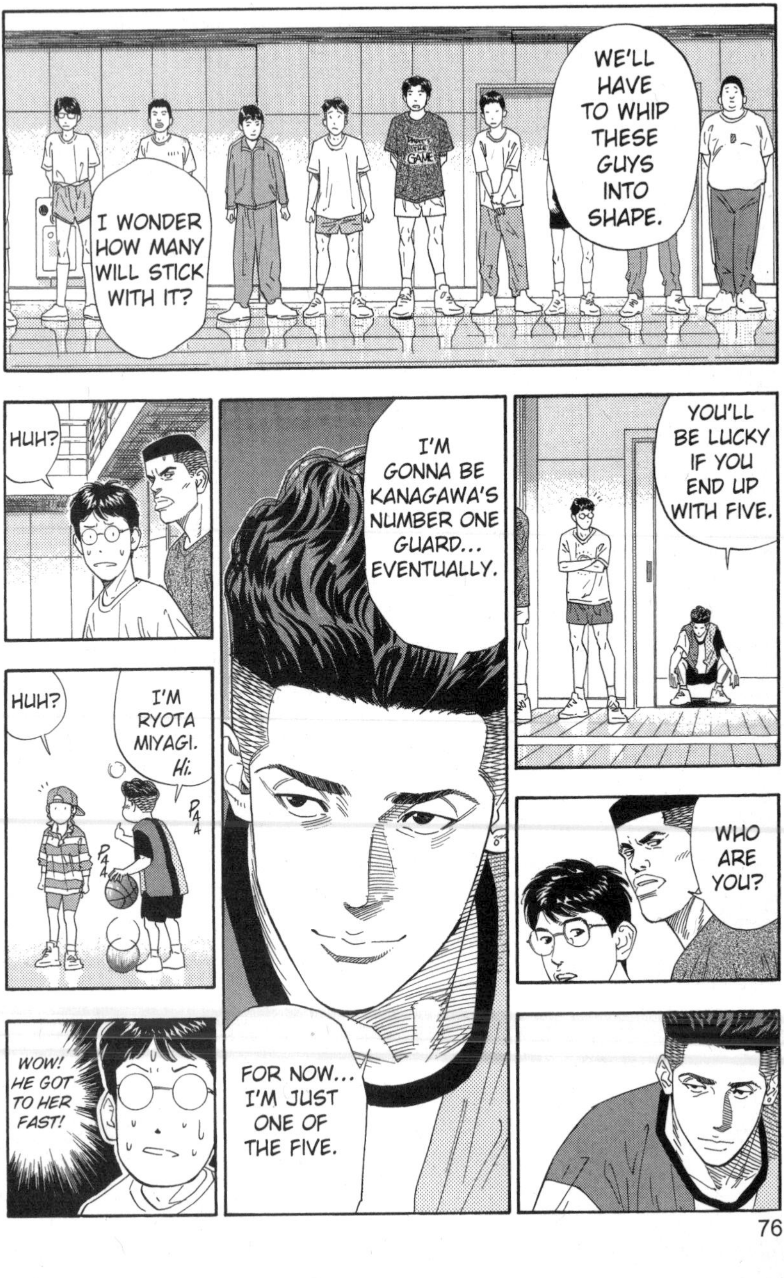

WE'LL HAVE TO WHIP THESE GUYS INTO SHAPE.
I WONDER HOW MANY WILL STICK WITH IT?
YOU'LL BE LUCKY IF YOU END UP WITH FIVE.
WHO ARE YOU?
I'M GONNA BE KANAGAWA'S NUMBER ONE GUARD... EVENTUALLY.
FOR NOW... I'M JUST ONE OF THE FIVE.
HUH?
I'M RYOTA MIYAGI.
Hi.
HUH?
WOW! HE GOT TO HER FAST!

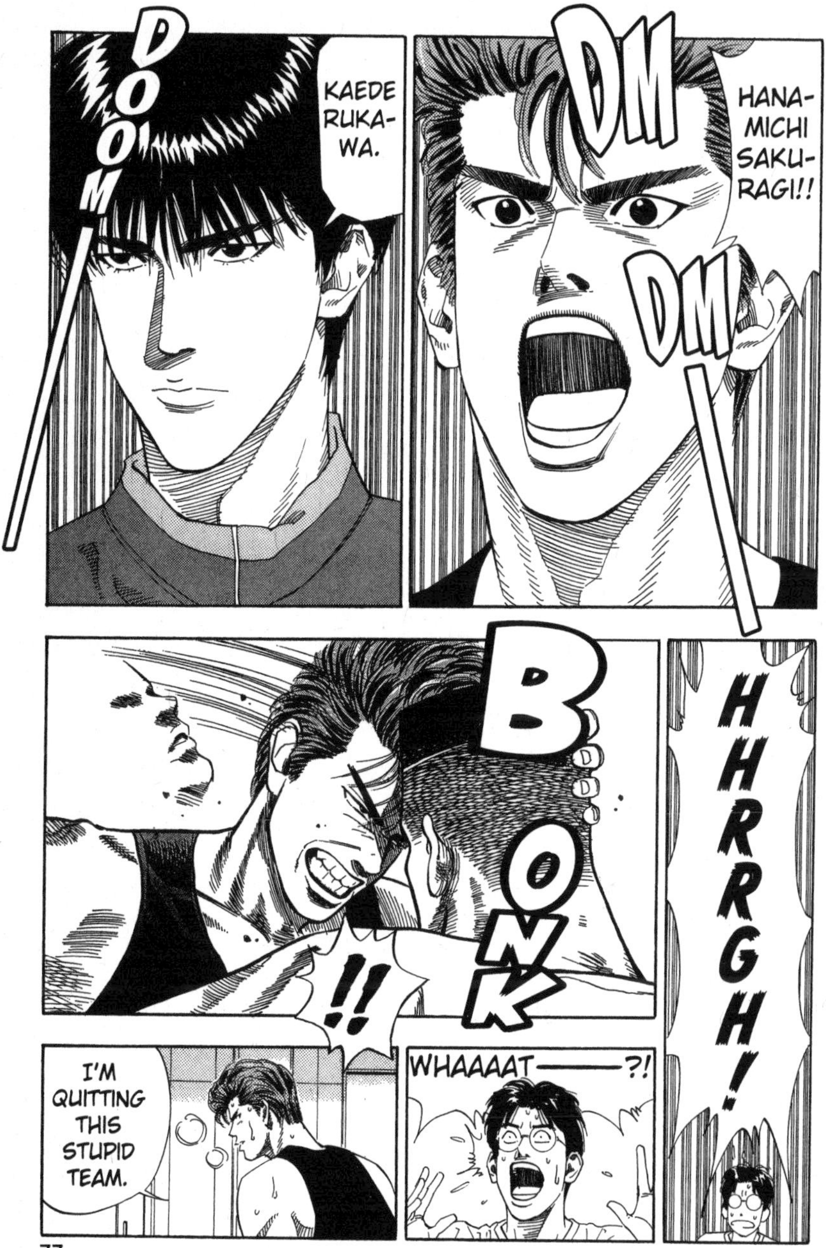
DM
HANA-MICHI SAKURAGI!!
DM
DOOM
KAEDE RUKAWA.
HHRRGH!
BONK
!!
WHAAAAT——?!
I'M QUITTING THIS STUPID TEAM.

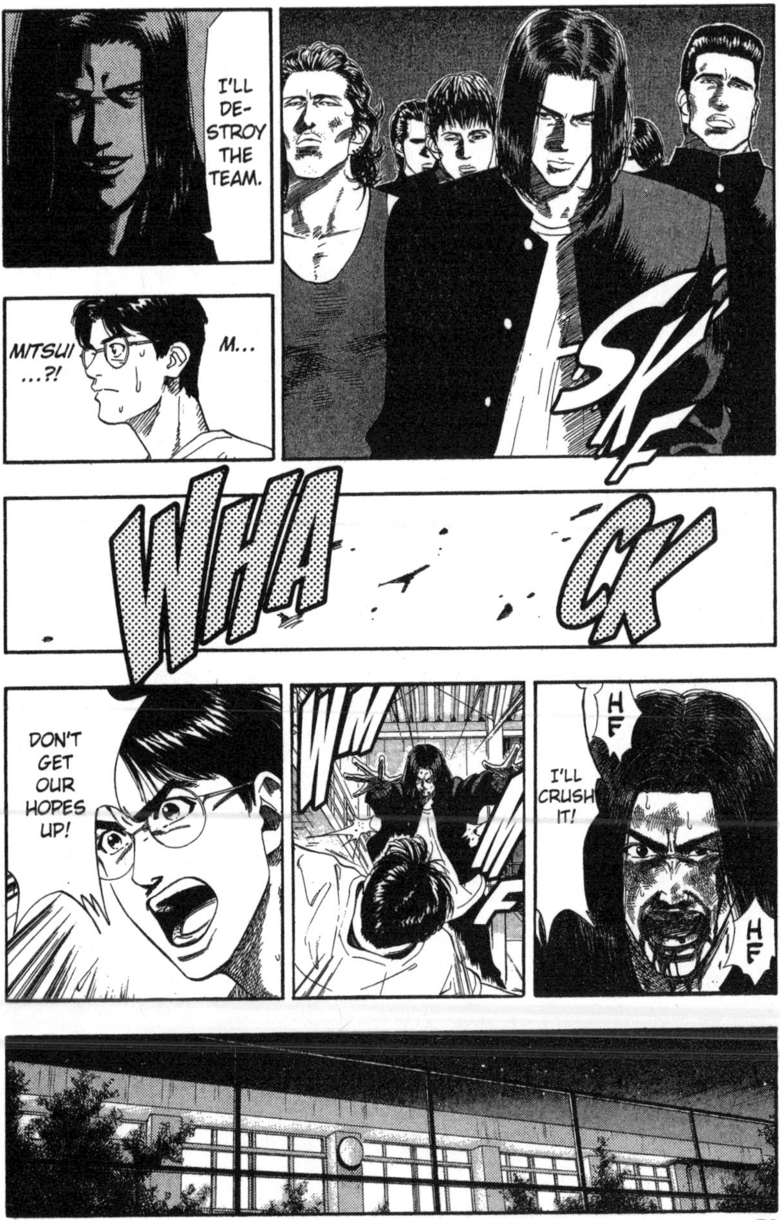
I'LL DE-STROY THE TEAM.
M...
MITSUI ...?!
WHACK
HF
I'LL CRUSH IT!
HF
DON'T GET OUR HOPES UP!

READ THIS WAY

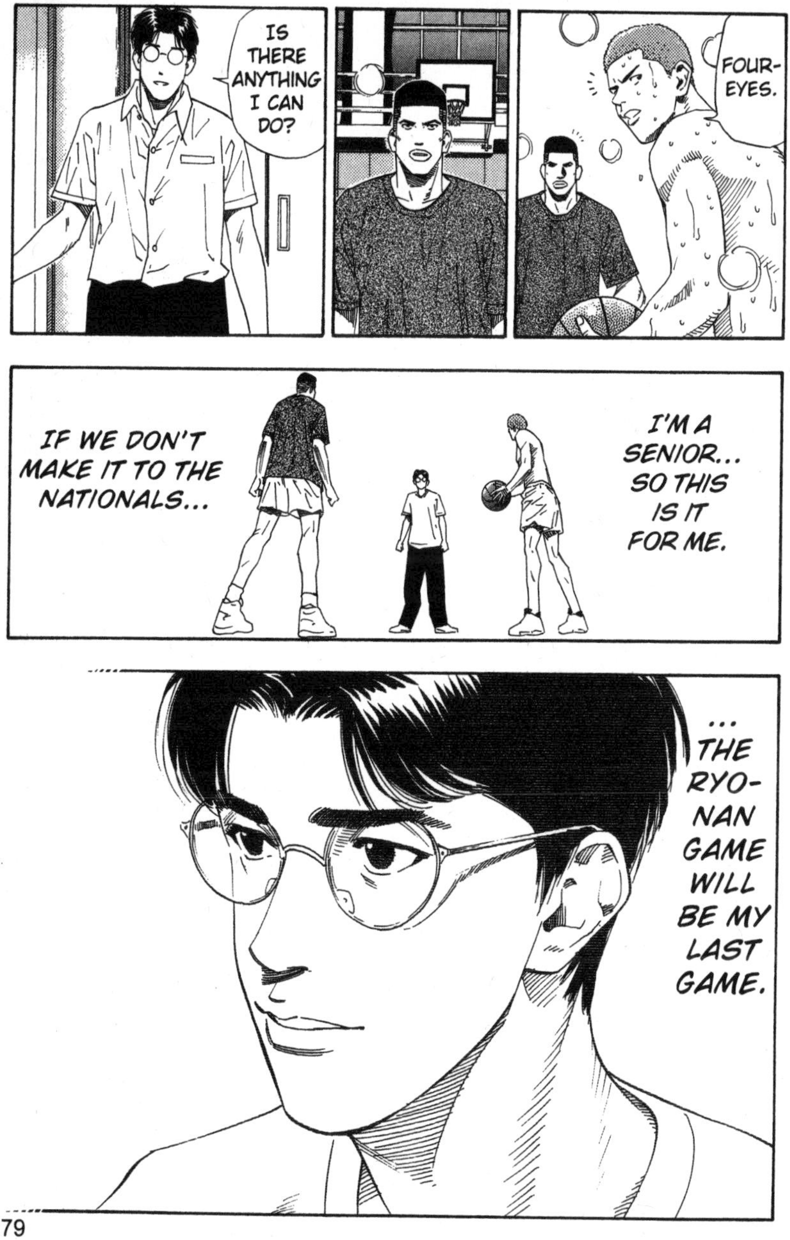
FOUR-EYES.
IS THERE ANYTHING I CAN DO?
I'M A SENIOR... SO THIS IS IT FOR ME.
IF WE DON'T MAKE IT TO THE NATIONALS...
...THE RYO-NAN GAME WILL BE MY LAST GAME.

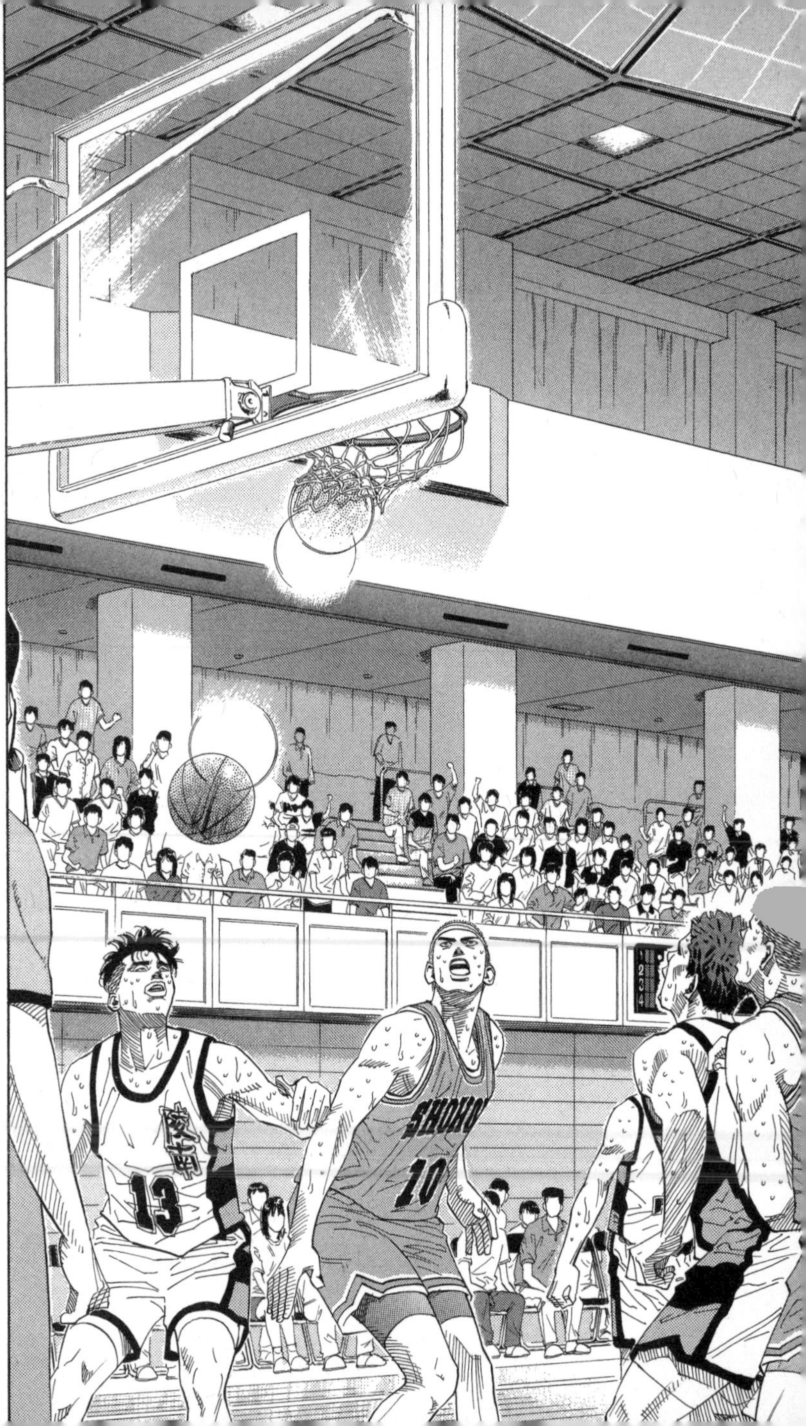

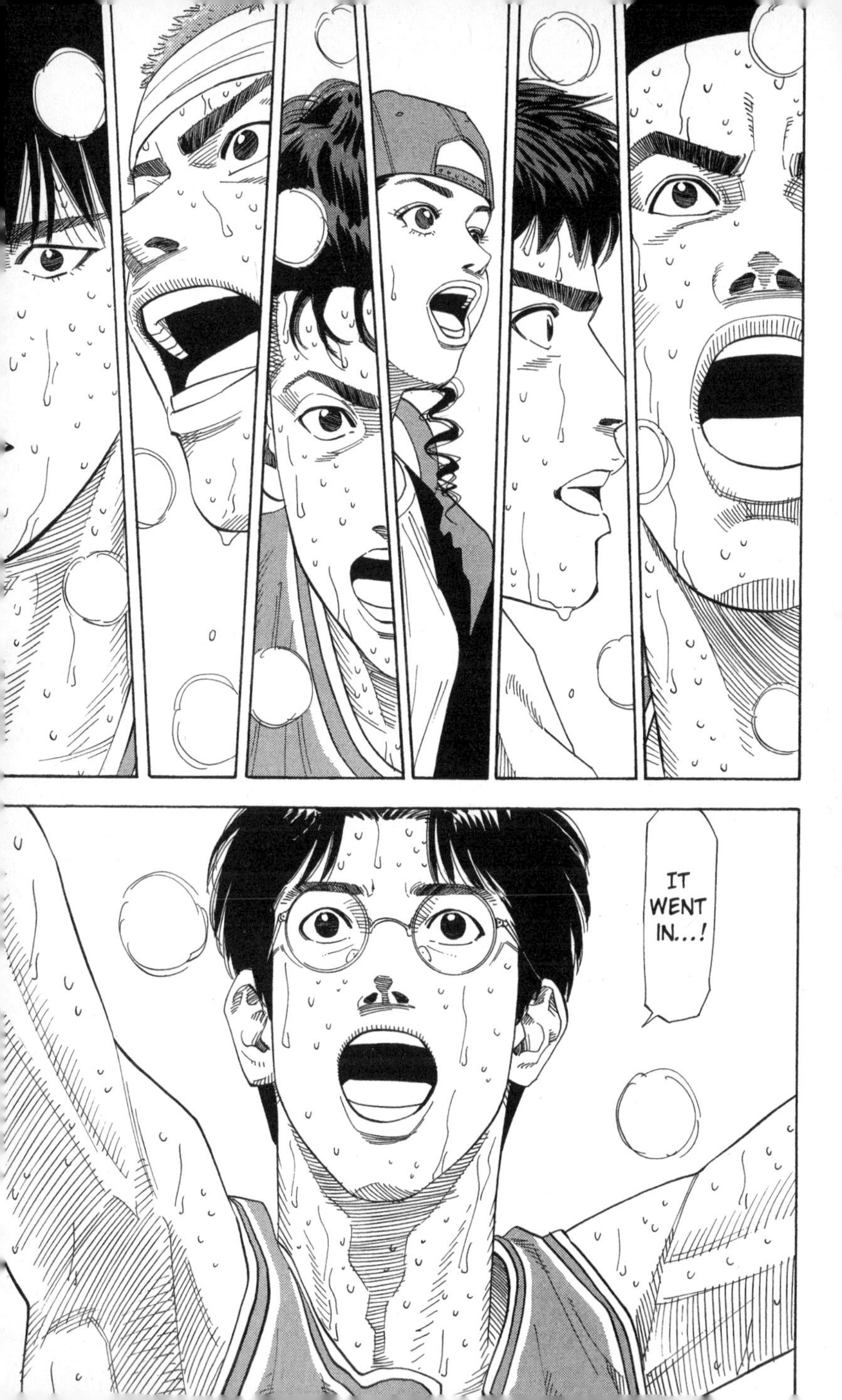
IT WENT IN...!

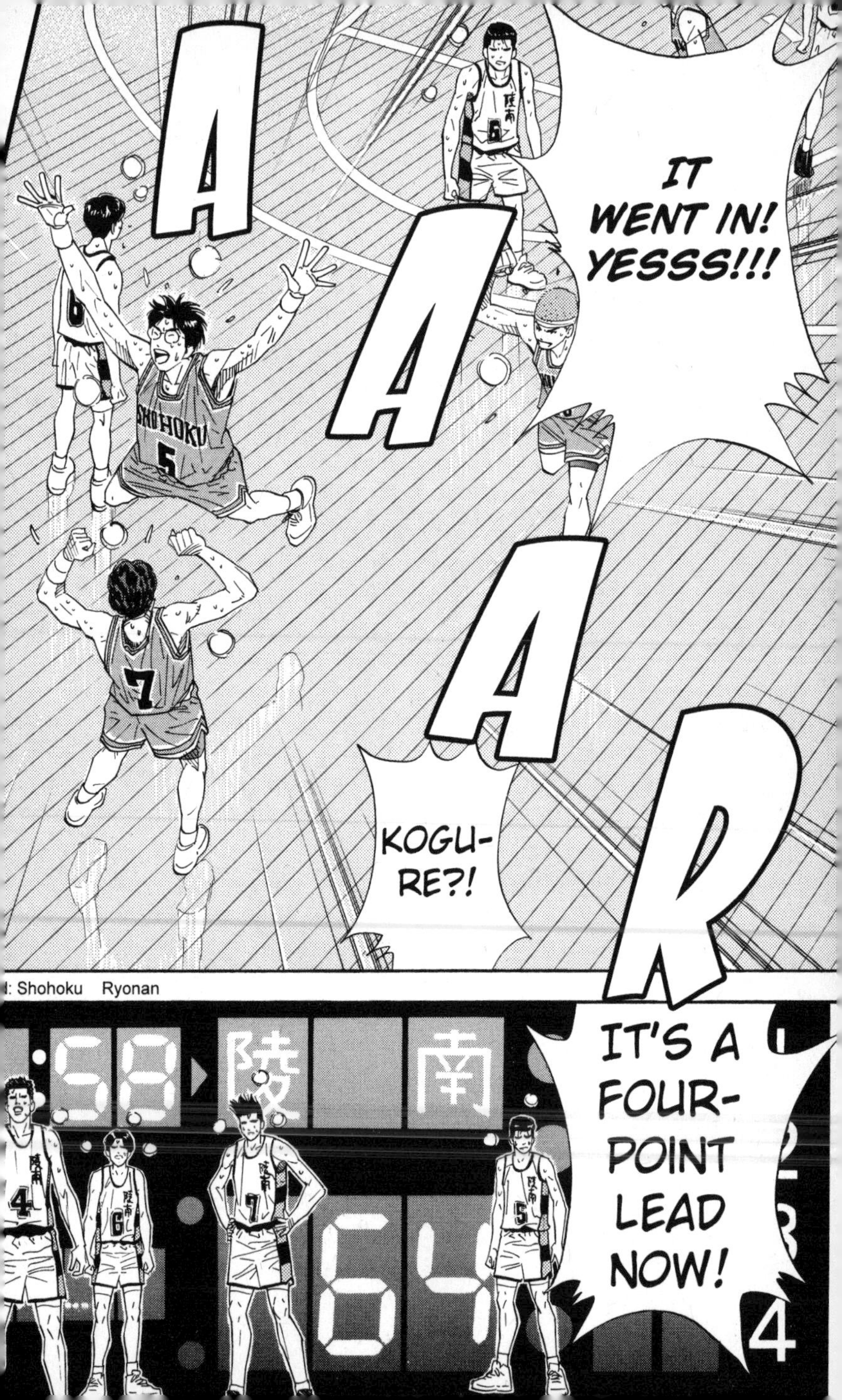

IT WENT IN! YESSS!!!
AAAR
KOGU-RE?!
: Shohoku Ryonan
陵南
IT'S A FOUR-POINT LEAD NOW!

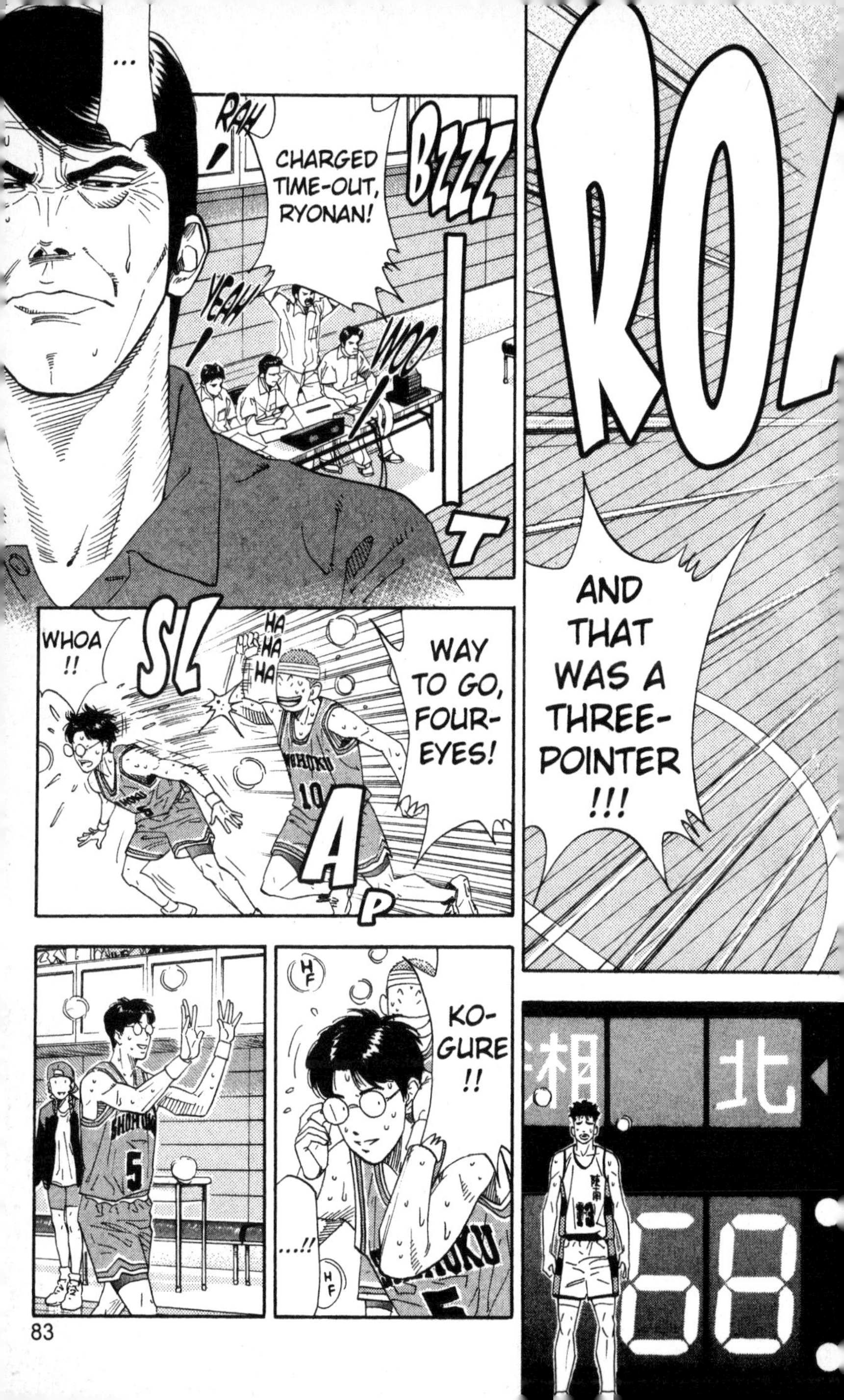
ROL
AND THAT WAS A THREE-POINTER !!!
BZZZ
CHARGED TIME-OUT, RYONAN!
RAH!
...
WOO!
YEAH!
T
WAY TO GO, FOUR-EYES!
HA HA HA HA
SL
WHOA !!
A
P
湘
北
KO-GURE !!
HF
...!!
HF

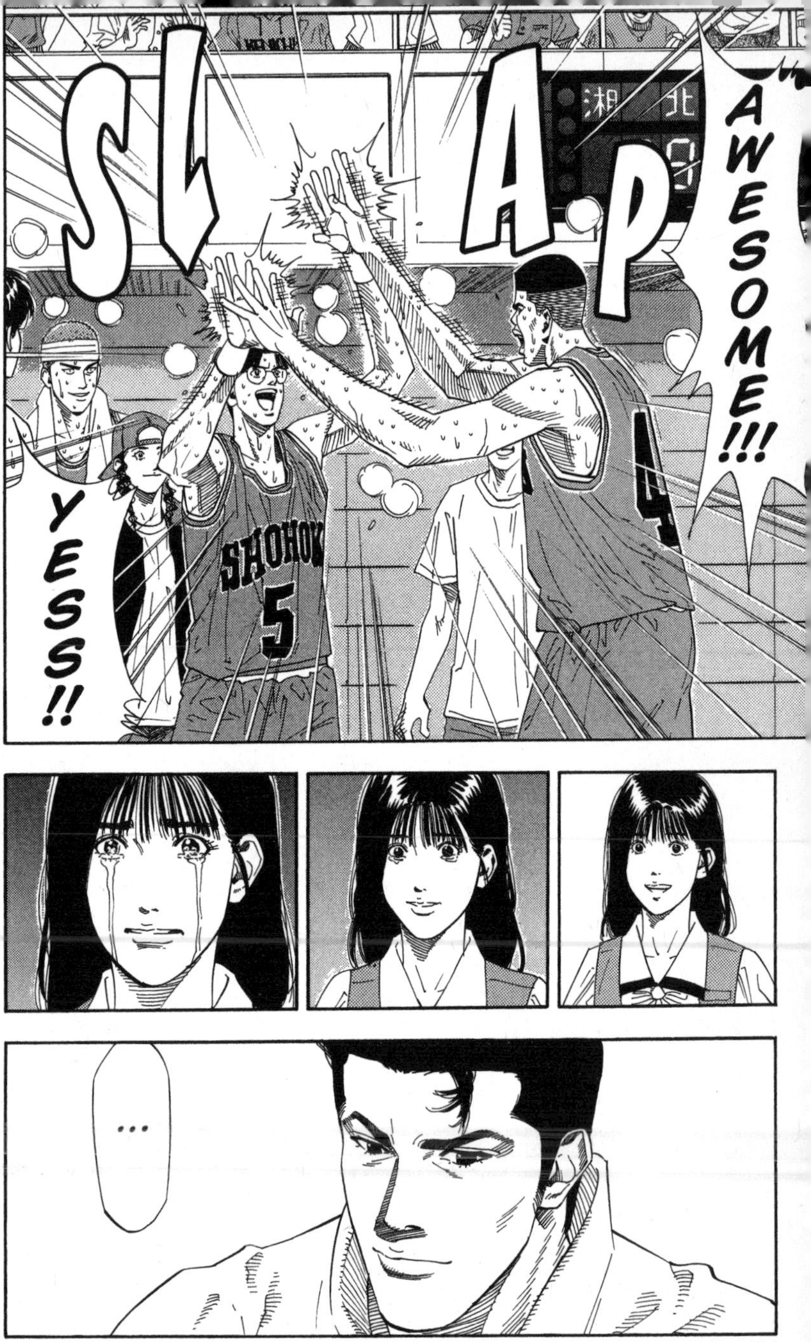
AWESOME!!!
湘北
SLAP
YESS!!
SHOHOKU
...

READ THIS WAY

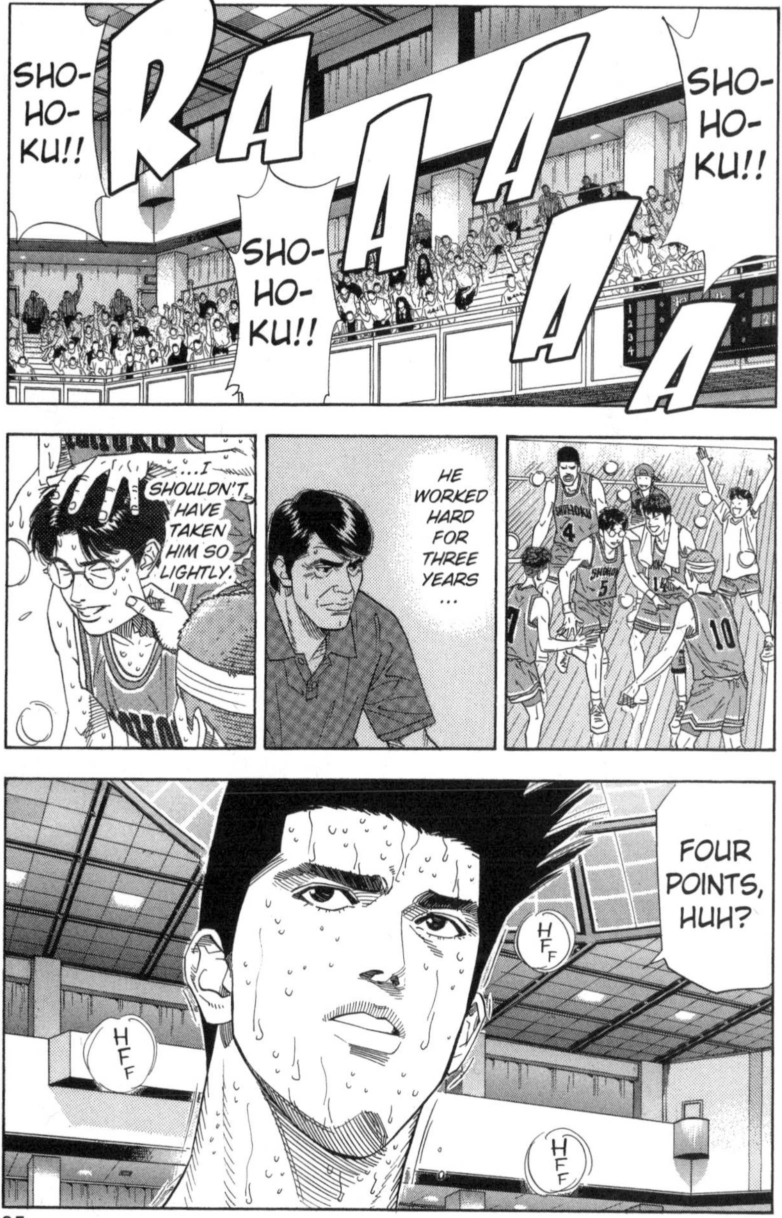
SHO-HO-KU!!
RAAAAAAA
SHO-HO-KU!!
SHO-HO-KU!!
HE WORKED HARD FOR THREE YEARS ...
...I SHOULDN'T HAVE TAKEN HIM SO LIGHTLY.
FOUR POINTS, HUH?
HFF
HFF
HFF

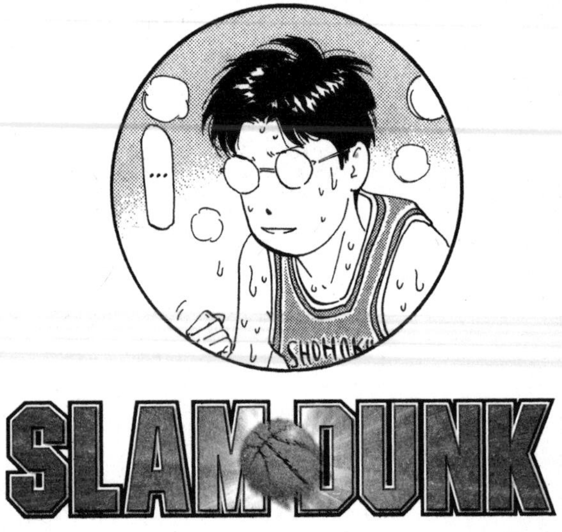
...

SLAM DUNK

WIN/LOSS

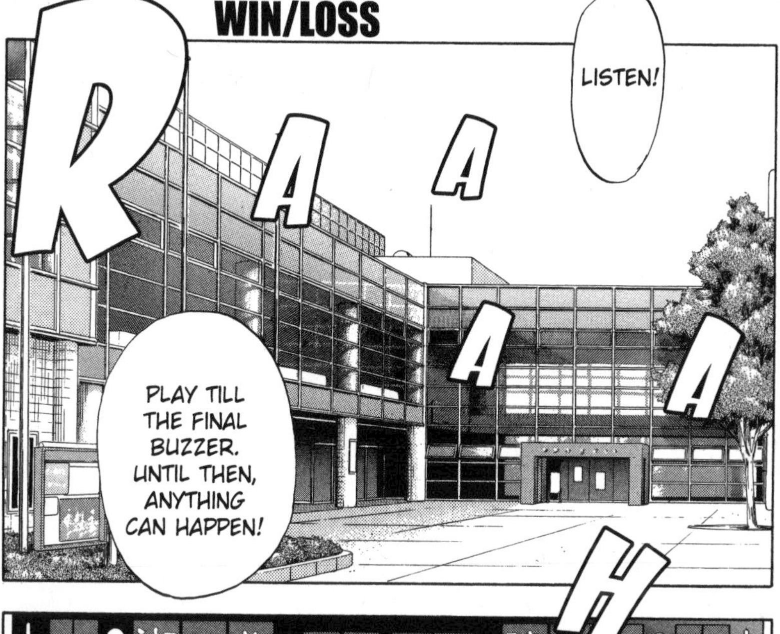
LISTEN!
RAAAAH
PLAY TILL THE FINAL BUZZER. UNTIL THEN, ANYTHING CAN HAPPEN!

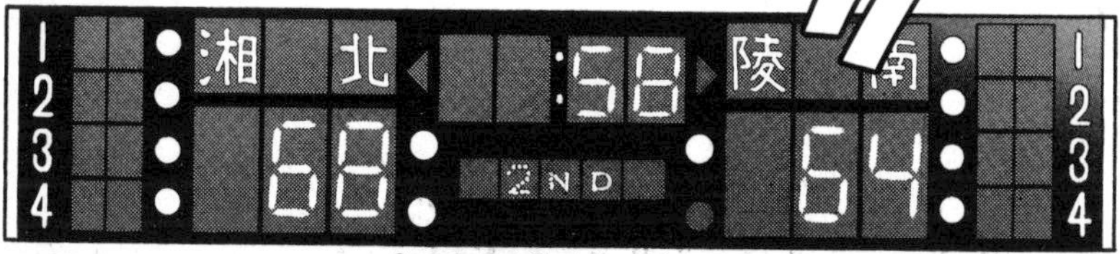
1 2 3 4
湘北
58
陵南
68
2ND
64
1 2 3 4

Scoreboard: Shohoku Ryonan

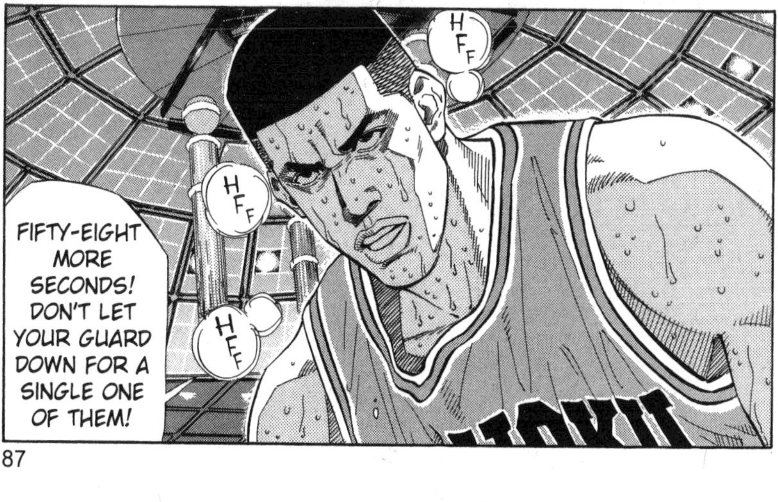
HFF
HFF
HFF
FIFTY-EIGHT MORE SECONDS! DON'T LET YOUR GUARD DOWN FOR A SINGLE ONE OF THEM!

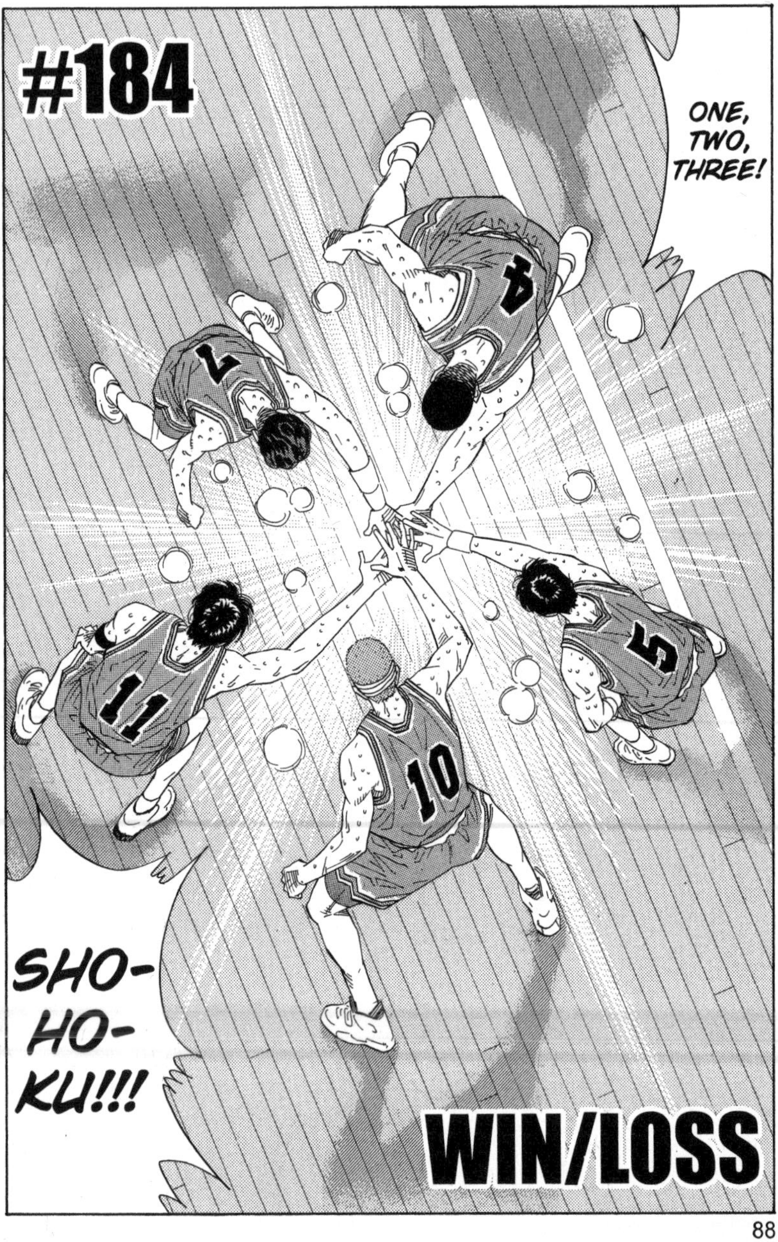
#184
ONE, TWO, THREE!
SHO-HO-KU!!!
WIN/LOSS

READ THIS WAY

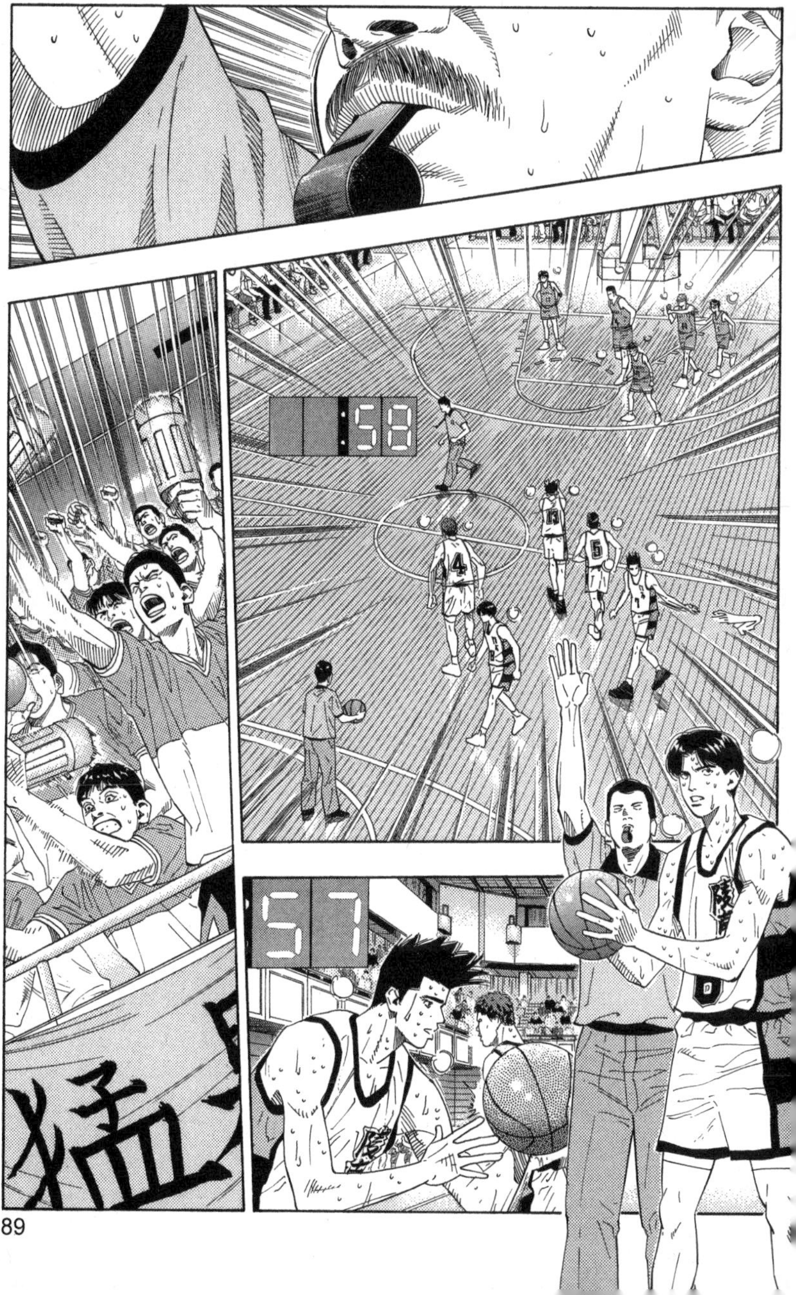
58
57
猛

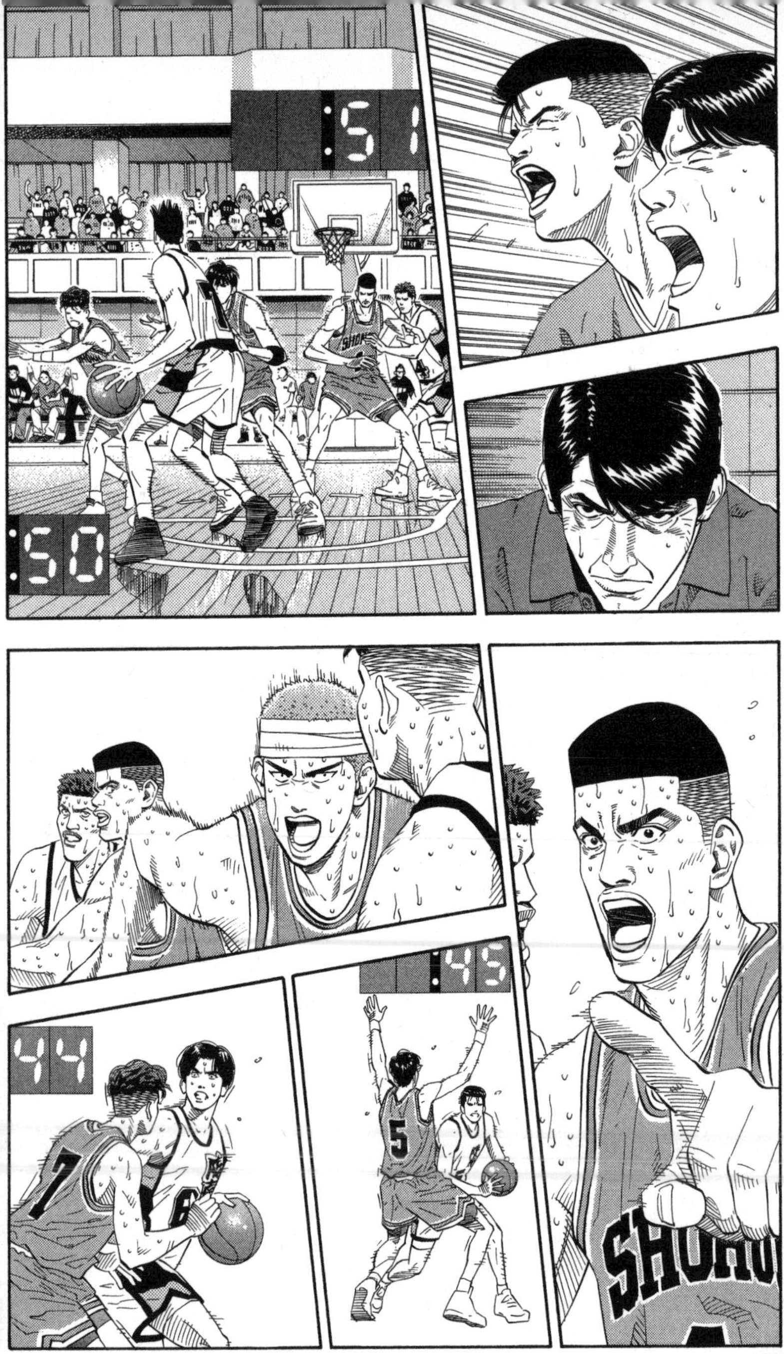
51
50
45
44

READ THIS WAY

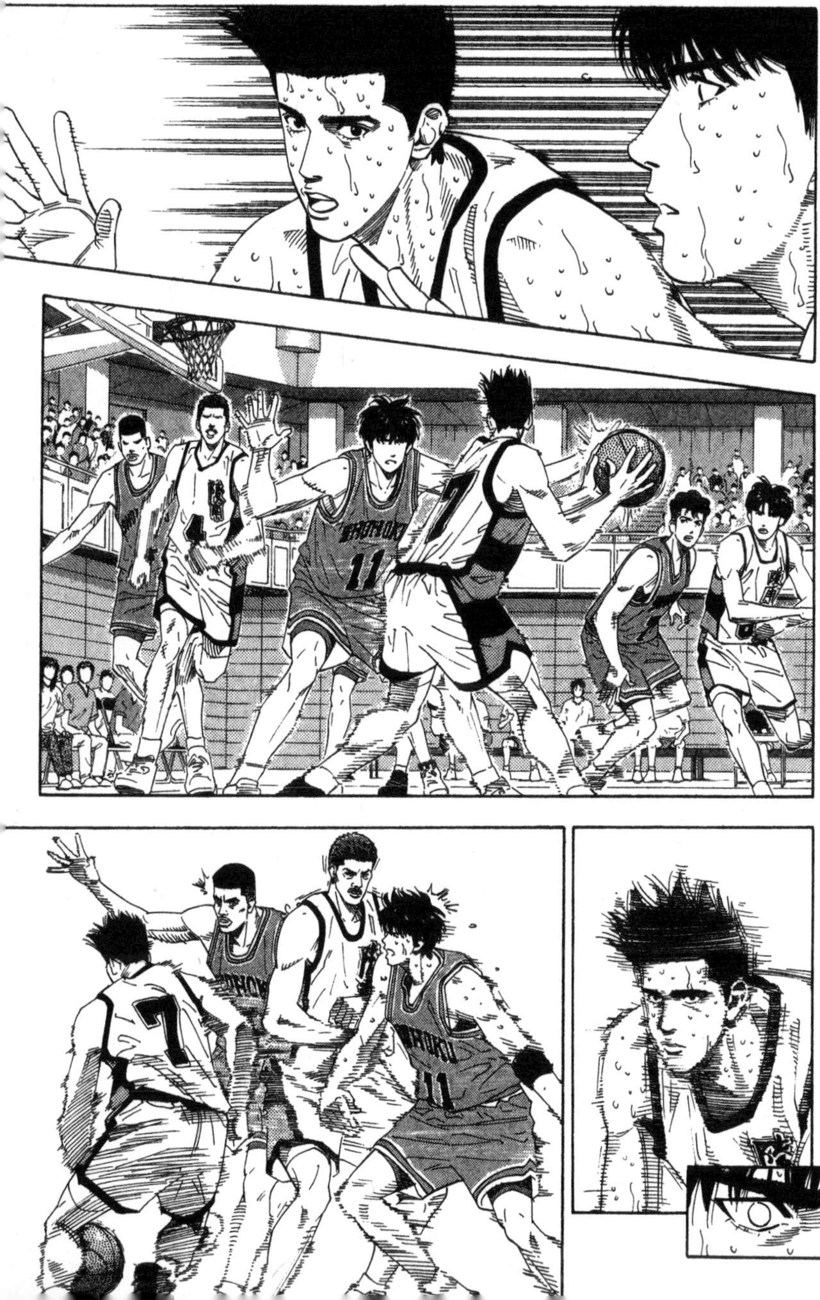

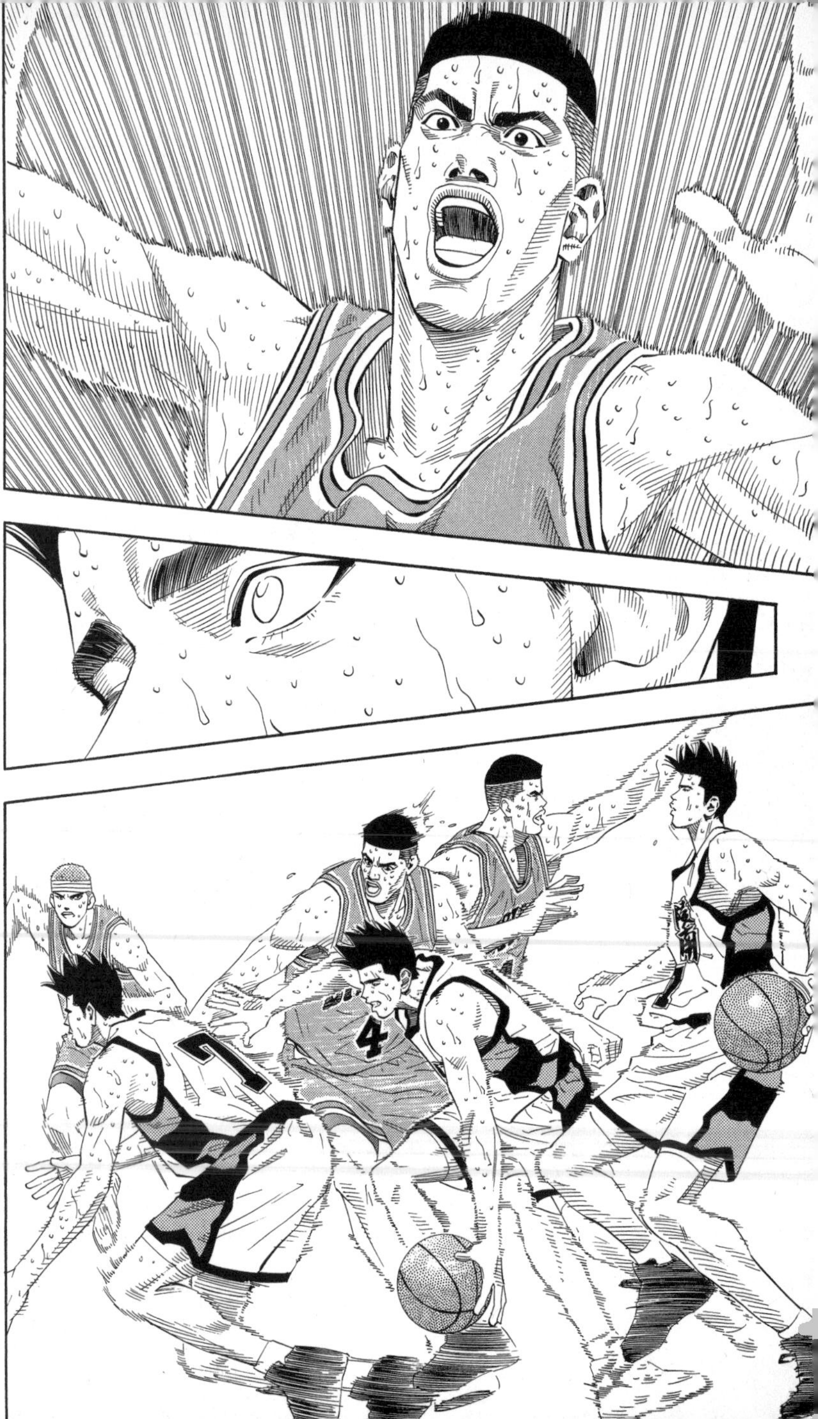

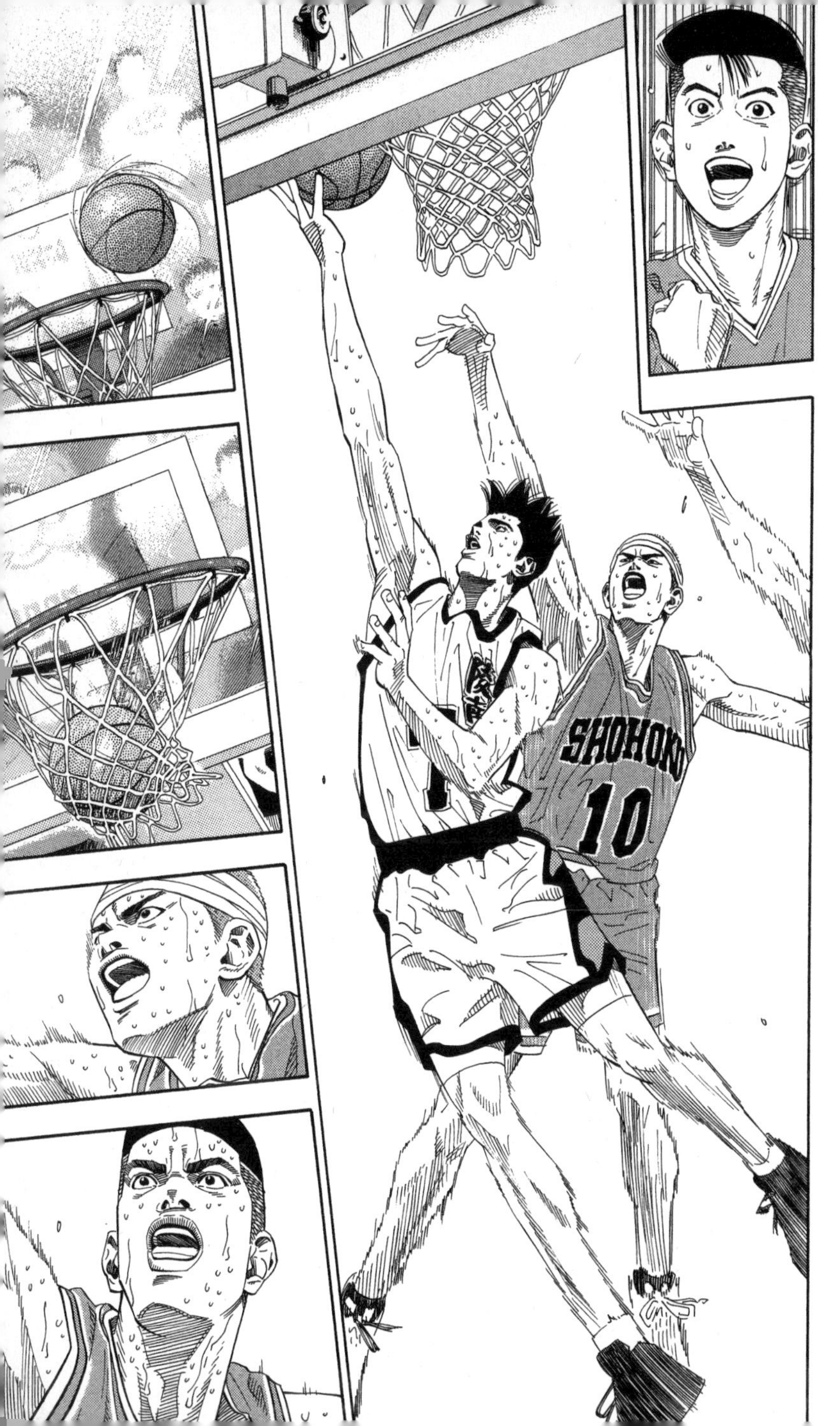
SHOHOKU
10

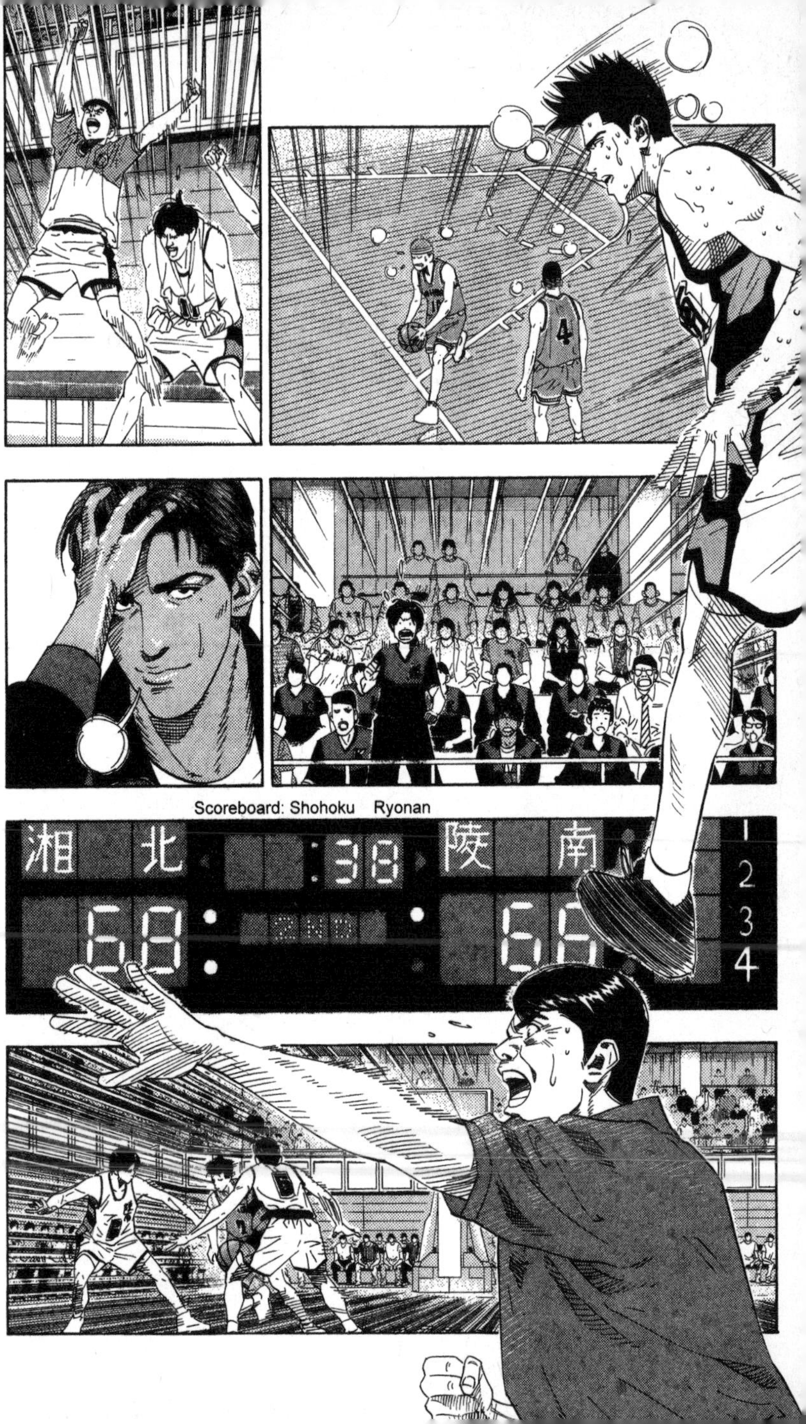
Scoreboard: Shohoku Ryonan
湘北
陵南
38
68
66
1
2
3
4

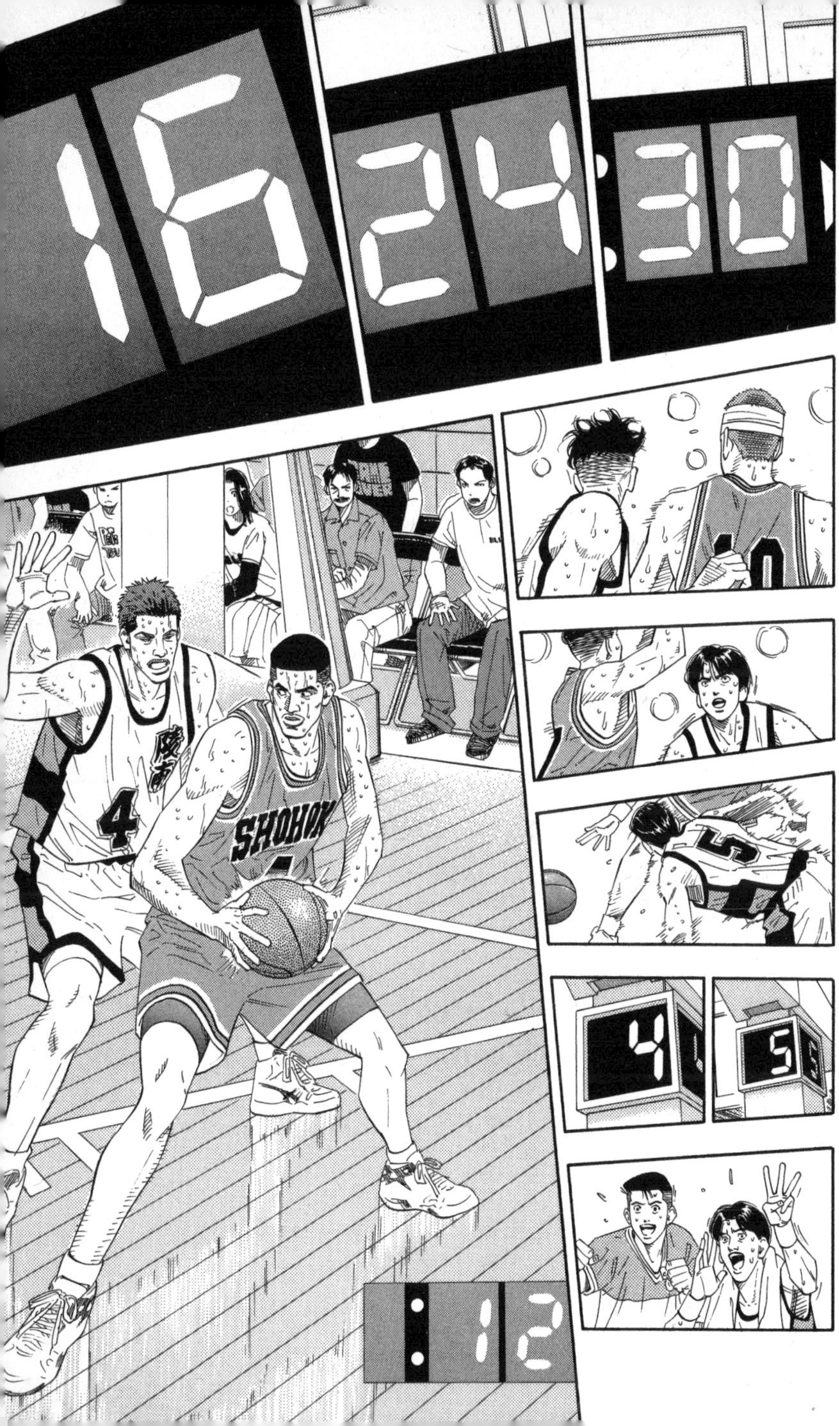
16 24:30
5
4
12

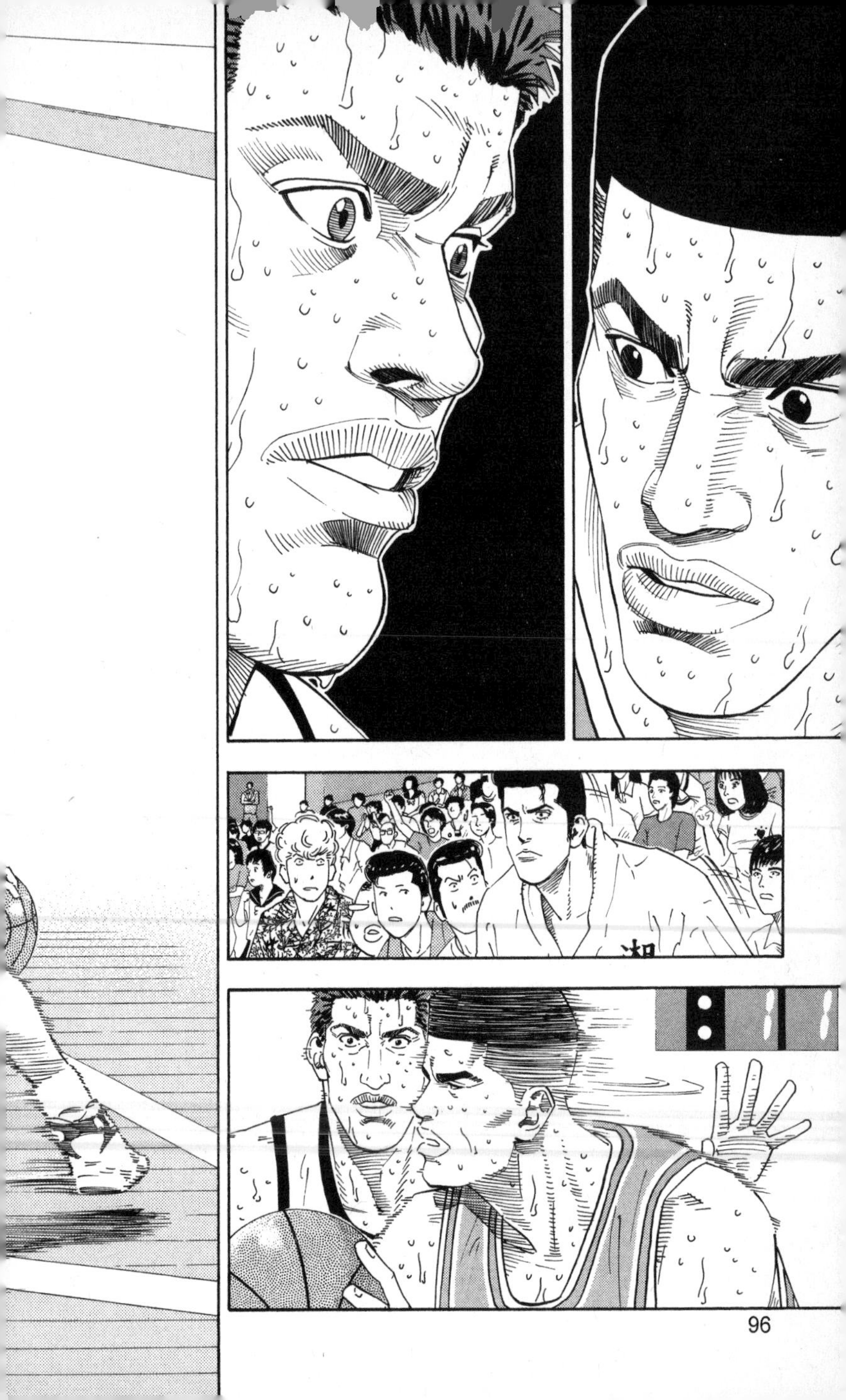

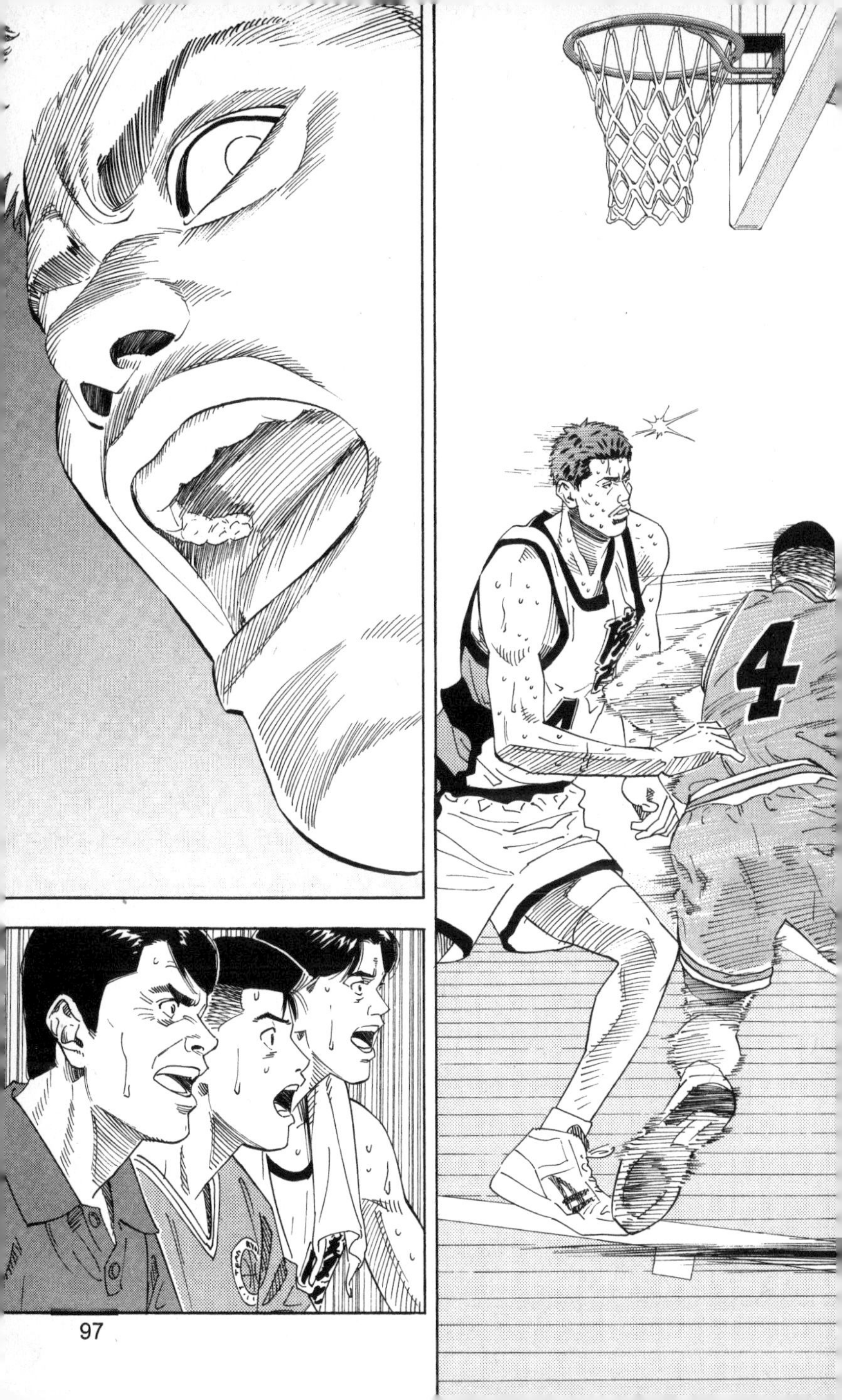

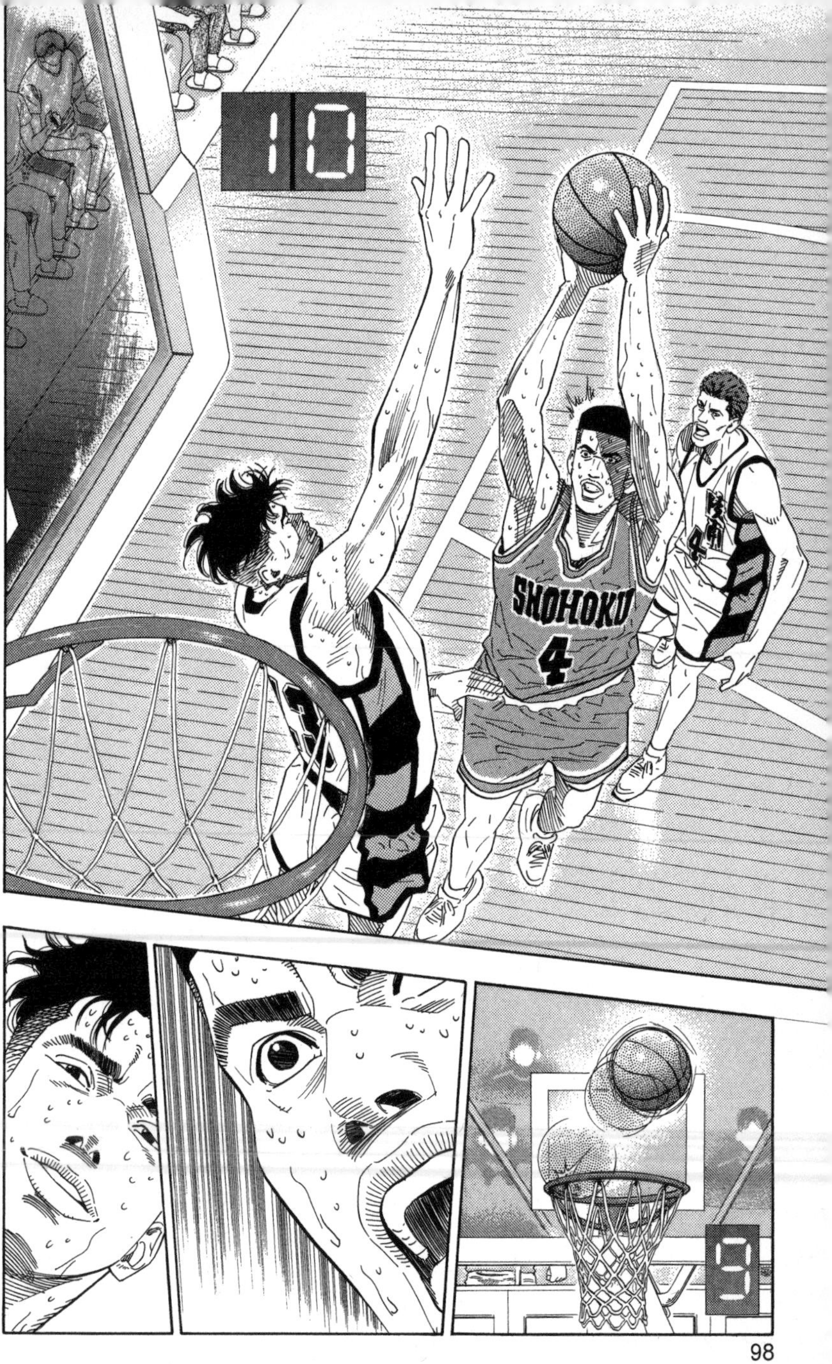
10
SHOHOKU
4
9

READ THIS WAY

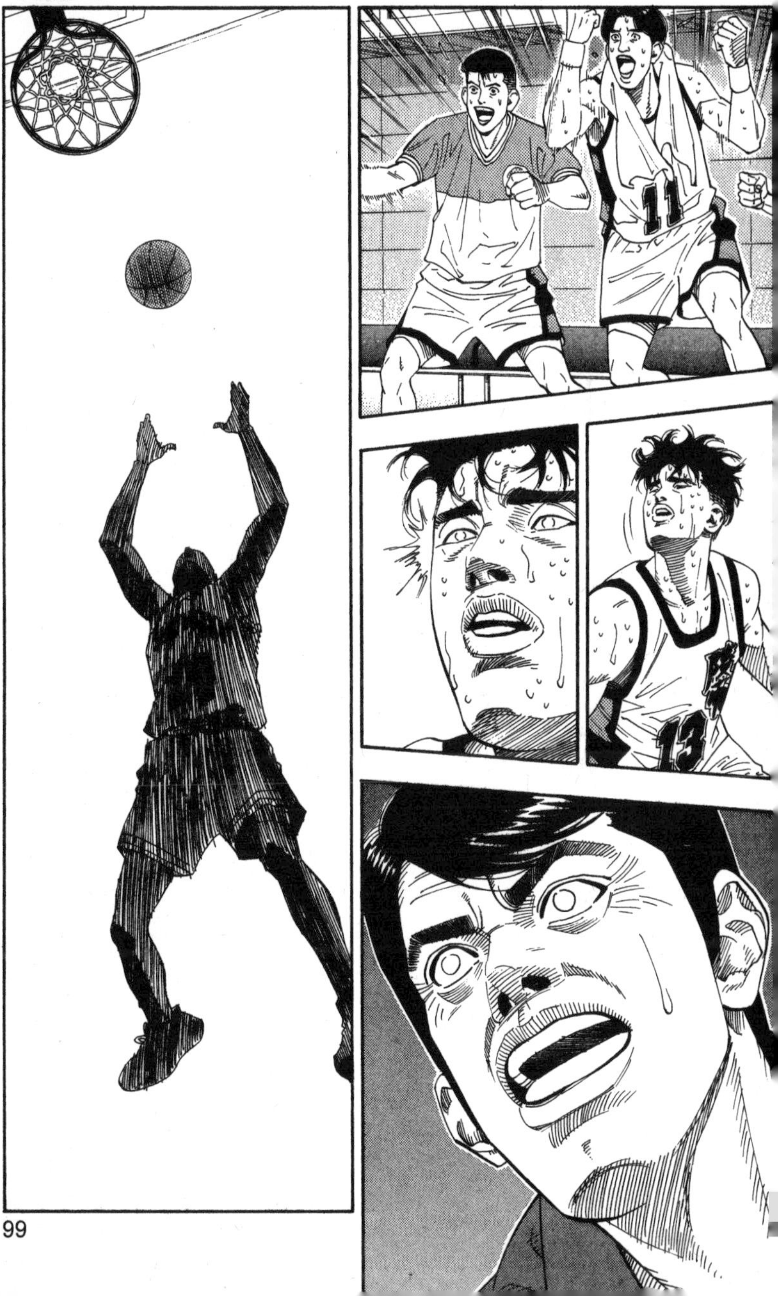

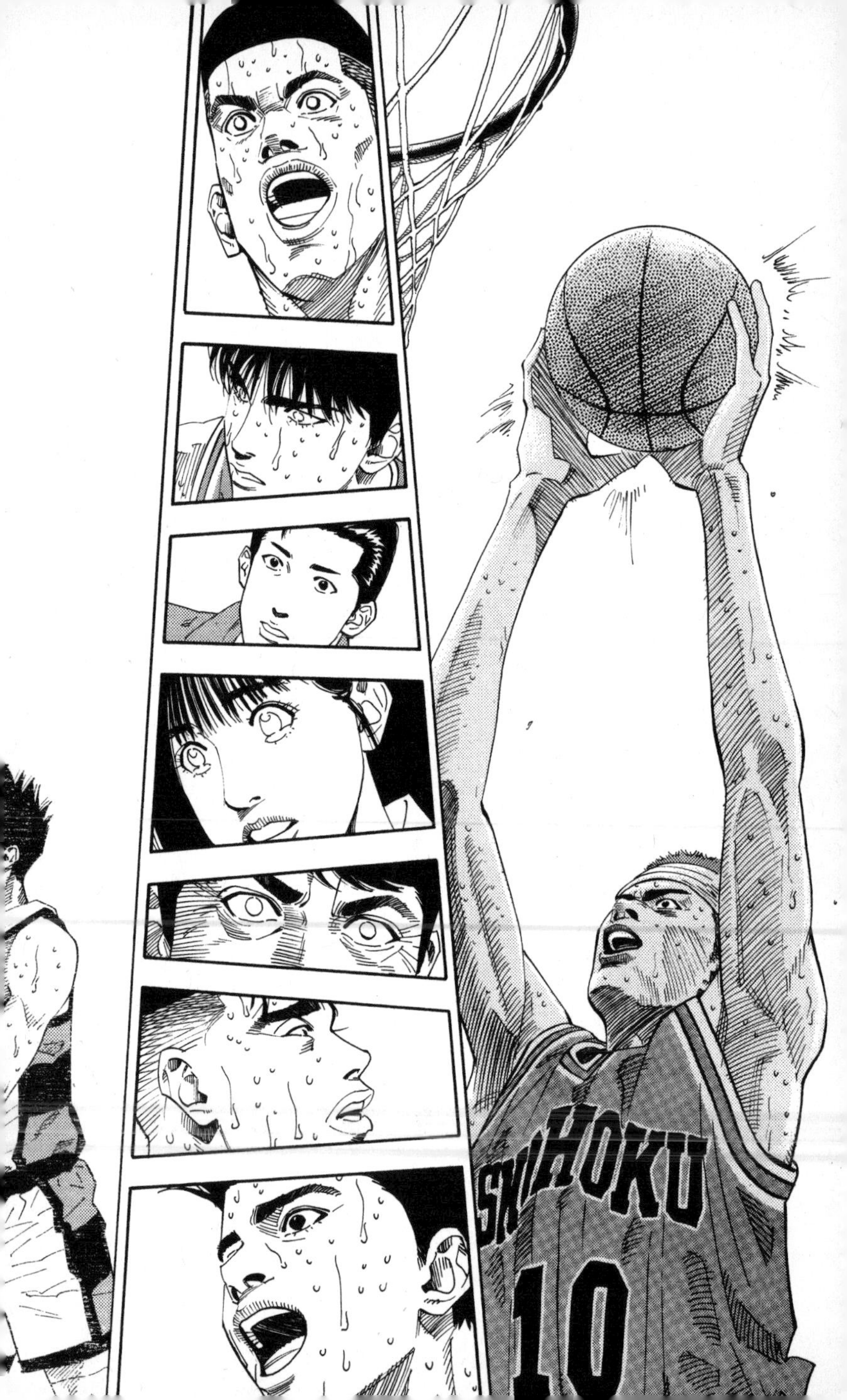
SHOHOKU
10

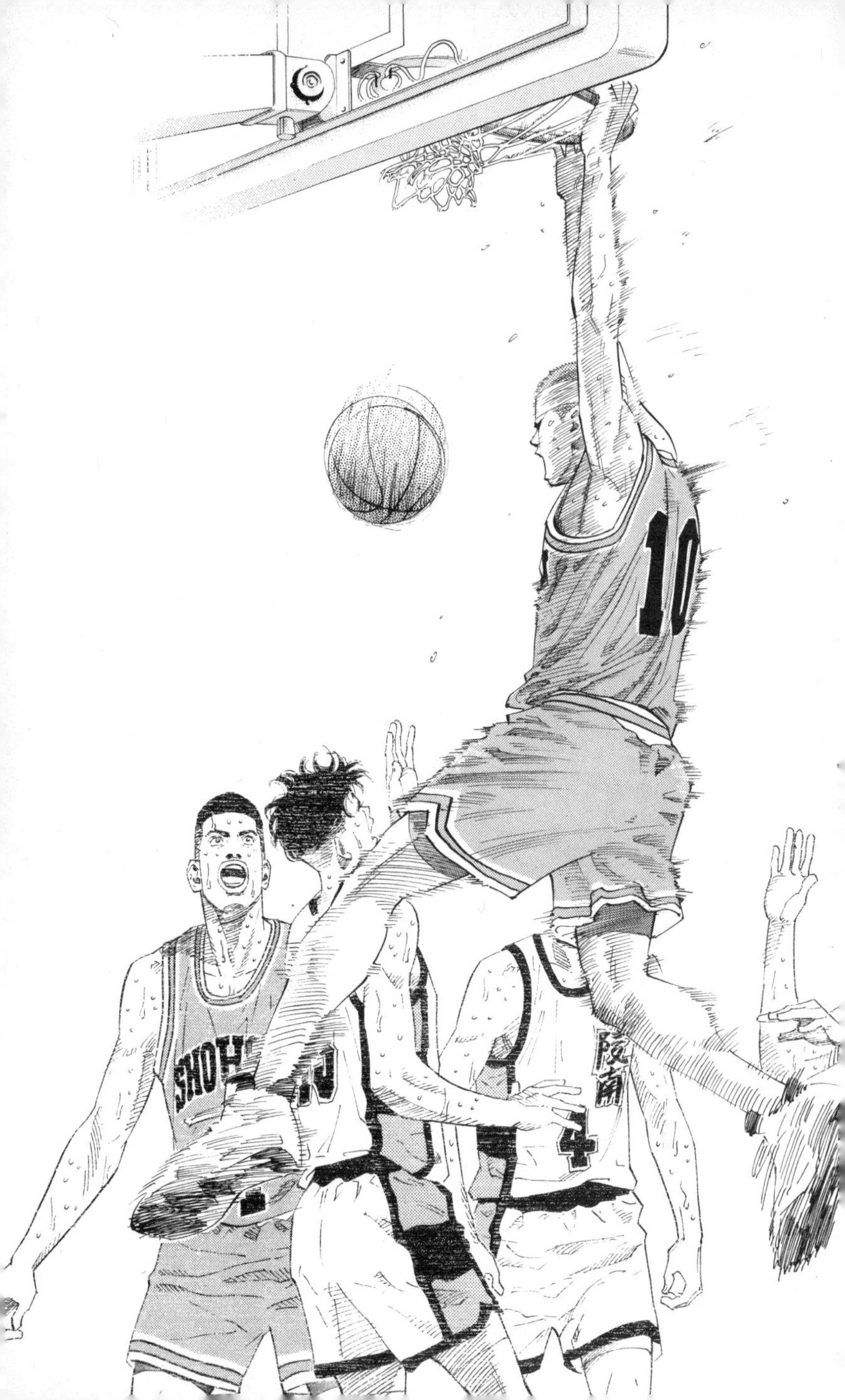

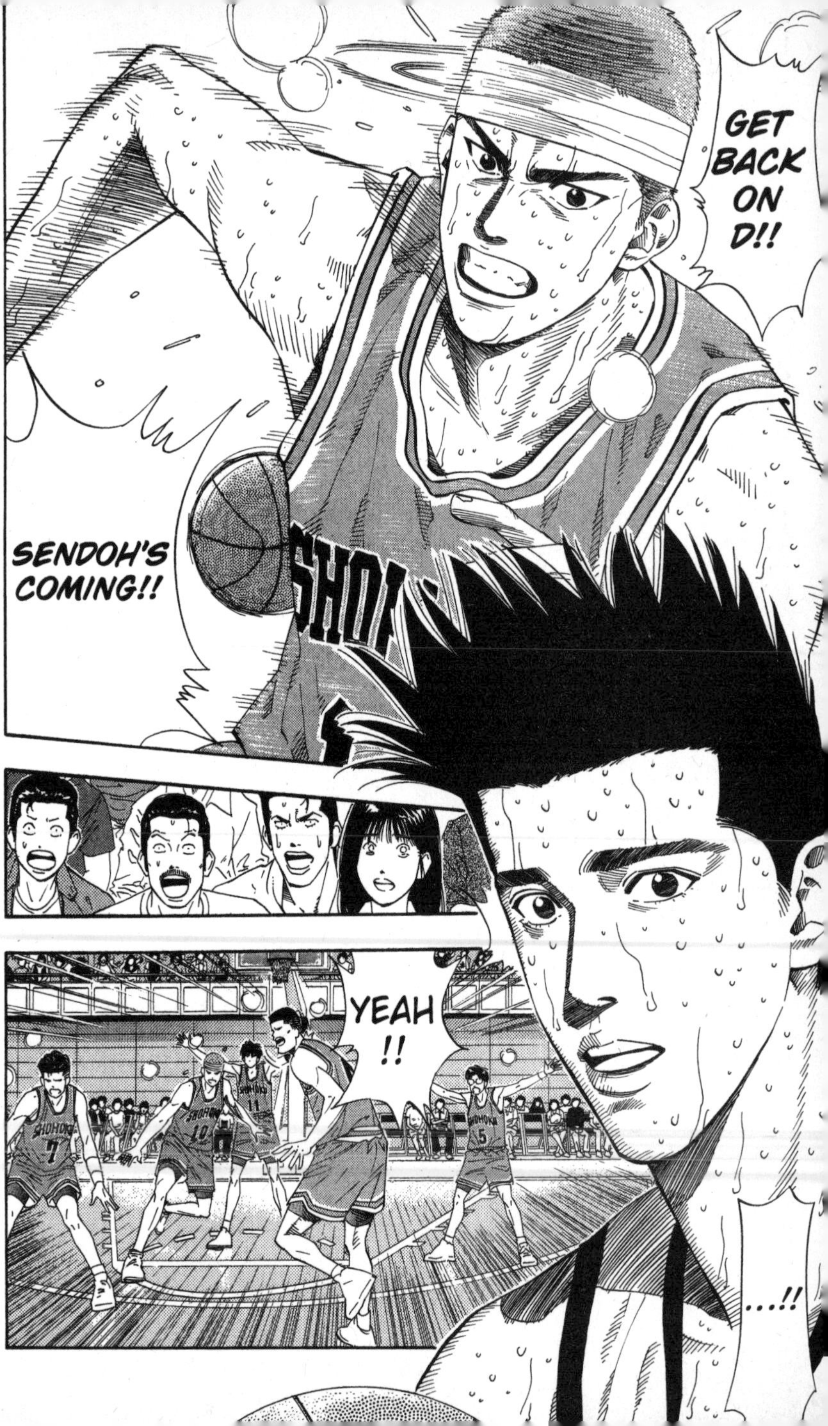
GET BACK ON D!!
SENDOH'S COMING!!
...!!
YEAH !!

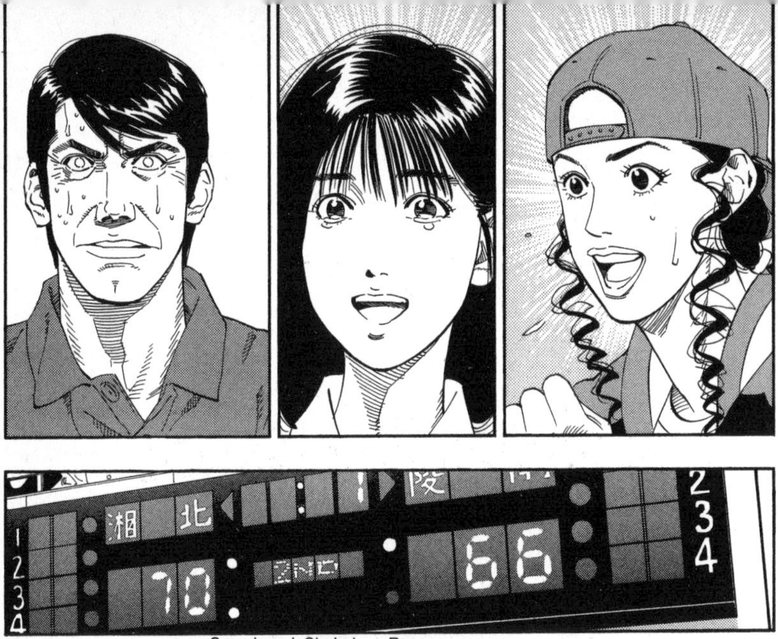
66
2ND
湘北
70
Scoreboard: Shohoku Ryonan

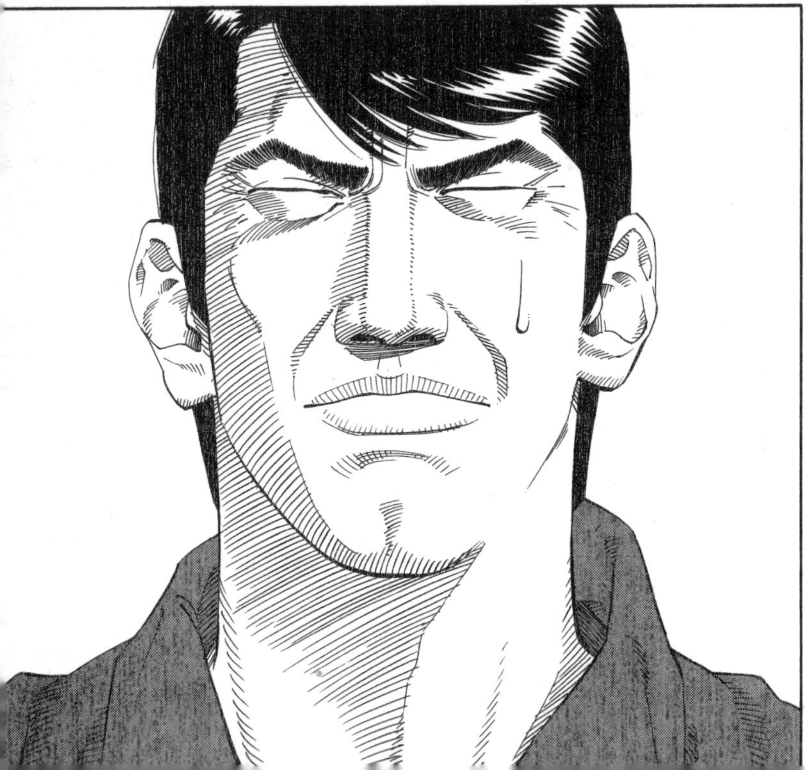

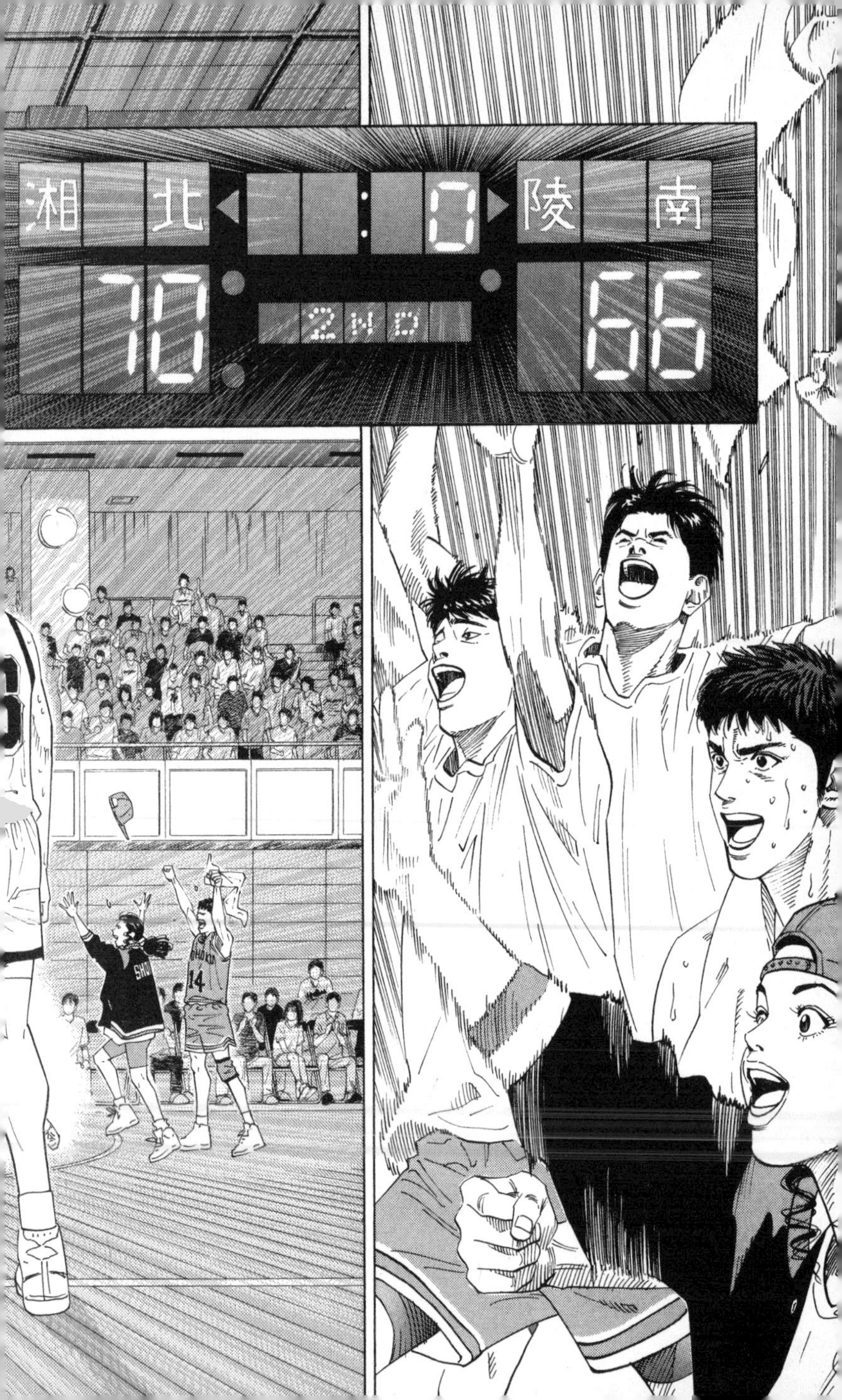
湘北
0
陵南
70
2ND
66

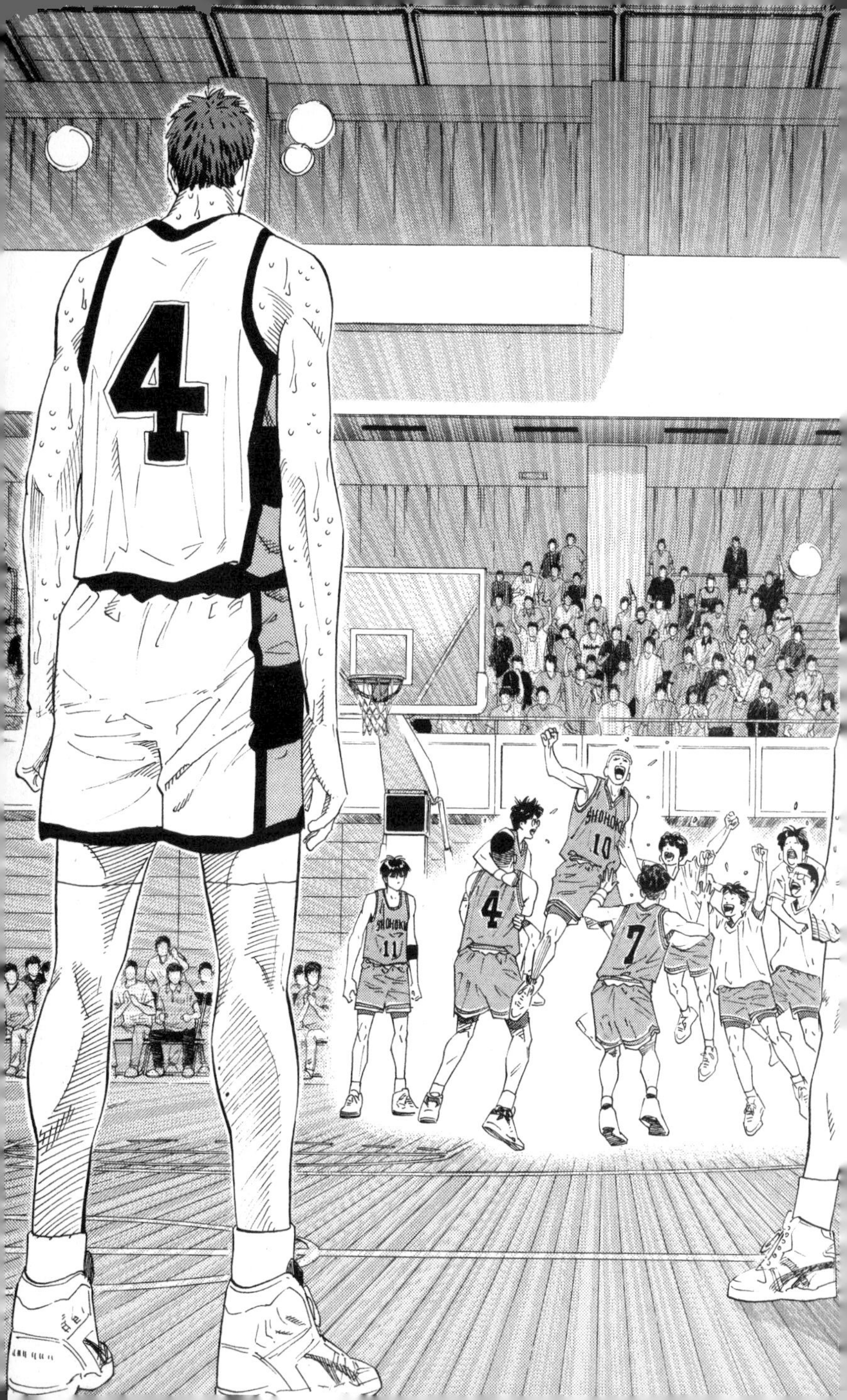

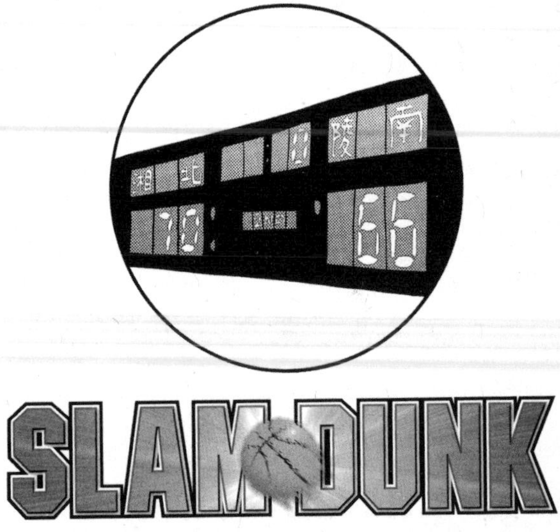
陵南
70
66

SLAM DUNK

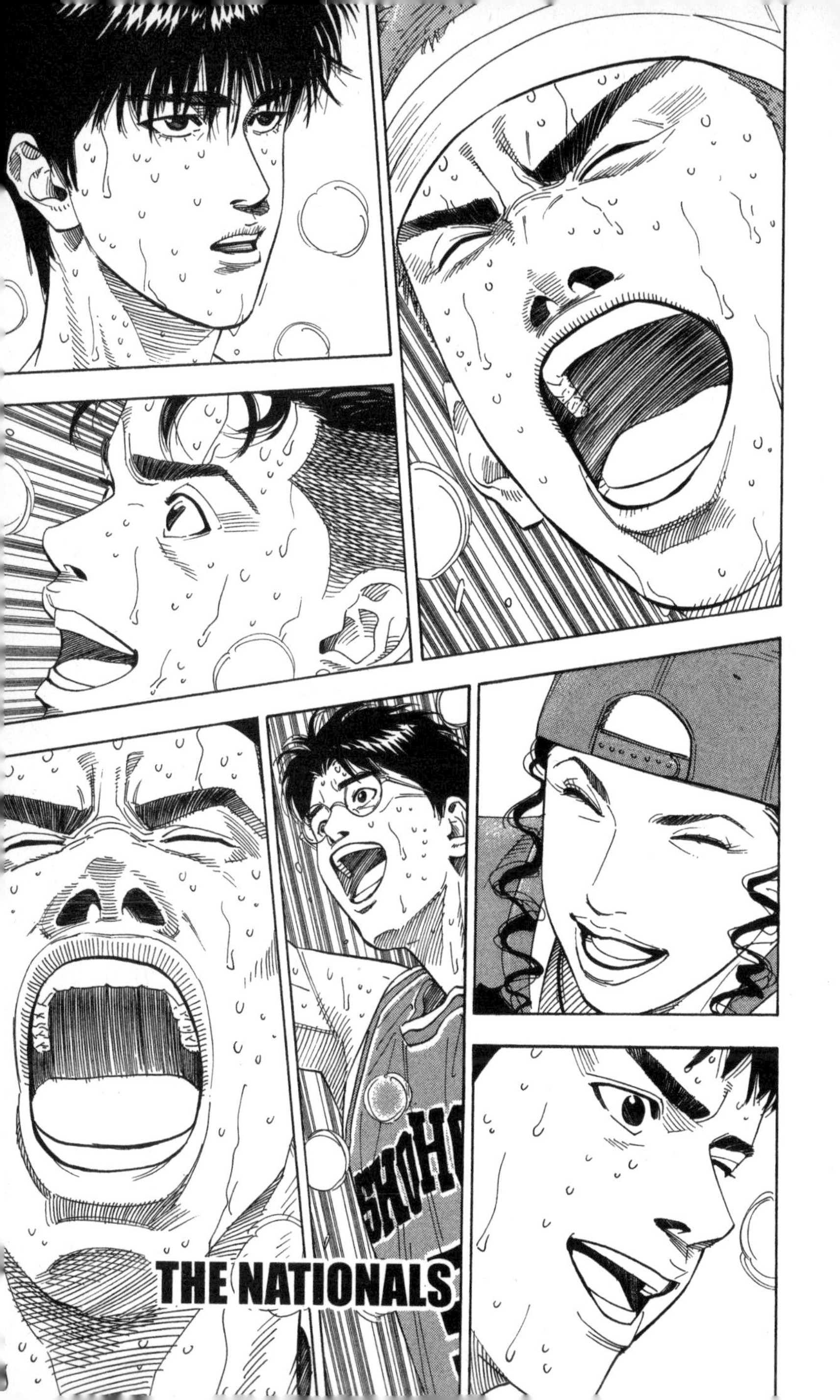
THE NATIONALS

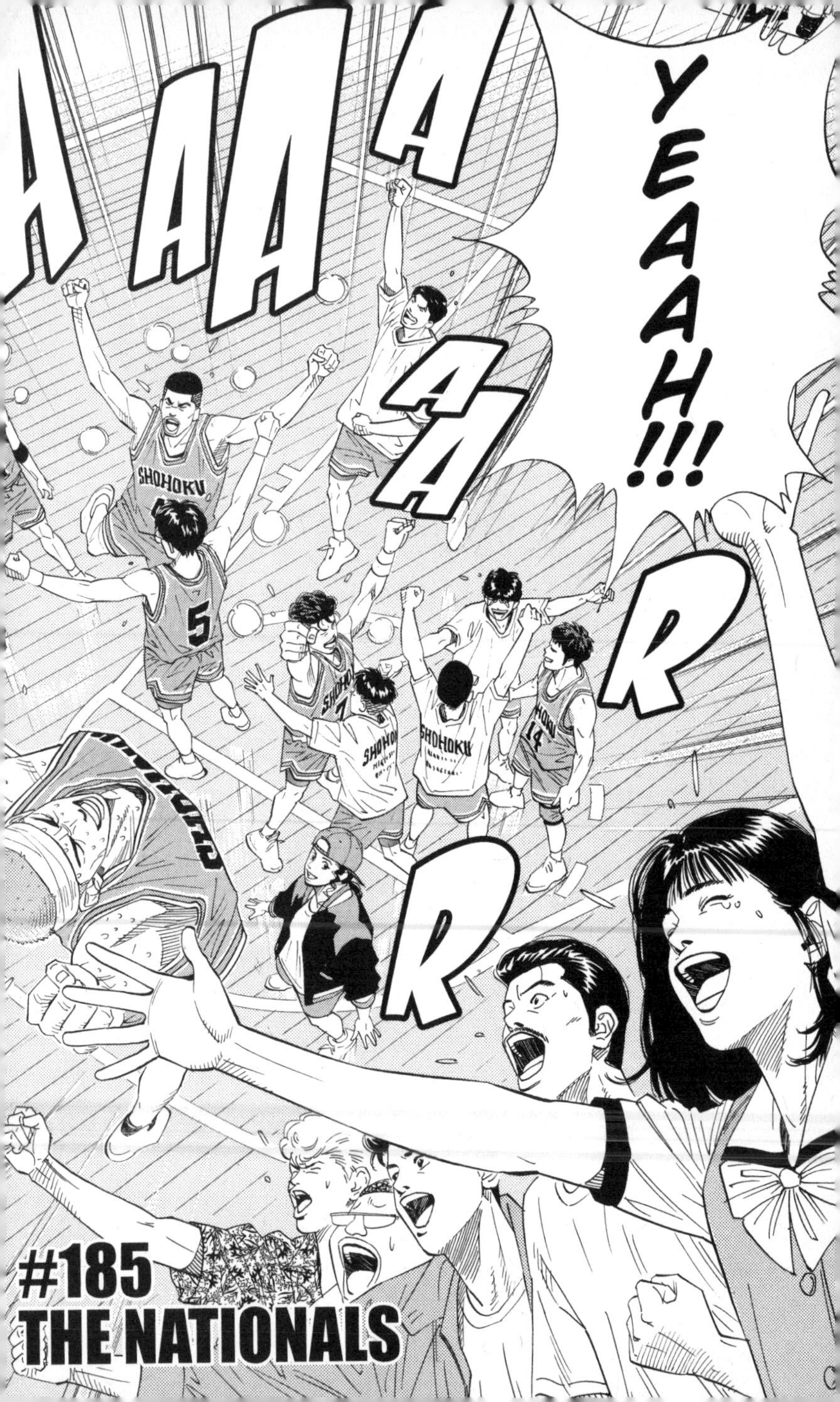
YEAAAH!!!
AAAAAARR

#185 THE NATIONALS

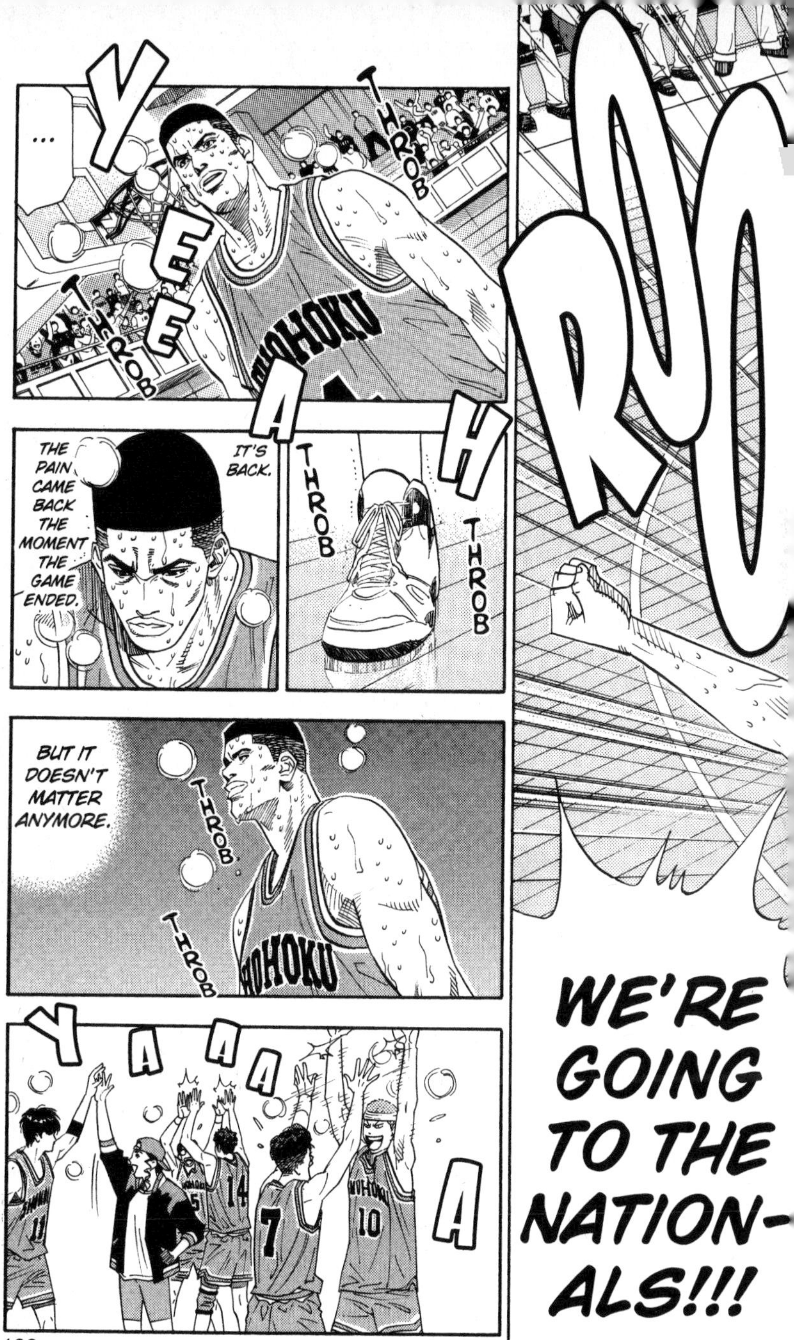
ROO
WE'RE GOING TO THE NATION-ALS!!!
...
YEEAH
THROB
THROB
THROB
THROB
IT'S BACK.
THE PAIN CAME BACK THE MOMENT THE GAME ENDED.
BUT IT DOESN'T MATTER ANYMORE.
THROB
THROB
YAAAA

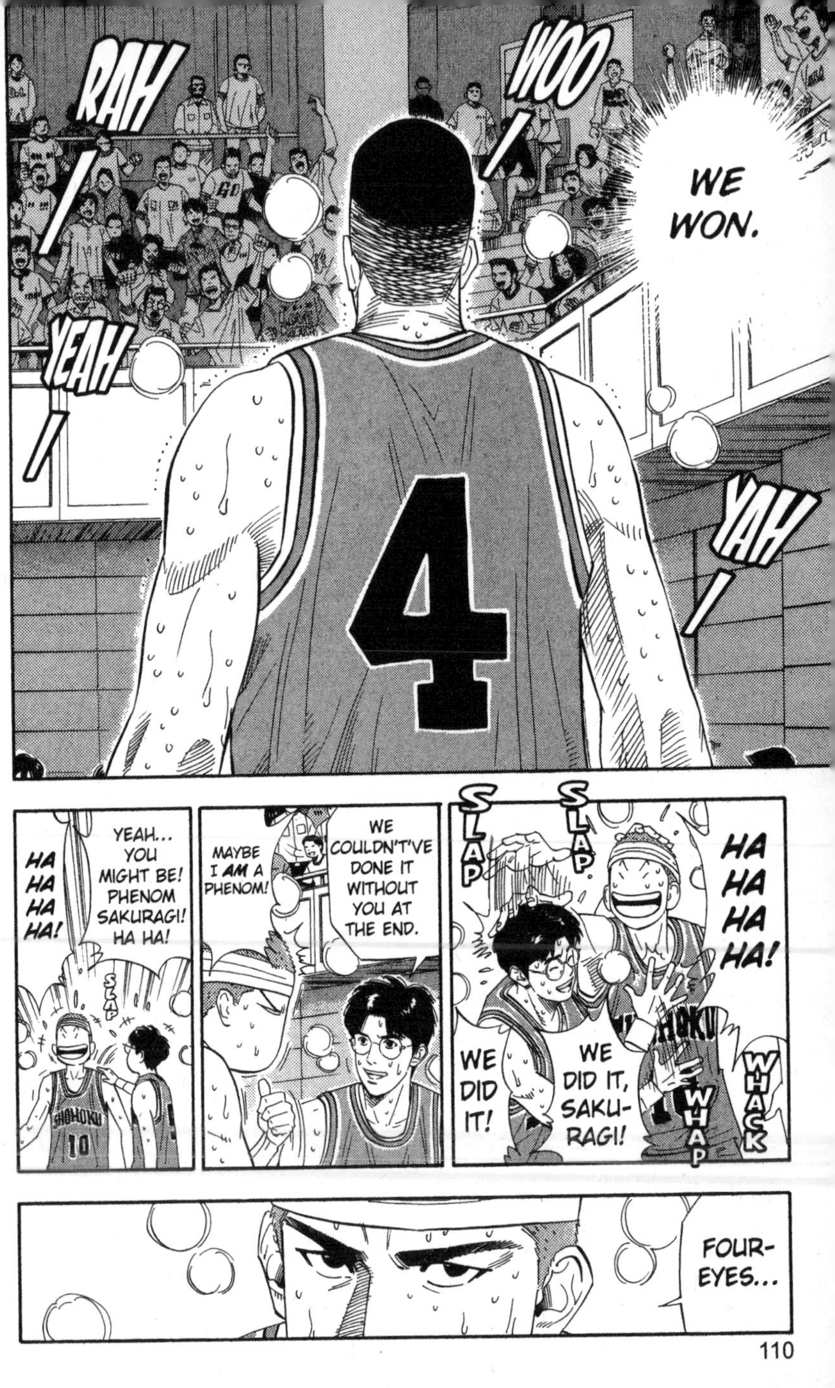
WOO!
WE WON.
RAH!
YAH!
YEAH!
SLAP
SLAP
HA HA HA HA!
WE DID IT, SAKURAGI!
WE DID IT!
WHAP
WHACK
WE COULDN'T'VE DONE IT WITHOUT YOU AT THE END.
MAYBE I *AM* A PHENOM!
YEAH... YOU MIGHT BE! PHENOM SAKURAGI! HA HA!
HA HA HA HA!
SLAP
FOUR-EYES...

READ THIS WAY

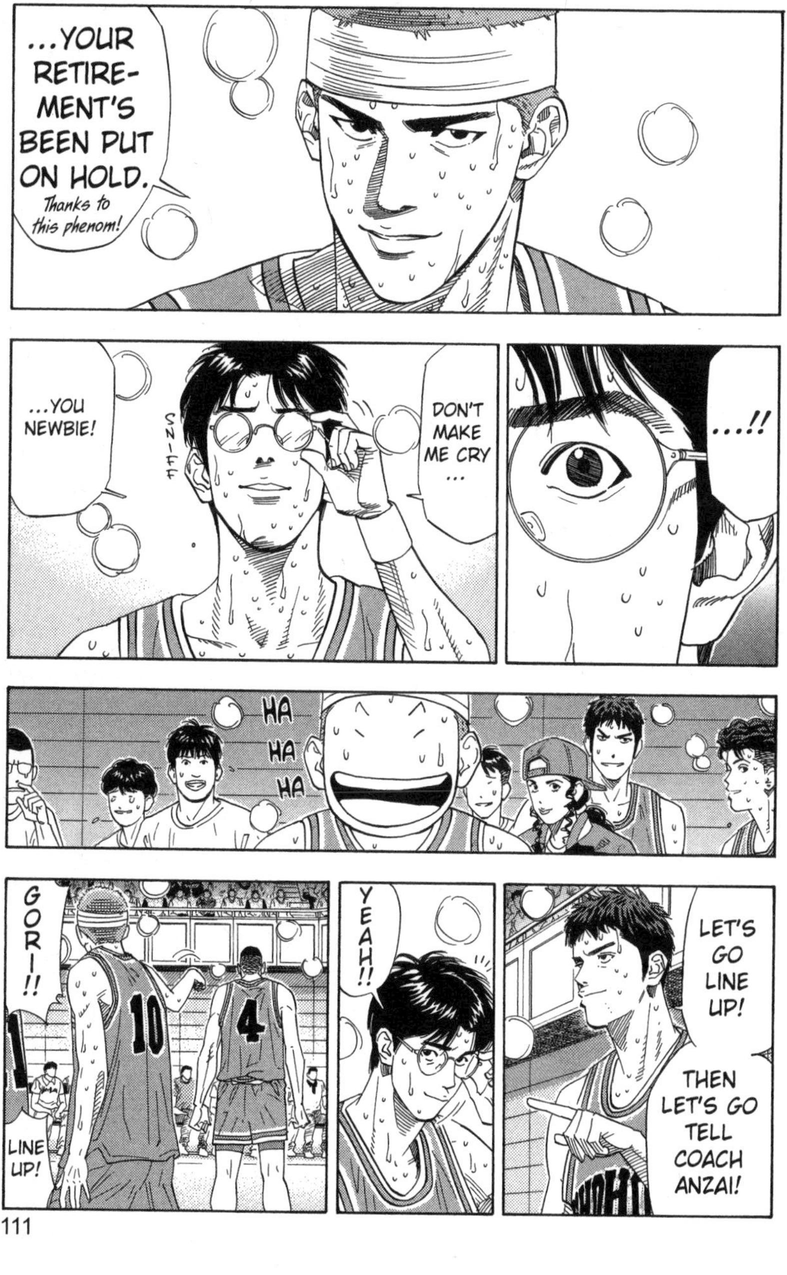

...YOUR RETIREMENT'S BEEN PUT ON HOLD.
Thanks to this phenom!
...!!
DON'T MAKE ME CRY...
SNIFF
...YOU NEWBIE!
HA HA HA
LET'S GO LINE UP!
THEN LET'S GO TELL COACH ANZAI!
YEAH!!
GORI!!
LINE UP!

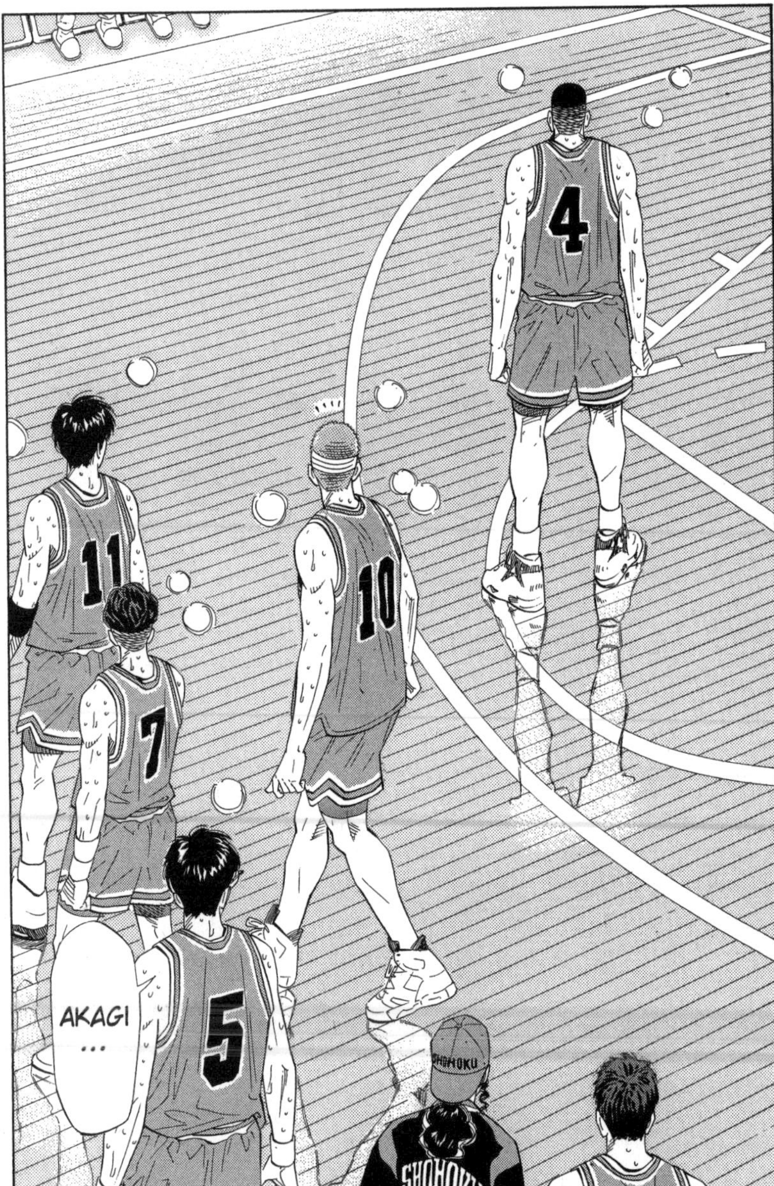
AKAGI ...
SHOHOKU
SHOHOKU

READ THIS WAY

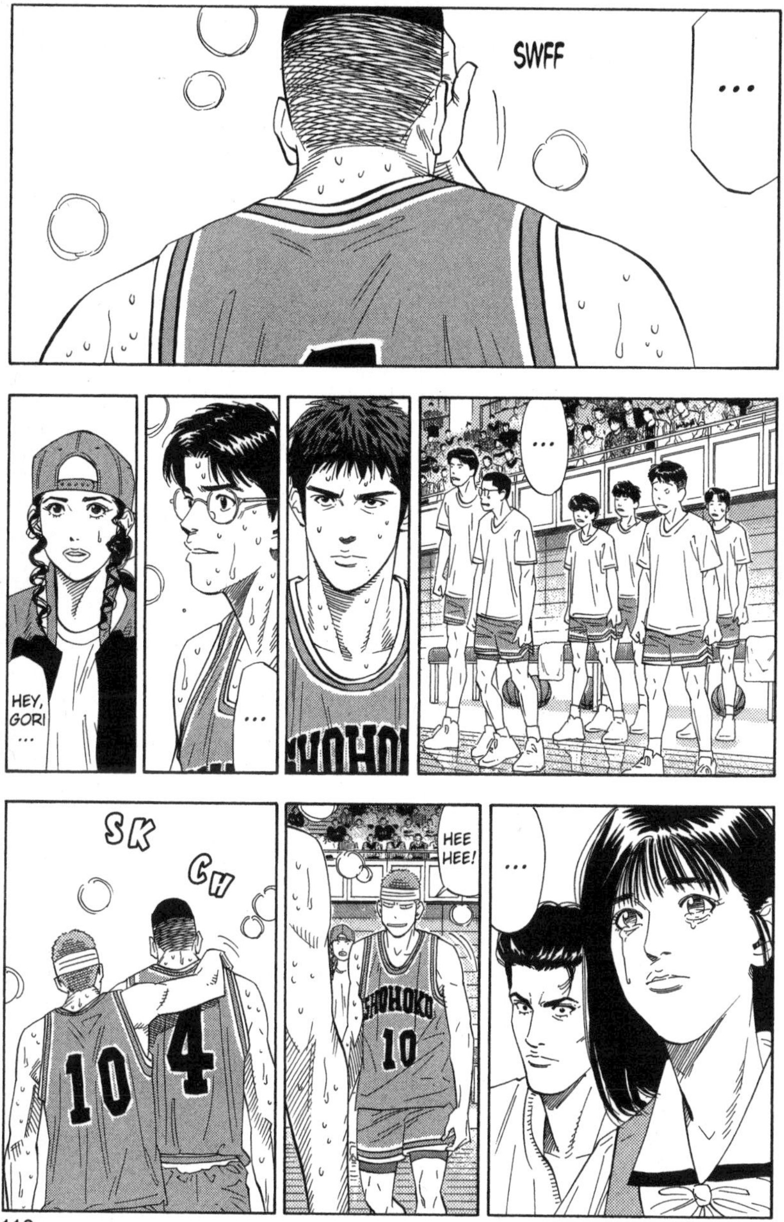
...
SWFF
...
...
HEY, GORI ...
...
HEE HEE!
SK CH

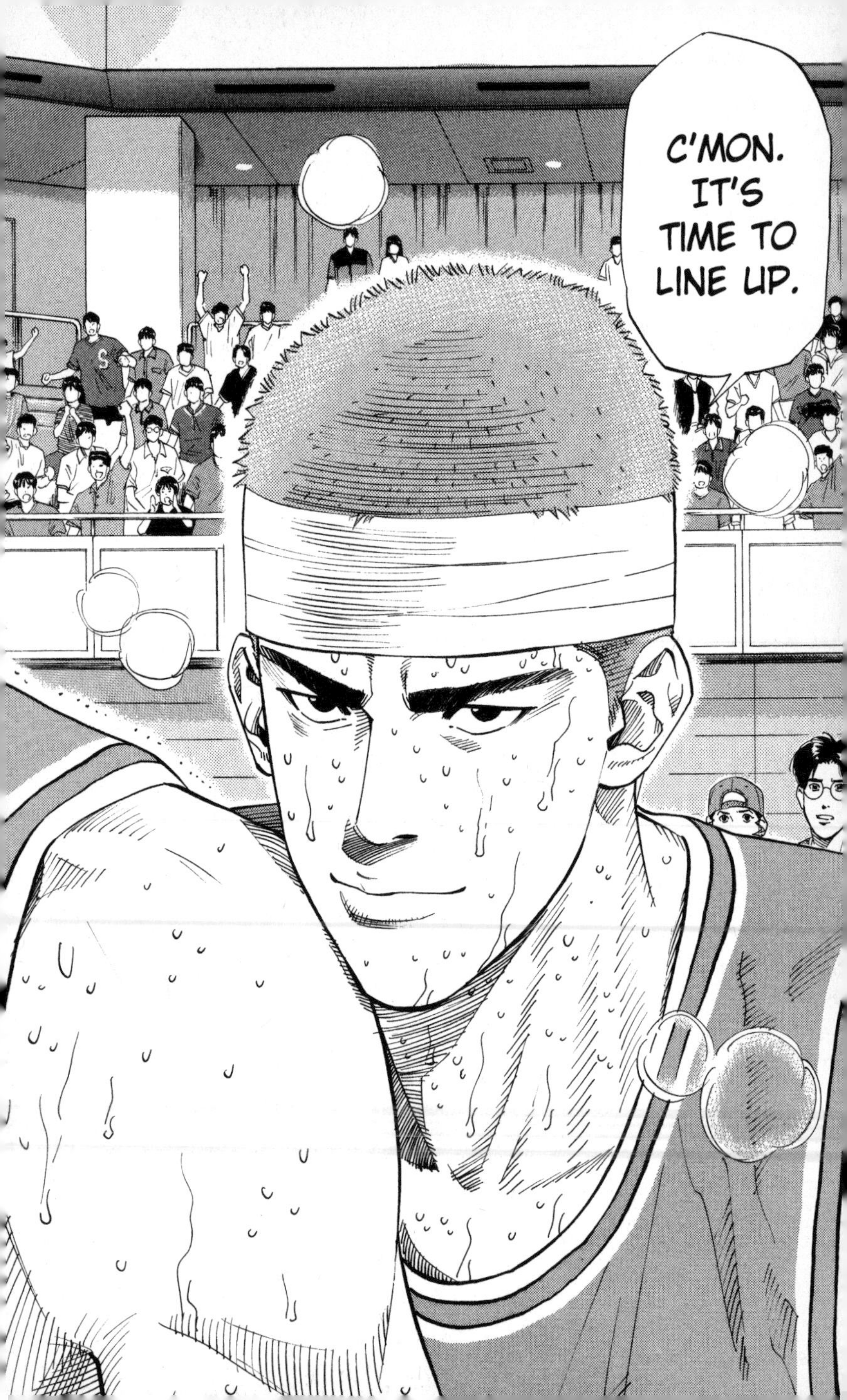
C'MON. IT'S TIME TO LINE UP.

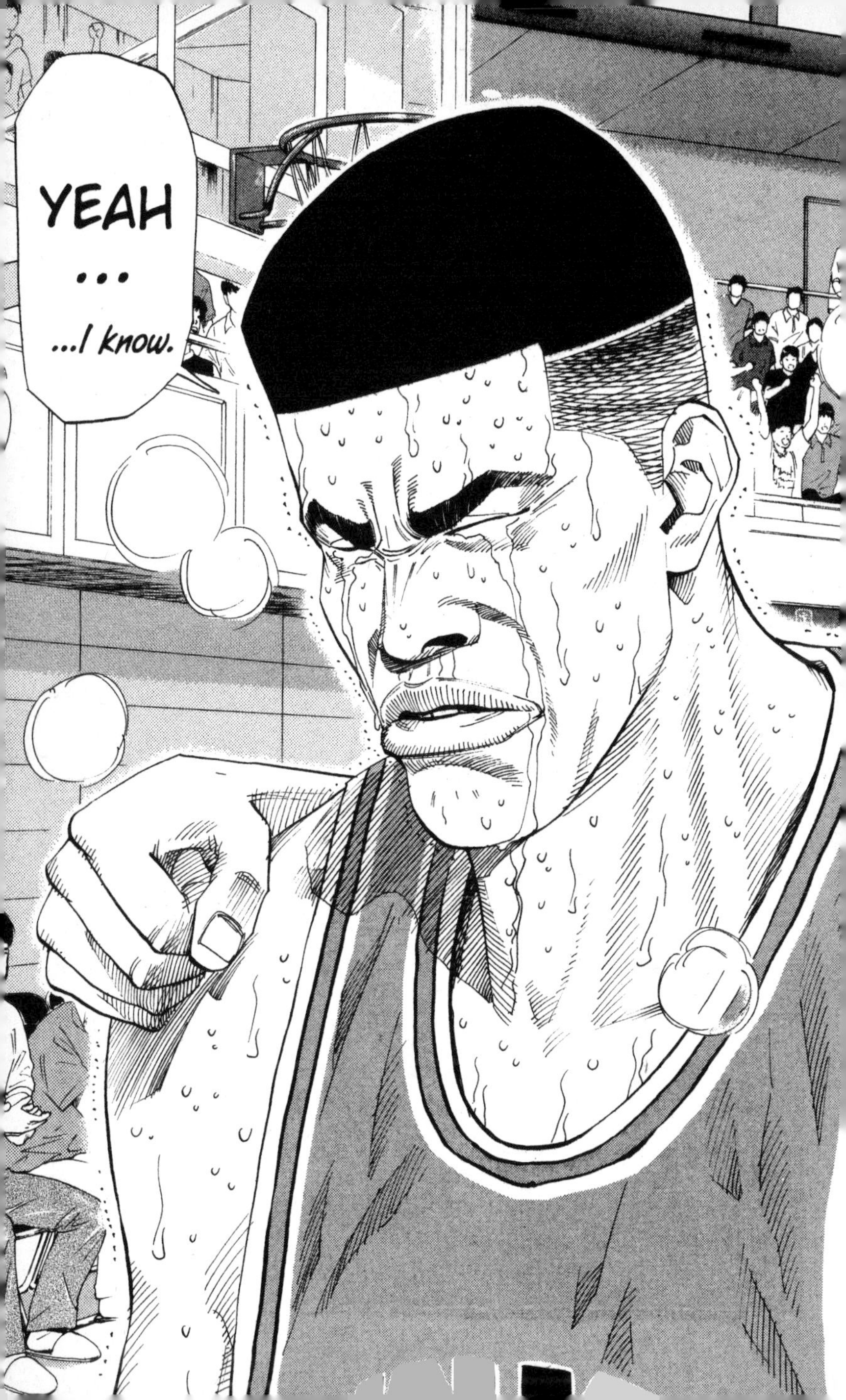
YEAH
...
...I know.

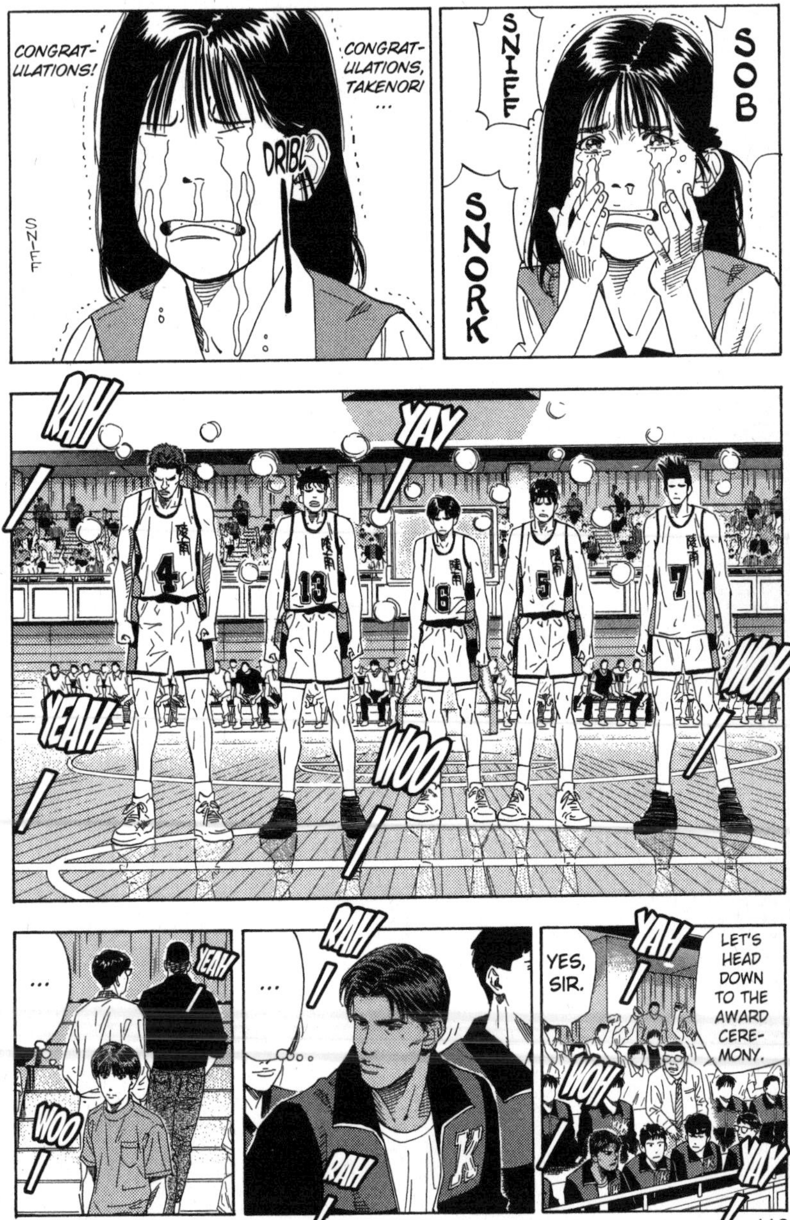
SOB
SNIFF
SNORK
CONGRAT-ULATIONS, TAKENORI ...
CONGRAT-ULATIONS!
DRIBL
SNIFF
YAY
RAH
WOH
WOO
YEAH
LET'S HEAD DOWN TO THE AWARD CERE-MONY.
YAH
YES, SIR.
WOH
YAY
RAH
...
RAH
YEAH
...
WOO

READ THIS WAY

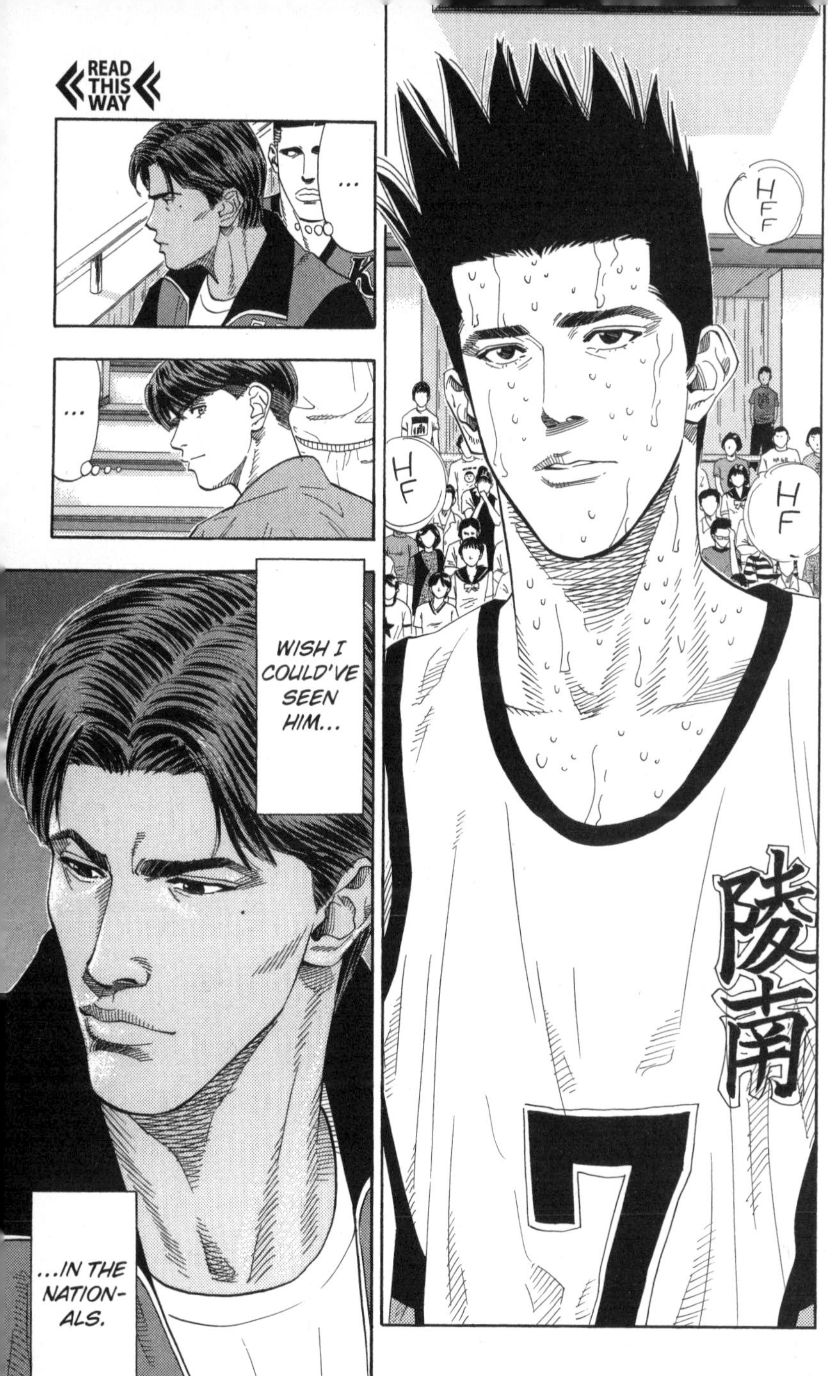
HFF
HF
HF
陵南
7
...
...
WISH I COULD'VE SEEN HIM...
...IN THE NATIONALS.

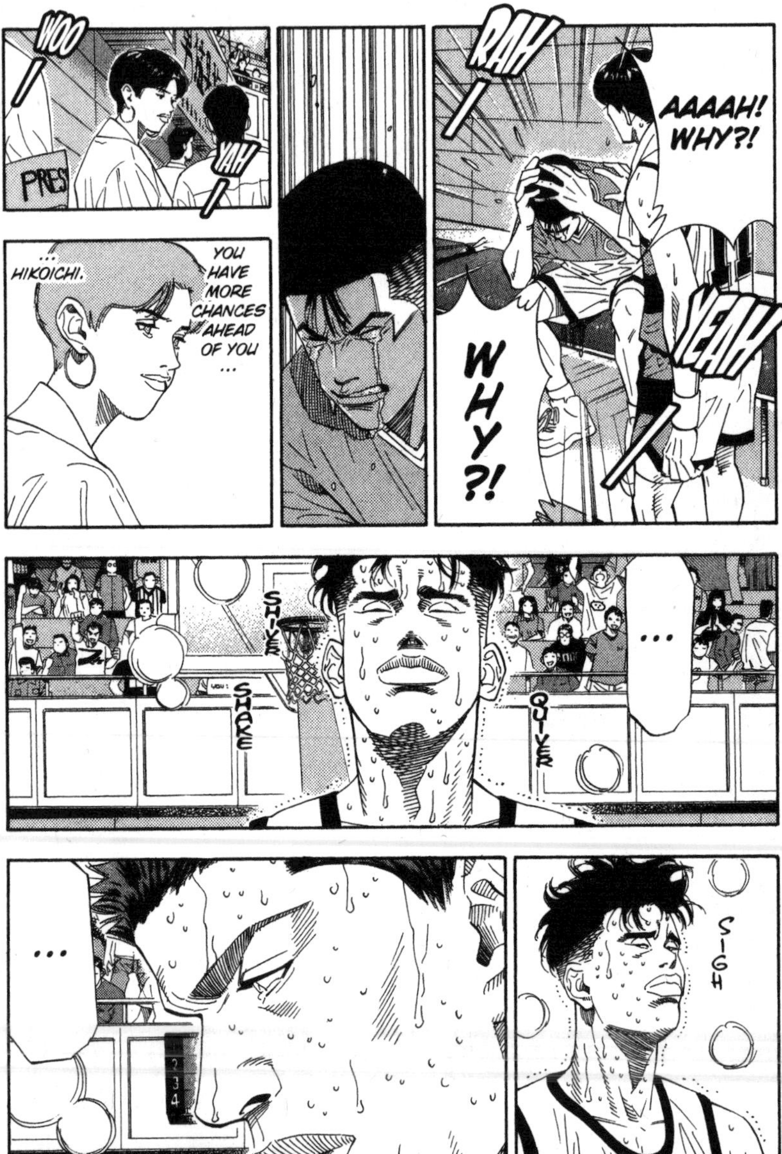
RAH
AAAAH! WHY?!
YEAH
WHY?!
WOO
YAH
... HIKOICHI.
YOU HAVE MORE CHANCES AHEAD OF YOU ...
...
QUIVER
SHIVER
SHAKE
SIGH
...

READ THIS WAY

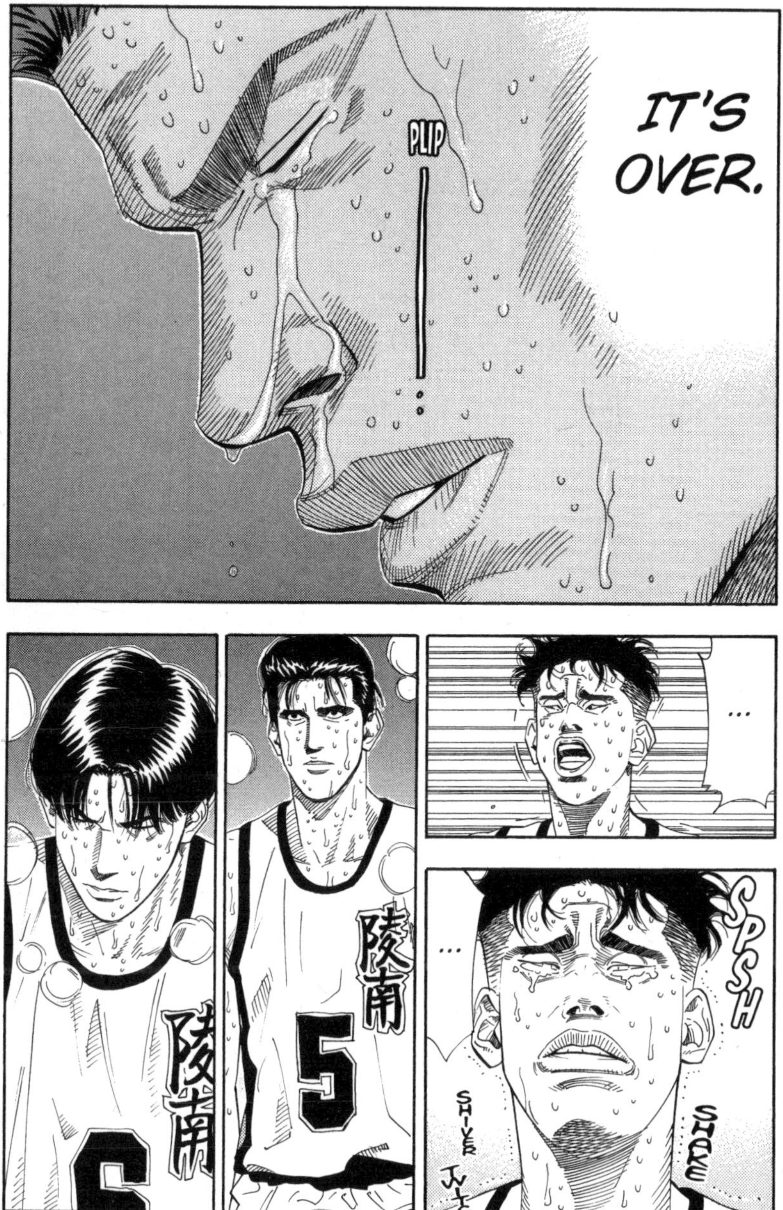
IT'S OVER.
PLIP
...
SPSH
...
SHAKE
SHIVER
TWITCH

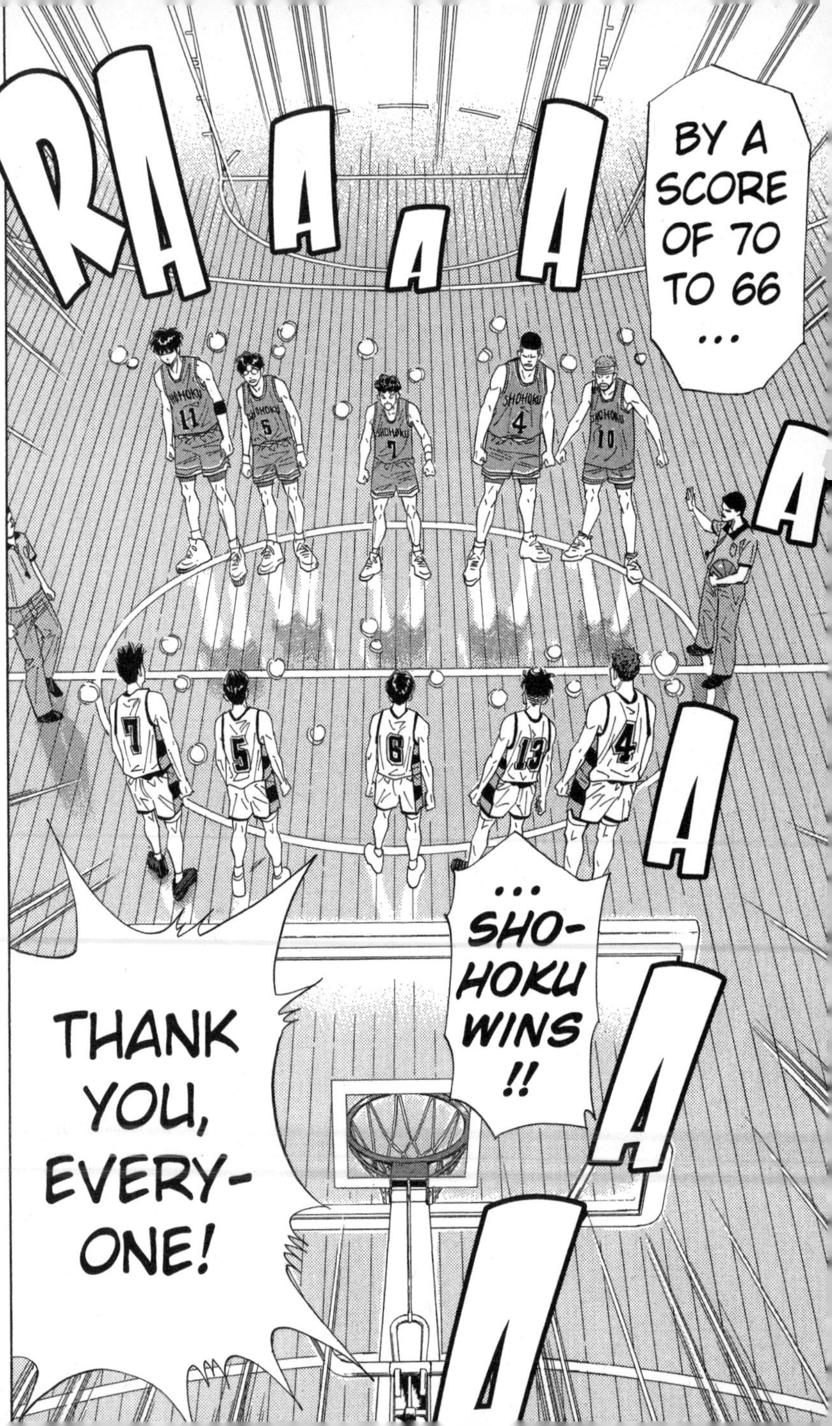
BY A SCORE OF 70 TO 66 ...
RAAAAAAAA
... SHO-HOKU WINS!!
THANK YOU, EVERY-ONE!

READ THIS WAY

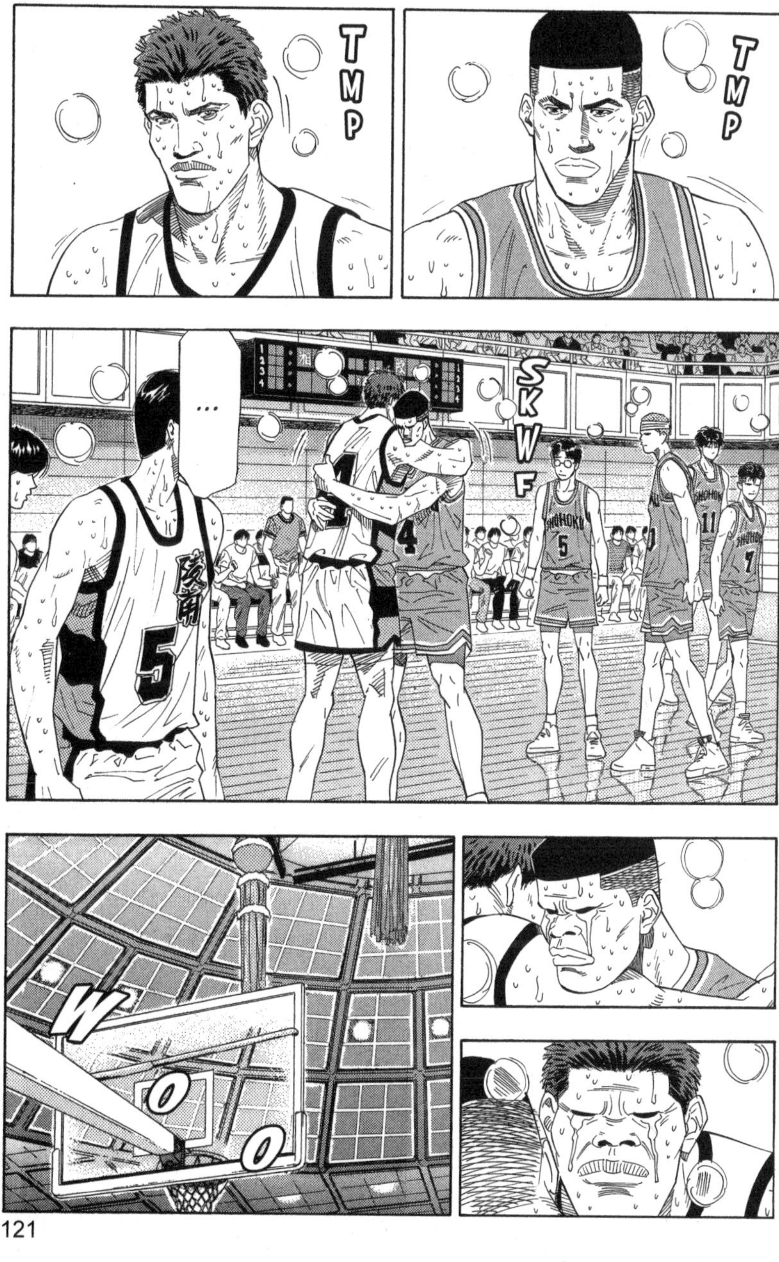
TMP
TMP
...
SKWF
WOO

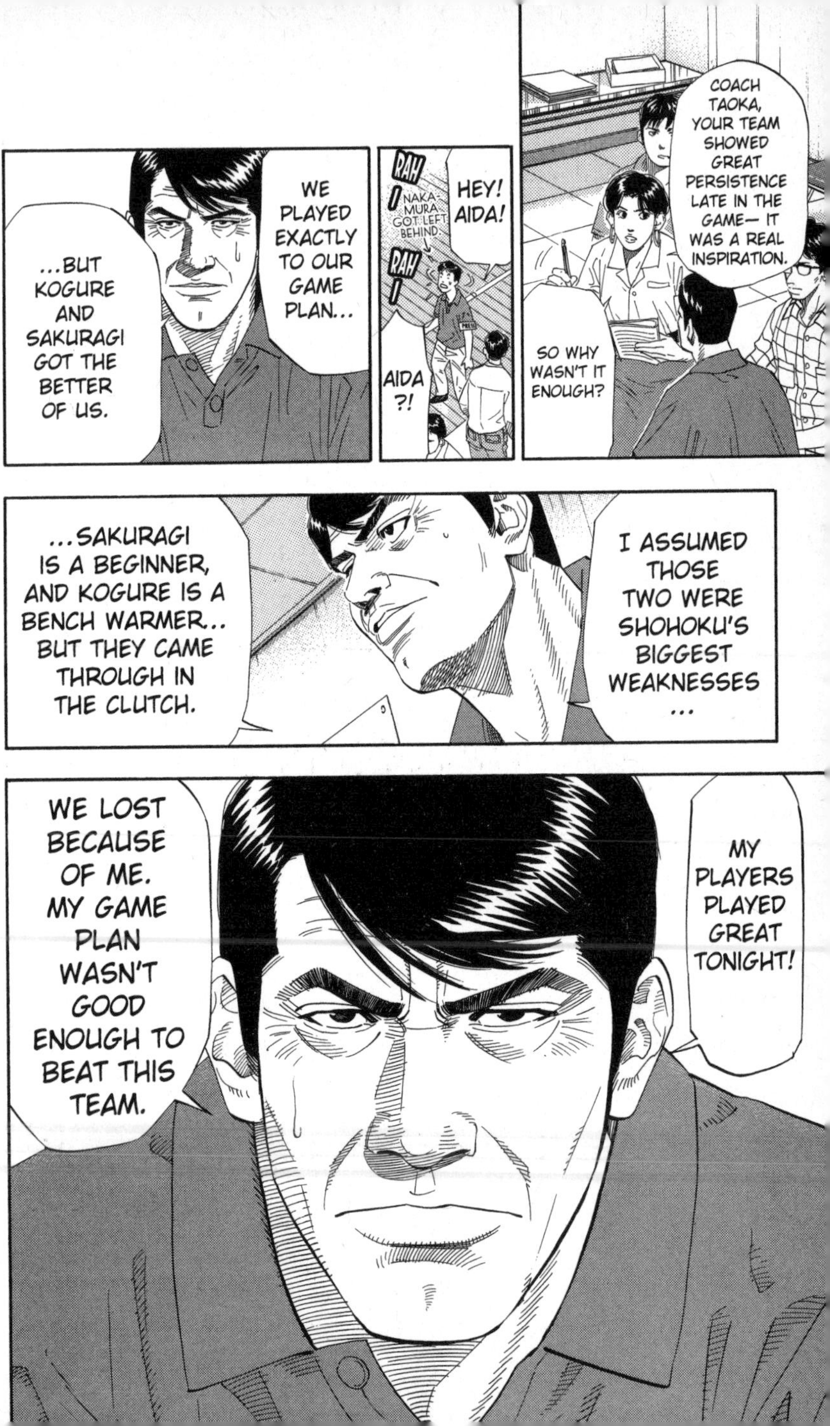
COACH TAOKA, YOUR TEAM SHOWED GREAT PERSISTENCE LATE IN THE GAME— IT WAS A REAL INSPIRATION.
SO WHY WASN'T IT ENOUGH?
HEY! AIDA!
RAH
RAH
NAKA-MURA GOT LEFT BEHIND.
AIDA ?!
WE PLAYED EXACTLY TO OUR GAME PLAN...
...BUT KOGURE AND SAKURAGI GOT THE BETTER OF US.
I ASSUMED THOSE TWO WERE SHOHOKU'S BIGGEST WEAKNESSES ...
...SAKURAGI IS A BEGINNER, AND KOGURE IS A BENCH WARMER... BUT THEY CAME THROUGH IN THE CLUTCH.
MY PLAYERS PLAYED GREAT TONIGHT!
WE LOST BECAUSE OF ME. MY GAME PLAN WASN'T GOOD ENOUGH TO BEAT THIS TEAM.

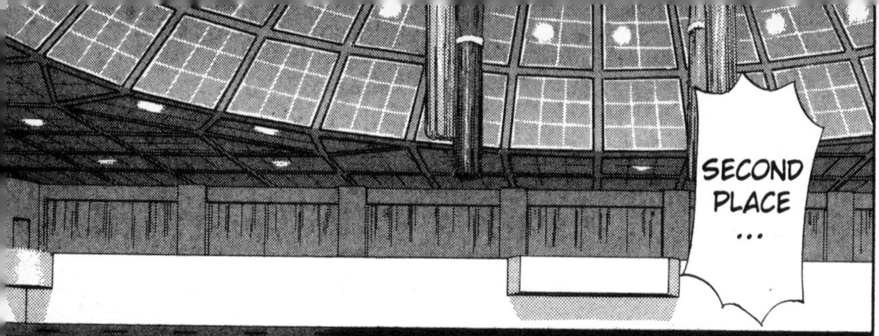
SECOND PLACE ...

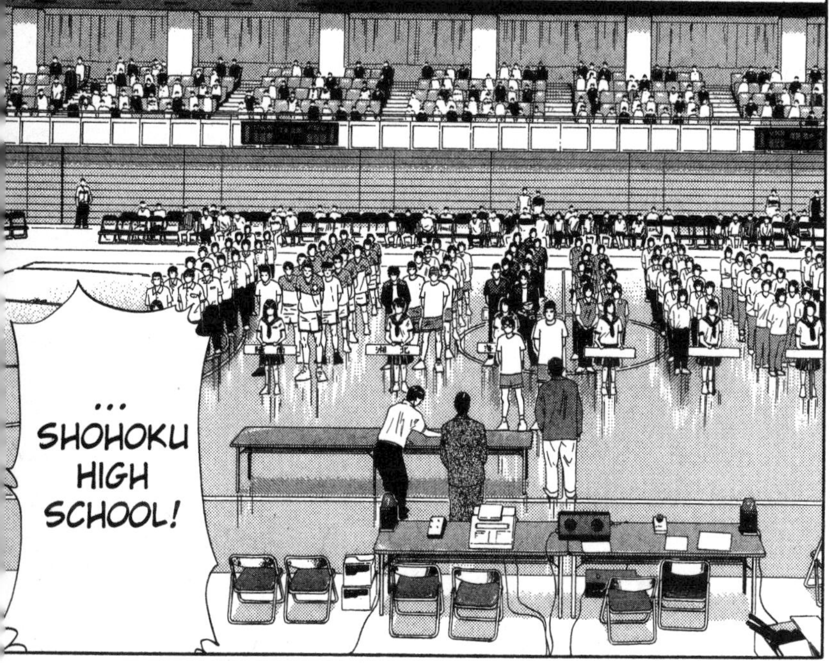
... SHOHOKU HIGH SCHOOL!

Final standings

	Kai	Sho	Ryo	Take	Win/Loss/Standing
Kainan Univ.		○ 90-88	○ 89-83	○ 98-51	3 Wins 1st
Shohoku	× 88-90		○ 70-66	○ 120-81	2 wins 1 loss 2nd
Ryonan	× 83-89	× 66-70		○ 117-64	1 win 2 losses 3rd
Takezato	× 51-98	× 81-120	× 64-117		3 losses 4th

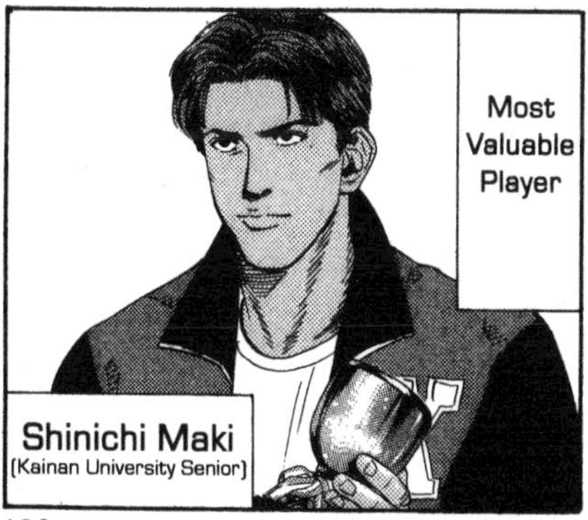
Most Valuable Player
Shinichi Maki
(Kainan University Senior)

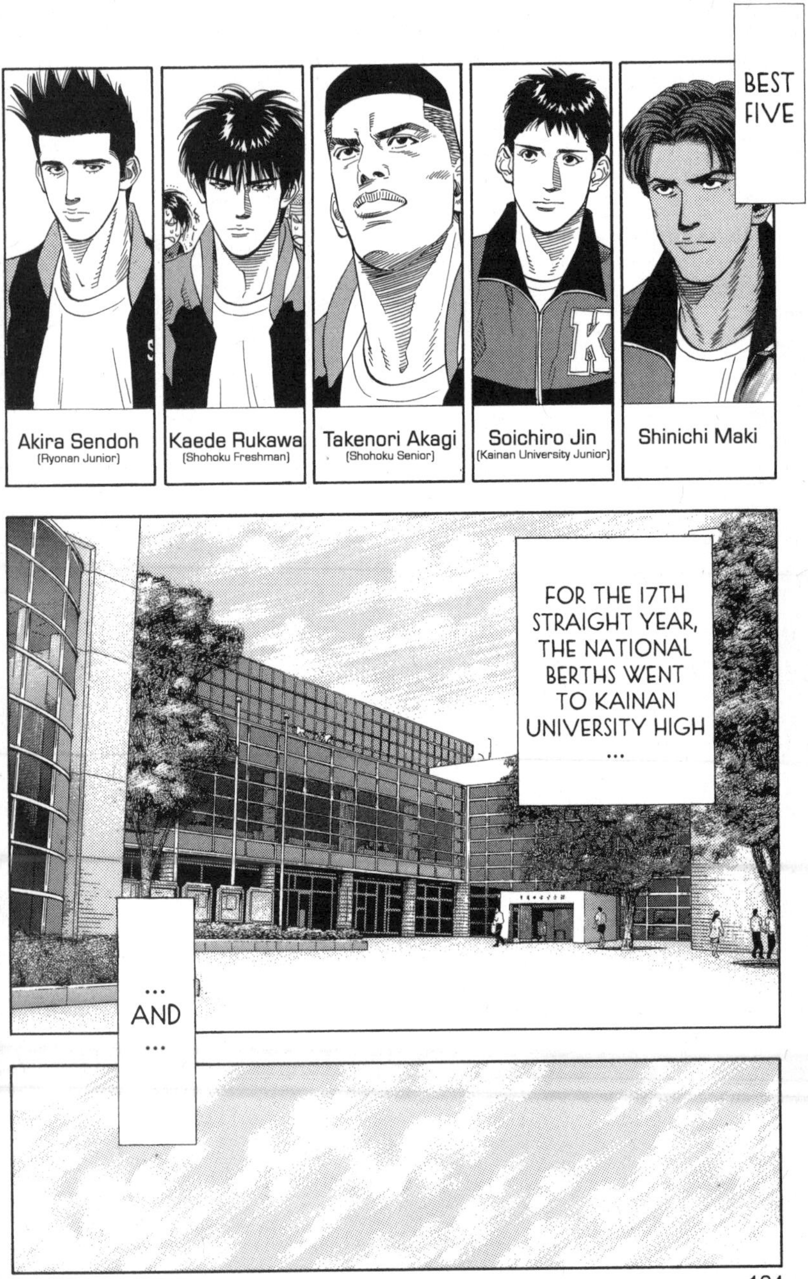
BEST FIVE
Shinichi Maki
Soichiro Jin
(Kainan University Junior)
Takenori Akagi
(Shohoku Senior)
Kaede Rukawa
(Shohoku Freshman)
Akira Sendoh
(Ryonan Junior)
FOR THE 17TH STRAIGHT YEAR, THE NATIONAL BERTHS WENT TO KAINAN UNIVERSITY HIGH ...
... AND ...

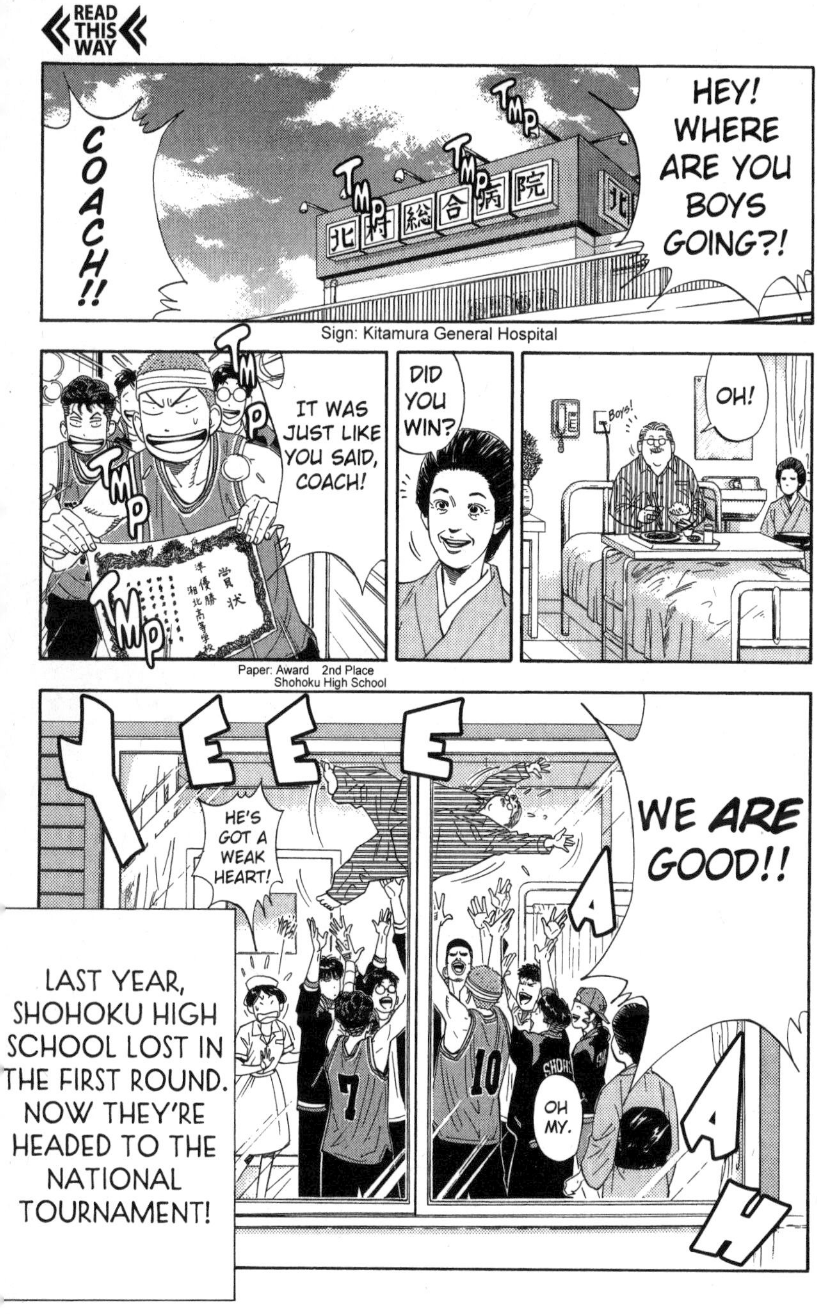
READ THIS WAY
HEY! WHERE ARE YOU BOYS GOING?!
TMP
TMP
TMP
北村総合病院
COACH!!
Sign: Kitamura General Hospital
OH!
Boys!
DID YOU WIN?
IT WAS JUST LIKE YOU SAID, COACH!
TMP
TMP
TMP
Paper: Award 2nd Place Shohoku High School
WE ARE GOOD!!
YEEEAAAH
HE'S GOT A WEAK HEART!
10
7
OH MY.
LAST YEAR, SHOHOKU HIGH SCHOOL LOST IN THE FIRST ROUND. NOW THEY'RE HEADED TO THE NATIONAL TOURNAMENT!

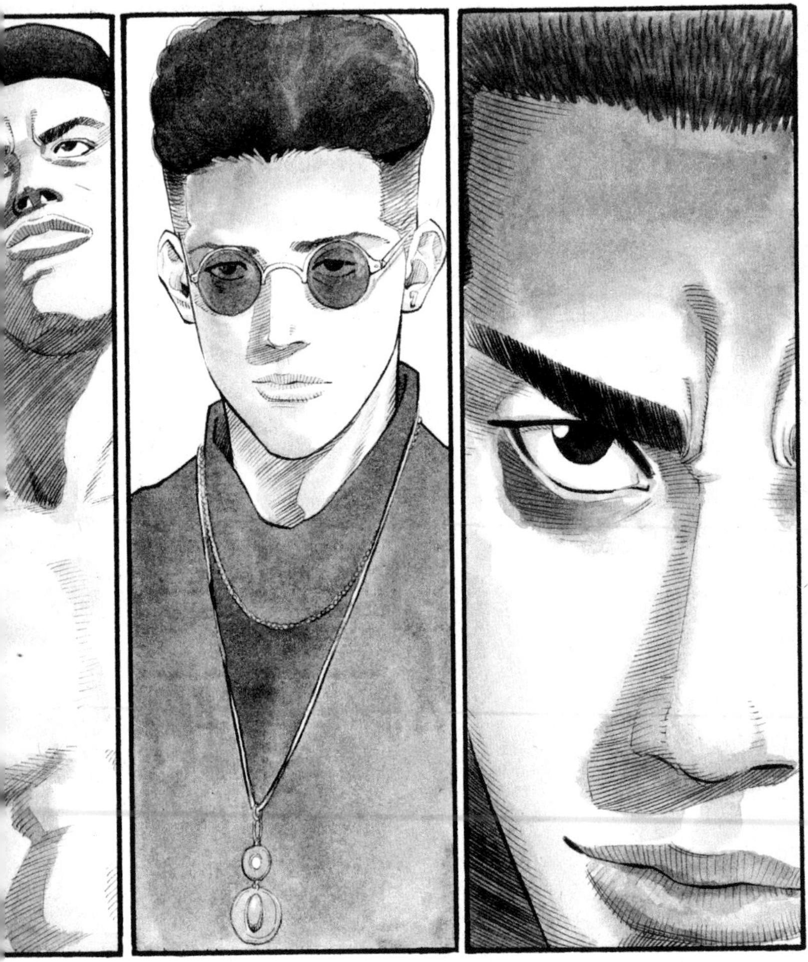

STAR OF AICHI

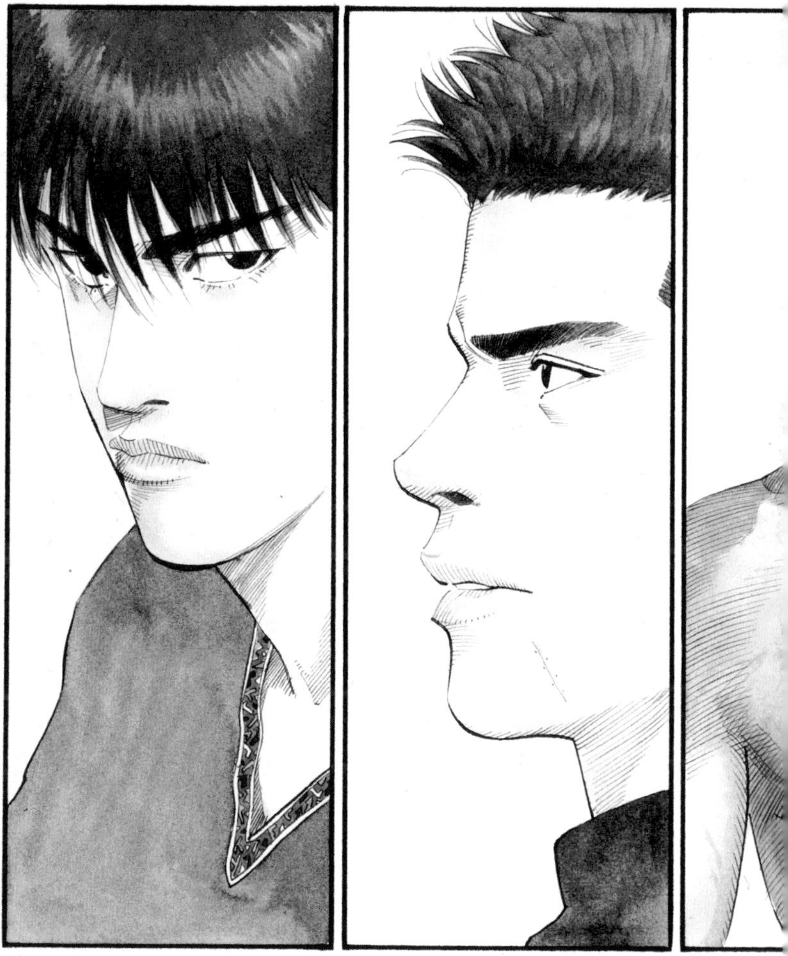

#186

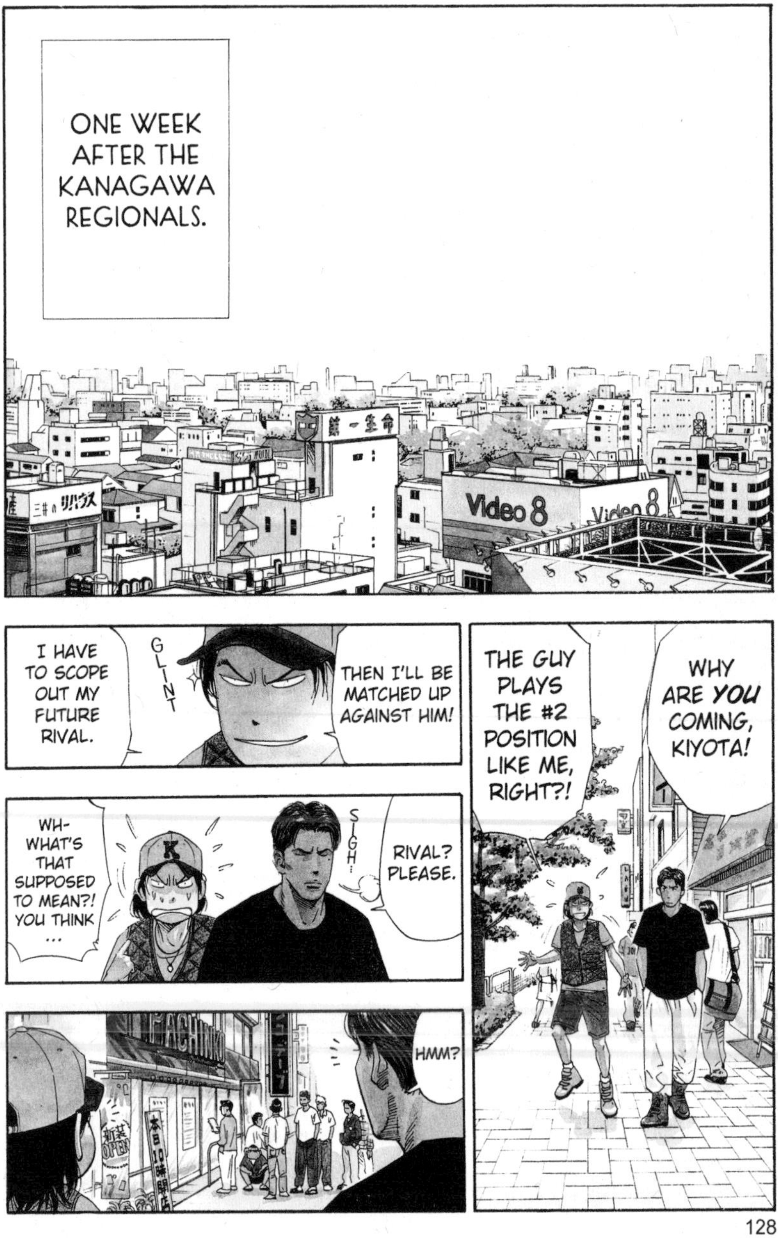
ONE WEEK AFTER THE KANAGAWA REGIONALS.
第一生命
Video 8
Video 8
三井のリハウス
WHY ARE YOU COMING, KIYOTA!
THE GUY PLAYS THE #2 POSITION LIKE ME, RIGHT?!
THEN I'LL BE MATCHED UP AGAINST HIM!
GLINT
I HAVE TO SCOPE OUT MY FUTURE RIVAL.
RIVAL? PLEASE.
SIGH…
WH- WHAT'S THAT SUPPOSED TO MEAN?! YOU THINK …
HMM?
PACHINKO
新装 OPEN
本日10時開店

READ THIS WAY

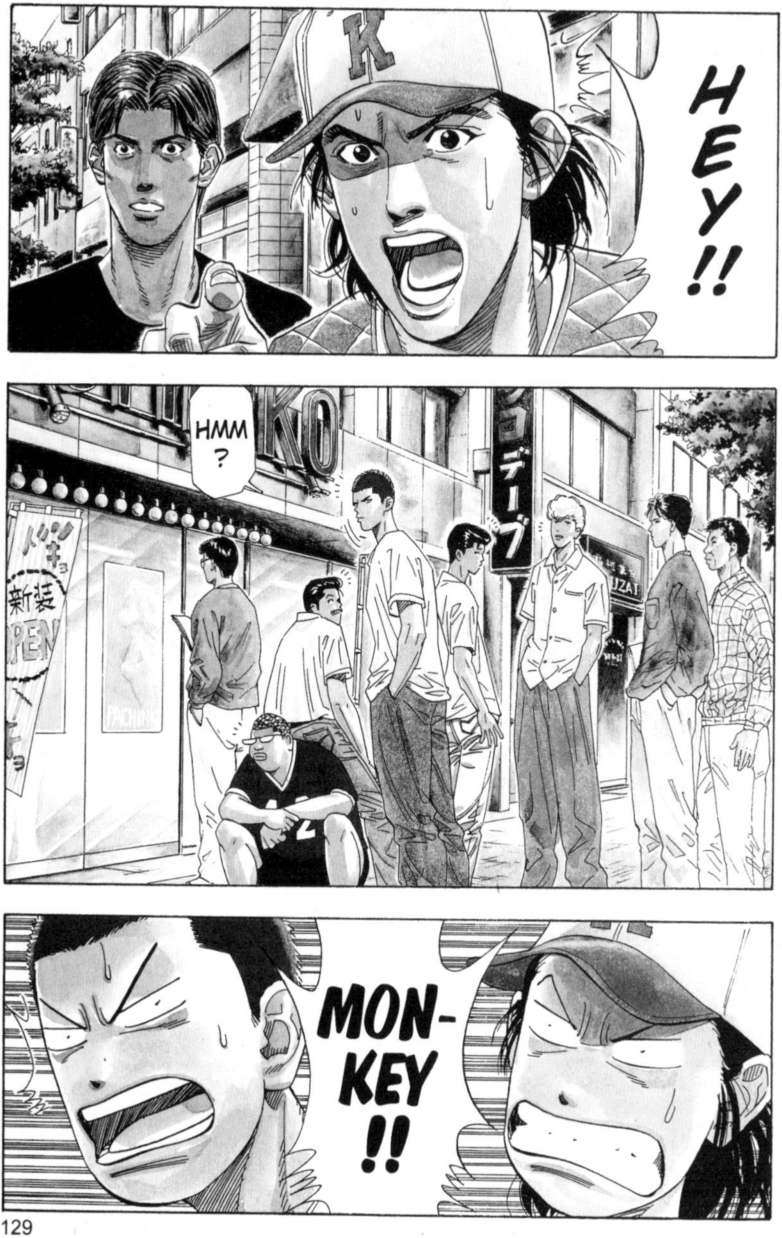
HEY!!
HMM ?
新装
MON-KEY !!

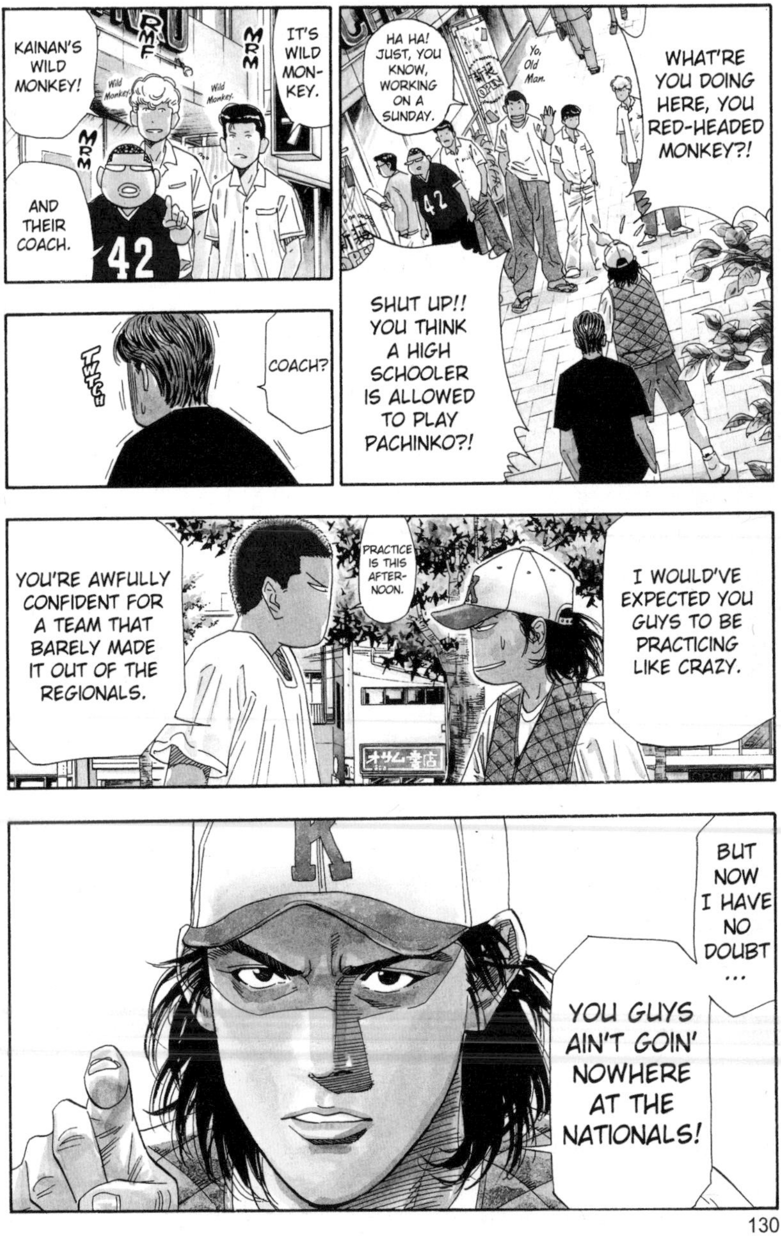
WHAT'RE YOU DOING HERE, YOU RED-HEADED MONKEY?!
Yo, Old Man.
HA HA! JUST, YOU KNOW, WORKING ON A SUNDAY.
SHUT UP!! YOU THINK A HIGH SCHOOLER IS ALLOWED TO PLAY PACHINKO?!
IT'S WILD MON-KEY.
MRM
Wild Monkey.
RMF
Wild Monkey!
KAINAN'S WILD MONKEY!
MRM
AND THEIR COACH.
COACH?
TWITCH
I WOULD'VE EXPECTED YOU GUYS TO BE PRACTICING LIKE CRAZY.
PRACTICE IS THIS AFTER-NOON.
YOU'RE AWFULLY CONFIDENT FOR A TEAM THAT BARELY MADE IT OUT OF THE REGIONALS.
オサム書店
BUT NOW I HAVE NO DOUBT ...
YOU GUYS AIN'T GOIN' NOWHERE AT THE NATIONALS!

READ THIS WAY

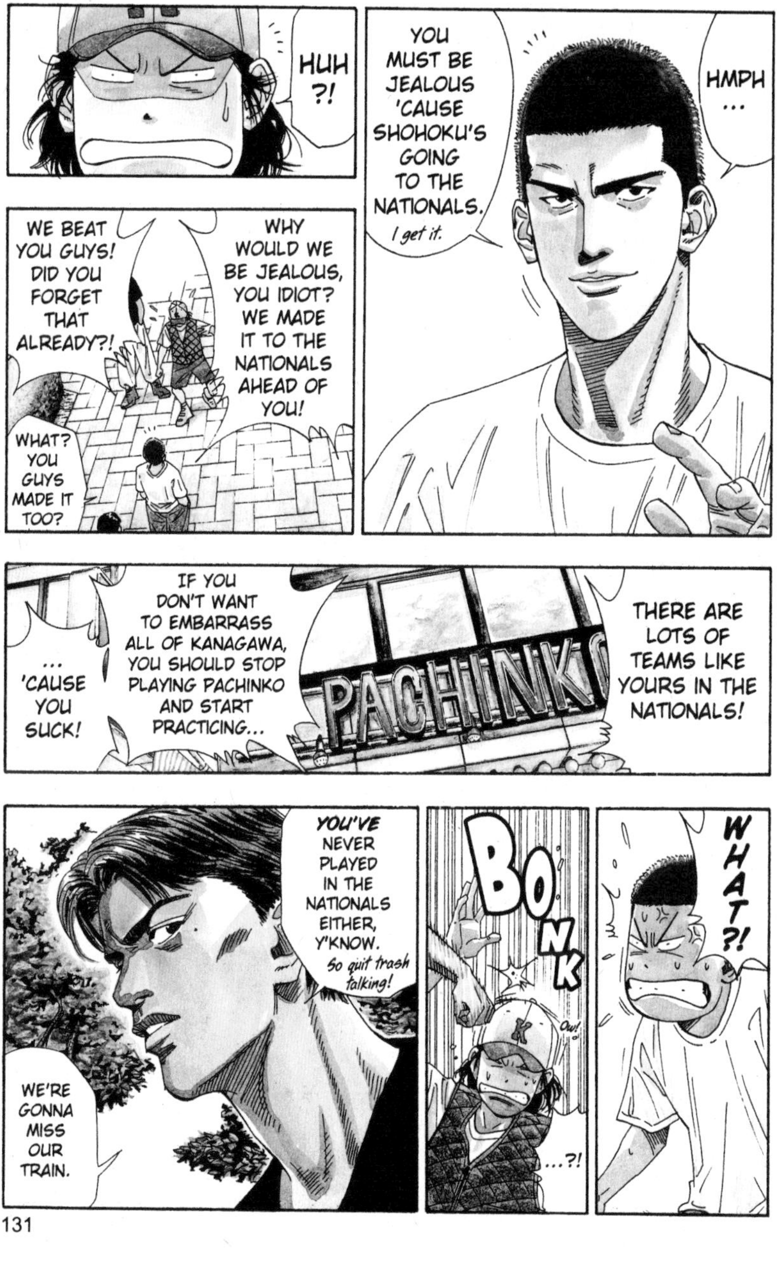
HMPH ...
YOU MUST BE JEALOUS 'CAUSE SHOHOKU'S GOING TO THE NATIONALS.
I get it.
HUH ?!
WHY WOULD WE BE JEALOUS, YOU IDIOT? WE MADE IT TO THE NATIONALS AHEAD OF YOU!
WE BEAT YOU GUYS! DID YOU FORGET THAT ALREADY?!
WHAT? YOU GUYS MADE IT TOO?
THERE ARE LOTS OF TEAMS LIKE YOURS IN THE NATIONALS!
PACHINKO
IF YOU DON'T WANT TO EMBARRASS ALL OF KANAGAWA, YOU SHOULD STOP PLAYING PACHINKO AND START PRACTICING...
... 'CAUSE YOU SUCK!
WHAT?!
BONK
Ow!
...?!
YOU'VE NEVER PLAYED IN THE NATIONALS EITHER, Y'KNOW.
So quit trash talking!
WE'RE GONNA MISS OUR TRAIN.

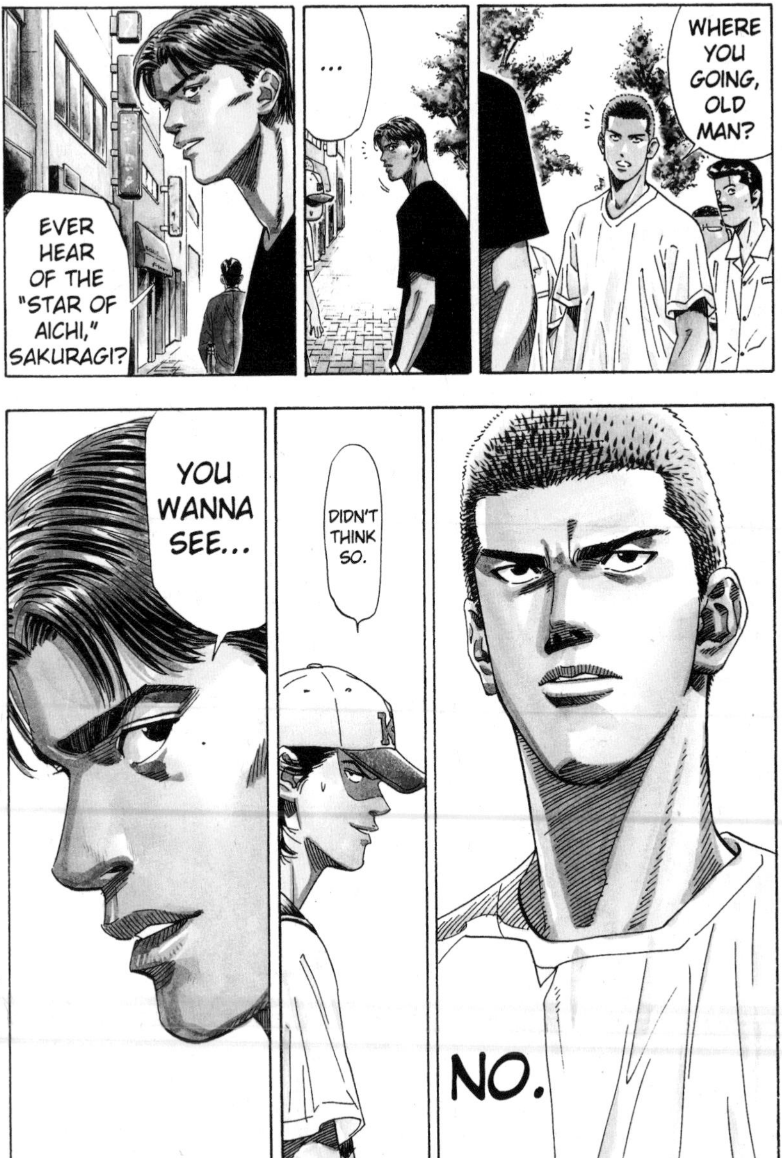
WHERE YOU GOING, OLD MAN?
...
EVER HEAR OF THE "STAR OF AICHI," SAKURAGI?
NO.
DIDN'T THINK SO.
YOU WANNA SEE...

READ THIS WAY

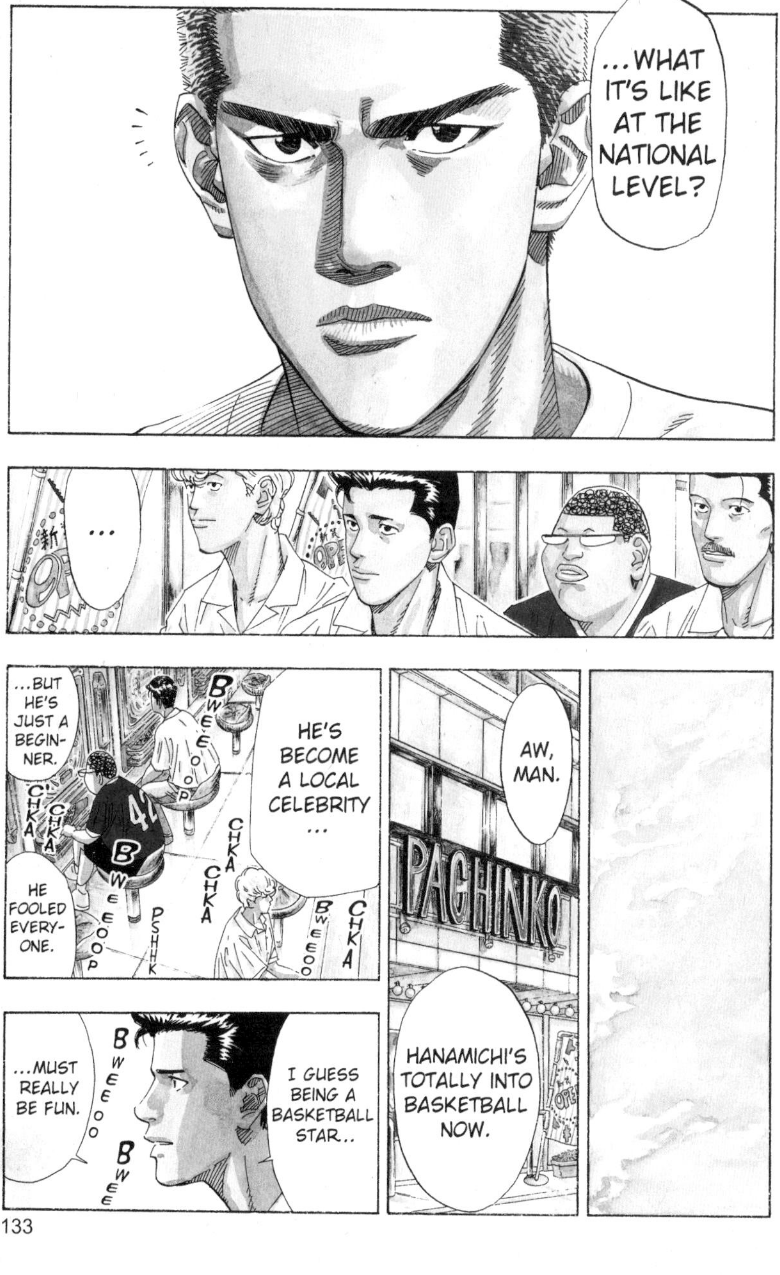

...WHAT IT'S LIKE AT THE NATIONAL LEVEL?
...
AW, MAN.
HANAMICHI'S TOTALLY INTO BASKETBALL NOW.
BWEEOOP
HE'S BECOME A LOCAL CELEBRITY...
...BUT HE'S JUST A BEGINNER.
CHKA
CHKA
CHKA
CHKA
BWEEOO
CHKA
PSHHK
BWEEOOP
HE FOOLED EVERYONE.
I GUESS BEING A BASKETBALL STAR...
BWEEOO
...MUST REALLY BE FUN.
BWEE

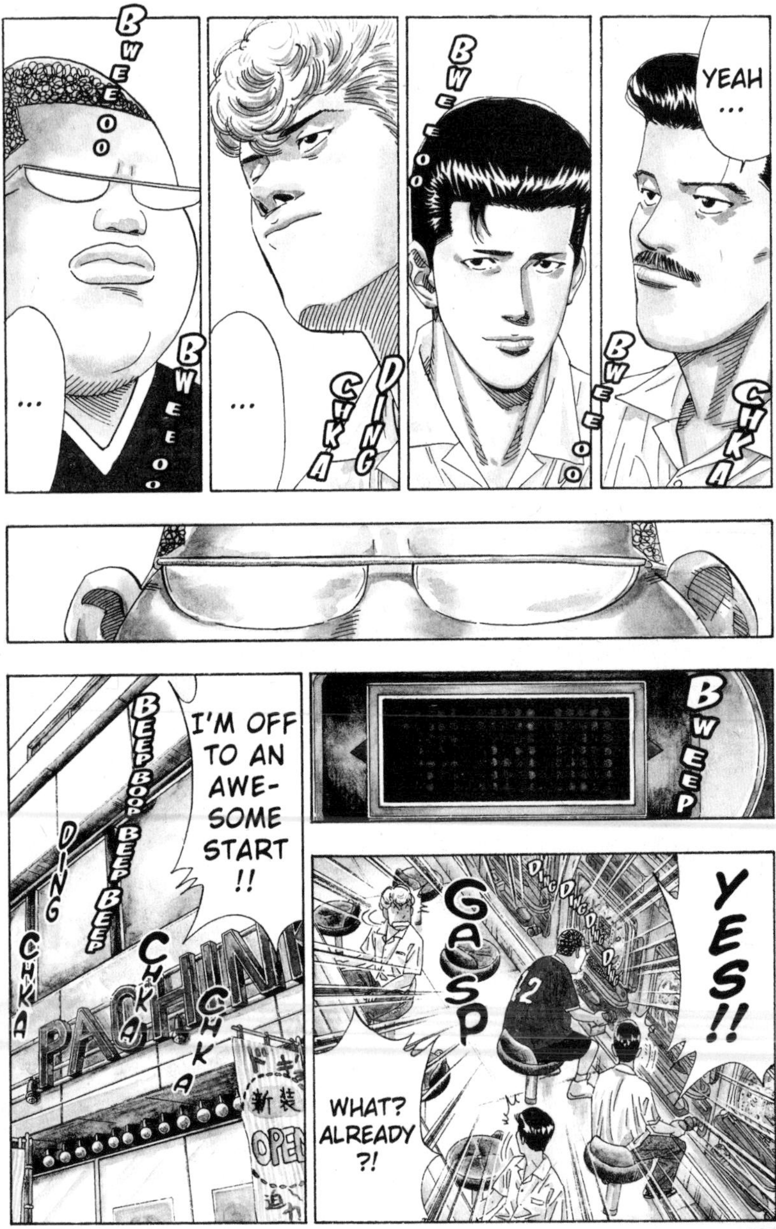

YEAH ...
BWEEOO
CHKA
BWEEOO
BWEEOO
CHKA
DING
...
BWEEOO
...
BWEEOO
BWEEP
YES!!
DING DING DING DING
GASP
WHAT? ALREADY ?!
I'M OFF TO AN AWE-SOME START !!
BEEP BOOP BEEP BEEP
DING
CHKA
CHKA
CHKA
PACHIN
新装
OPE

READ THIS WAY

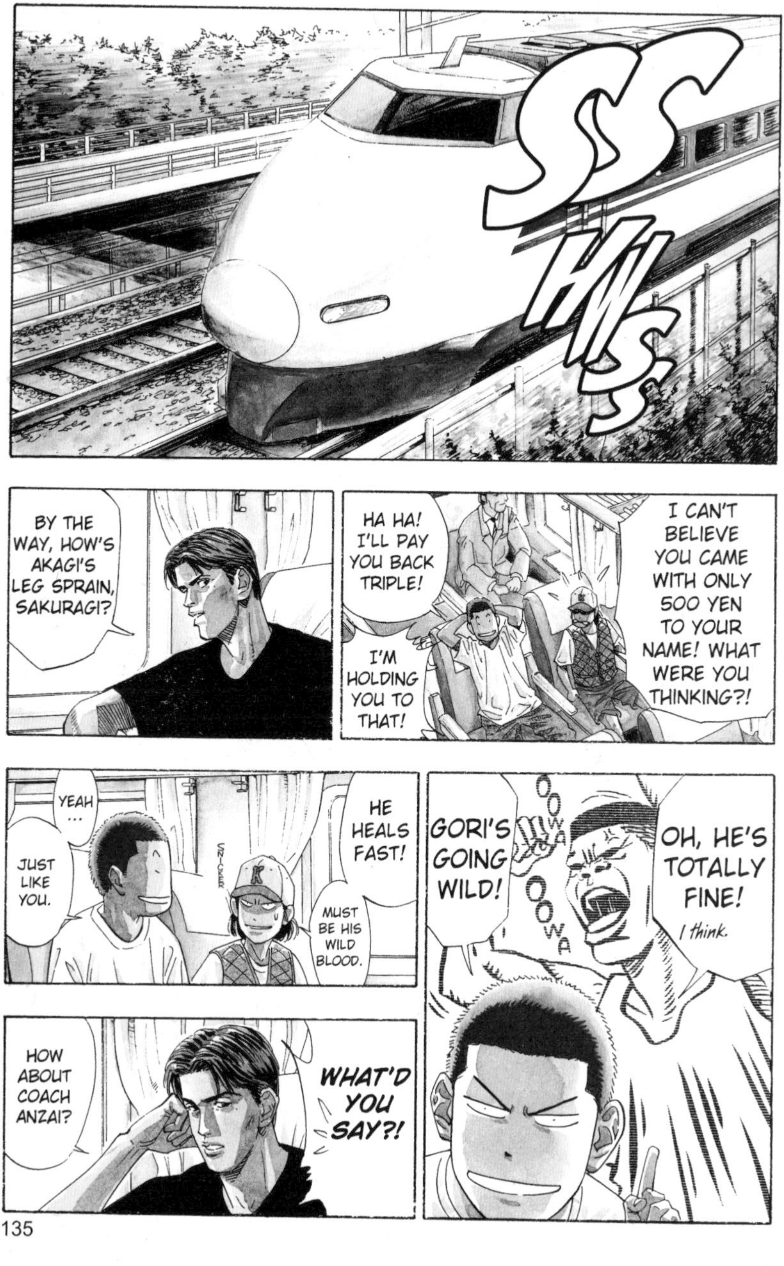
SSHWSS
I CAN'T BELIEVE YOU CAME WITH ONLY 500 YEN TO YOUR NAME! WHAT WERE YOU THINKING?!
HA HA! I'LL PAY YOU BACK TRIPLE!
I'M HOLDING YOU TO THAT!
BY THE WAY, HOW'S AKAGI'S LEG SPRAIN, SAKURAGI?
OH, HE'S TOTALLY FINE!
I think.
OOWA
OOWA
GORI'S GOING WILD!
HE HEALS FAST!
MUST BE HIS WILD BLOOD.
SNICKER
YEAH ...
JUST LIKE YOU.
WHAT'D YOU SAY?!
HOW ABOUT COACH ANZAI?

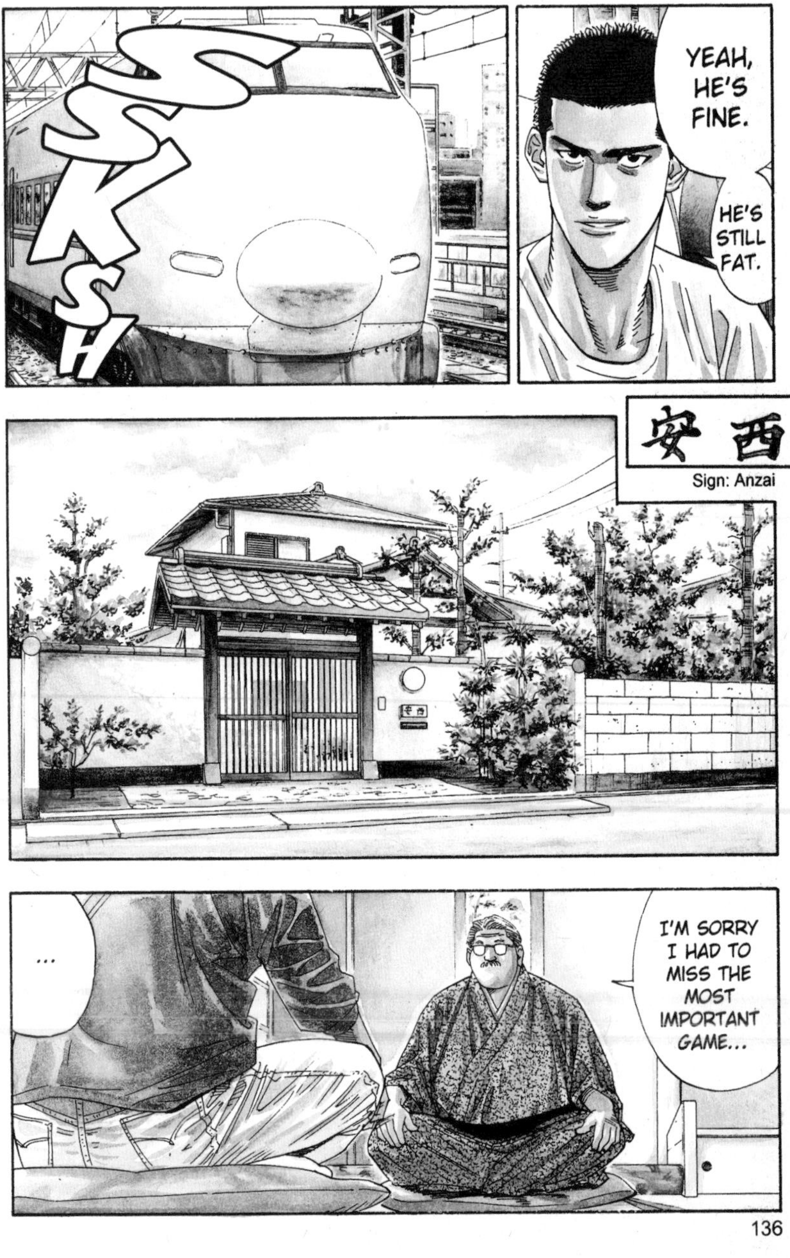

YEAH, HE'S FINE.
HE'S STILL FAT.
SSKSH
安西
Sign: Anzai
I'M SORRY I HAD TO MISS THE MOST IMPORTANT GAME...
...

READ THIS WAY

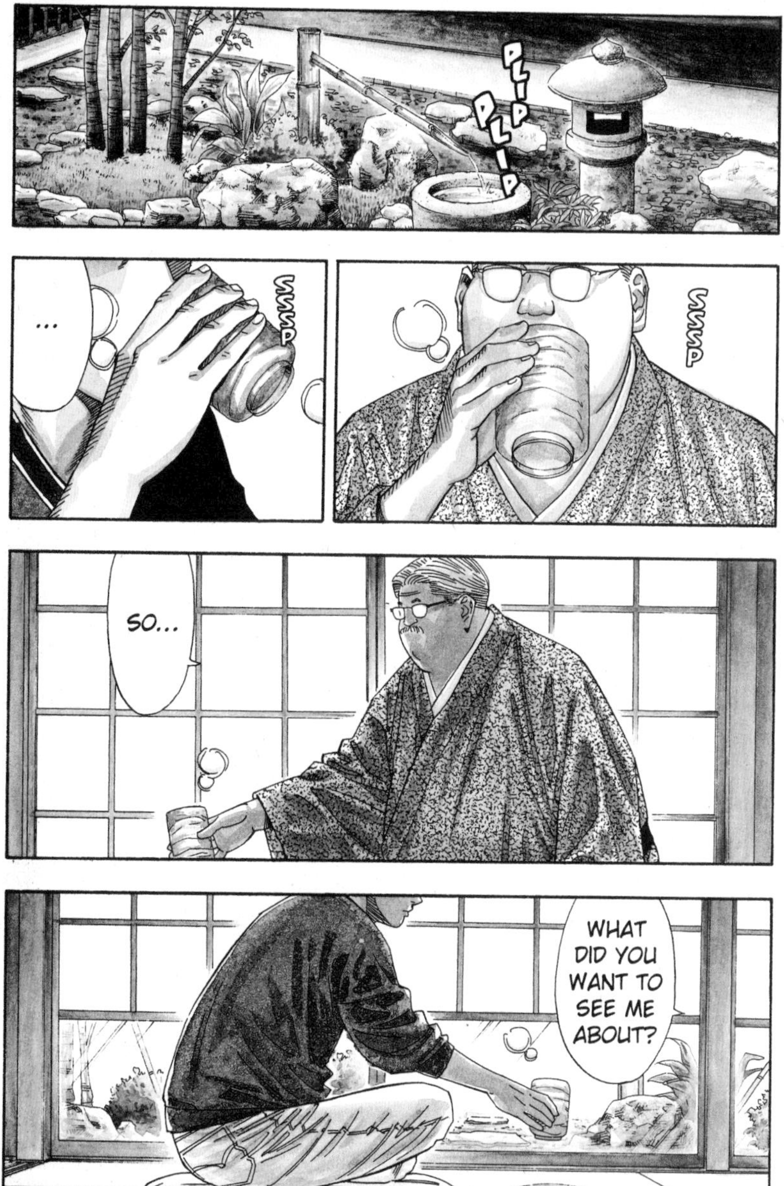
PLIP
PLIP
PLIP
SSSP
...
SSSP
SO...
WHAT DID YOU WANT TO SEE ME ABOUT?

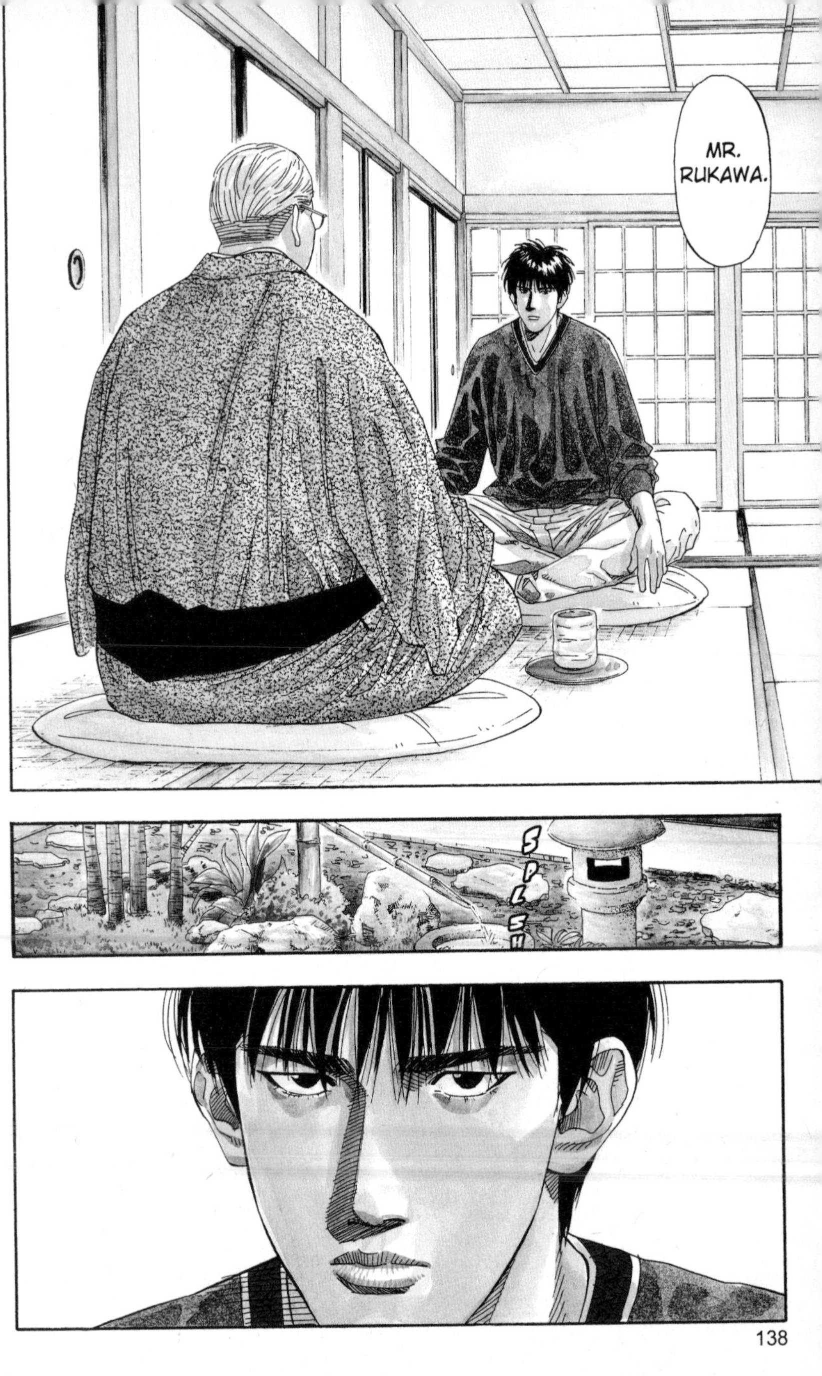
MR. RUKAWA.
SPLSH

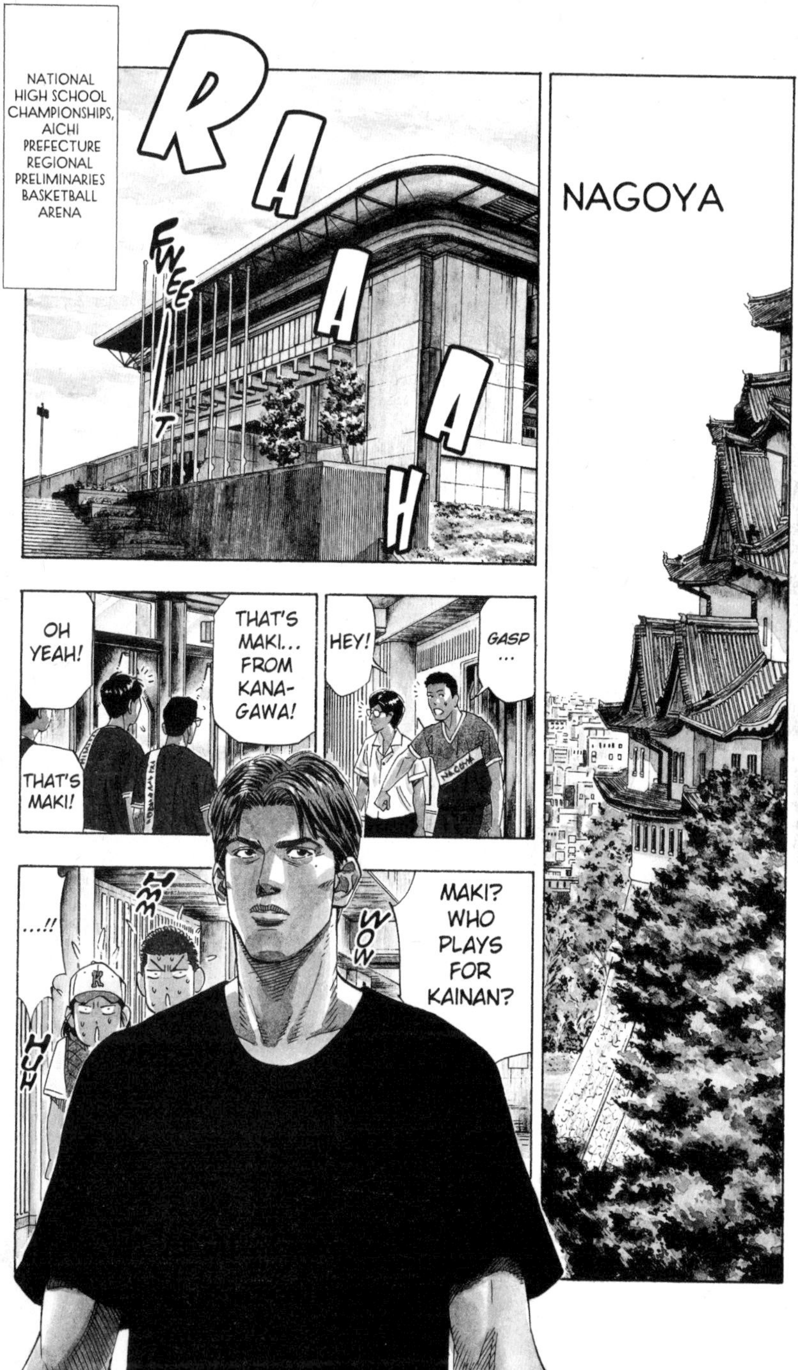
NAGOYA
NATIONAL HIGH SCHOOL CHAMPIONSHIPS, AICHI PREFECTURE REGIONAL PRELIMINARIES BASKETBALL ARENA
RAAAAH
FWEEEET
GASP...
HEY!
THAT'S MAKI... FROM KANA-GAWA!
OH YEAH!
THAT'S MAKI!
MAKI? WHO PLAYS FOR KAINAN?
WOW
HMM
...!!
HUH

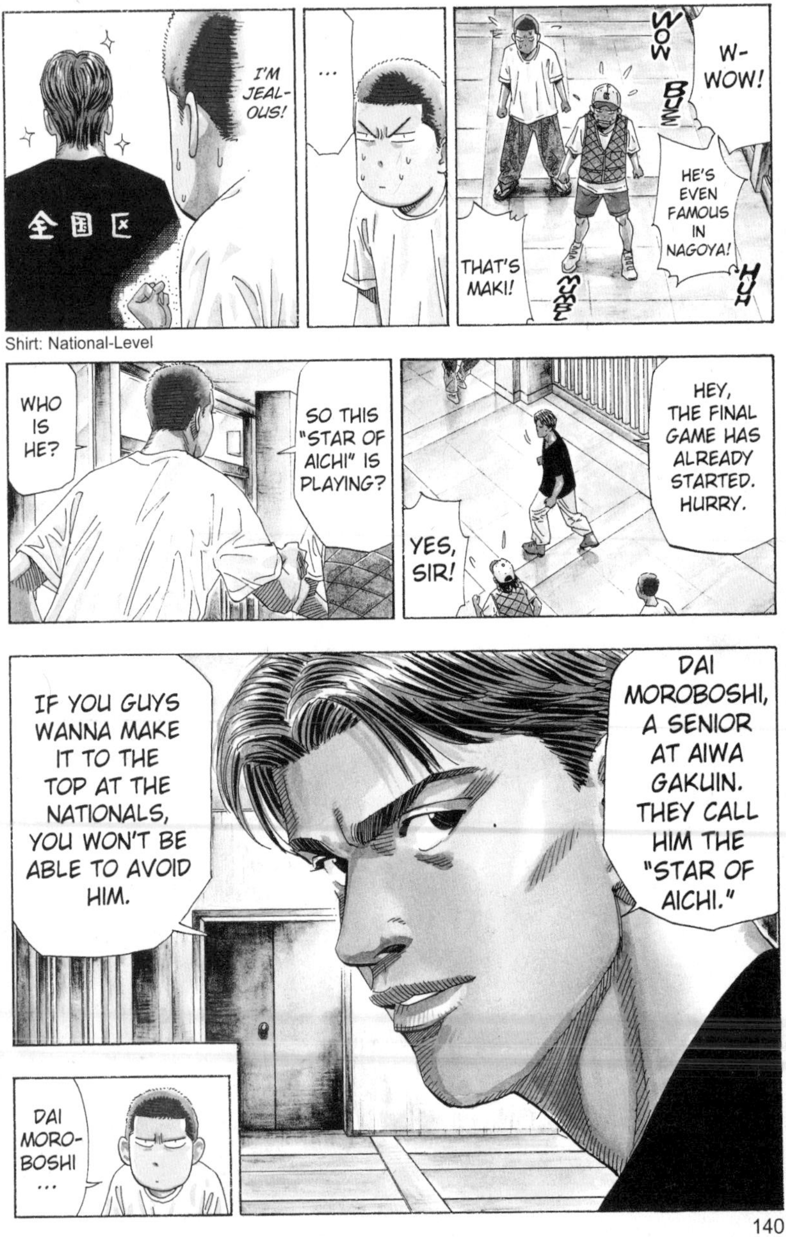
W-WOW!
WOW
BUZZ
HE'S EVEN FAMOUS IN NAGOYA!
HUH
THAT'S MAKI!
MUMBLE
...
I'M JEALOUS!
全国区
HEY, THE FINAL GAME HAS ALREADY STARTED. HURRY.
YES, SIR!
SO THIS "STAR OF AICHI" IS PLAYING?
WHO IS HE?
DAI MOROBOSHI, A SENIOR AT AIWA GAKUIN. THEY CALL HIM THE "STAR OF AICHI."
IF YOU GUYS WANNA MAKE IT TO THE TOP AT THE NATIONALS, YOU WON'T BE ABLE TO AVOID HIM.
DAI MOROBOSHI...

Shirt: National-Level

READ THIS WAY

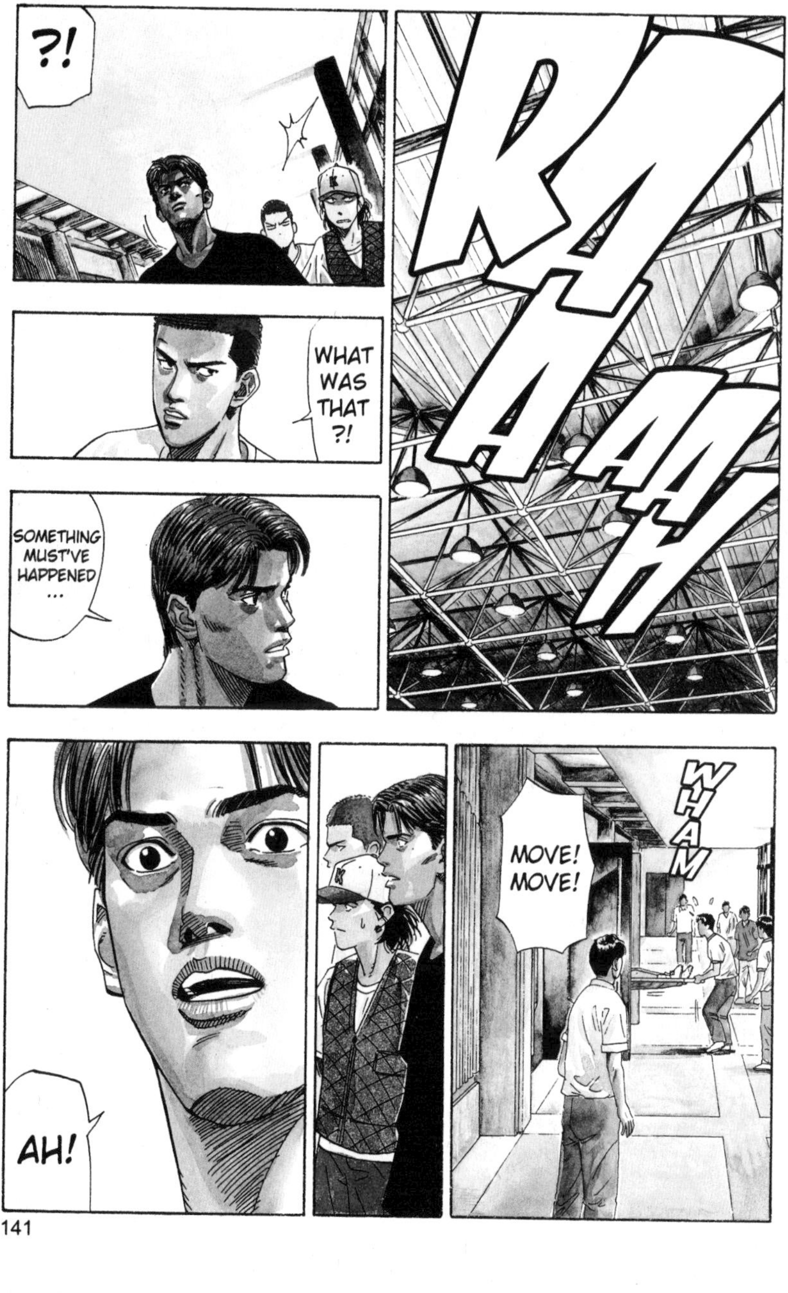
KRAAAH
?!
WHAT WAS THAT ?!
SOMETHING MUST'VE HAPPENED ...
WHAM
MOVE! MOVE!
AH!

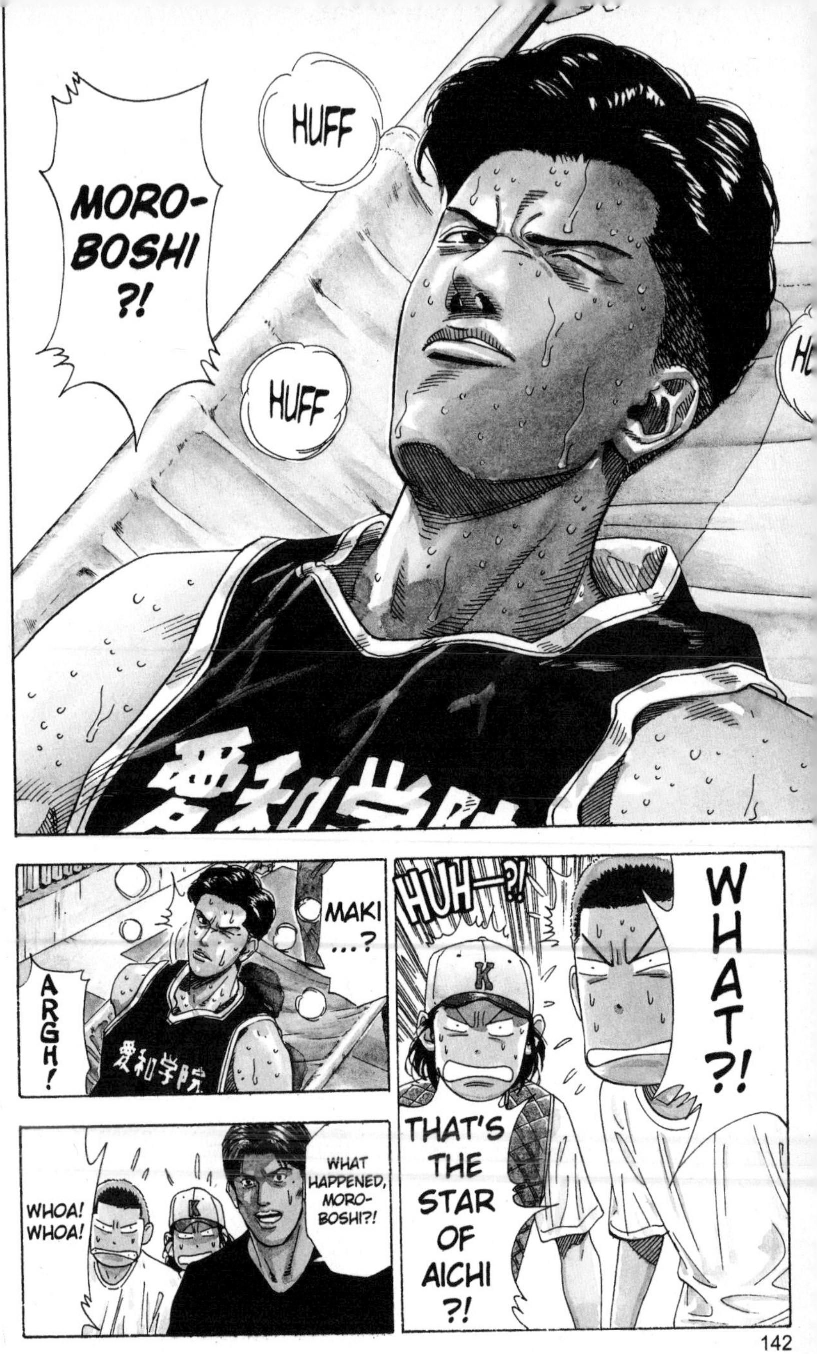
HUFF
MORO-BOSHI?!
HUFF
WHAT?!
HUH—?!
THAT'S THE STAR OF AICHI?!
MAKI...?
ARGH!
愛和学院
WHAT HAPPENED, MOROBOSHI?!
WHOA! WHOA!

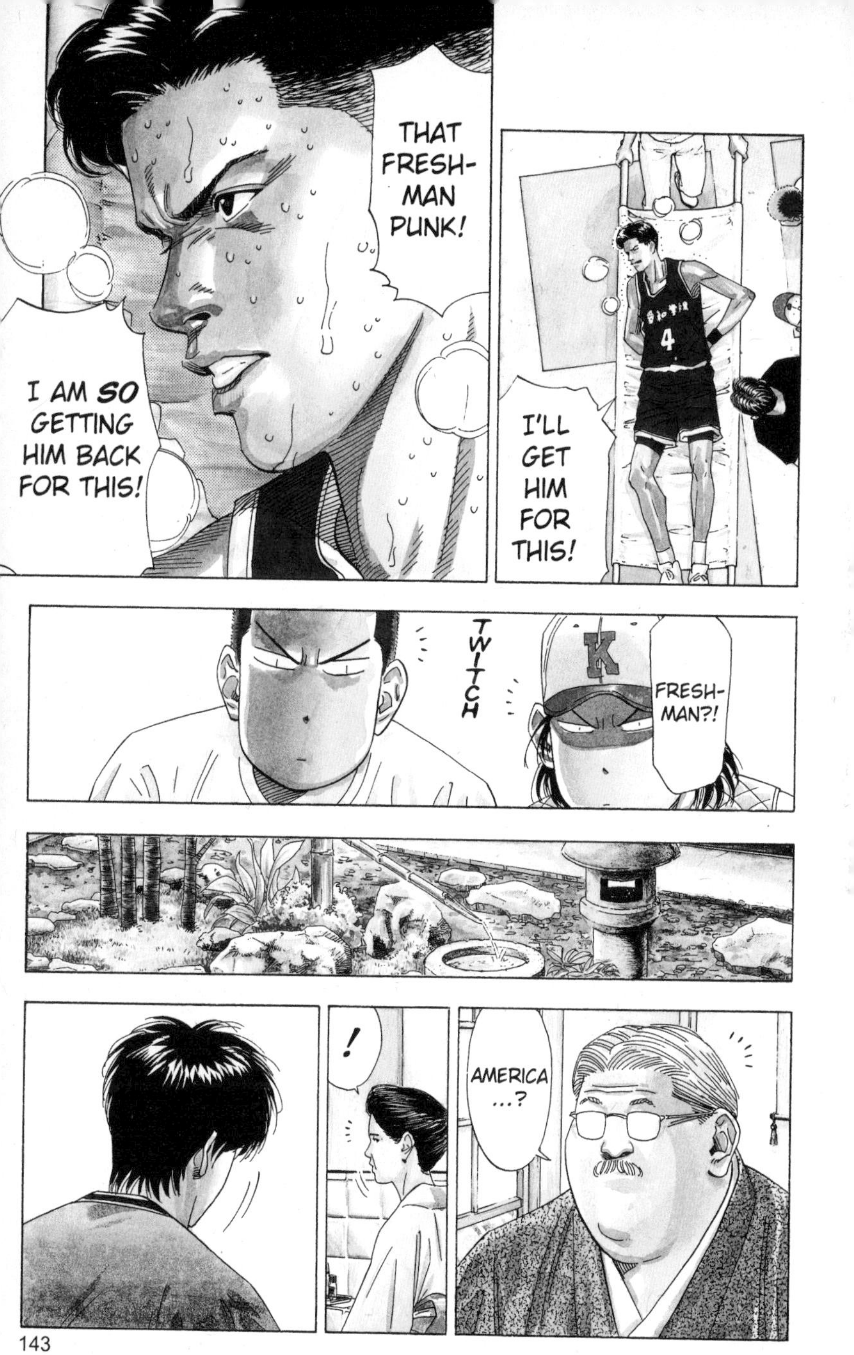
I'LL GET HIM FOR THIS!
THAT FRESH-MAN PUNK!
I AM SO GETTING HIM BACK FOR THIS!
FRESH-MAN?!
TWITCH
AMERICA ...?
!

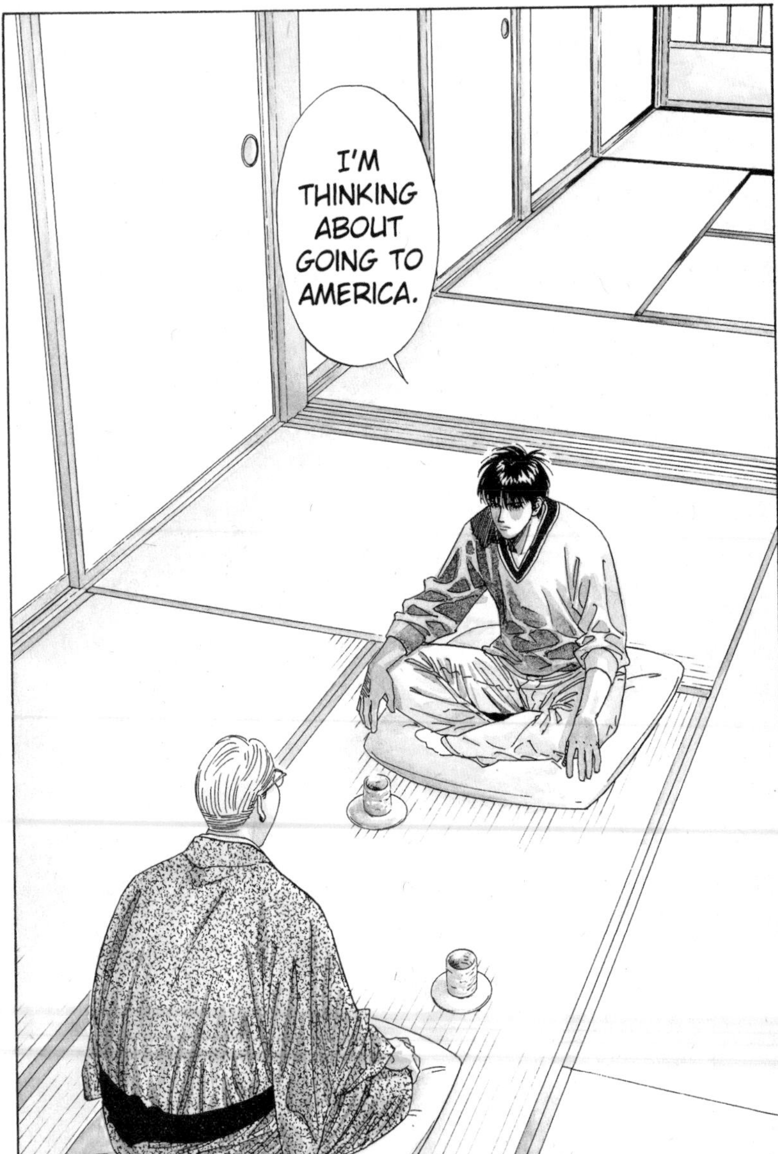
I'M THINKING ABOUT GOING TO AMERICA.

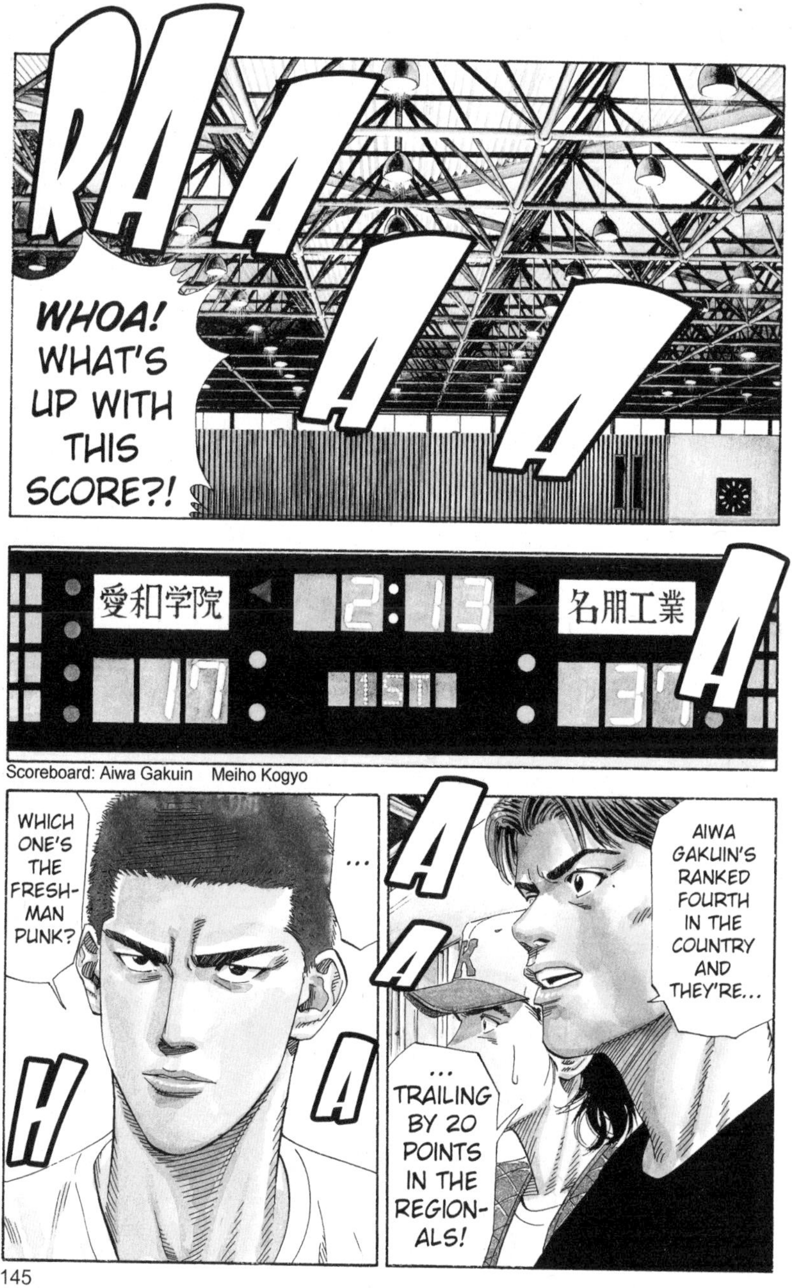
RAAAA
WHOA! WHAT'S UP WITH THIS SCORE?!
愛和学院
2:13
名朋工業
17
1ST
37
A
Scoreboard: Aiwa Gakuin Meiho Kogyo
AIWA GAKUIN'S RANKED FOURTH IN THE COUNTRY AND THEY'RE...
...TRAILING BY 20 POINTS IN THE REGIONALS!
AA
...
WHICH ONE'S THE FRESHMAN PUNK?
HA

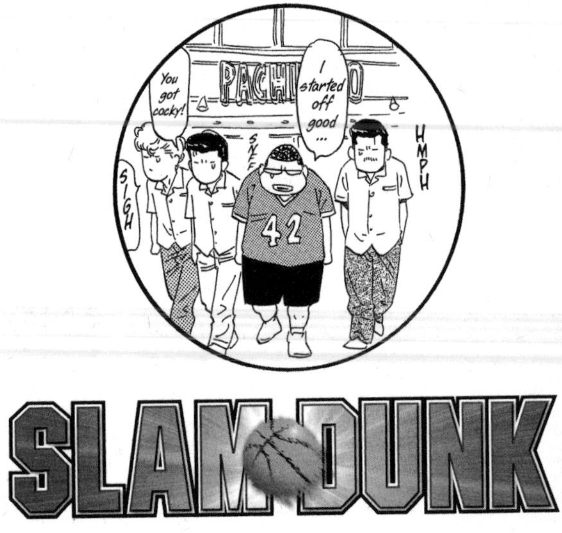
HMPH
I started off good ...
SNIFF
You got cocky!
SIGH

SLAM DUNK

#187 FRESHMAN PUNK

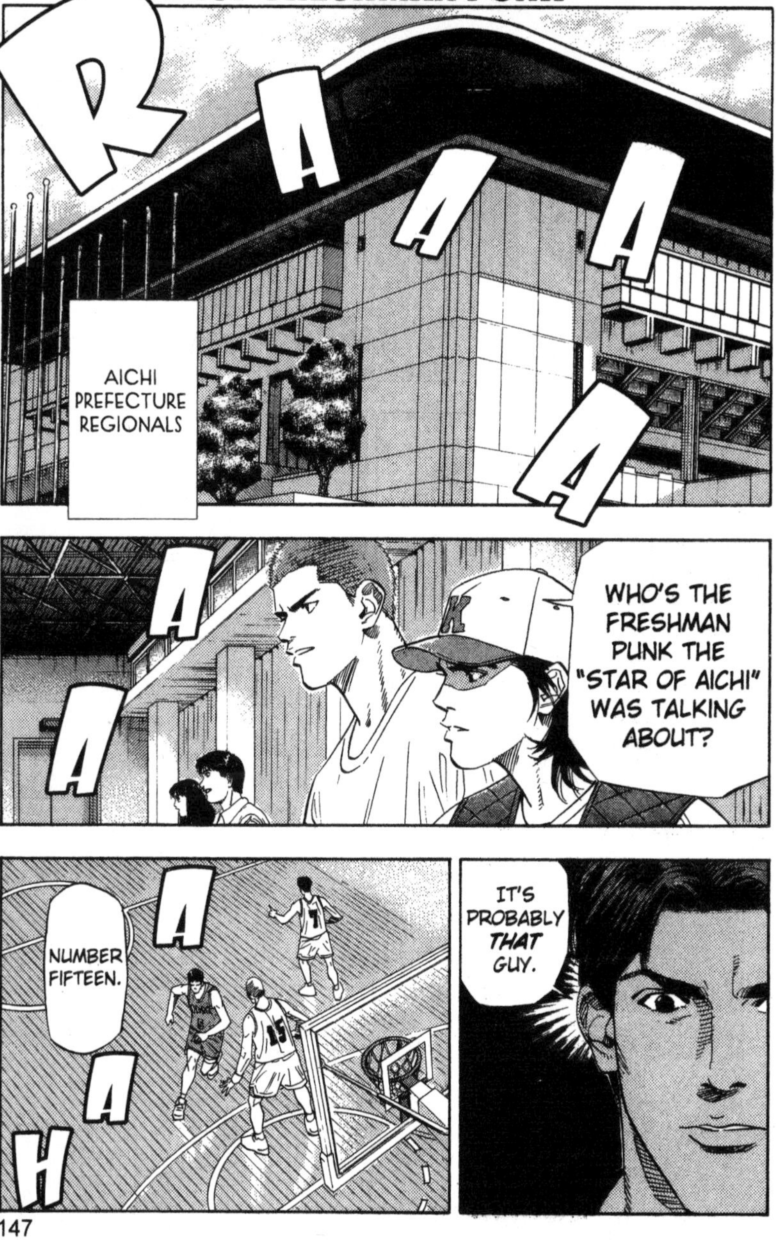
RAAAA
AICHI PREFECTURE REGIONALS
WHO'S THE FRESHMAN PUNK THE "STAR OF AICHI" WAS TALKING ABOUT?
AA
IT'S PROBABLY *THAT* GUY.
NUMBER FIFTEEN.
AAH

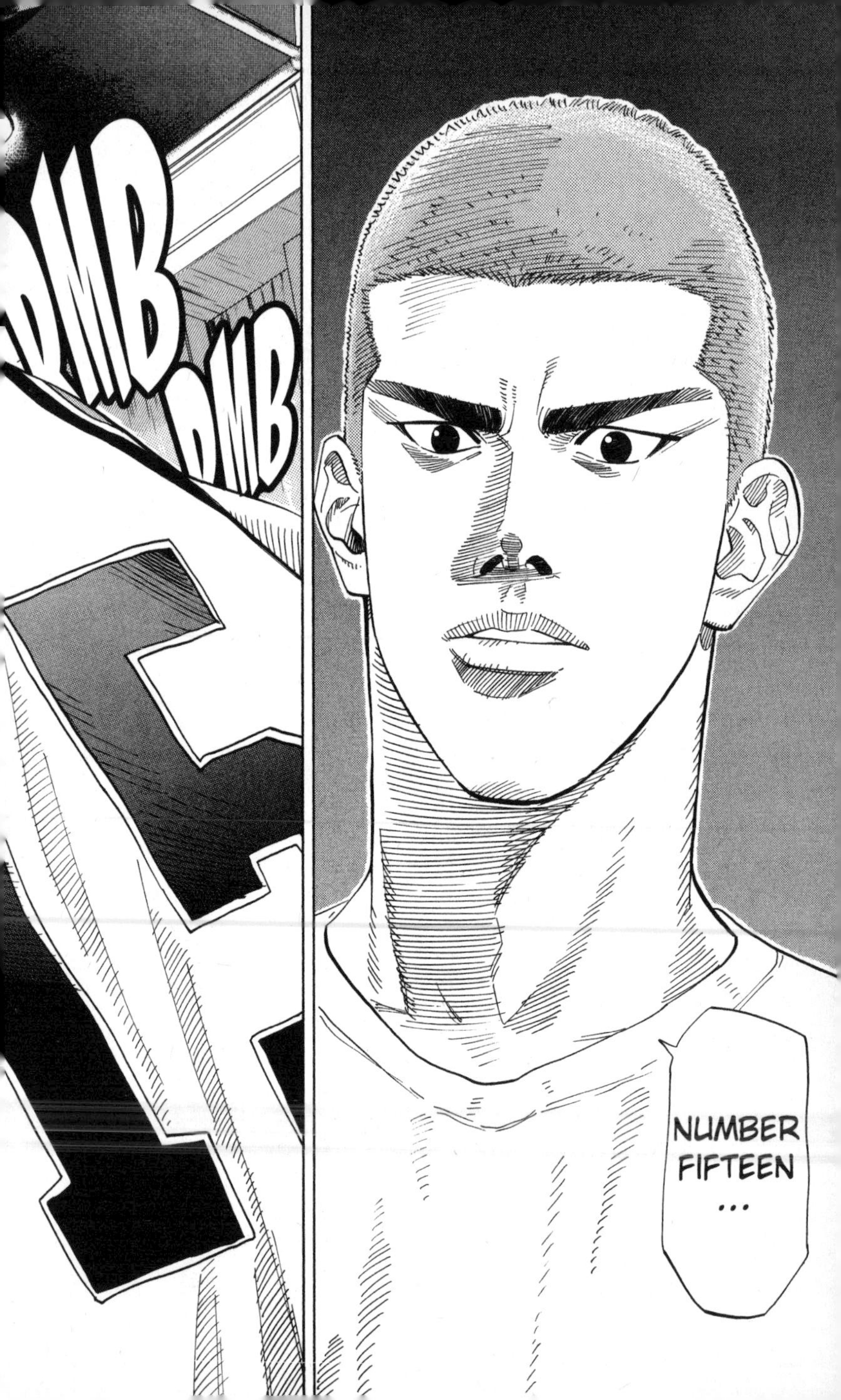
NUMBER FIFTEEN ...
DMB
DMB

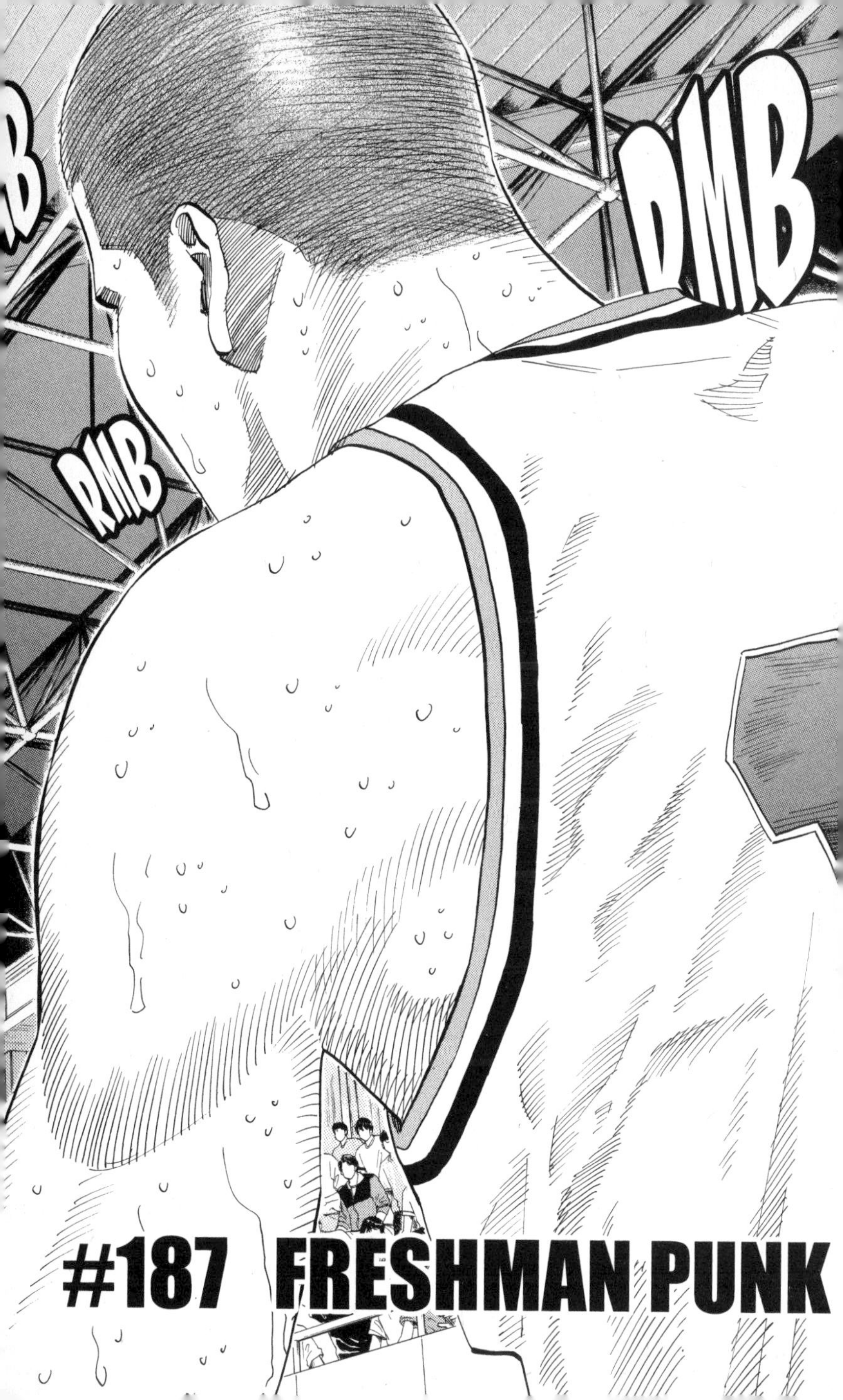
DMB
RMB

#187 FRESHMAN PUNK

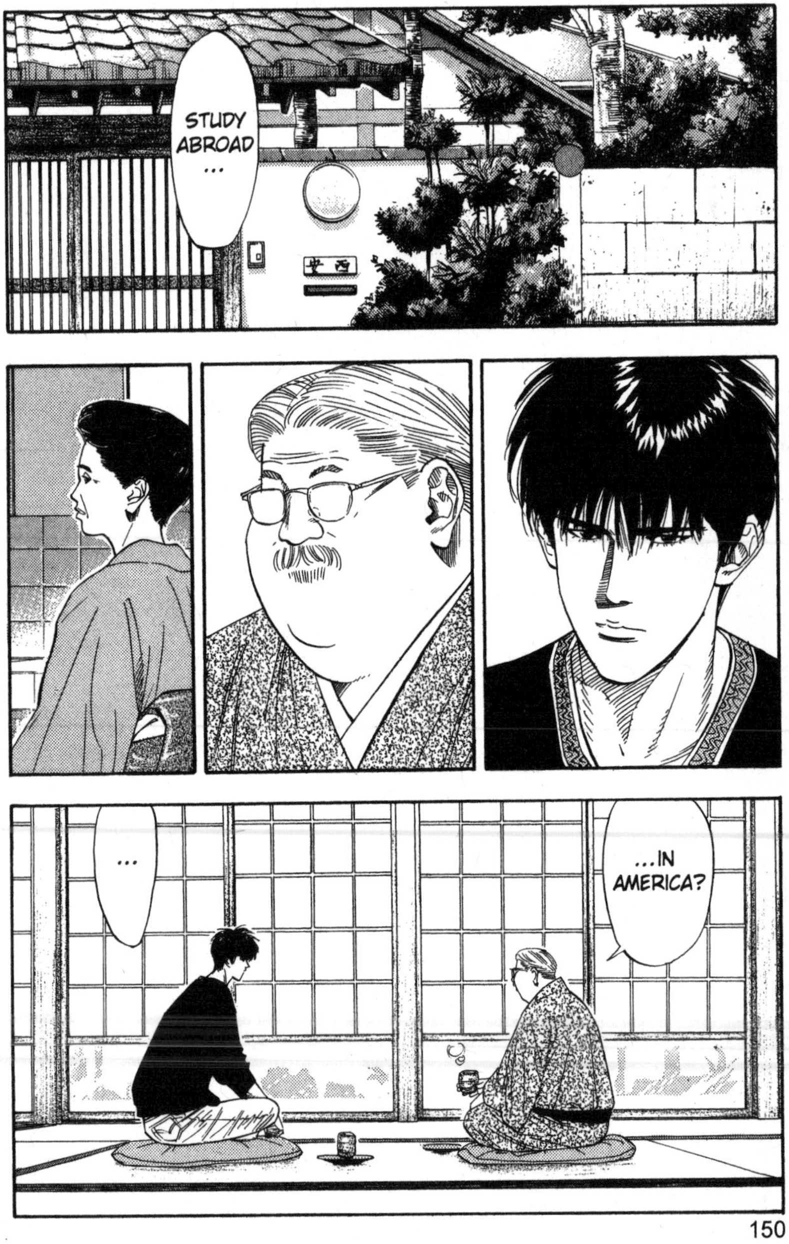
STUDY ABROAD ...
...IN AMERICA?
...

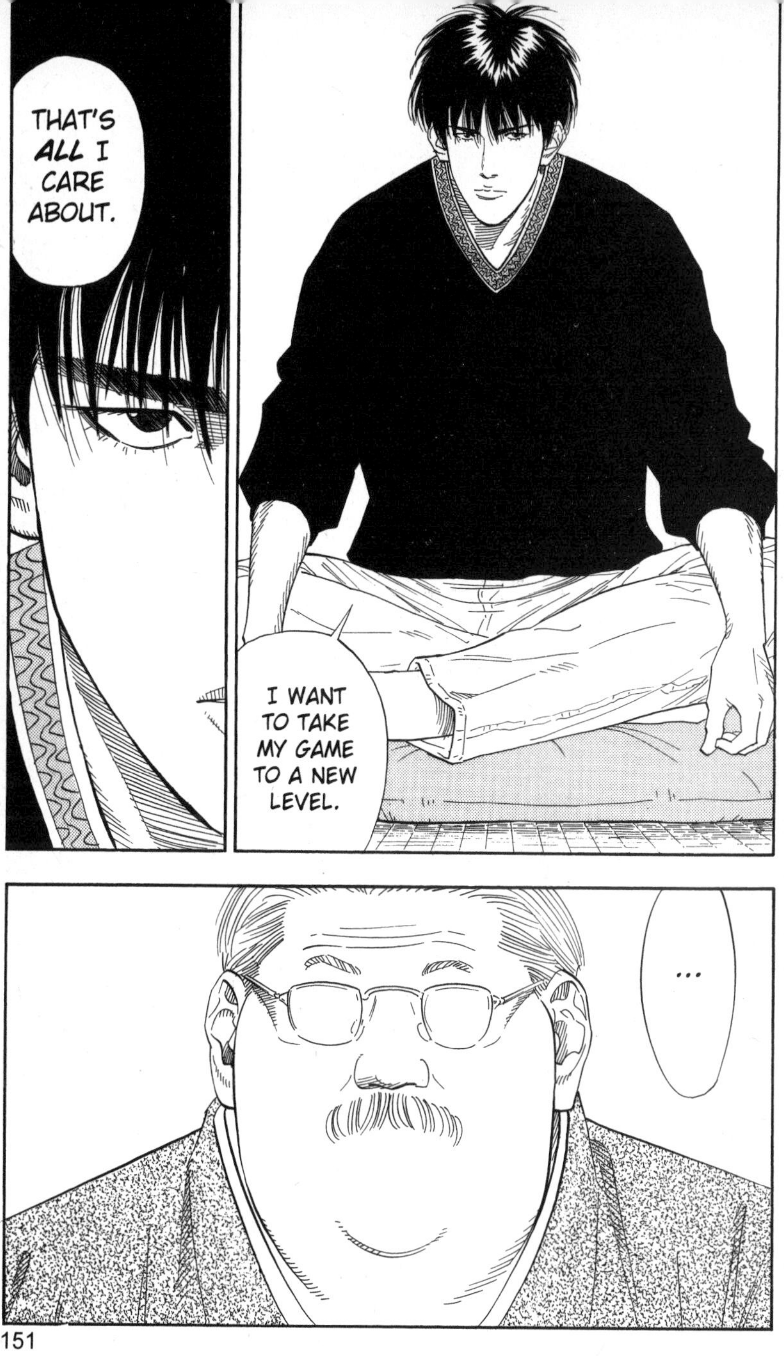
I WANT TO TAKE MY GAME TO A NEW LEVEL.
THAT'S ALL I CARE ABOUT.
...

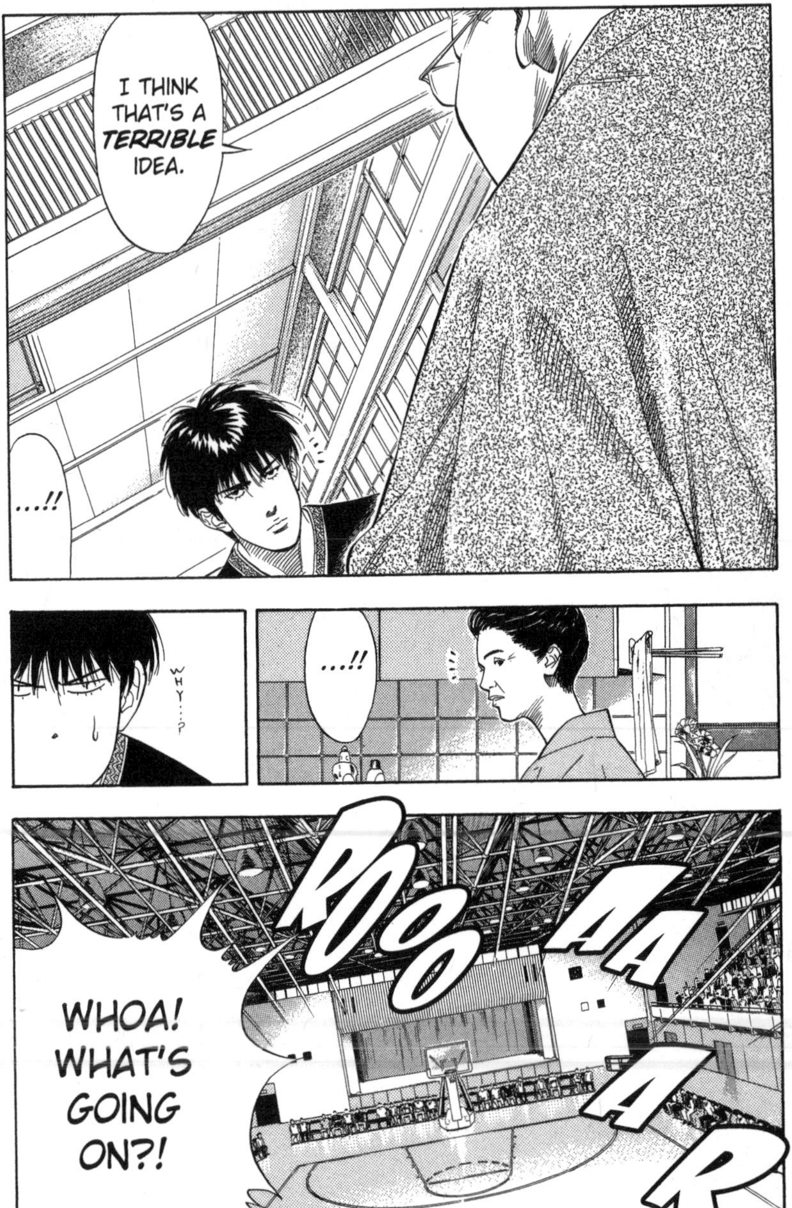
I THINK THAT'S A *TERRIBLE* IDEA.
...!!
...!!
WHY...?
ROOOAAAR
WHOA! WHAT'S GOING ON?!

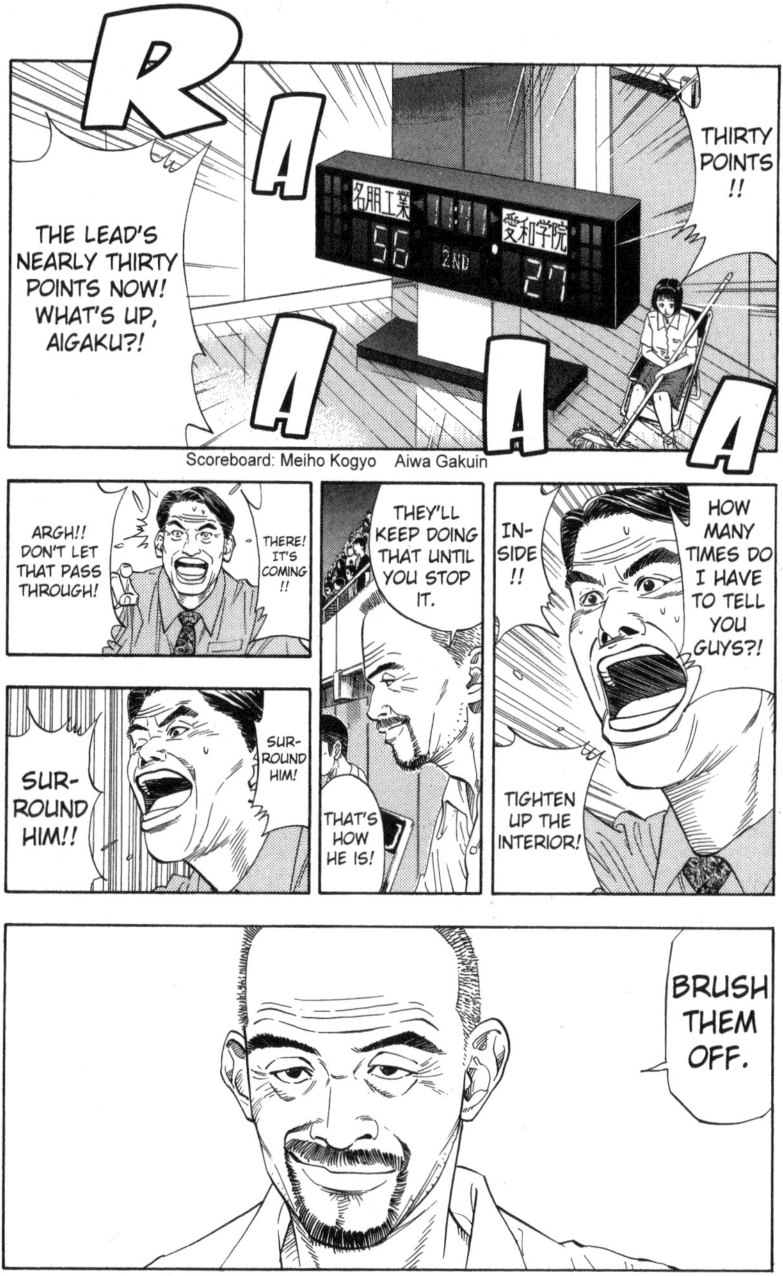
THIRTY POINTS!!
THE LEAD'S NEARLY THIRTY POINTS NOW! WHAT'S UP, AIGAKU?!
RAAAA
名朋工業 56
2ND
愛和学院 27
Scoreboard: Meiho Kogyo Aiwa Gakuin
HOW MANY TIMES DO I HAVE TO TELL YOU GUYS?!
INSIDE!!
TIGHTEN UP THE INTERIOR!
THEY'LL KEEP DOING THAT UNTIL YOU STOP IT.
THAT'S HOW HE IS!
THERE! IT'S COMING!!
ARGH!! DON'T LET THAT PASS THROUGH!
SURROUND HIM!
SURROUND HIM!!
BRUSH THEM OFF.

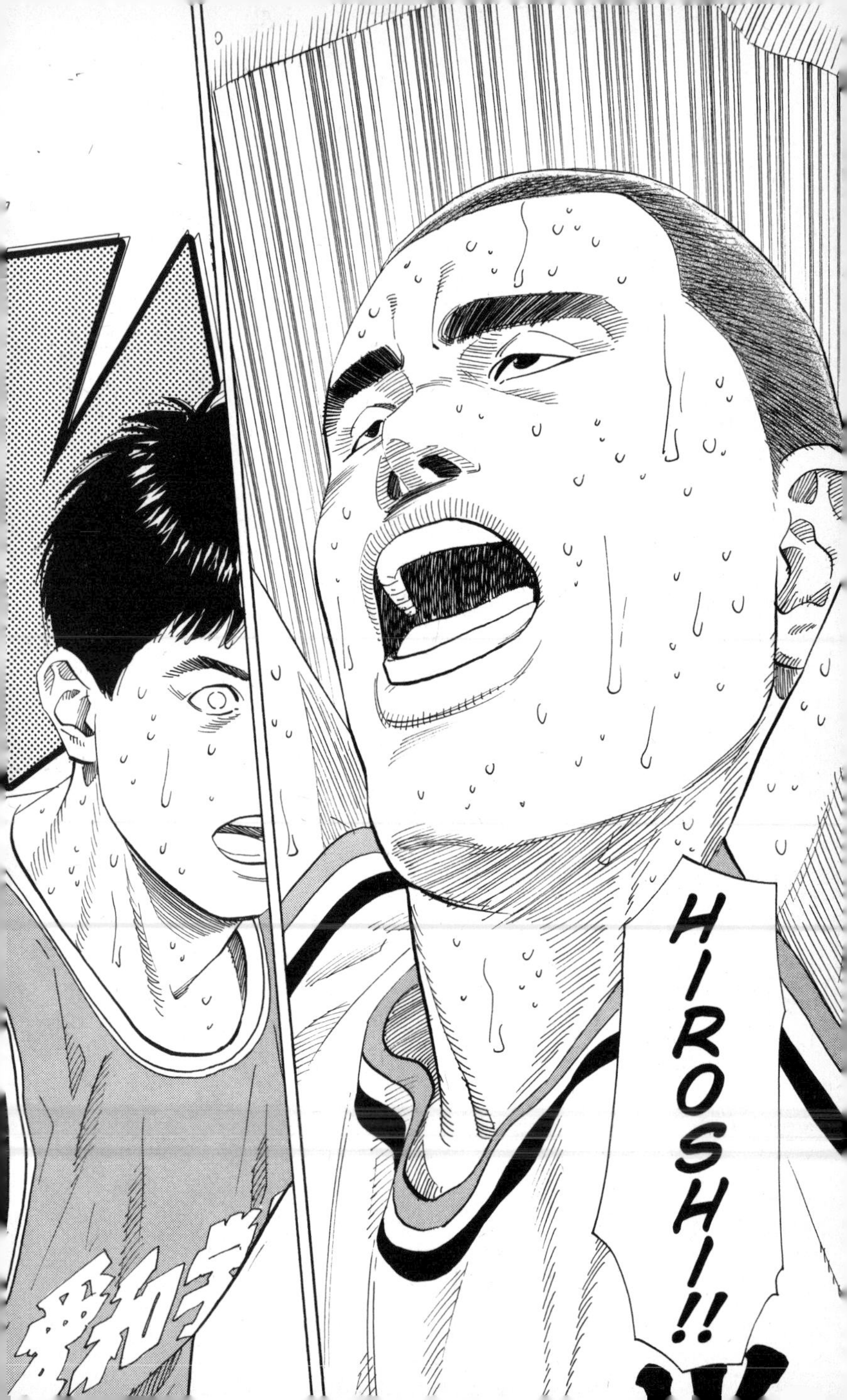
HIROSHI!!

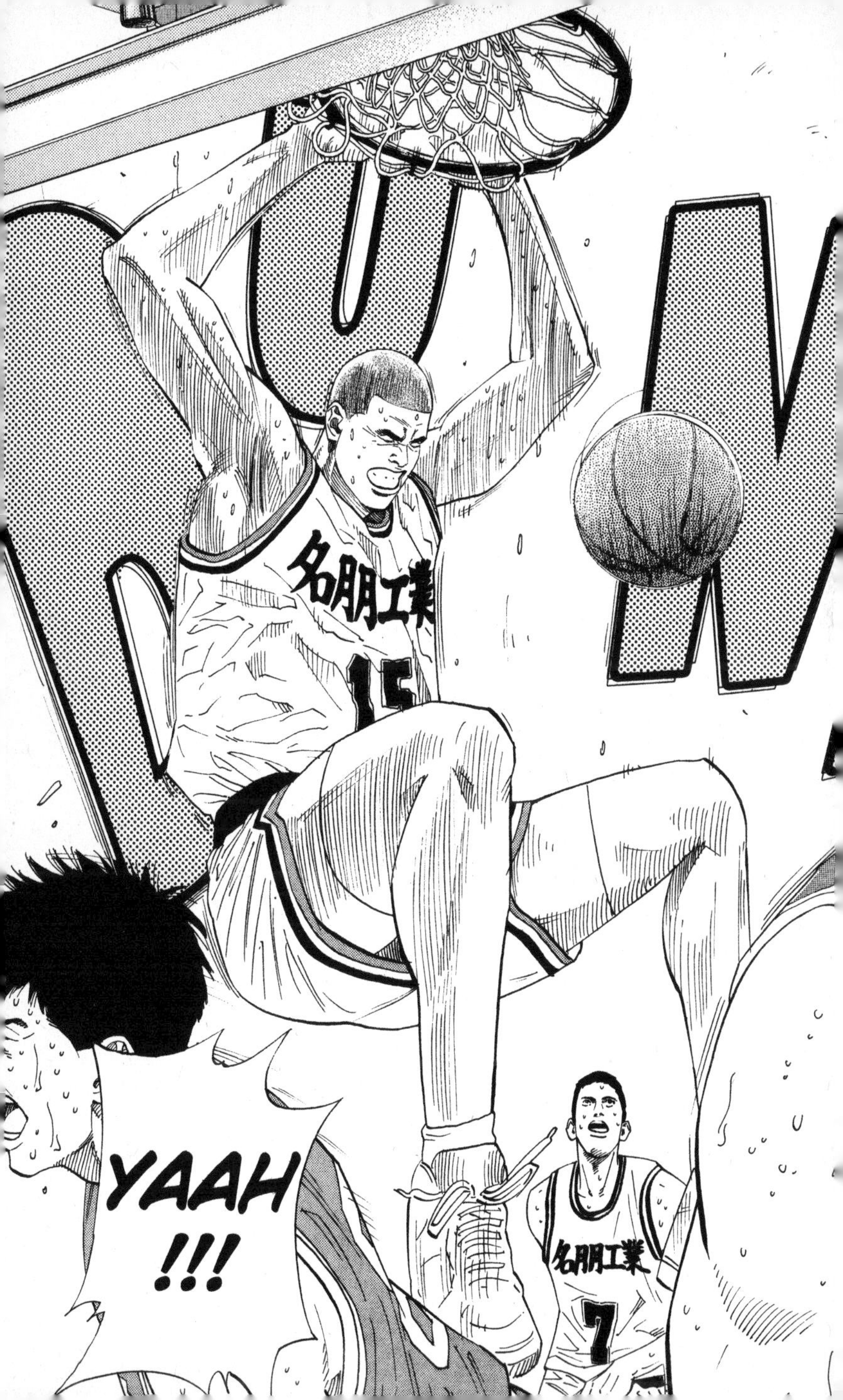
名朋工業
15
YAAH
!!!
名朋工業
7

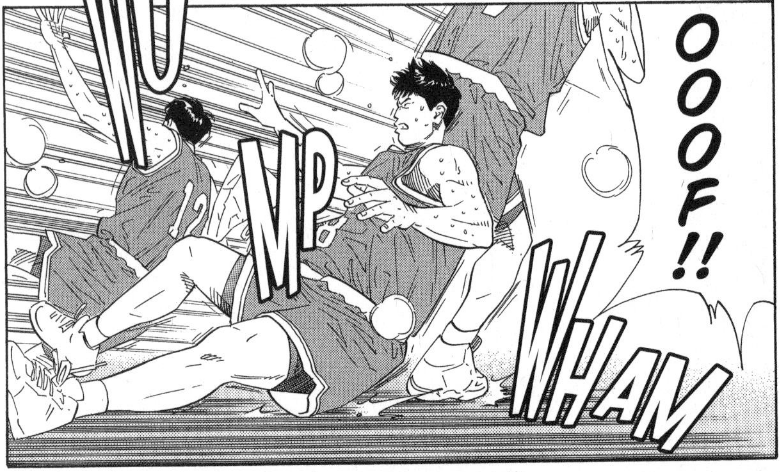
OOOOF!!
WUMP
WHAM

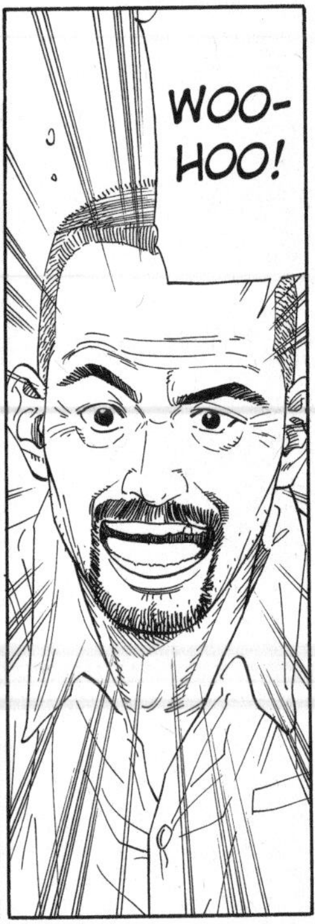
WOO-
HOO!

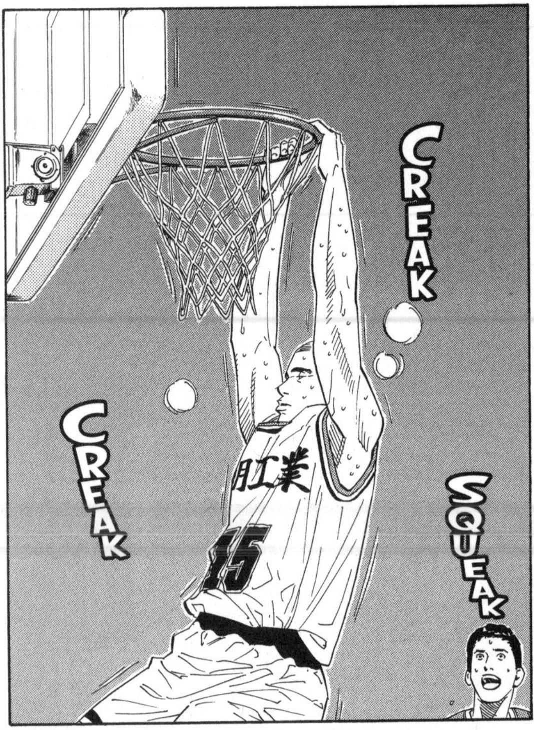
CREAK
CREAK
SQUEAK

READ THIS WAY

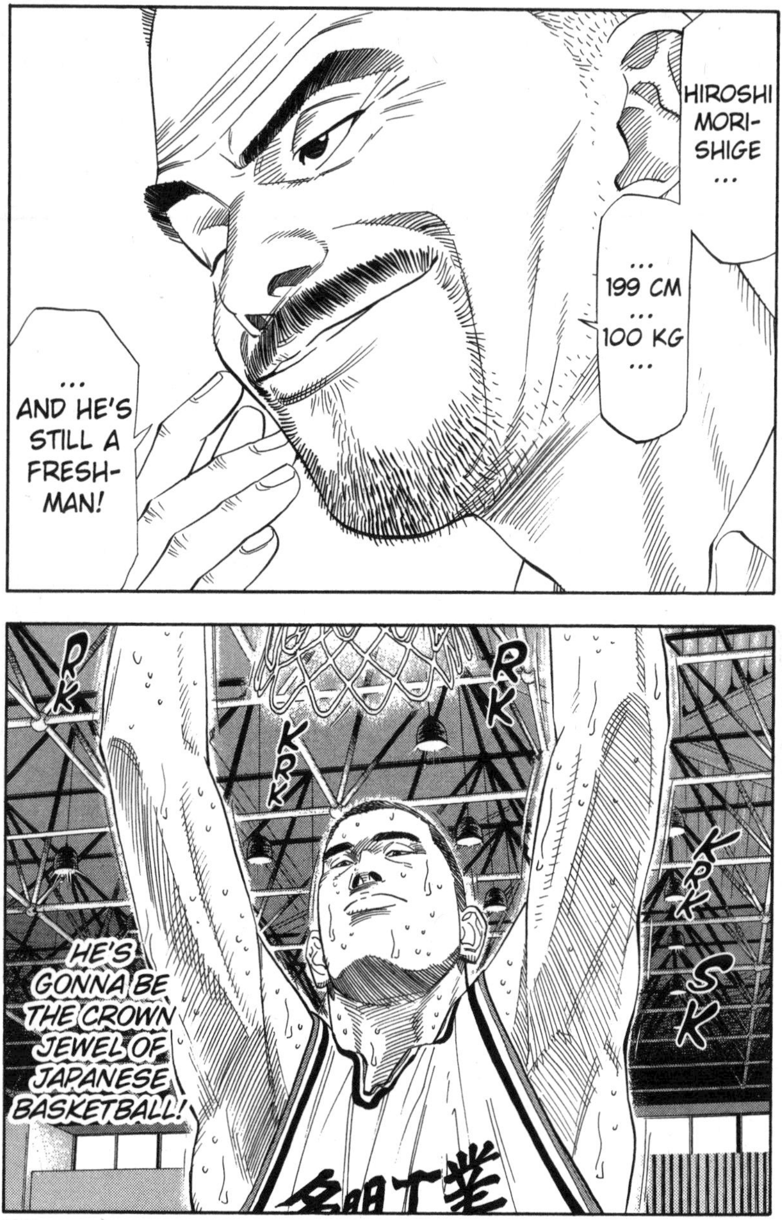
HIROSHI MORI-SHIGE ...
... 199 CM ... 100 KG ...
... AND HE'S STILL A FRESH-MAN!
RK
RK
KRK
KRK
SK
HE'S GONNA BE THE CROWN JEWEL OF JAPANESE BASKETBALL!

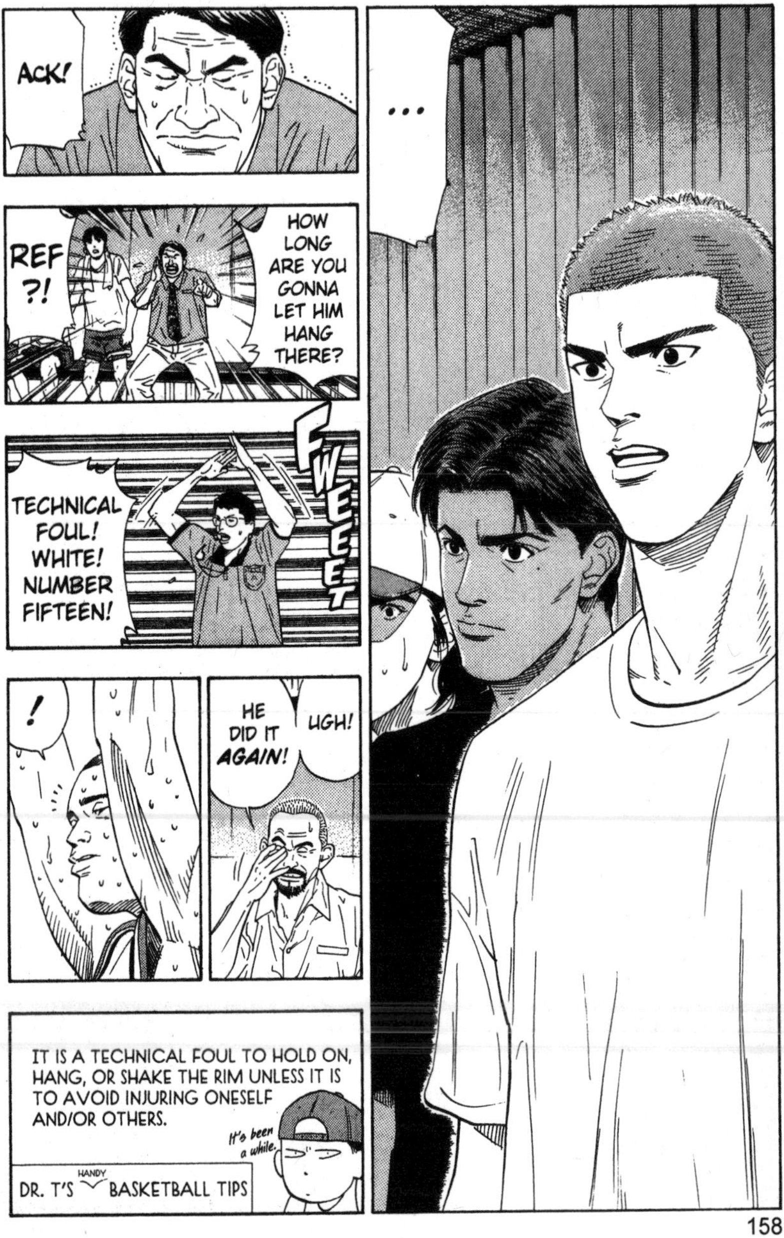
...
ACK!
HOW LONG ARE YOU GONNA LET HIM HANG THERE?
REF ?!
FWEEET
TECHNICAL FOUL! WHITE! NUMBER FIFTEEN!
UGH!
HE DID IT **AGAIN!**
!
IT IS A TECHNICAL FOUL TO HOLD ON, HANG, OR SHAKE THE RIM UNLESS IT IS TO AVOID INJURING ONESELF AND/OR OTHERS.
It's been a while.
DR. T'S HANDY BASKETBALL TIPS

READ THIS WAY

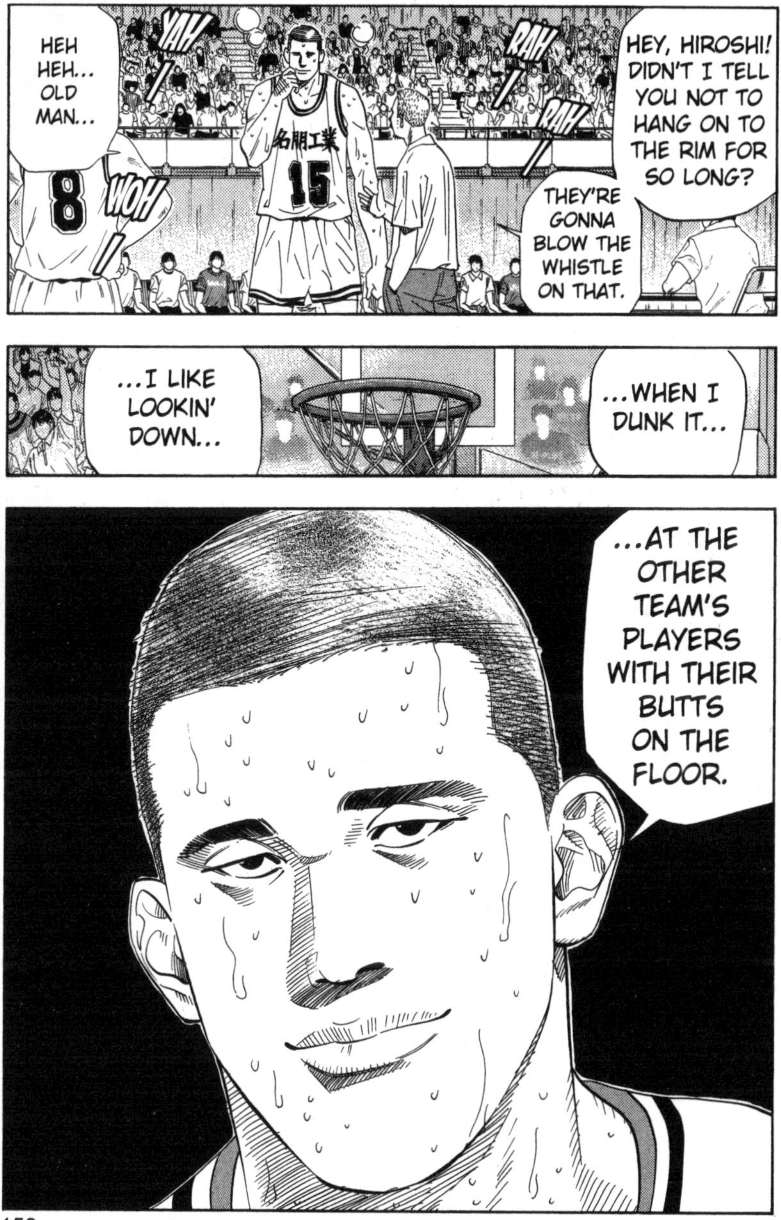
HEY, HIROSHI! DIDN'T I TELL YOU NOT TO HANG ON TO THE RIM FOR SO LONG?
RAH RAH
THEY'RE GONNA BLOW THE WHISTLE ON THAT.
YAH
WOH
HEH HEH... OLD MAN...
...WHEN I DUNK IT...
...I LIKE LOOKIN' DOWN...
...AT THE OTHER TEAM'S PLAYERS WITH THEIR BUTTS ON THE FLOOR.

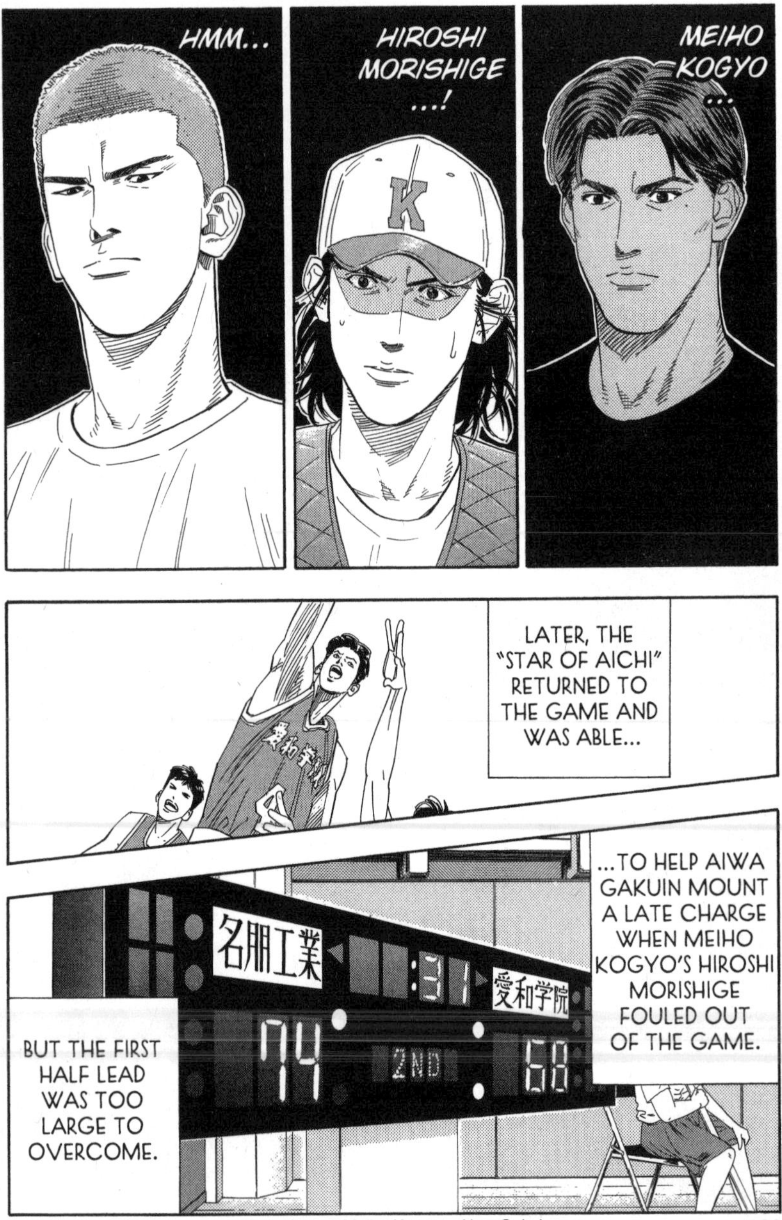
MEIHO KOGYO ...
HIROSHI MORISHIGE ...!
HMM...
LATER, THE "STAR OF AICHI" RETURNED TO THE GAME AND WAS ABLE...
...TO HELP AIWA GAKUIN MOUNT A LATE CHARGE WHEN MEIHO KOGYO'S HIROSHI MORISHIGE FOULED OUT OF THE GAME.
名朋工業
愛和学院
74
2ND
BUT THE FIRST HALF LEAD WAS TOO LARGE TO OVERCOME.

Scoreboard: Meiho Kogyo Aiwa Gakuin

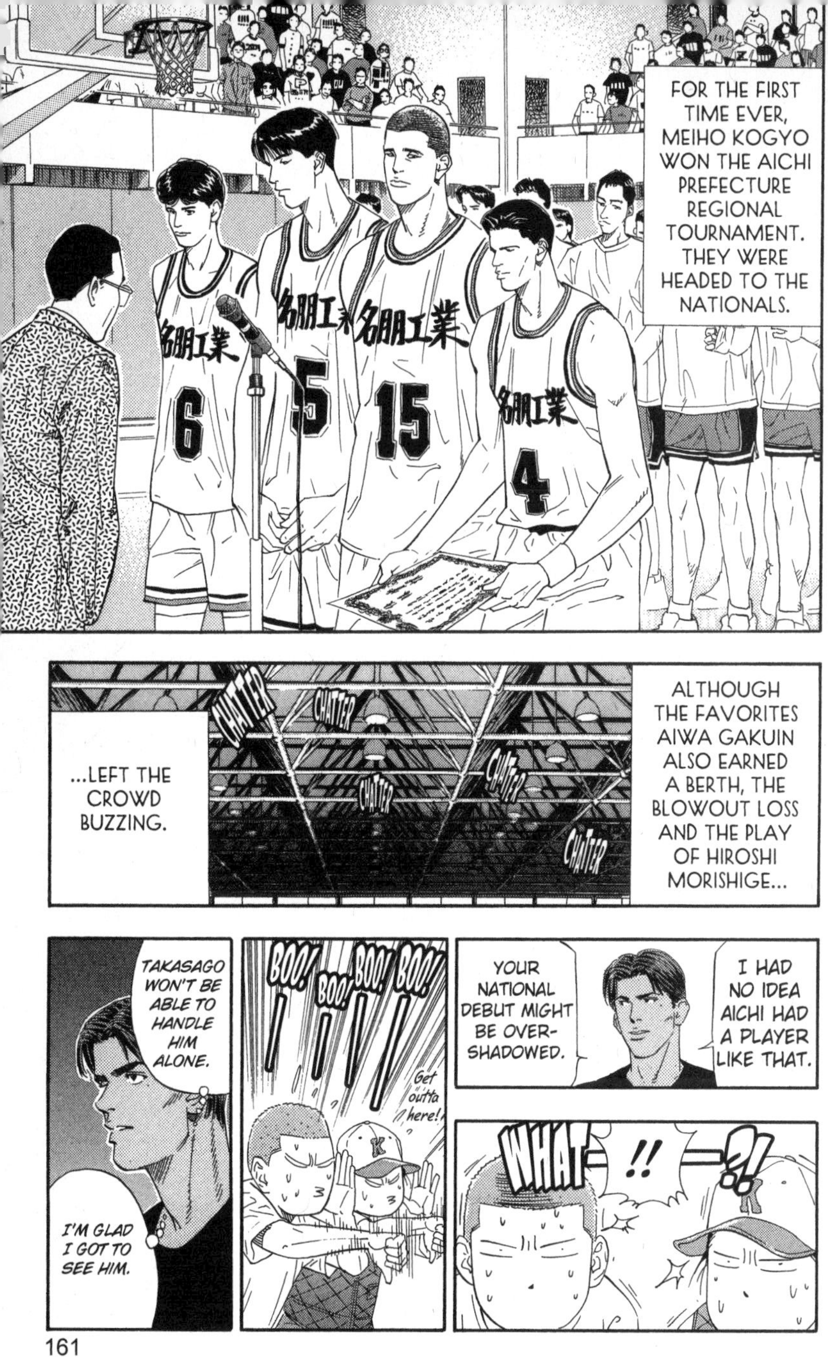
FOR THE FIRST TIME EVER, MEIHO KOGYO WON THE AICHI PREFECTURE REGIONAL TOURNAMENT. THEY WERE HEADED TO THE NATIONALS.
ALTHOUGH THE FAVORITES AIWA GAKUIN ALSO EARNED A BERTH, THE BLOWOUT LOSS AND THE PLAY OF HIROSHI MORISHIGE...
CHATTER
CHATTER
CHATTER
CHATTER
CHATTER
...LEFT THE CROWD BUZZING.
I HAD NO IDEA AICHI HAD A PLAYER LIKE THAT.
YOUR NATIONAL DEBUT MIGHT BE OVER-SHADOWED.
WHAT— !!
—?!
BOO! BOO! BOO! BOO!
Get outta here!
TAKASAGO WON'T BE ABLE TO HANDLE HIM ALONE.
I'M GLAD I GOT TO SEE HIM.

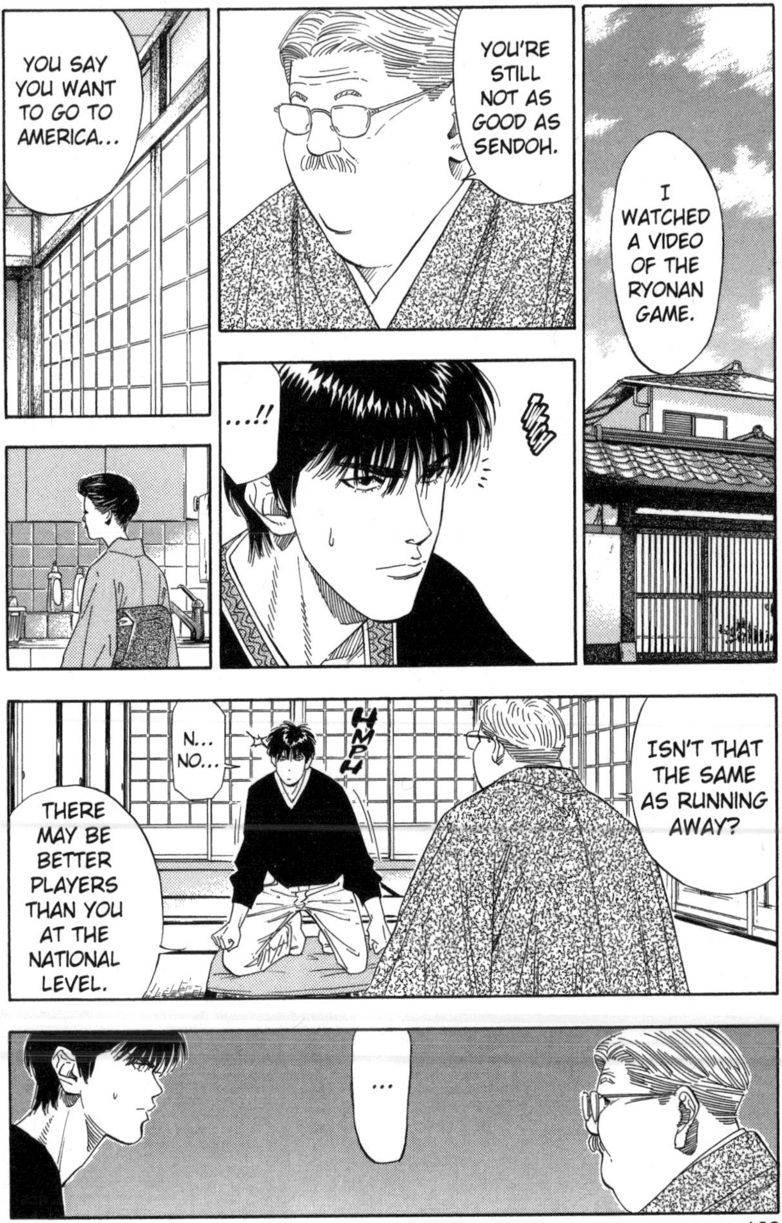
I WATCHED A VIDEO OF THE RYONAN GAME.
YOU'RE STILL NOT AS GOOD AS SENDOH.
...!!
YOU SAY YOU WANT TO GO TO AMERICA...
ISN'T THAT THE SAME AS RUNNING AWAY?
HMPH
N... NO...
THERE MAY BE BETTER PLAYERS THAN YOU AT THE NATIONAL LEVEL.
...

READ THIS WAY

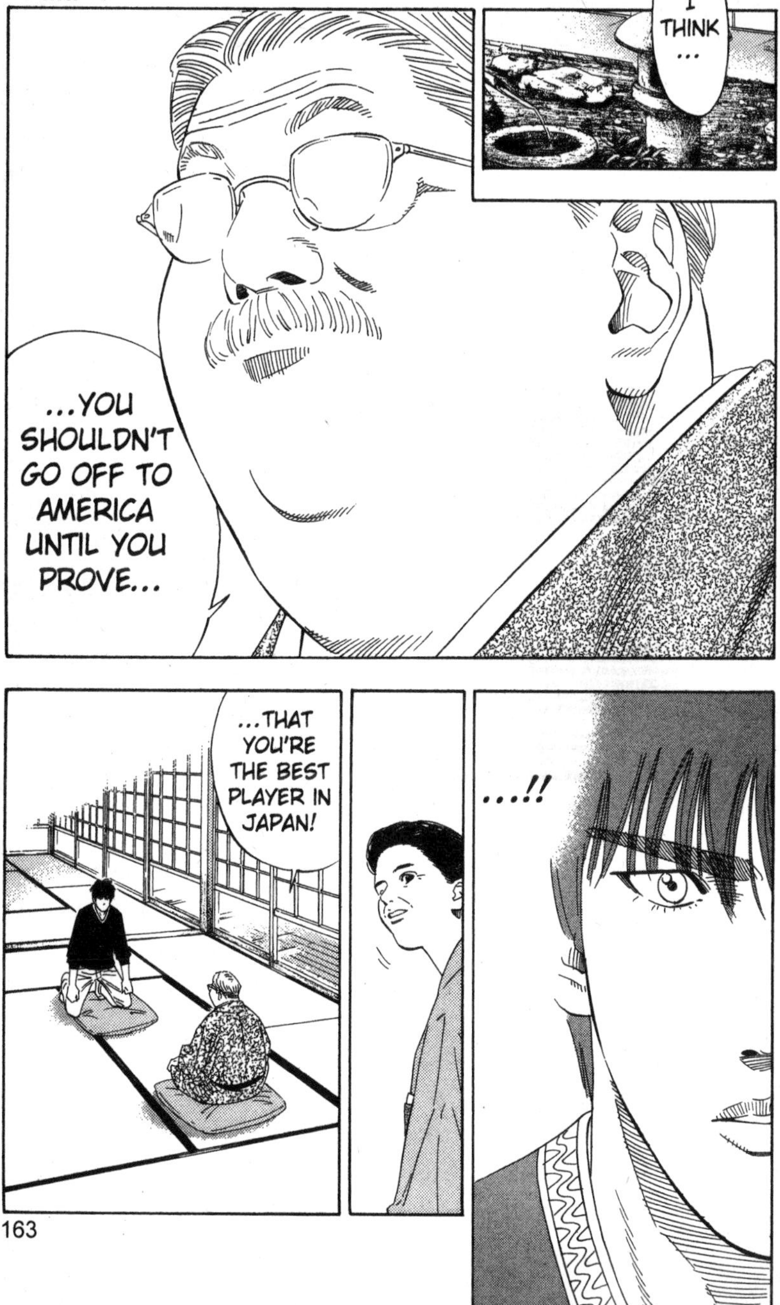
I THINK...
...YOU SHOULDN'T GO OFF TO AMERICA UNTIL YOU PROVE...
...!!
...THAT YOU'RE THE BEST PLAYER IN JAPAN!

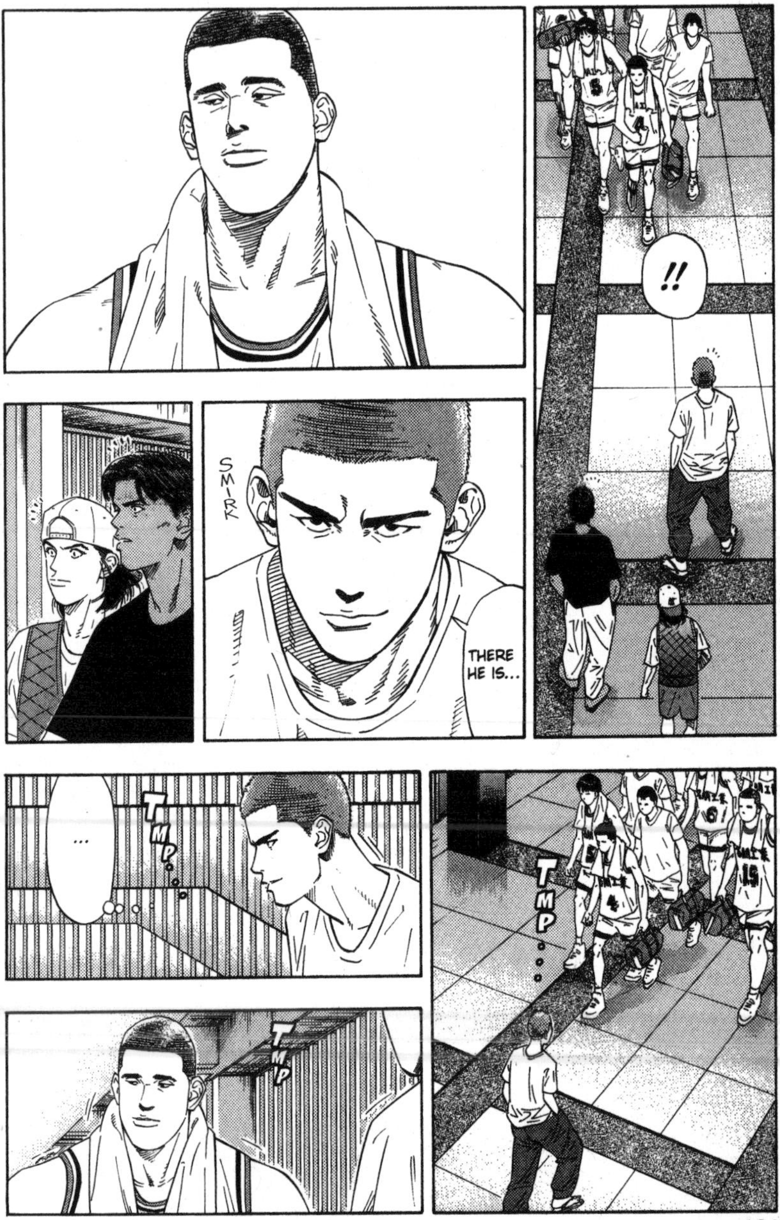
!!
SMIRK
THERE HE IS...
TMP...
...
TMP...
TMP

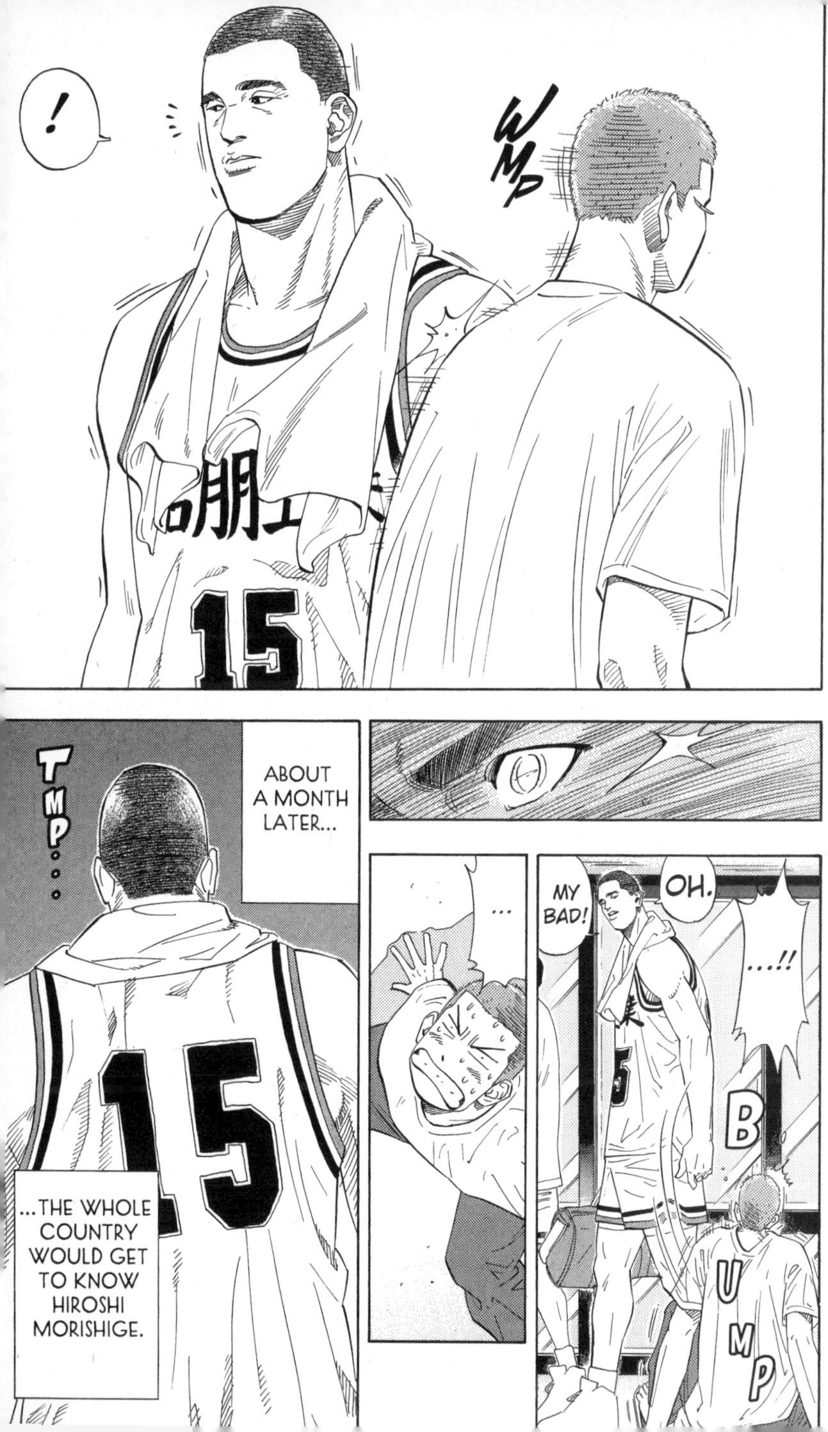

WMP
!
OH.
MY BAD!
...!!
BUMP
...
TMP...
ABOUT A MONTH LATER...
...THE WHOLE COUNTRY WOULD GET TO KNOW HIROSHI MORISHIGE.

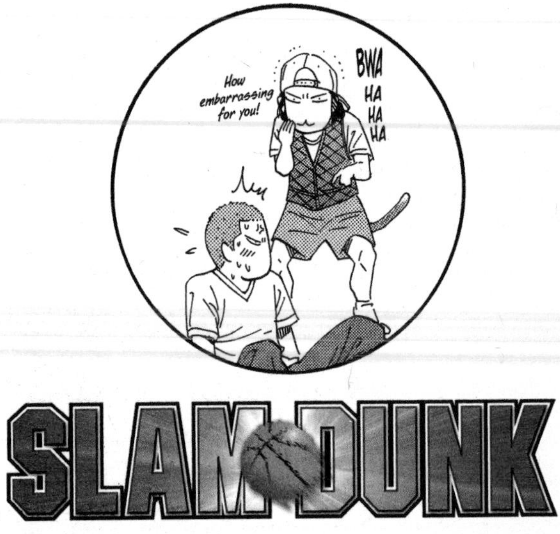
How embarrassing for you!
BWA HA HA HA

#188
HIKOICHI RETURNS TO OSAKA

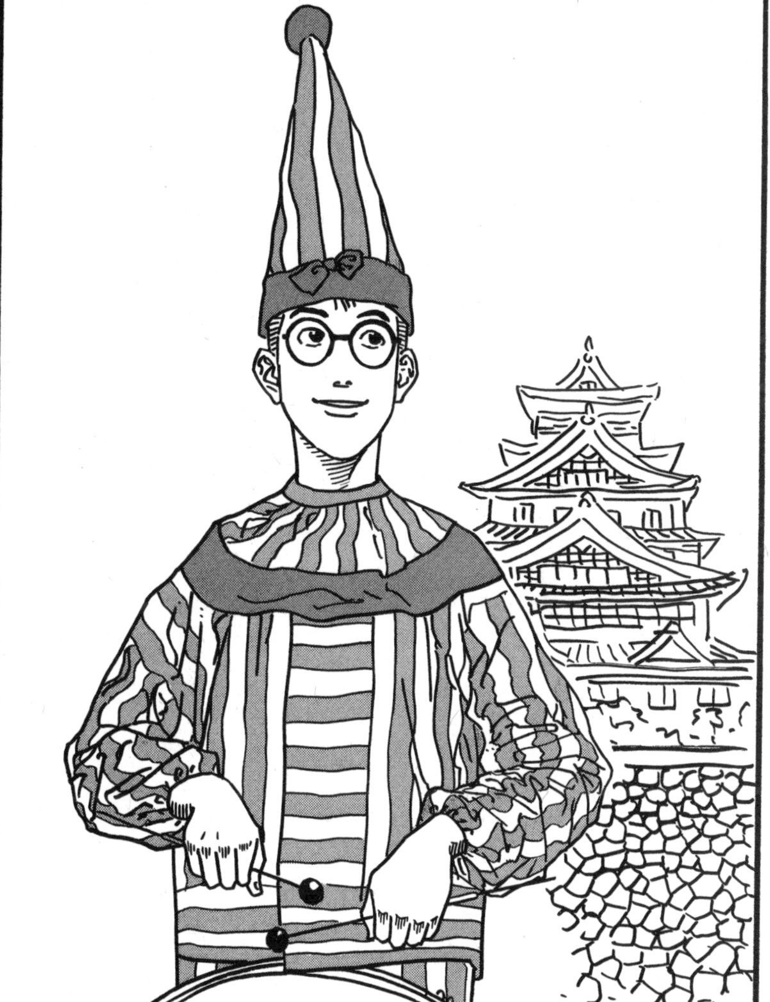

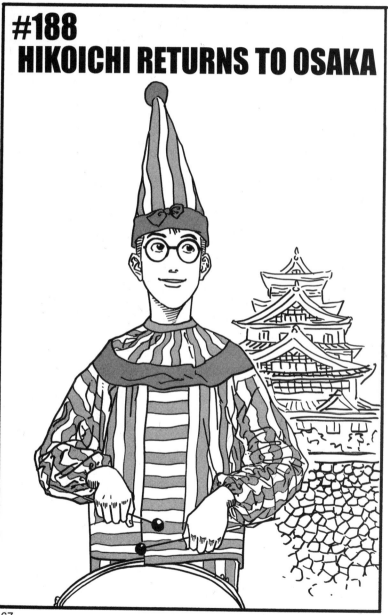

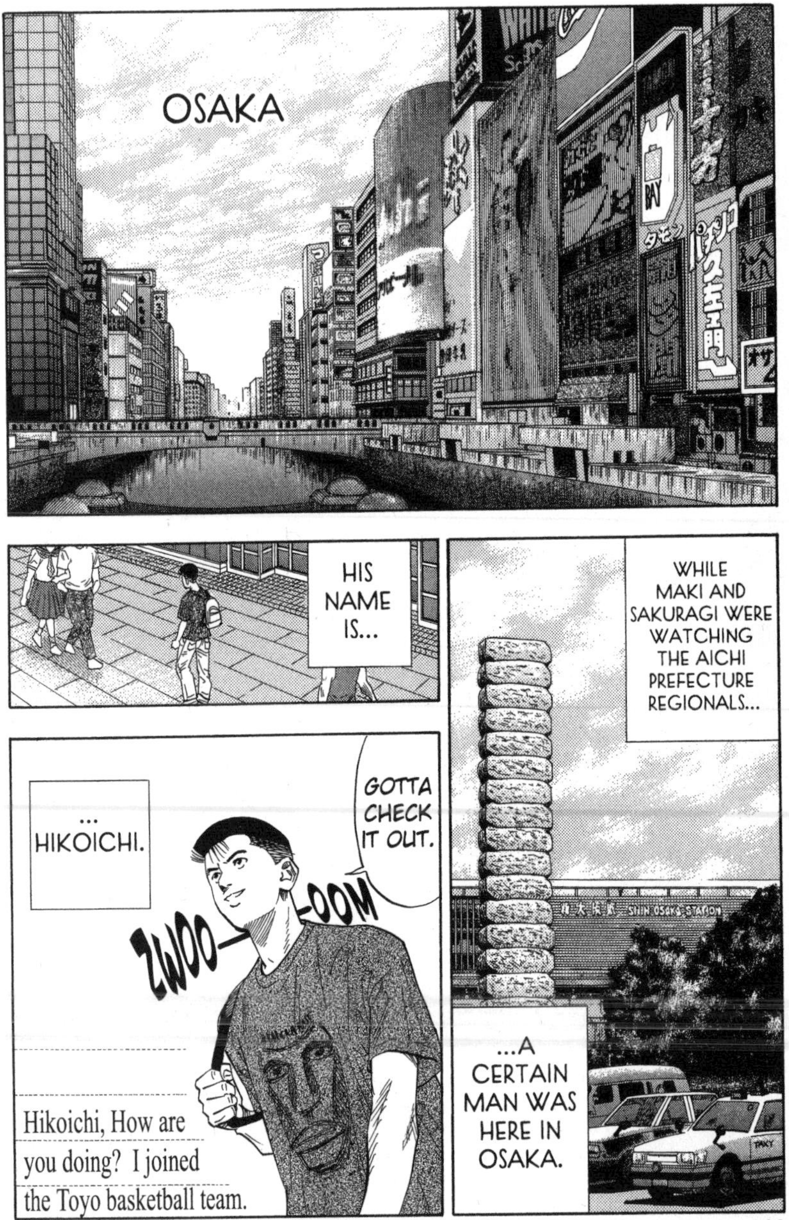
OSAKA
WHILE MAKI AND SAKURAGI WERE WATCHING THE AICHI PREFECTURE REGIONALS...
SHIN OSAKA STATION
...A CERTAIN MAN WAS HERE IN OSAKA.
HIS NAME IS...
GOTTA CHECK IT OUT.
... HIKOICHI.
ZWOO—OOM
Hikoichi, How are you doing? I joined the Toyo basketball team.

READ THIS WAY

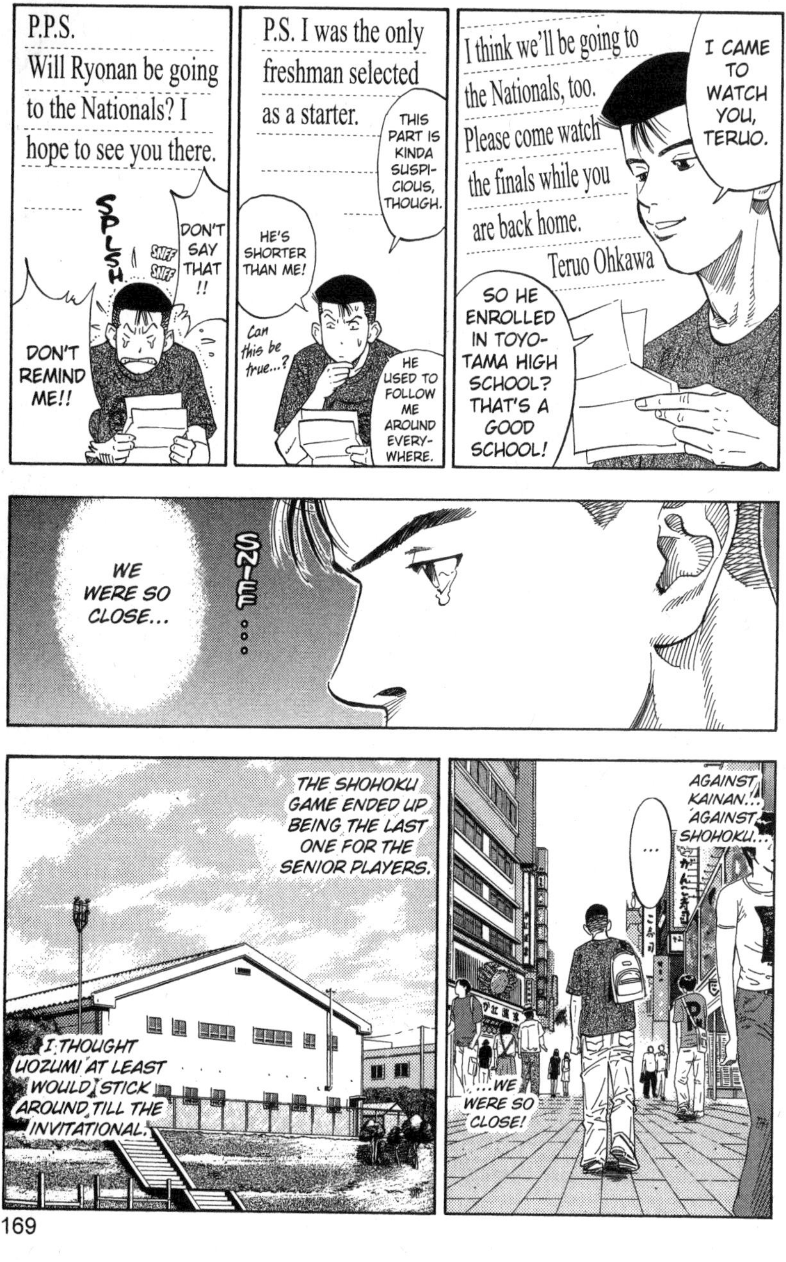
I CAME TO WATCH YOU, TERUO.
I think we'll be going to the Nationals, too. Please come watch the finals while you are back home.
Teruo Ohkawa
SO HE ENROLLED IN TOYOTAMA HIGH SCHOOL? THAT'S A GOOD SCHOOL!
P.S. I was the only freshman selected as a starter.
THIS PART IS KINDA SUSPICIOUS, THOUGH.
HE'S SHORTER THAN ME!
Can this be true...?
HE USED TO FOLLOW ME AROUND EVERYWHERE.
P.P.S. Will Ryonan be going to the Nationals? I hope to see you there.
DON'T SAY THAT!!
SNFF SNFF
SPLSH
DON'T REMIND ME!!
SNIFF...
WE WERE SO CLOSE...
AGAINST KAINAN... AGAINST SHOHOKU...
...
...WE WERE SO CLOSE!
THE SHOHOKU GAME ENDED UP BEING THE LAST ONE FOR THE SENIOR PLAYERS.
I THOUGHT UOZUMI AT LEAST WOULD STICK AROUND TILL THE INVITATIONAL.

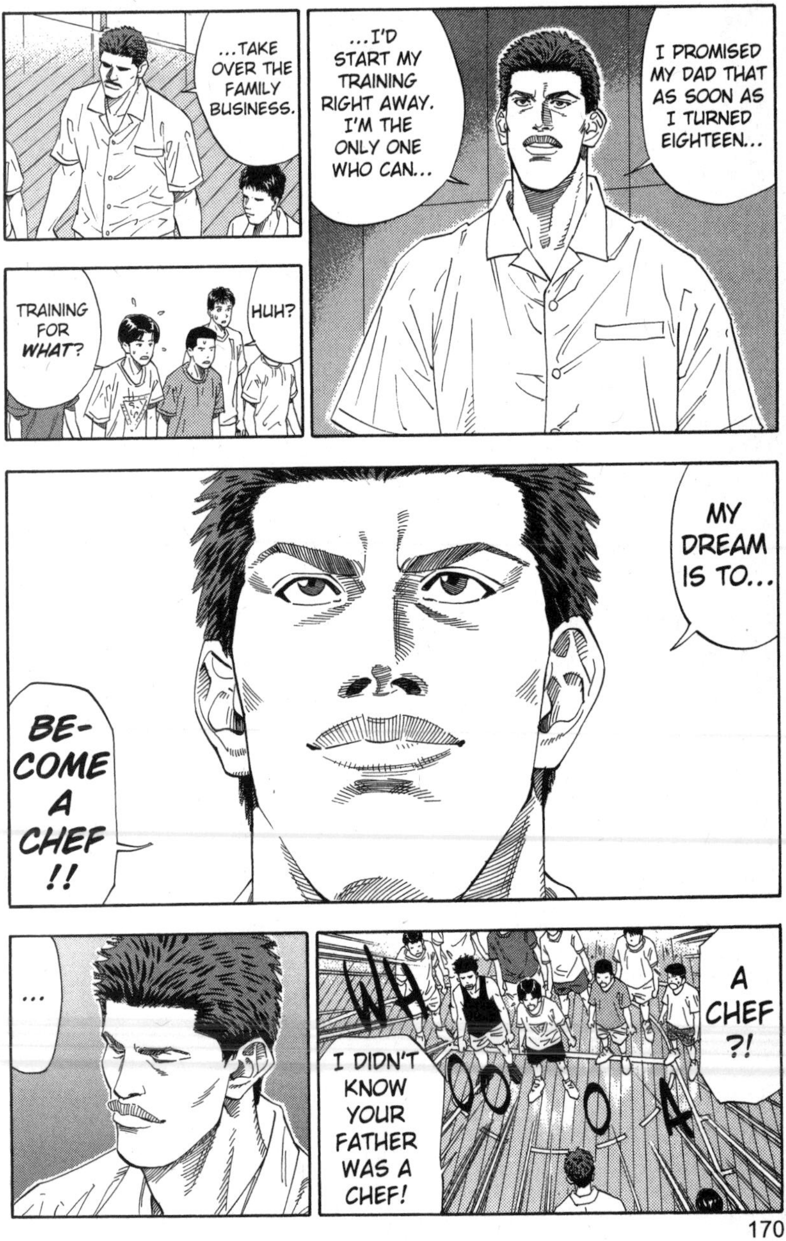
I PROMISED MY DAD THAT AS SOON AS I TURNED EIGHTEEN...
...I'D START MY TRAINING RIGHT AWAY. I'M THE ONLY ONE WHO CAN...
...TAKE OVER THE FAMILY BUSINESS.
HUH?
TRAINING FOR *WHAT?*
MY DREAM IS TO...
BE-COME A CHEF!!
A CHEF?!
WHOOOA
I DIDN'T KNOW YOUR FATHER WAS A CHEF!
...

READ THIS WAY

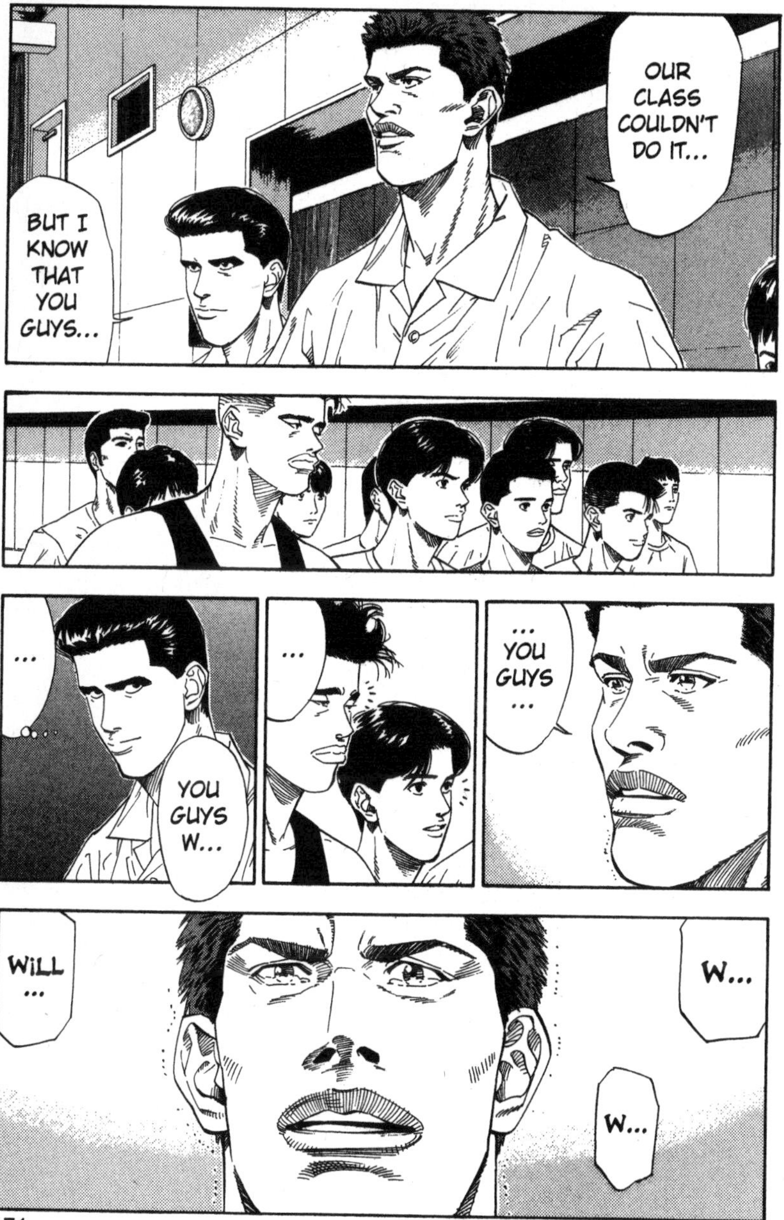

OUR CLASS COULDN'T DO IT...
BUT I KNOW THAT YOU GUYS...
... YOU GUYS ...
...
...
YOU GUYS W...
W...
W...
WILL ...

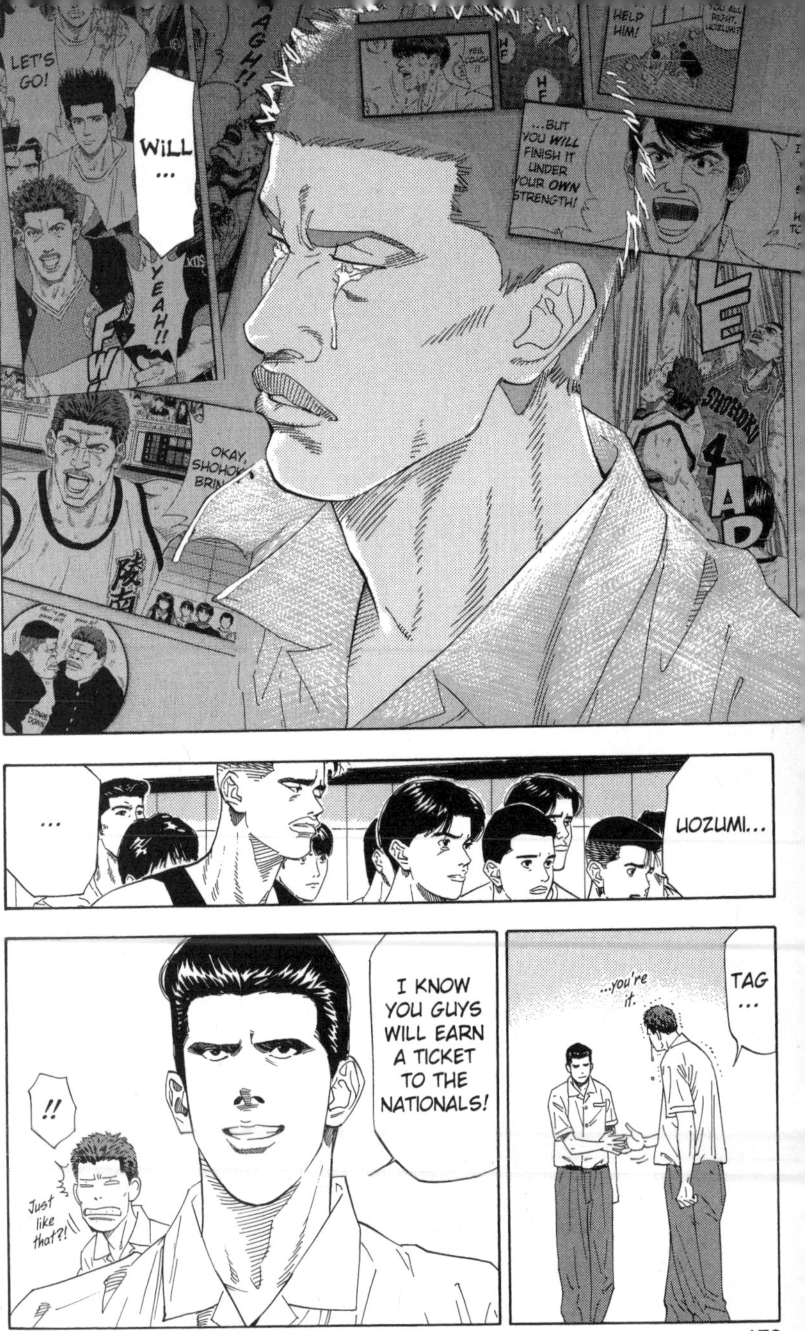
YOU ALL RIGHT, UOZUMI?
HELP HIM!
...BUT YOU WILL FINISH IT UNDER YOUR OWN STRENGTH!
AGH!!
WILL ...
YEAH!!
LET'S GO!
UOZUMI...
...
TAG ...
...you're it.
I KNOW YOU GUYS WILL EARN A TICKET TO THE NATIONALS!
!!
Just like that?!

READ THIS WAY

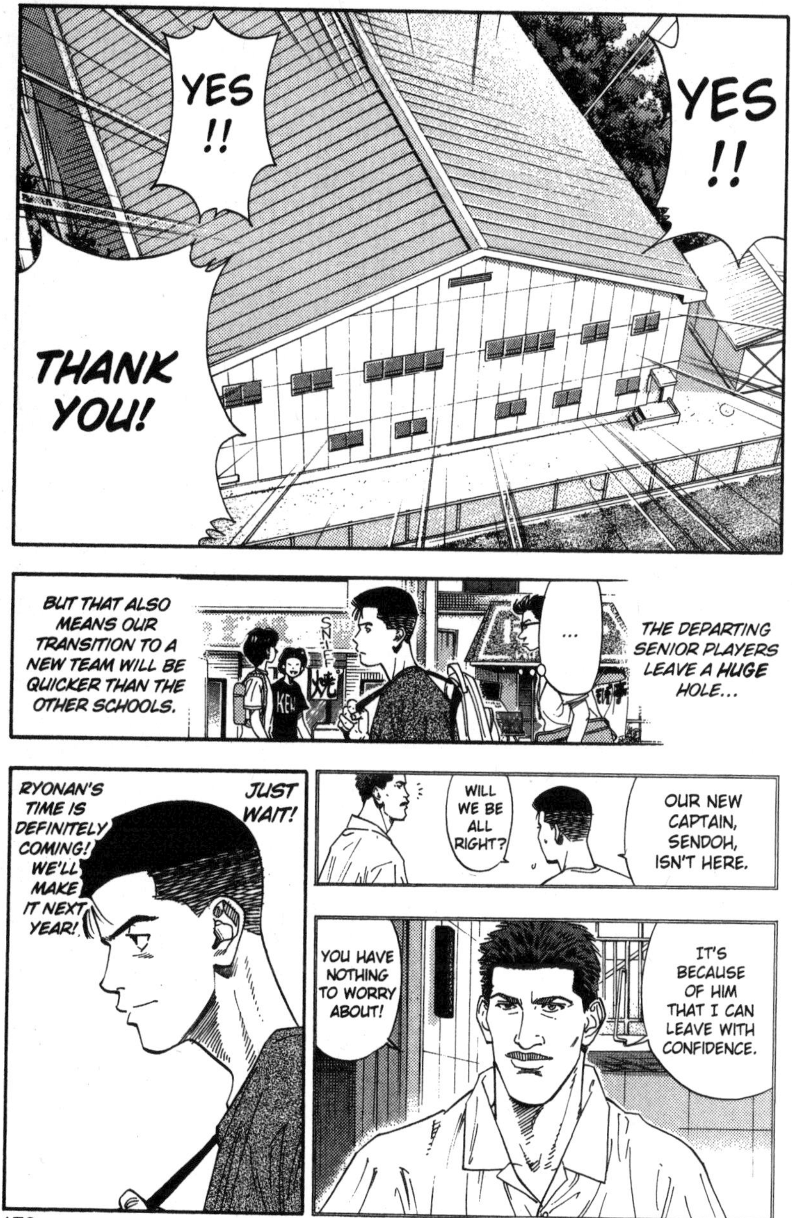
YES !!
YES !!
THANK YOU!
THE DEPARTING SENIOR PLAYERS LEAVE A HUGE HOLE...
...
BUT THAT ALSO MEANS OUR TRANSITION TO A NEW TEAM WILL BE QUICKER THAN THE OTHER SCHOOLS.
OUR NEW CAPTAIN, SENDOH, ISN'T HERE.
WILL WE BE ALL RIGHT?
IT'S BECAUSE OF HIM THAT I CAN LEAVE WITH CONFIDENCE.
YOU HAVE NOTHING TO WORRY ABOUT!
JUST WAIT!
RYONAN'S TIME IS DEFINITELY COMING! WE'LL MAKE IT NEXT YEAR!

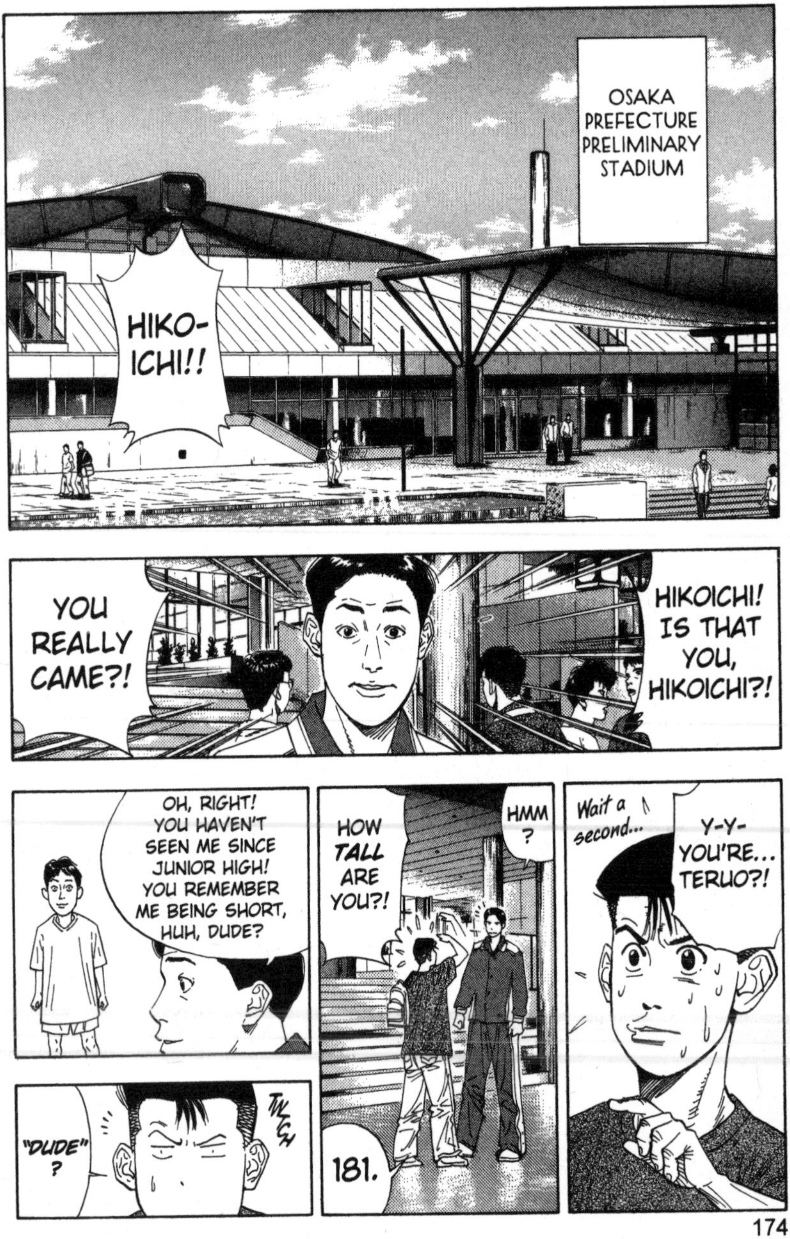
OSAKA PREFECTURE PRELIMINARY STADIUM
HIKO-ICHI!!
HIKOICHI! IS THAT YOU, HIKOICHI?!
YOU REALLY CAME?!
Y-Y-YOU'RE... TERUO?!
Wait a second...
HMM?
HOW TALL ARE YOU?!
181.
OH, RIGHT! YOU HAVEN'T SEEN ME SINCE JUNIOR HIGH! YOU REMEMBER ME BEING SHORT, HUH, DUDE?
TWITCH
"DUDE"?

READ THIS WAY

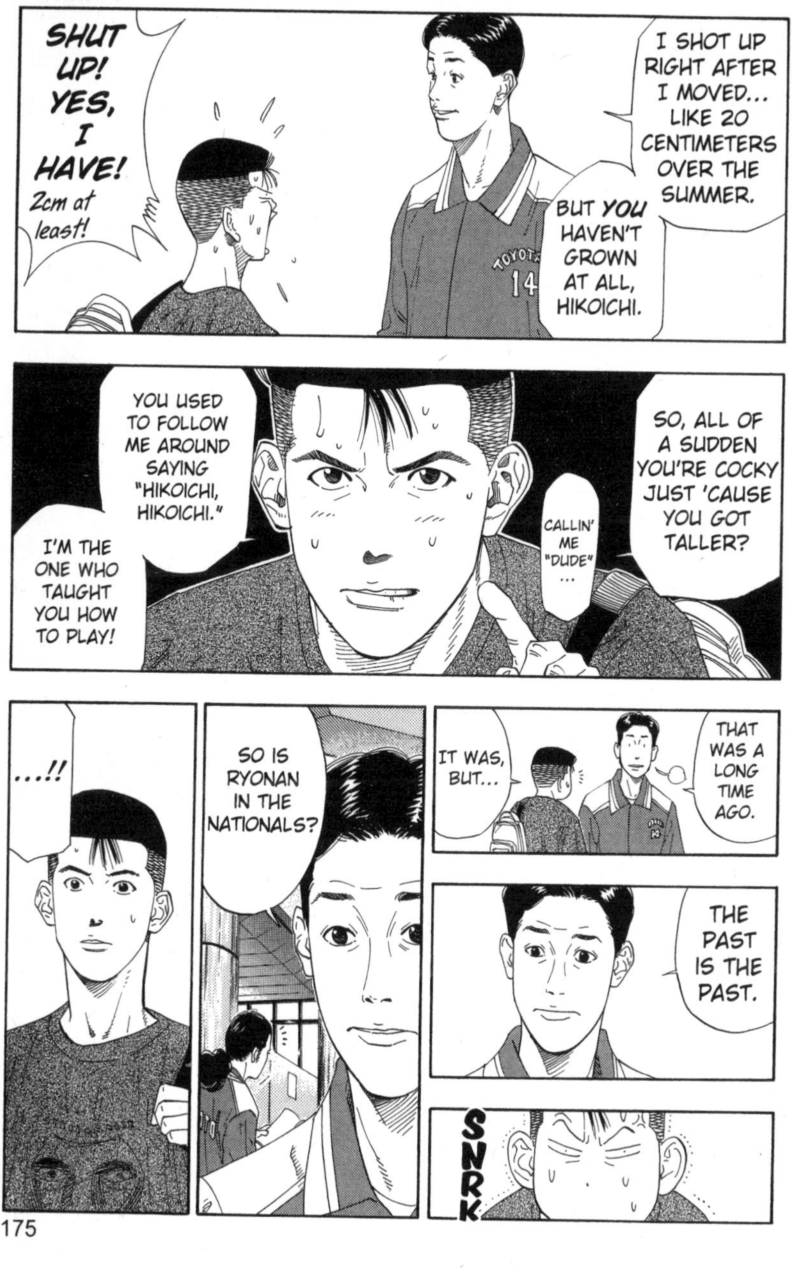

I SHOT UP RIGHT AFTER I MOVED... LIKE 20 CENTIMETERS OVER THE SUMMER.
BUT YOU HAVEN'T GROWN AT ALL, HIKOICHI.
SHUT UP! YES, I HAVE! 2cm at least!
SO, ALL OF A SUDDEN YOU'RE COCKY JUST 'CAUSE YOU GOT TALLER?
CALLIN' ME "DUDE"...
YOU USED TO FOLLOW ME AROUND SAYING "HIKOICHI, HIKOICHI."
I'M THE ONE WHO TAUGHT YOU HOW TO PLAY!
THAT WAS A LONG TIME AGO.
IT WAS, BUT...
THE PAST IS THE PAST.
SNRK
SO IS RYONAN IN THE NATIONALS?
...!!

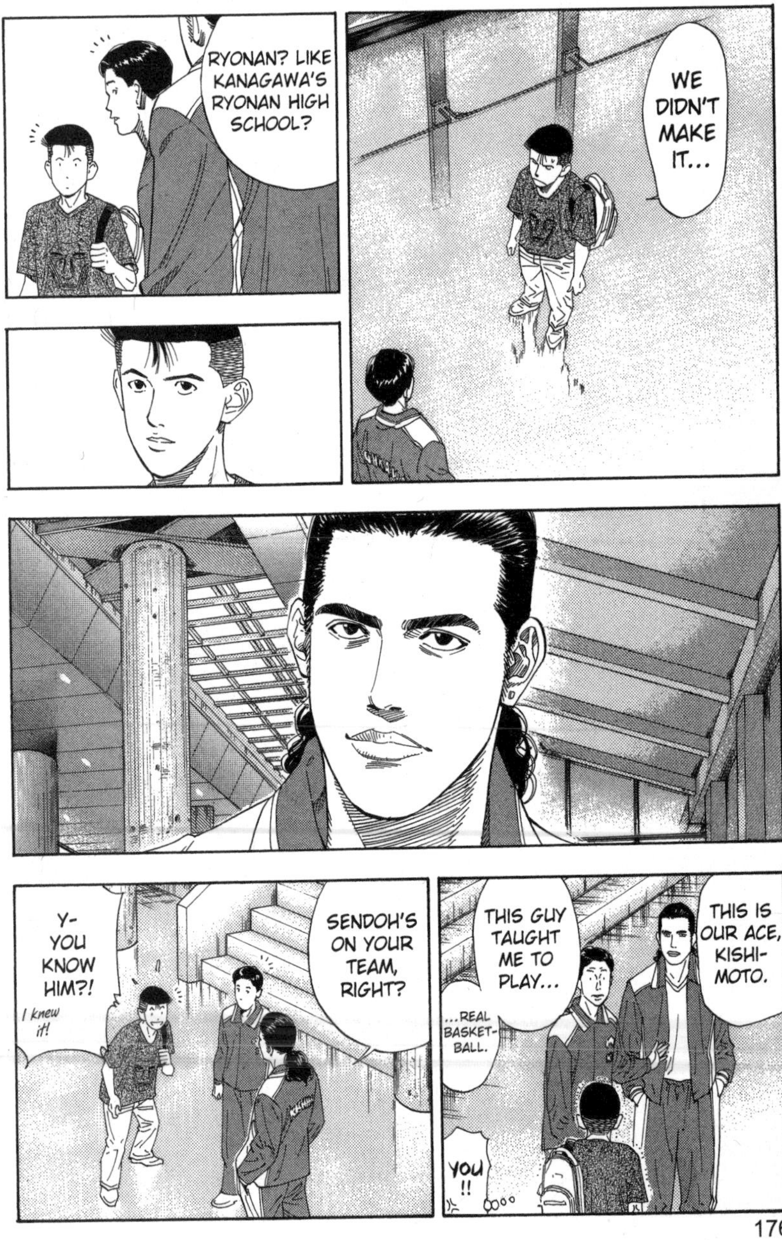
WE DIDN'T MAKE IT...
RYONAN? LIKE KANAGAWA'S RYONAN HIGH SCHOOL?
THIS IS OUR ACE, KISHI-MOTO.
THIS GUY TAUGHT ME TO PLAY...
...REAL BASKET-BALL.
YOU !!
SENDOH'S ON YOUR TEAM, RIGHT?
Y-YOU KNOW HIM?!
I knew it!

READ THIS WAY

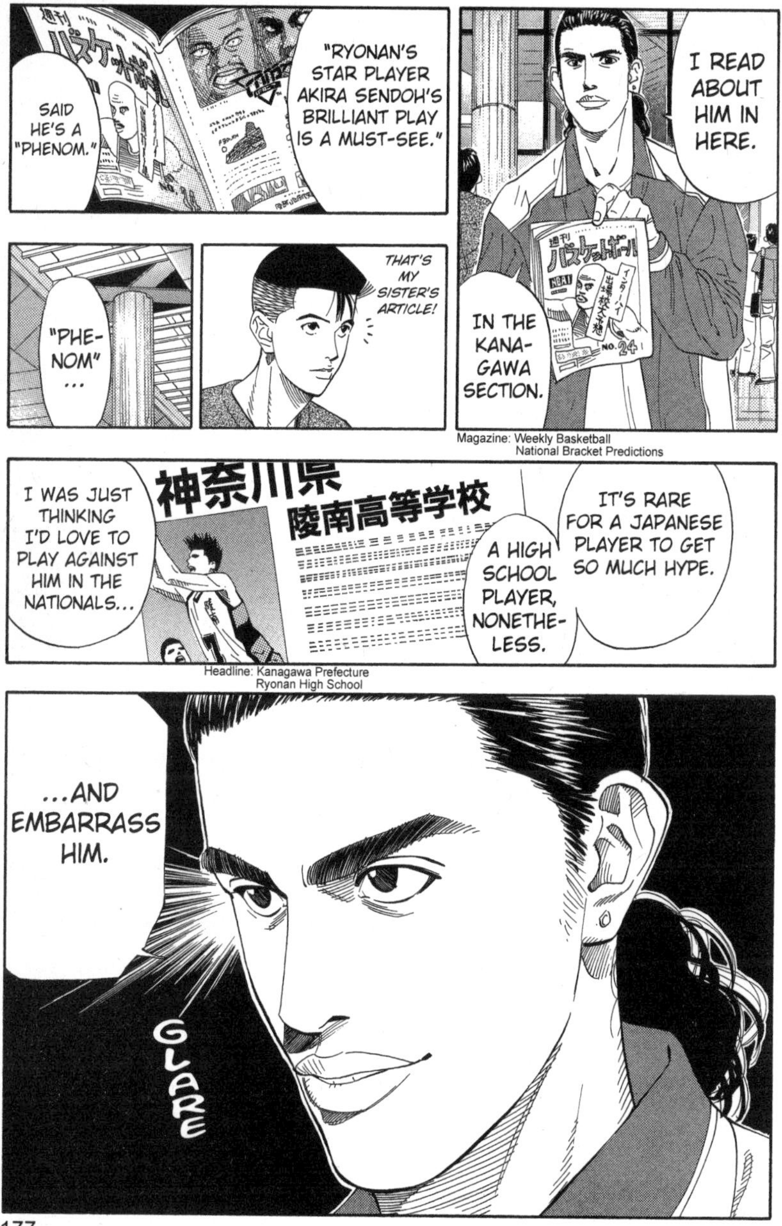
I READ ABOUT HIM IN HERE.
IN THE KANAGAWA SECTION.
Magazine: Weekly Basketball
National Bracket Predictions
"RYONAN'S STAR PLAYER AKIRA SENDOH'S BRILLIANT PLAY IS A MUST-SEE."
SAID HE'S A "PHENOM."
THAT'S MY SISTER'S ARTICLE!
"PHE-NOM" ...
IT'S RARE FOR A JAPANESE PLAYER TO GET SO MUCH HYPE.
A HIGH SCHOOL PLAYER, NONETHE-LESS.
神奈川県
陵南高等学校
I WAS JUST THINKING I'D LOVE TO PLAY AGAINST HIM IN THE NATIONALS...
Headline: Kanagawa Prefecture
Ryonan High School
...AND EMBARRASS HIM.
GLARE

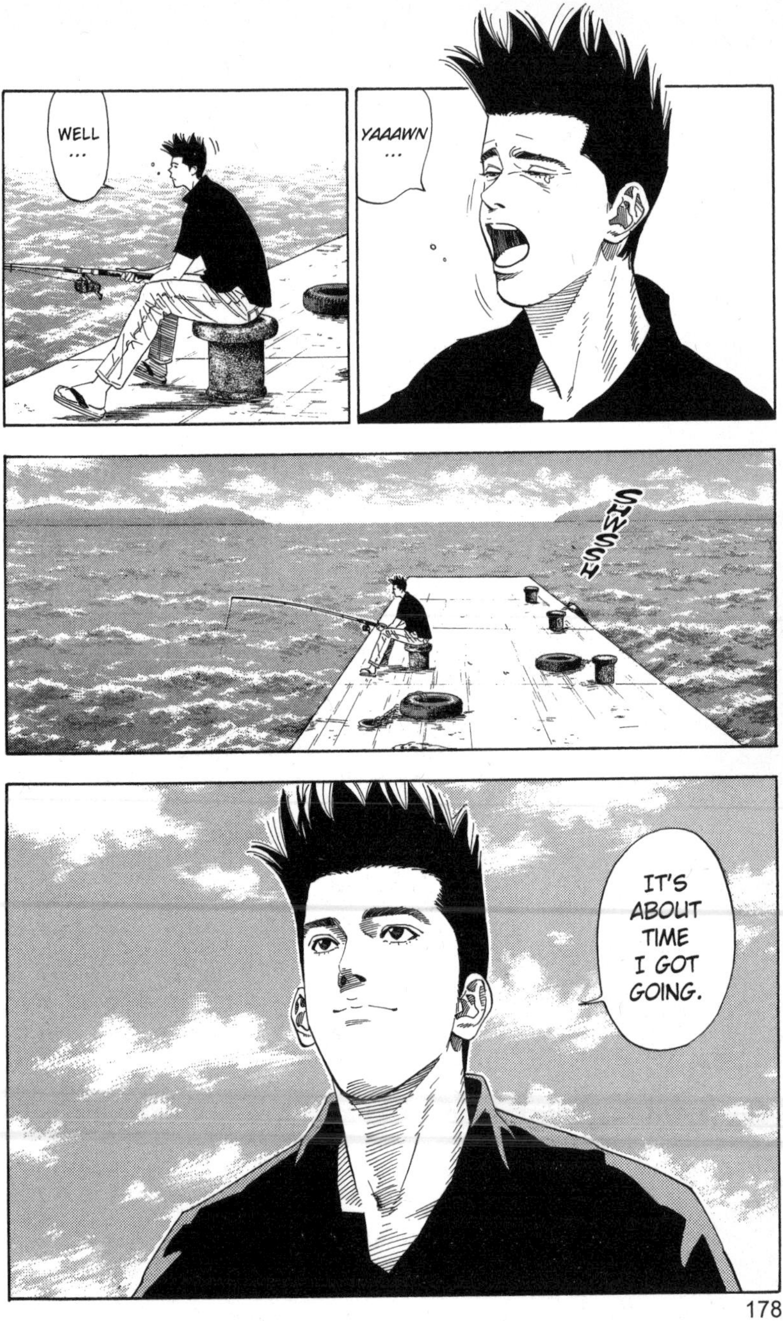
YAAAWN ...
WELL ...
SHWSSSH
IT'S ABOUT TIME I GOT GOING.

READ THIS WAY

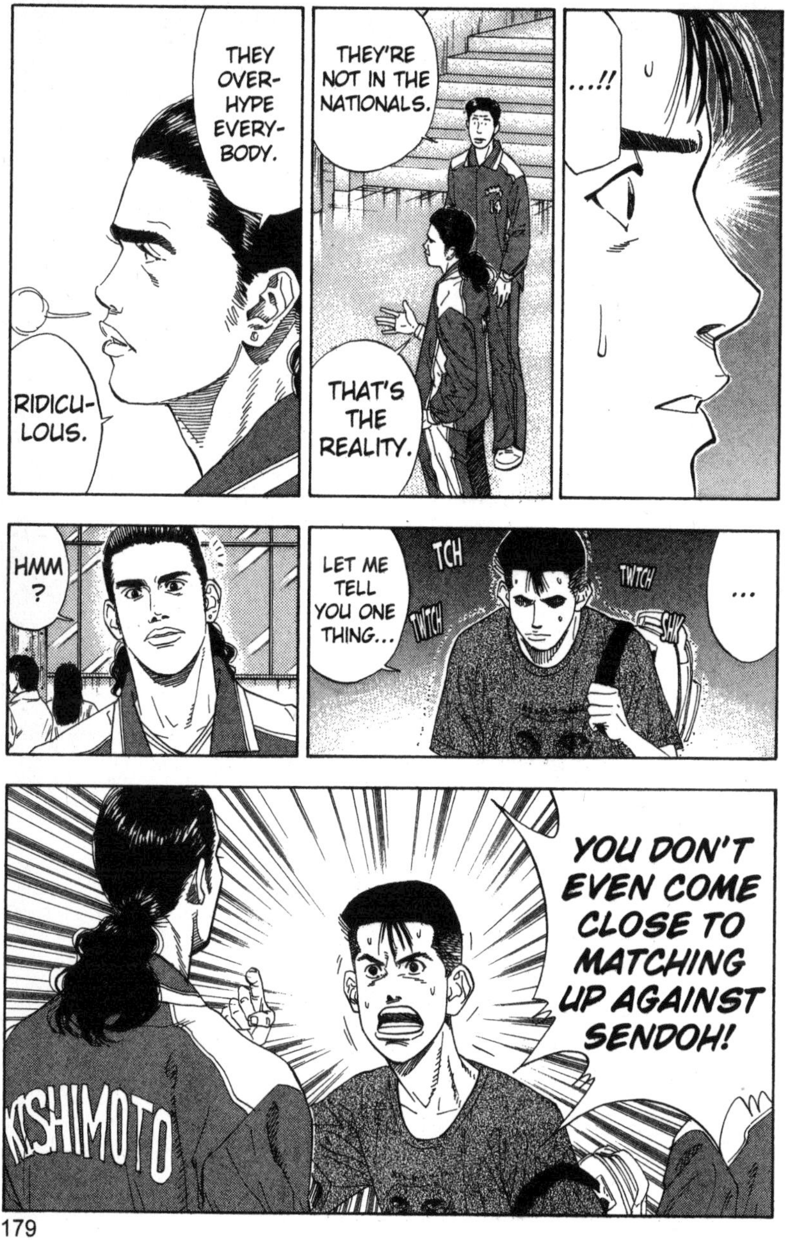

...!!
THEY'RE NOT IN THE NATIONALS.
THAT'S THE REALITY.
THEY OVER-HYPE EVERY-BODY.
RIDICU-LOUS.
...
TWTCH
SHK
TCH
TWTCH
LET ME TELL YOU ONE THING...
HMM?
YOU DON'T EVEN COME CLOSE TO MATCHING UP AGAINST SENDOH!
KISHIMOTO

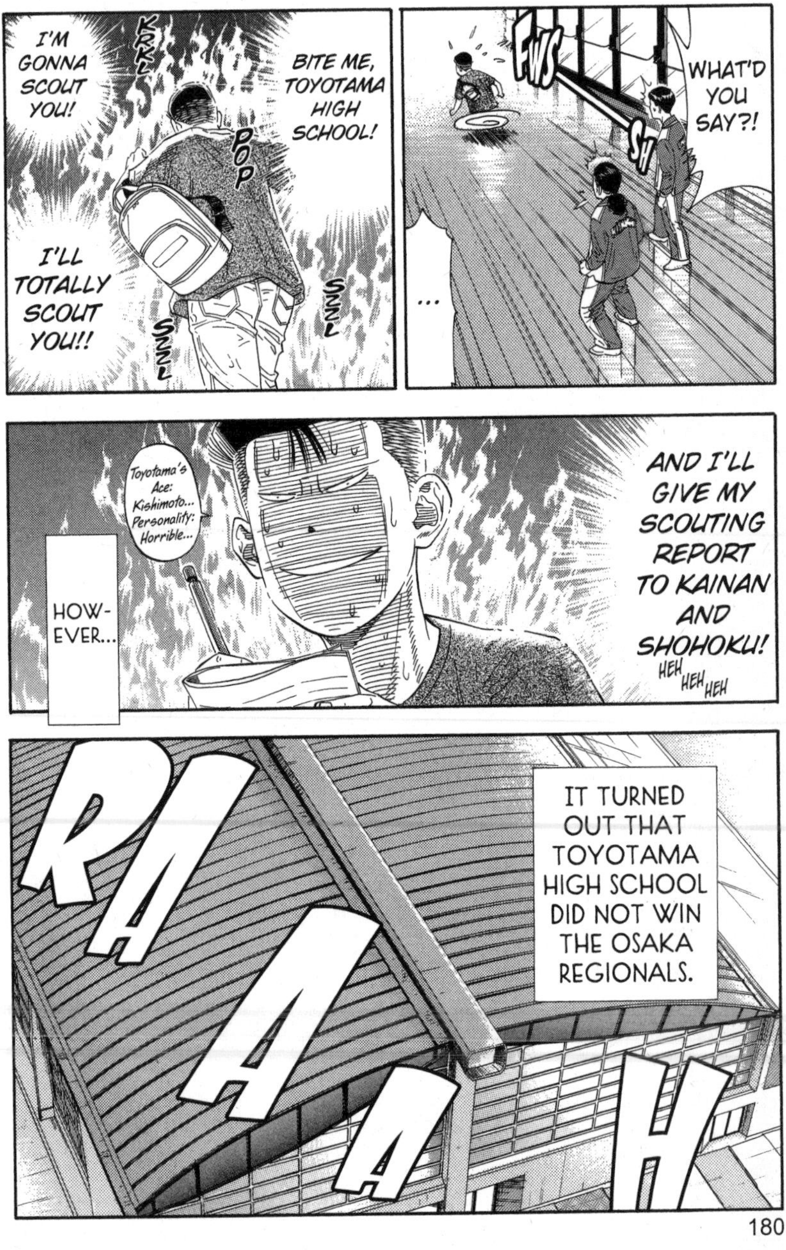
FWS
WHAT'D YOU SAY?!
SH
...
BITE ME, TOYOTAMA HIGH SCHOOL!
KRKL
I'M GONNA SCOUT YOU!
POP
SZZL
I'LL TOTALLY SCOUT YOU!!
SZZL
AND I'LL GIVE MY SCOUTING REPORT TO KAINAN AND SHOHOKU!
HEH HEH HEH
Toyotama's Ace: Kishimoto... Personality: Horrible...
HOW-EVER...
IT TURNED OUT THAT TOYOTAMA HIGH SCHOOL DID NOT WIN THE OSAKA REGIONALS.
RAAAAH

READ THIS WAY

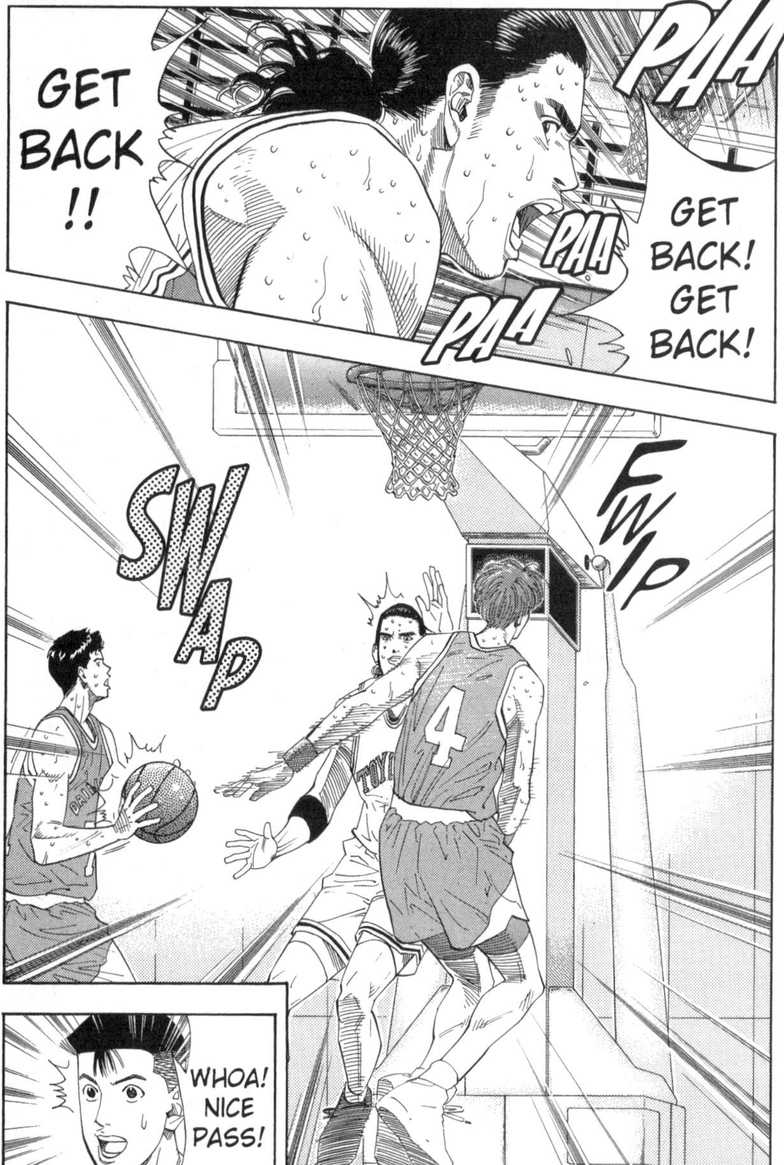

PAA
GET BACK! GET BACK!
PAA
PAA
GET BACK !!
FWIP
SWAP
WHOA! NICE PASS!

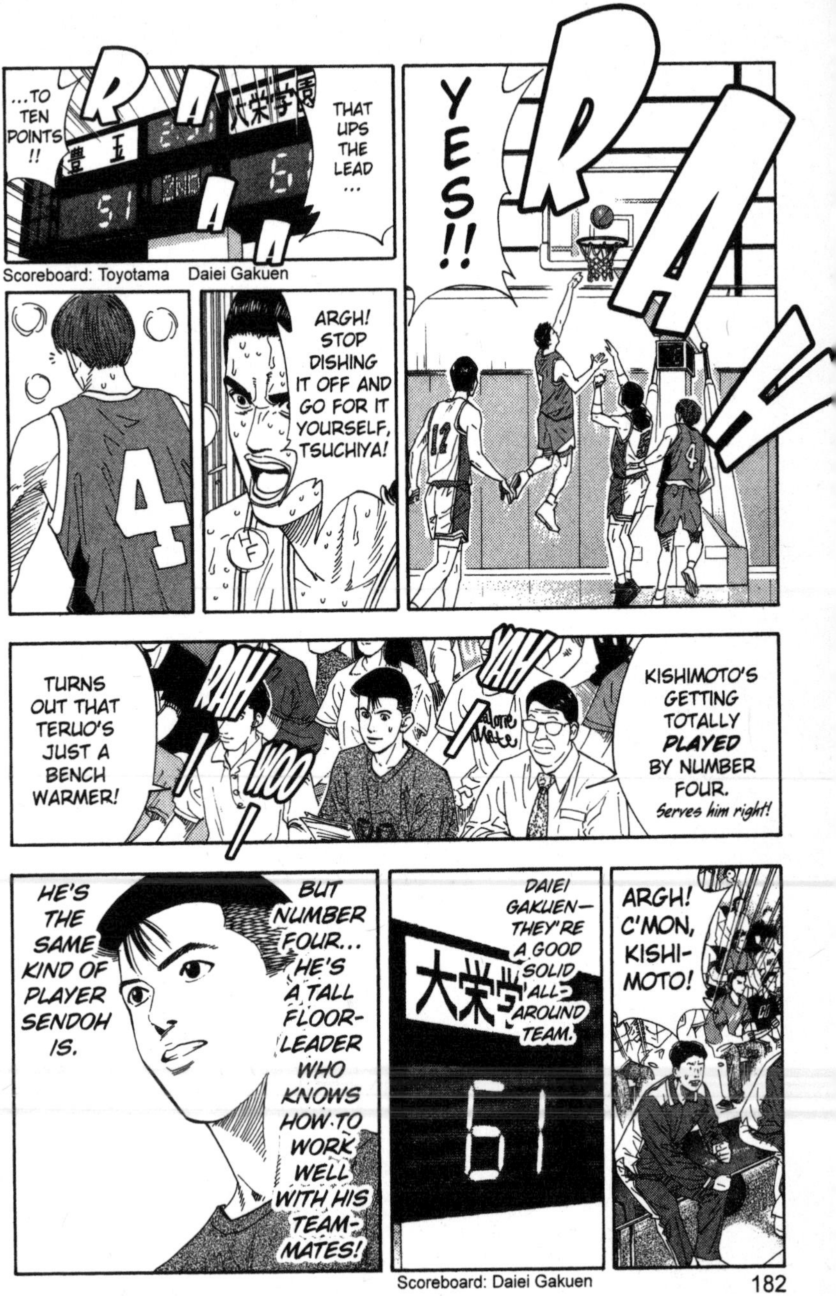
YES!!
RAAH
THAT UPS THE LEAD...
...TO TEN POINTS!!
RAAA
ARGH! STOP DISHING IT OFF AND GO FOR IT YOURSELF, TSUCHIYA!
KISHIMOTO'S GETTING TOTALLY ***PLAYED*** BY NUMBER FOUR.
Serves him right!
YAH
WOO
RAH
TURNS OUT THAT TERUO'S JUST A BENCH WARMER!
ARGH! C'MON, KISHI-MOTO!
DAIEI GAKUEN—THEY'RE A GOOD SOLID ALL-AROUND TEAM.
BUT NUMBER FOUR... HE'S A TALL FLOOR-LEADER WHO KNOWS HOW TO WORK WELL WITH HIS TEAM-MATES!
HE'S THE SAME KIND OF PLAYER SENDOH IS.

Scoreboard: Toyotama Daiei Gakuen

Scoreboard: Daiei Gakuen

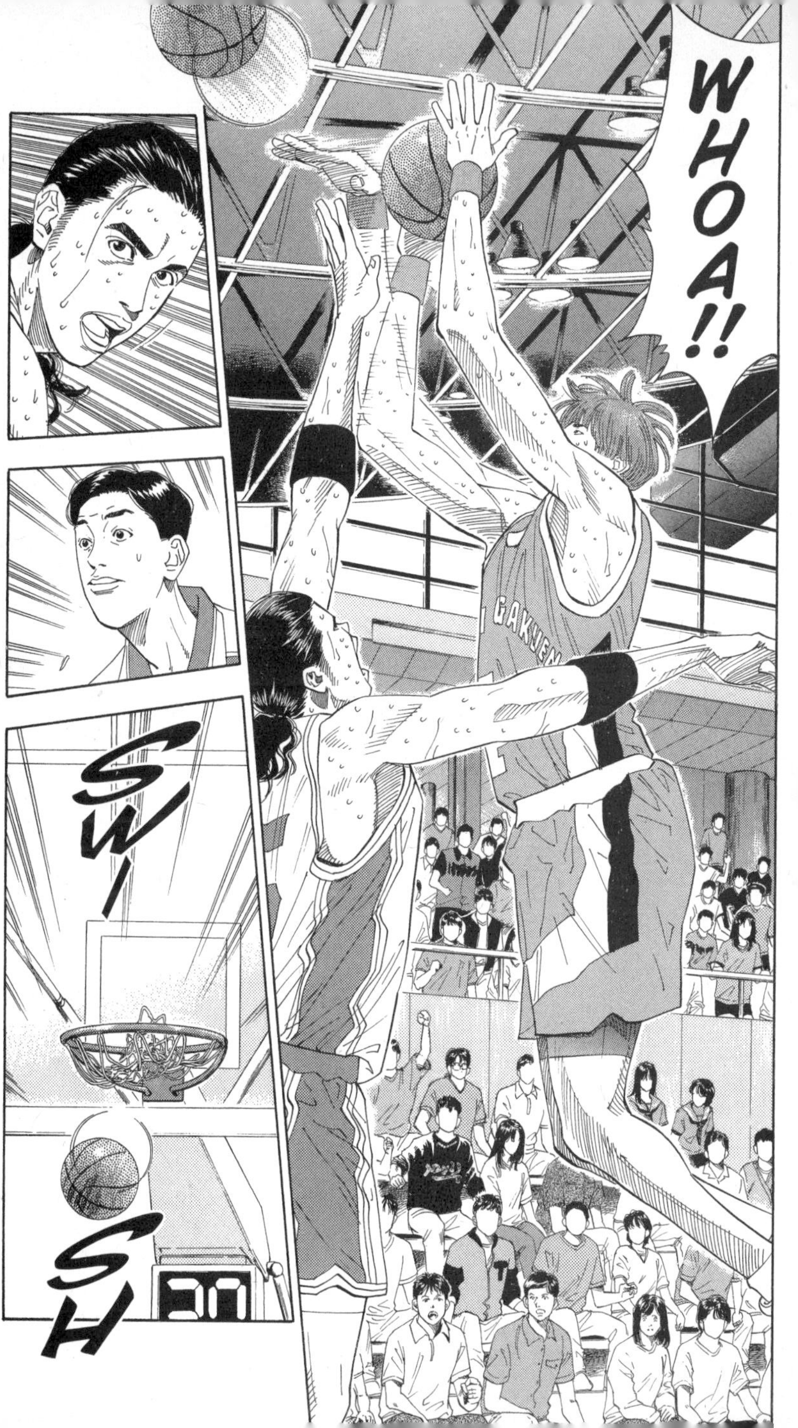
WHOA!!
GAKUEN
SWISH

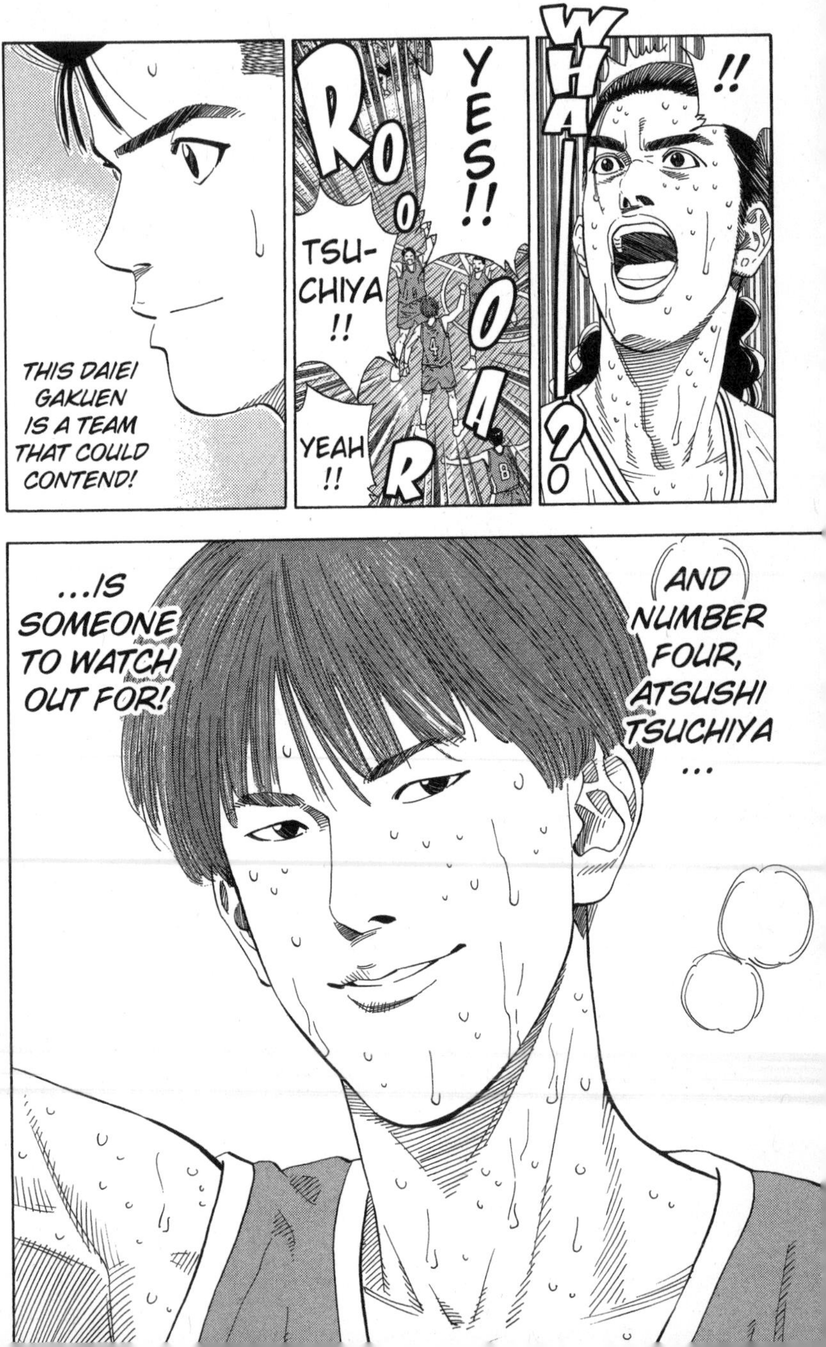
WHA!!?
ROOOOAR
YES!!
TSU-CHIYA!!
YEAH!!
THIS DAIEI GAKUEN IS A TEAM THAT COULD CONTEND!
AND NUMBER FOUR, ATSUSHI TSUCHIYA...
...IS SOMEONE TO WATCH OUT FOR!

READ THIS WAY

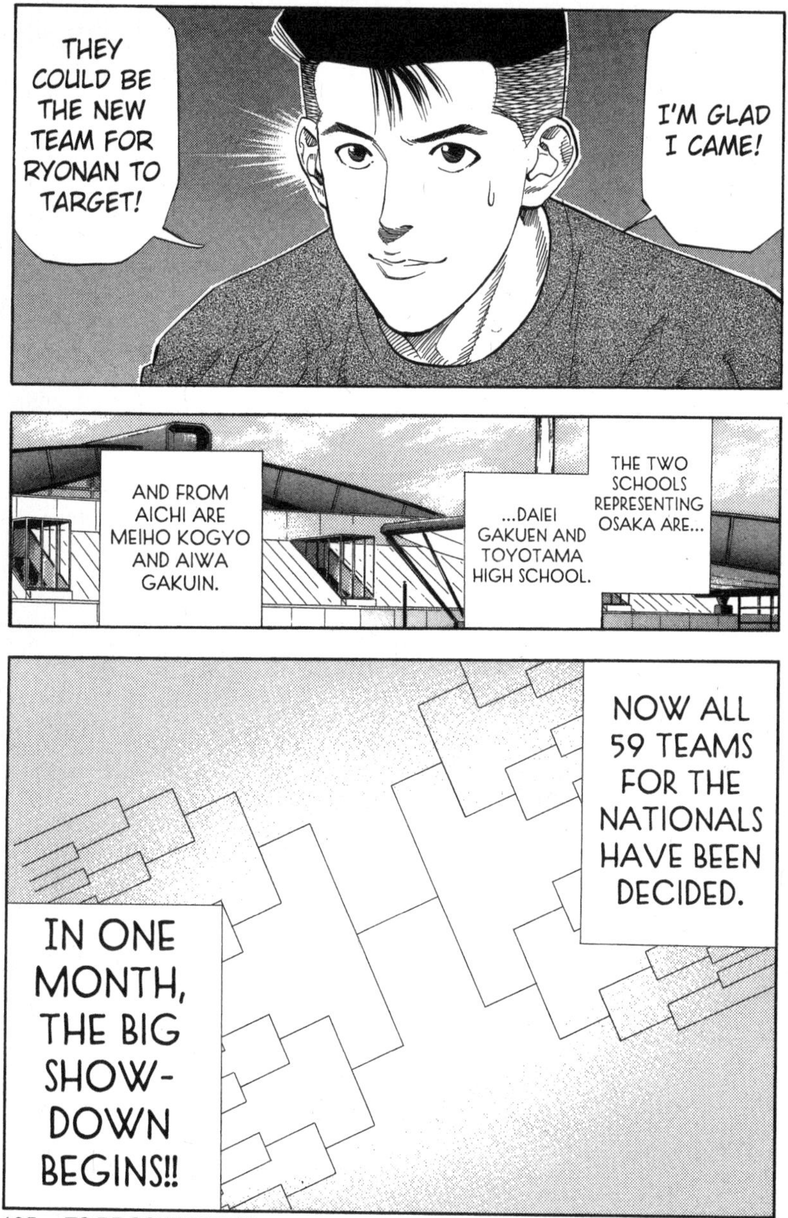

I'M GLAD I CAME!
THEY COULD BE THE NEW TEAM FOR RYONAN TO TARGET!
THE TWO SCHOOLS REPRESENTING OSAKA ARE...
...DAIEI GAKUEN AND TOYOTAMA HIGH SCHOOL.
AND FROM AICHI ARE MEIHO KOGYO AND AIWA GAKUIN.
NOW ALL 59 TEAMS FOR THE NATIONALS HAVE BEEN DECIDED.
IN ONE MONTH, THE BIG SHOW-DOWN BEGINS!!

TO BE CONTINUED!

Coming Next Volume

For the Shohoku High players, the past echoes in the present, as Rukawa learns something about Coach Anzai that leaves him determined to be the best high school player in Japan. With ten days remaining until the start of the national tournament, Coach Anzai sends the Shohoku High team to Shizuoka for a week of practice with another local team. But Sakuragi stays behind for a special practice session that will push him to the limit and improve his individual skills for the crucial games ahead.

ON SALE JUNE 2012

By Tite Kubo, creator of *ZOMBIEPOWDER*.

THE SECRETS OF THE SOUL SOCIETY REVEALED!

Become an unofficial Soul Reaper with the official *BLEACH* character book containing 326 pages of:

- Character and storyline info from vol. 1-22
- The original *BLEACH* one shot
- Bonus manga
- An interview with series creator Tite Kubo

Plus, exclusive stickers and poster!

COMPLETE your *BLEACH* collection with the *BLEACH SOULs.* Official Character Book— GET YOURS TODAY!

On sale at **www.shonenjump.com**
Also available at your local bookstore and comic store.

bleach.viz.com

RATED **T** FOR TEEN ratings.viz.com

viz media
www.viz.com

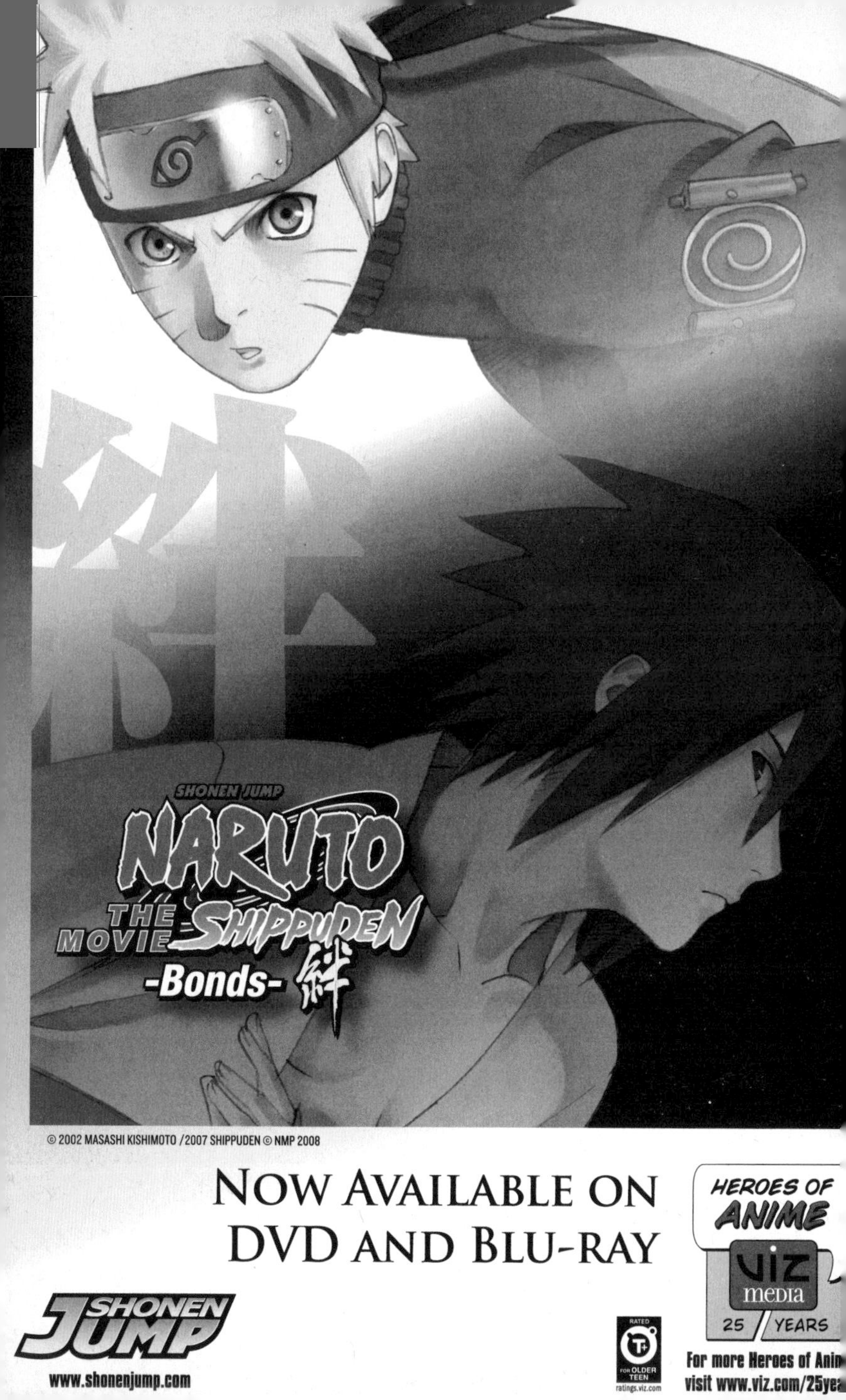
SHONEN JUMP
NARUTO
THE MOVIE SHIPPUDEN
-Bonds- 絆

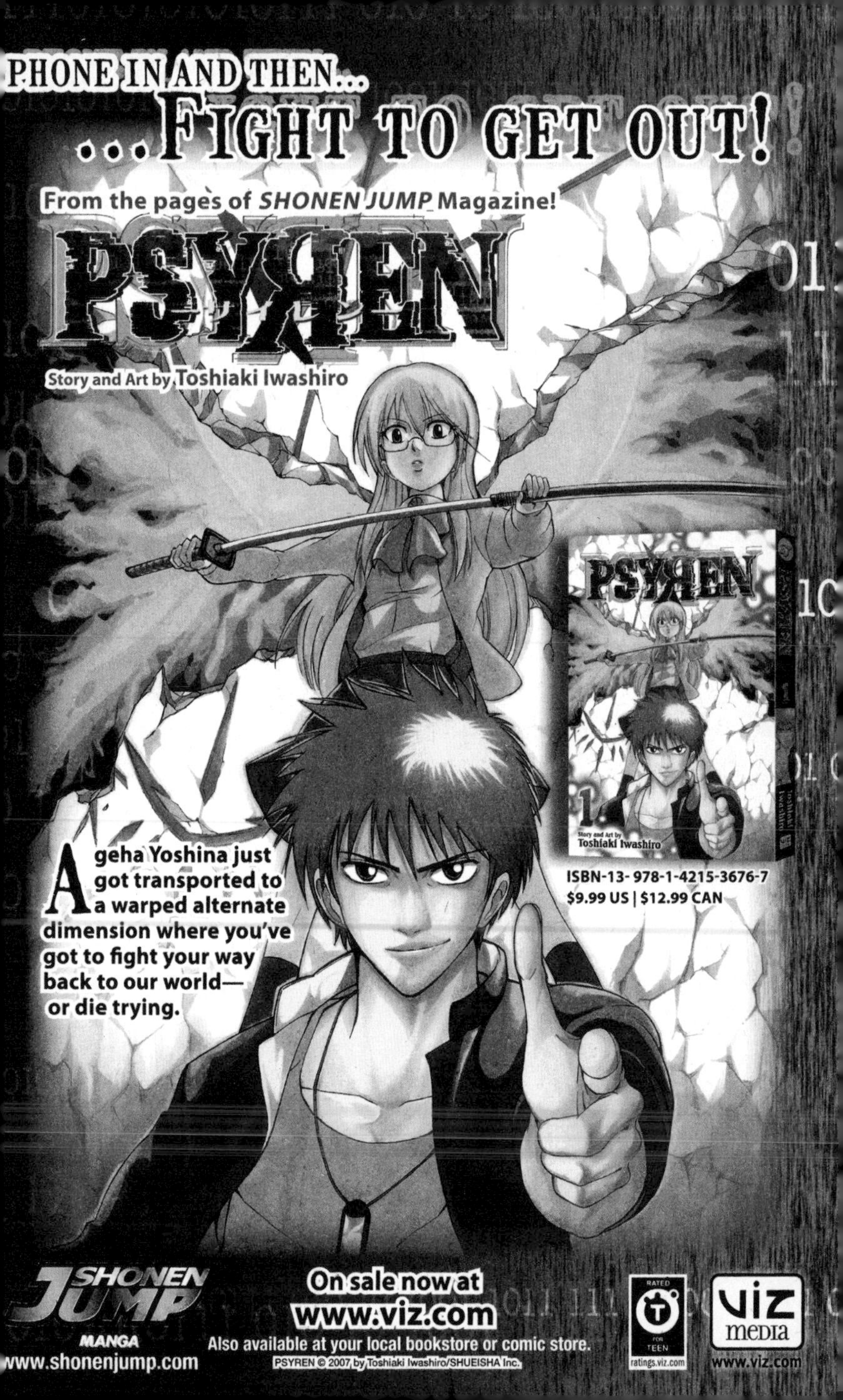
PHONE IN AND THEN...
...FIGHT TO GET OUT!
From the pages of SHONEN JUMP Magazine!
PSYREN
Story and Art by Toshiaki Iwashiro
PSYREN
1
Story and Art by Toshiaki Iwashiro
ISBN-13- 978-1-4215-3676-7
$9.99 US | $12.99 CAN
Ageha Yoshina just got transported to a warped alternate dimension where you've got to fight your way back to our world—or die trying.
SHONEN JUMP
MANGA
www.shonenjump.com
On sale now at
www.viz.com
Also available at your local bookstore or comic store.
PSYREN © 2007 by Toshiaki Iwashiro/SHUEISHA Inc.
RATED
T
FOR TEEN
ratings.viz.com
VIZ media
www.viz.com

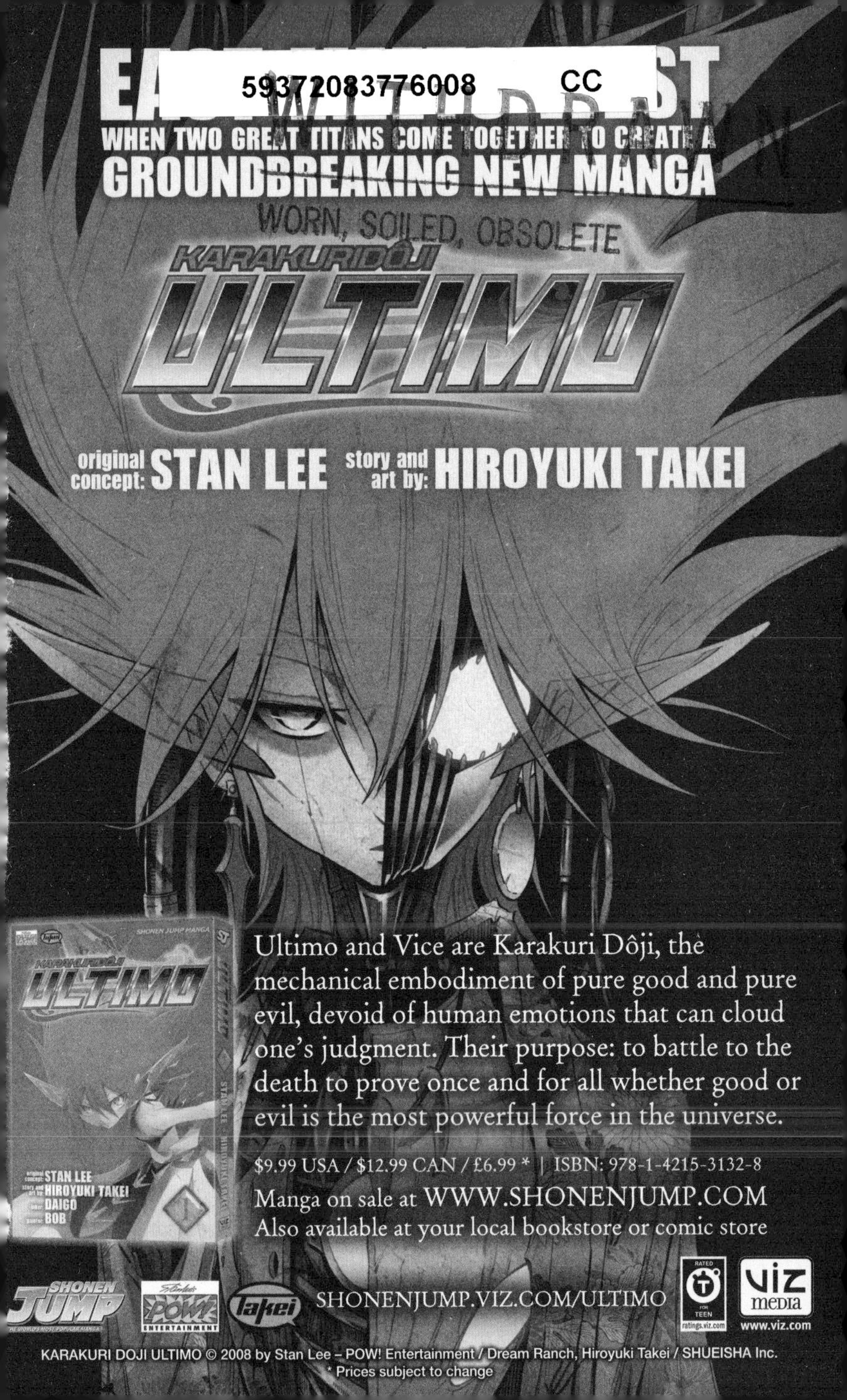